Records
of Indentured Servants
and
of Certificates for Land
Northumberland County
Virginia
1650-1795

Compiled by
W. Preston Haynie

HERITAGE BOOKS
2008

HERITAGE BOOKS
AN IMPRINT OF HERITAGE BOOKS, INC.

Books, CDs, and more—Worldwide

For our listing of thousands of titles see our website
at
www.HeritageBooks.com

Published 2008 by
HERITAGE BOOKS, INC.
Publishing Division
100 Railroad Ave. #104
Westminster, Maryland 21157

Copyright © 1996 W. Preston Haynie

Other books by the author:
Northumberland County, Virginia Apprenticeships, 1650-1750
Northumberland County, Virginia Apprenticeships, 1750-1852
Northumberland County, Virginia Bookshelf and Old Books, 1650-1852

All rights reserved. No part of this book may be reproduced or transmitted in any form or by any means, electronic or mechanical, including photocopying, recording or by any information storage and retrieval system without written permission from the author, except for the inclusion of brief quotations in a review.

International Standard Book Number: 978-0-7884-0425-2

TABLE OF CONTENTS

Preface v

Introduction 1

Documents 23

Index 317

PREFACE

The aim of this book is (1) to give one a view of indentured servitude and (2) to aid in genealogical research. Without a study of servants, one's view of colonial life would be incomplete. Their work provided the comfort and manner in which a planter may have been able to live. It is only just that we look at their entry into a world of servitude, their hardships, and their conduct. They did, after all, constitute a major proportion of the population. One may also locate an ancestor among the headrights or see his name among the court records involving servants. If one's ancestor were a planter, more than likely his name will be among those receiving a certificate for land, buying a servant, or defending himself in court against the suit of a servant.

Hopefully historians will make use of the book as well in addressing larger questions. What were the fates of the Northumberland servants after they completed their terms of indenture? How many remained in the county? What were their points of origin? How closely do the punishments of the county court follow the laws of the colony? The book is only the beginning of many fascinating studies of a system that endured in the county for almost 150 years.

The court records, for the most part, have been transcribed as they were written. In some cases a comma or a period has been inserted for clarity, and Record Book (RB) and Order Book (OB) have been abbreviated for brevity. One will notice that a name may be spelled differently within a document. One should look for all possible spellings of a name. Some local names have undergone changes over the years; it is difficult, at times, to prove these changes in spelling.

Generally, spelling did not become standardized until Samuel Johnson's *Dictionary* in 1755. Then, in 1768, Benjamin Franklin published *A Scheme for a New Alphabet and a Reformed Mode of Spelling.* In 1763, It was Noah Webster who, in his *Grammatical Institute of the English Language*, achieved a divorce between English and American practice. Since the documents in this work end in 1795, we can understand more clearly the spelling of words as we know them today. We also have to take into account the clerk's ability to spell or the ability of the person copying the documents in the record or order books, certainly a tedious task. A rare example of a word being consistently misspelled is the word gaol, meaning jail. The clerk or the person copying the court order has spelled it goal.

Unfortunately, there are no record books between 1672 and 1706; some deeds and wills were rerecorded in *Record Book 1706-20*. Also the record book for the years 1729 to 1738 has been missing for a number of years. Surely some servants would have been mentioned in these books. All order books are available for research.

My appreciation goes to the clerk of the court, Steve Thomas, and staff— Linda L. Booth, Eleanor R. Morrison, and Emily D. Thomas—who, as custodians of county records, recognize the importance of seventeenth- and eighteenth-century records. At all times they have been helpful, friendly, and courteous. I owe a deep sense of gratitude to Carolyn H. Jett, who spent hours in studying names to make certain that we transcribed them correctly. And I would like to thank Jim and Joanne Foster, who prepared the manuscript. Joanne was quick to question any inconsistencies and to raise flags concerning possible errors. Lastly, I am grateful to Heritage Books for publishing this work, thus making available valuable records to those interested in the colonial life of Northumberland County.

INTRODUCTION

One frequently reads about plantation life and prominent planters; without a study of servants, however, no one can have a complete picture of life during the colonial and revolutionary periods. This compilation of court records includes names of those persons receiving certificates for land, headrights, and servants.

Headrights
"The term headrights," according to Nell Marion Nugent, "in connection with a patent for land has been subject to no little misunderstanding. For the purpose of stimulating immigration and the settlement of the Colony the London Company ordained that any person who paid his own way to Virginia should be assigned 50 acres of land 'for his owne personal adventure,' and if he transported 'at his own cost' one or more persons he should, for each person whose passage he paid, be awarded fifty acres of land."[1]

A majority of the first 150 documents are certificates for land, most for relatively small amounts. Some received a substantial number of acres. William Presly was granted 1,000 acres in July 1657 (Document 112). Robert Clarke received 1,200 acres on 21 September 1651 (Document 117). Richard Wright was granted 850 acres on 20 July 1658 (Document 135) and then 800 acres on 20 May 1659 (Document 153). Maj. George Colclough received 1,050 acres of land on 5 September 1660 for the transportation of 20 persons (Document 180). One of the largest grants was to John Lee; he received 4,700 acres on 20 April 1664 for the transportation of 94 persons (Document 313).

Among the names of the headrights may be the person himself or herself, members of his or her family, friends, or indentured servants. In looking at the names, we cannot always tell whether a person paid his own passage, was a friend or a member of the family although not carrying the family surname, or an indentured servant. Arthur Marsh, for example, in 1666 was a bond servant

---

1. Nell Marion Nugent, *Cavaliers and Pioneers 1623–1800* (Richmond: Press of the Dietz Printing Co., 1934) vol. 1, XXLV.

to Thomas Gayner and was to serve him for five years[2]; yet he appears as a headright in Ambrose Feilding's certificate for land (Document 549). It is possible Gayner sold his title of a headright, in this case Arthur Marsh, to Feilding. Documents 491, 492, and 494 indicate some of the complexity in the headright system.

Surely a number of the headrights were indentured servants, and primarily for that reason they have been included in this study.

Servants

"Indentured servitude had its roots in the widespread poverty and human dislocation of seventeenth-century England. Still a largely backward economy with a great part of its population permanently unemployed, England was moving toward more modern methods in industry and agriculture; yet in the short run some of the improvements greatly added to the unemployed."[3] The colonies needed laborers, especially Virginia because of its tobacco economy. Thus, for nearly two centuries from London, "as well as from many lesser ports and inland towns, the English poor, lured, seduced, or forced into the emigrant stream, kept coming to America."[4] They provided much of the labor supply until they "were substantially replaced by slaves . . . during the course of the eighteenth century."[5]

The vast majority of the indentured servants were white; however, some African-Americans were among the headrights. Henry, Dick, and Jack are among those listed in John Lee's certificate for land (Document 384).* Indian children could be servants, with permission of their parents, provided they were brought up in the Christian religion.[6] Some of the Indian children were as young as 4 or 5 years old.** Margrett Rheine, a servant to Capt. William Jones, was whipped for having a bastard child; however, she was acquitted of having to pay a fine or serve additional time because the hundreth Act did not apply to the natives of this country. Jones, however, appealed to the governor

---

2. Peter Wilson Coldham, *The Bristol Registers of Servants Sent to Foreign Plantations 1654–1686* (Baltimore: Genealogical Publishing Co., Inc., 1988), 224.
3. Richard Hofstadter, *America at 1750 A Social Portrait* (London: Jonathan Cape, 1972), 34, 35.
4. Ibid., 35.
5. Ibid., 34.
* Other documents listing African-Americans: 26, 87, 180, 313, 712, 714, 784, 833, 834, 864.
6. William Waller Hening, *The Statutes at Large* (Charlottesville: University of Virginia Press, 1969), vol. 1, 410.
** Other documents mentioning Indians: 751, 808, 865, 955, 1327.

and council (Document 955).

During a major portion of these two centuries, the importation of servants became a big business.

> Without the money to pay their own way across the ocean they [servants] had bartered four years or more of their lives in return for the privilege of spending two months on a ship making the voyage to America. The man who carried them over or paid their passage gained the title to their labor for a period of years and might sell that title as he chose. The importation of servants was actually a business in itself, in which a number of middlemen profited before the servant reached his final master. Sometimes dealers known as 'soul-drivers' purchased whole shiploads of servants and drove them through the countryside, selling them like so many pots and pans to whoever would buy. More often a ship carrying servants would anchor off Leedstown or Yorktown, where a dealer would advertise the cargo and those who needed servants would come and purchase them.[7]

Because at times there were at least two tobacco warehouses on the Coan River, two on the Great Wicomico, and one on Dividing Creek, it only stands to reason that vessels containing cargo and servants would dock at these ports as well as at Leedstown and Yorktown, as Morgan mentioned in his work. After a ship unloaded its cargo of servants and commodities needed by colonists in the new world, the vessel sailed with a cargo of tobacco. Documents 532, 562, and 672 mention ships and their arrival into the Wicomico or Great Wicomico River.

Even after being purchased by one person, a servant might soon find himself being sold to someone else. In a court deposition of February 1662/63, Edward Salmon stated that John Hull sold Thomas Levett one maid servant for one hammock and one hogshead of sweet-scented tobacco. Levett also agreed to pay William Thomas a sum of money owed by Hull (*RB 1658–66*, 99).

People within the county often would enter into agreements for someone to buy a servant for them. In January 1650/51, the court ordered, because of a prior agreement, that John Hiller deliver to William Harding two servants and a cask of spirits. One servant was to be a tailor, age 18 to 25, with his

---

7. Edmund S. Morgan, *Virginians at Home* (Williamsburg: Colonial Williamsburg Foundation, 1987), 56.

shears, pressing iron, and bedding; the other servant was to be above the age of 16 (*RB 1650–52, 69*). In a court order dated 20 August 1655, because Hugh Lee had not delivered a servant to John Kent, Lee was ordered to pay by November 1,580 pounds of good tobacco and cask (Document 80). George Durant, in another court order, was to purchase for Rice Maddocke a man servant between the ages of 16 and 30 to serve for four years. Durant was ordered to deliver the servant to Maddocke and pay the cost of the suit (Document 182).

Very few of the court documents reveal the captain or persons responsible for bringing the servants into the country. In a testimony given by Thomas Speke on 4 November 1653, he stated that four or five years previously Mr. Winter Chapman had brought into this country two brothers, Henry and Thomas West, to sell (Documents 59, 60). On 17 April 1700, Katherine and Owen Sivillivant complained to the court that Capt. William Thornton, on whose ship they arrived, kept their indentures (Document 1173).

The indenture or contract was a vital part of the business transaction between master and servant. For those who had indentures, there would be no reason for their going to court unless there was a conflict to be resolved. As early as 1662, every master who bought a servant without an indenture was required by law to carry him to court within four months after the purchase to have his age judged.[8]

Disputes over indentures were settled in court, where the master or the servant very often sought to benefit himself. John Dalton, servant to Walter Dunne, brought before the court to have his age judged, stated that his indenture was supposed to come into the country by another ship. He was given one month to produce such an indenture; if he was unable to, he was to serve his master according to law (Document 988). Rosamond Wells, having been bound by two indentures, on 18 July 1706 was released from Isaac Hester, the court declaring the contracts were not good (Document 1329). John Nuball, servant to Ebenezer Sanders, was ordered on 20 December 1688 to serve his master according to law unless he produced an indenture. On 17 April 1689, he presented an indenture to the court, but it was declared void because Nicholas Ley, master of the vessel, did not have the authority to indent him (Document 873). On 20 September 1652, the court ordered that William Linsey didn't have to serve William Reynolds but four years, according to his original indenture, even though Thomas Hawkens sold him for five years (Document 38). Phebe Whitters als Cooke agreed in court to serve John Cockrell 10 years, a period of time longer than required by law after she stated

---

8. Hening, *Statutes at Large*, vol. 2, 169.

that the contract was in no way clandestinely procured or meant to entrap her (Document 1209).

During the late 1600s and early 1700s, half-grown boys and young men comprised one of the largest groups of servants. Many of these, one can be certain, were kidnapped, picked up off the streets of London or nearby towns, sold by their parents, or sent from orphanages for service in Virginia. They were one of the main sources of help to the planters during this period. The influx of young men reached its peak in the late 1600s. Every document between 1017 (18 May 1698) and 1147 (22 June 1699), with the exception of documents 1045, 1064, 1103, 1104, and 1144, concerns itself with one or more servants being brought to court to have their ages judged.* Young girls as well as young boys frequently were brought before the court to determine their ages, some as young as 9 years old.**

Many historians contend that most of the indentured servants coming to Virginia were unskilled. Certainly the young men were not skilled in any trade, and because of the demand for labor in the fields, some of the older servants who may have had skills were forced to forsake their trades. Those who knew trades were able to negotiate with their masters. William Taite agreed to give Dennis McCarty two years of his service provided McCarty would teach Taite's Negro man Jacob the blacksmith's trade as well as the trades of a cooper, smith brazier, and tinsmith (Document 1917). Robert Leitch, servant to Samuel Heath, agreed to give up his freedom dues provided the executors of Heath's estate would release him from any further service after making all of the clothes for the Negroes that year (Document 1623). Apparently Leitch knew he could do well as a tailor on his own. William Higgens, servant to William Grinstead, agreed to serve his master one additional year provided his master would keep him at his trade as a tailor and teach him to cut out clothes, a portion of the trade he apparently hadn't mastered (Document 1499). The threat of having to work in the fields was always a possibility any tradesman feared. Michael Melton, servant to John Coutanceau, asked the court that he not be employed in any work other than his trade as a tailor (Document 561). John Roach complained to the court that his master had employed him in base service. The court ordered that Thomas Mathew adhere to Roach's indenture and that Roach be employed only as a merchant (Document 500). Silvester Nono, shoemaker to William Taite, agreed to serve his master an additional year provided he would not have to do

---

* Some documents listing numbers of children: 187, 441, 519, 527, 559, 568, 623, 637, 650, 667, 696, 698, 713, 840, 941, 976, 986.

** Documents containing names of young girls: 410, 411, 413, 434, 458, 483, 821.

any planter's work (Document 1694). Thomas Floyd, a servant of Nicholas Cary, agreed to serve his master two additional years in consideration of his master keeping him employed as a blacksmith (Document 1734). Peter Faushew, servant to George Ball, agreed to serve Ball one additional year after his indented time provided Ball buy him from his former master and employ him as a miller (Document 1736).

Several documents express a desire on the part of the servants to learn a trade. Mary Jinkins, servant of Thomas Webster, agreed to serve her master two years beyond her indented time provided he would teach her to read, write, knit, spin, and do household work (Document 1632). In March 1724/25, Ann Conner als Prichard agreed to serve Cary Keble four years provided he give her a new suit of clothes, provide her with sufficient clothes, diet, and lodging, and teach her to sew, knit, and spin, and at the end of her service, Keble was to give her a new suit, a gown and petticoat, two shifts, two aprons, two caps, two handkerchiefs, a pair of shoes and stockings, a heifer and sow with pigs (Document 1580). Probably because this was one of the most prosperous periods in the colony's history, Conner was able to negotiate a good bargain for herself and at the same time learn trades useful to her in later life.

Historians have made frequent references to servants having been convicts, especially a number coming to the new world around 1728. Of the 1,988 documents in this study, 1,620 are dated before 1728. Court records in themselves would not necessarily reveal that a person had been a convict. Two documents do. Peter Bateman, a convict servant to Richard Lee, was charged with breaking and entering the storehouse of Charles Campbell and the house of Richard Booth (Document 1832). Sufficient evidence was found for him to be tried at the next General Court in Williamsburg. Anne Taylor, a convict servant of Thomas Ball, was found guilty of stealing a silver spoon valued at four shillings. The court ordered that she receive 39 lashes on her bare back well laid on (Document 1868).

According to Richard Hofstadter, "Indentured servants were put to arduous field labor by owners whose goal it was to get a maximum yield of labor in the four or five years contracted for. The chief temptation to the master was to drive the servant beyond his powers in the effort to get as much as possible out of him during limited years of service."[9]

Both servant and master had access to the courts. One common complaint of the servants was of ill usage. Jane Mills complained to the court against her master, Nathaniel Wilson. The court ordered that she be sold for the term of three years and six months and that the produce of the sale be paid

---

9. Hofstadter, *America at 1750*, 44, 45.

to Wilson (Document 1959). Richard Baker made a complaint against his master for ill usage but failing to make out the complaint, he was ordered to return to his master. The court did note that he was "bare & naked" and his master was ordered that he be well clothed (Document 1271). Roger Kaine and Henry Voy, servants of David Beatham, complained that their master did not keep them with sufficient diet and clothing. The court ordered that they be given two good shirts, a pair of summer drawers, and warm winter clothing as servants usually wear (Document 1636). Margery Worsly, servant to Daniel Neale, complained to the court that her mistress, Daniel's wife, had been too rigid and severe to her. After hearing testimony of Margery and some of the members of the court, the court ordered that she be free and her mistress be barred from having any Christian woman servant "unless she give caution for her better behaviour" (Document 874).

Mary Stephens, servant to Thomas Foulks, was released from one year's service after diverse women testified that Mary had "been most basely & inhumanly beaten and abused by her sd master" (Document 903). Jane Owen, a servant of Capt. Richard Budd, made a complaint before the court of physical abuse. Mrs. Morris and Mrs. Hawley testified that Jane "had about twelve markes black & blew [blue] about her" (Document 89).

Several servants complained to the court of physical abuse on the part of their master, Richard Cole. Frances Newman stated that Cole gave her unreasonable blows and hard usage. The court told Cole that he had the liberty of selling his servant, and if he did not, she was to be brought to the next court for further orders (Document 291). Mary Earle testified that Cole "hath very much abused her by very unlawfull & causeless beatinge." She was to remain at the house of James Magregor until the next court, when Cole was to appear (Document 221). The case of Alice English against Cole was carried to the General Court in James City. Cole failed to appear, and he was ordered to pay Peter Knight, sheriff of Northumberland, 100 pounds of tobacco and cask for his trouble (Document 337). Document 343 mentions Cole as well, but the servant is not named.*

In addition to servants going to court for ill usage, they also went to court to seek their freedom. These documents give information beyond the servant's petition for his or her freedom. In Document 237, for example, the court ordered that Dorothy Lockwitt, servant to Henry Winter, be given her freedom and, with it, three barrels of corn, two pairs of shoes and stockings, two shifts, one coarse cloth suit and canvas petticoat, and four caps. Henry Howard, servant to Thomas Webb, in petitioning the court for his freedom, presented

---

* Other documents mentioning abuse: 91, 394, 398, 522.

a copy of his indenture from someone—the name of the person is not legible—in Bristol (Document 706). Thomas Sims, servant to James Johnson, also produced an indenture signed by John Burrage, merchant, when Sims went to court to seek his freedom (Document 869). Michael Kendy contended he had an indenture signed by the Lord Mayor of Dublin and that he came into this country on the *Anne,* William Thornton being its master. He said the indenture was taken from him and destroyed. Dennis McFarley, under oath, stated that he was a shipmate to Michael and had seen and read the indenture. After hearing the evidence, the court ordered that Michael be free and his master, John Taylor, pay him corn and clothes according to law (Document 1234). Richard Staples, servant to Capt. John Haynie, complained to the court that his master refused to free him. Haynie, a former member of the House of Burgesses and a King's attorney, failed to appear in court. He was represented there by his son Richard Haynie, who also was to serve in the House of Burgesses. Captain Haynie was ordered to appear at the next court to answer Staples's complaint. Haynie evidently gave Staples his freedom and dues as there is no record of a court appearance (Document 965). Thus, we see one of the largest landowners in the county taking advantage of what amounted to almost free labor.*

The court did not always grant a servant's request for freedom. Some servants may have been trying to get free; others may have been ignorant of what their indentures stated. John McDaniell was clearly attempting to see whether he could obtain his freedom when he petitioned the court on 16 December 1691. An order of the county court was produced, dated 21 May 1690, in which McDaniell and his wife agreed to serve three years. He and his wife were ordered to return to their master and remain until his full term had expired (Document 916). Edward Watts, a servant to Capt. Thomas Mathew, produced an indenture that the court declared was forged. He was ordered to return to his master (Document 767). On 21 October 1702, Patrick Quiff was sold by Captain Voyer to John Cockrell, but Quiff didn't know for how long. The court declared that he be set "free the fourth of Christmas next" (Document 1239). Mary James, a servant to John Champion, petitioned the court for her freedom. Because she was formerly ordered to serve according to law, her request was denied (Document 783). William Fitzgerrad complained to the court that his master, Charles Vallen, was detaining him. A trial by jury was held, and William was ordered to return to his master's service (Document 936).

---

* Other documents in which servants sought freedom: 246, 567, 615, 675, 766, 810, 824, 921, 1236, 1240, 1527, 1647, 1676, 1722.

In a number of instances, servants were set free but were not paid their freedom dues. The court ordered that Josias Dameron pay to Mary Anley, his former servant, "fifteen bushels of corn and forty shillings current money or the value thereof in goods" (Document 1525). Servants sometimes had to petition the estates of their former masters for their freedom dues. Thomas Watts petitioned the court against the estate of Ambrose Fielding for his corn and clothes (Document 656). John Roberts, former servant to Josias Gaskins, deceased, also went to court to seek his corn and clothes (Document 1273). John Guy complained to the court that his late master refused to pay the accustomed corn, two hoes, and an ax. Adam Yarrett was ordered to pay Guy three barrels of corn, one hoe, and one ax, plus costs of suit (Document 907). Hanah Malony stated that she was entitled to her freedom dues. The court, after hearing both sides, decided that she had been set free early; therefore, there was nothing due her (Document 1566).*

Because of the prosperity of the colony during the 1730s, 1740s, and 1750s, there were opportunities for those who were ambitious and hardworking; thus, a number of servants felt life had more to offer than the meager freedom dues to be received at the expiration of their term of service. They also longed to be free from the rule of a master or overseer and to have lives of their own. A number of these were women, including Barbary Jones (Document 1751), Grace Payne (Document 1882), Magdalan Pingo (Document 1839), Anne Waters (Document 1844), and Janet Hunter (Document 1688). With men far outnumbering women, any young girl could easily enter into the institution of marriage.

Peter Runey and John Stephen agreed to forgive their masters their freedom dues in consideration of their masters' setting them free (Documents 1794, 1802). Beause of more prosperous times, other men bargained for their releases. James Guttry, a servant of John Routt, agreed to give up his freedom dues in consideration of his master's discharging him from his service and paying him 150 pounds of tobacco (Document 1855). Richard Rapson agreed to discharge his master of his freedom dues provided "he be this day discharged" (Document 1600). Timothy Harris, servant to George Conway, agreed to quit his freedom dues in consideration of his master's forgiving two months of his service (Document 1639).

Many servants, in an attempt to get out from under the service of their masters, sought ones who would be less cruel and not overly demanding in their work. Word of how servants were treated spread in the community, and

---

* Other documents in which servants sought freedom dues: 72, 604, 765, 912, 1270, 1296, 1297, 1351, 1352, 1365, 1520, 1565, 1571, 1577, 1714.

the servants knew the planters who would be more humane to those working for them. Ann Enderby agreed to serve Robert Davis four years for his buying her from John Keine. Davis paid Keine 1,200 pounds of tobacco for his new servant (Document 1411). Jane Stevens agreed to serve William Knott three years above her indented time for his buying her from her former master, William Self (Document 1530). Frances Clarke agreed to serve John Nickless five years in consideration of Nickless buying her from Bartholomew Dameron (Document 922). Ginneter Conner came to court and agreed to serve Richard Denny one year more than her indented time in consideration of his buying her from her former master and for trying his best to cure her of an ailment (Document 1540). Mary Martin, formerly a servant of James Webb, agreed to serve John Basie one year above her indented time. She did ask for a good suit in addition to what was to be allowed for her freedom dues (Document 1612).*

Because of a fear of being sold, both Robert Phealand and John Hader agreed to serve their masters additional time. Phealand, servant to William James, agreed to serve his master six months beyond his indented time provided James would not sell him (Document 1692). Hader voluntarily agreed to serve John Coleman two years in addition to the terms of his indenture on the condition that his master would not sell him to any other person during the time of his servitude (Document 1704).

Very often servants, after being sold from one master to another, found themselves involved in disputes to be settled in court. Christopher Bryerly was sold by Thomas Penry to Thomas Matthew. Bryerley served Matthew five years even though Penry had sold him for only four. The court ordered that Matthew pay Bryerley for his last year's service 1,000 pounds of tobacco (Document 732).*

The court, in most cases, appears to have ruled that the servant should serve only the length of time designated in the indenture even though this may have been in conflict with the law at the time. Phil Hocar, servant to Hugh Baker (Document 532), and John Marson, servant to Edward Coles (Document 1466), had to serve only eight years even though each was only 11 years old when they were sold to their masters. The court ruled that Francis Jones, servant to Daniel Neale, had to serve only seven years, according to his indenture, even though he was only 12 when sold (Document 797).** As of

---

* Other documents in which servants agreed to serve additional time for persons buying them from former masters: 1283, 1471, 1558, 1572, 1627, 1684, 1721, 1736, 1749, 1774, 1810, 1864.

** Other documents relating to the selling of servants: 164, 429, 565, 578, 1410.

March 1661/62, a servant, if above the age of 16, was not to serve more than five years. If he was under the age of 16, he was to serve until 24. Because of the apparent inequities concerning age, in 1666 the law was changed and a servant judged to be 19 or older was to serve five years, "if under that age then to serve soe many yeares as he wants of twenty fowre yeares...."[10]

During the first quarter of the eighteenth century, some servants, apparently pleased with their masters, were willing to serve additional periods of time provided they were given certain items above those required by law upon the expiration of their indentures. Elizabeth McDermat's request was small: she was willing to serve an additional eighteen months for a gown and petticoat above what the law allowed (Document 1522). Elizabeth McColley agreed to serve two additional years in consideration of two suits, a pair of bodice, shoes and stockings, head clothes and gloves, a hood and shifts. One suit was to be given her upon her demand, the other items at the time of her freedom (Document 1504). Catherine Poor, who may have been a resident of the county at the time of her indenture to William Gill, demanded one suit at the signing of the agreement. She agreed to serve Gill five years and four months, during which time he was to provide her and her son, Richard, sufficient diet, washing, and lodging. At the expiration of her service she was to receive one good new gown and petticoat, one pair of shoes, two shifts, one pair of stockings, one apron, two new caps, and one handkerchief. She was also to be acquitted of any charges for the maintenance of her son (Document 1536). Alexander Solloman's indenture is even more complicated. Solloman agreed to serve Patrick Burn for four years. Burn was first to pay William Rust 600 pounds of tobacco for Solloman to pay widow Smith of Maryland 500 pounds of tobacco. Burn was to provide Alexander with sufficient meat, drink, washing, lodging, and apparel and at the end of his term give him one young mare 4 years old, one new saddle, bridle, and one new suit of clothes of kersey or serge (Document 1393).*

A serious threat to the master's investment was the possibility of the impairment of the health of his servants. A common disorder was distemper. Elizabeth Hazelwood complained to the court that her master, Christopher Dawson, neglected her. He was ordered to answer Elizabeth's complaint before Capt. Thomas Winder and Leonard Howson (Document 1277). John Baskafeild contended that he was detained by Philip Bustle, Edward Lewis and others under pretensions of curing him. The court ordered that he be

---

10. Hening, *Statutes at Large,* vol. 2, 113, 240.
* Other documents in which servants listed additional items to be given them at the end of their service: 1521, 1580.

discharged and that he apply himself to the churchwardens of St. Stephens parish for relief (Document 1467). Mary Smyth agreed to serve William Hartland seven years on condition that he cure her (Document 609). John Taylor asked that he might be free from paying any levy on his servant, William Edwards, because he was distempered (Document 1360). Bridgett Taylor, servant to William Mason, petitioned the court to have liberty to seek remedy for her distemper, her master having refused her request. The court ordered that she be allowed to seek help and her master was not to hinder her (Document 1305).

Ann Turner (Document 1793), Samuel Hoomes (Document 1886), John Abby and Anne Osborn (Document 1895), and Mary Wilson (Document 1885) wanted to be cured of the foul (venereal) disease. Each was willing to make certain concessions for a cure.*

The greatest problem confronting the master was that of his servant or servants running away. "People from the cities and from the mild English climate found the summer hard going in any colony from Maryland southward, especially on plantations where indentured servants were put to arduous field labor by owners whose goal it was to get a maximum yield of labor in the four or five years contracted for."[11] Working in tobacco fields was even more laborious than working in the corn fields, its season longer, and the tasks more strenuous.

Because the owner of the plantation, whether large or small, was involved in all aspects of work on the plantation, he did not have the time to search personally for his runaway servant; consequently, he paid someone else to find his runaways. This person was paid in tobacco, the amount based on the servant's absence from his master. The servant, in turn, served additional time. Sabrina Parker (Document 521), John Tayler (Document 540), and Joseph Elton (Document 1232) ran away from their masters during the busiest season or "in the height of the cropp," an expression commonly used. John Taylor was to serve two additional years for running away 11 weeks. Elton was absent from his master's service 102 days, surely a period longer than just the height of the crop. Ralph Smithhurst was ordered to receive 20 lashes on his bare back, and George Eskridge, executor for the deceased Mary Hues, had the liberty to put irons on him for running away (Document 1509).**

Servants from Northumberland escaped to Maryland; in turn, servants

---

* Other documents relating to health: 421, 589, 1412, 1505, 1879.
11. Hofstadter, *America at 1750*, 44.
** Other documents of runaways: 490, 792, 896, 973, 1272, 1364, 1509, 1519, 1830, 1893, 1894.

from Maryland crossed the Potomac to Northumberland. Robert Shiels and William Simmons, servants of Peter Presly, ran away into Maryland (Document 1703). William Simmons alias Roberts, servant of Peter Presly, on 9 April 1744 appeared in court after having crossed into Maryland. More than likely he had changed his name from Simmons to Roberts (Document 1763).* Alexander Duglas and John Parsons, both runaway servants from Isle of Kent in Maryland, were brought before the court on 1 March 1675/76. Robert Ross, also a runaway servant from Talbert County in Maryland, appeared before the court on 1 November 1726. Ross was taken up by Cary Keble. After remaining in jail 76 days, he was ordered to be sold (Document 1601). Mary Owens, a servant to John Ross of Maryland, was brought to the court as a runaway. Based on an affidavit of William Angell, the court declared that she had leave to be absent from her master (Document 1867).

Certificates were granted or taken to court for those picking up runaway slaves. Usually they were paid 180 or 200 pounds of tobacco. For some reason James Crain was paid only 90 pounds of tobacco for taking up Edward Davis, a servant belonging to William Garland of Richmond County (Document 1834). John Berry, servant of Henry Williams of Richmond County (Document 1700), and William Evers, a servant belonging to Susannah Grey (Document 1875), also of Richmond County, were picked up by Northumberland County residents. Samuel Snow, Simon Bowley, and Thomas Heath, Northumberland residents, presented certificates to the court for taking up runaway servants from Westmoreland County (Documents 1666, 1701, 1541).**

Some servants were captured some distance from their masters' homes. William Hill Jr. produced a certificate for taking up Thomas Hicks, a servant belonging to Andrew Cottrell (Document 1635). Thomas Burnell, a servant of Colonel Codd, had run away as far as the Rappahannock River (Document 553). A certificate was granted to Charles Dermott by the Assembly for taking up Patrick Farrell, a servant belonging to Joseph Palmer, some 15 miles from his master's home (Document 1103). Anne Geate, a servant belonging to William Wildey, was taken up by John Coutanceau above 10 miles from Wildey's residence (Document 583). It is not too amazing that Anne would run away since Wildey's wife, Elizabeth, took her husband to court for physical abuse and demanded separate maintenance.[12] Francis Roberts was

---

* Other runaways to Maryland: 1453, 1678, 1679, 1705.
** Other documents in which people were granted certificates for picking up slaves: 729, 1611, 1768, 1920.
12. *Order Book 1699–1713*, Part 1, 119.

granted a certificate for picking up three servants belonging to Captain Lightfoot (Document 587); however, the servants are not named.

In addition to running away, masters made other complaints before the court concerning the conduct of their servants. Patrick Martial (Document 1742), Terrence Smith (Document 1598), and Caron Clinton (Document 1533) were brought to court for striking their masters. Each was to serve an additional year for his offense. James Ecles, servant to Joseph Humphryes, having struck his master contrary to law, was ordered to serve his master for the default according to law (Document 1250). Elizabeth Lovell confessed in court that she laid violent hands on her mistress; she was ordered to serve one additional year after her indented time (Document 278). William Crue, servant to John Motley, beat his overseer and threatened his master. The court ordered that the sheriff give him "20 stripes on his bare back until the blood come"; however, as a result of the desire of his master and Crues, he was acquitted of the punishment (Document 513). Samuel Carter made a complaint to the court against Peter Bateman, a servant belonging to Richard Lee. He declared he was in danger of his life. The court ordered that Bateman receive 29 lashes well laid on and then be delivered to Carter (Document 1828).

One of the most serious offenses against a master was the suspected murder of Peter Presly by George Afflax, William Simmons, and Nicholas Meeds. The case was first brought to the court on 10 May 1750 (Document 1815). Bushrod Fauntleroy, William Harding, and John Foushee for Magdaline Pingo, his servant, gave evidence at the courthouse in the city of Williamsburg (Document 1816). Col. Peter Presly had encountered numerous problems with other servants as well.*

Servants were also found guilty of stealing. Sarah Garnett carried away goods from her master, Christopher Garlington, and absented herself from his service 11 months. She was to serve an additional three and a half years for her crime (Document 276). John Strickland and Darby Tool took a silver spoon belonging to John Lewis. They were to receive 39 lashes at the public whipping post and serve additional time according to law as well as nine extra days for the loss of time during that imprisonment (Document 1649). Two servants were found guilty of killing hogs (Documents 268, 287). George Wilson, a servant belonging to John Maith, was charged with breaking and entering the storehouse of William Smith and stealing two bottles and two quarts of rum. He was to receive 39 lashes at the whipping post (Document

---

* Documents in which other servants encountered difficulties with Presly: 1594, 1617, 1682, 1703, 1763, 1764.

1820).

Thomas Hicks admitted in court that he burned the tobacco house belonging to his master, Andrew Cottrell, and the tobacco house belonging to Abner Neale, but he denied burning the tobacco house of George Curtis. He was to be tried at the General Court (Document 1650). John Longerwood, a servant belonging to Ralph Wormly, was suspected of burning the jail. The court, after hearing the witnesses, ordered that he receive 39 lashes (Document 1872).

On two occasions William Taite complained to the court about the behavior of his servant, James Fitzmorris. No specifics were given. In one instance James was to receive 39 lashes; in the other, 10 (Documents 1888, 1891). Mrs. Anne Taite, the wife of William Taite, complained that Nanny Taylor, a servant, resisted her. Taylor was to receive 39 lashes and ordered to serve an additional year for threatening to strike her mistress and burn her house down (Document 1865).

John and Mary MacDaniell and Duglasse Watts were brought to court for scandalizing their masters. Watts was to receive 20 stripes on her bare back and ask the forgiveness of her master (Document 336). John MacDaniell was to receive 31 lashes on his bare back well laid on; however, because Mary was pregnant, she was to receive her punishment at a convenient time after the birth of her child (Document 892). Dennis Clark confessed that she had lied when she told Mr. Rogers, Mr. Allerton, and Mr. Jones that she had been beaten and abused by her master (Document 349).

One needs to be objective about the behavior of servants. By observing closely all documents, one can see a discernible pattern in which some masters had difficulty with a number of servants. Richard Pemberton, for example, had problems with some of his servants. Priscilla Dixon evidently had gotten her freedom but had not received her freedom dues. On 20 May 1681, she petitioned the court for the accustomed clothes and one ax and one hoe (Document 908). The document is also of interest because it indicates she more than likely worked in the fields along with the men. It's possible she continued to work for Pemberton or at least worked close by. On 16 November 1692, she declared, under oath, that Dr. Pemberton was the father of her base child. He was to pay £10 sterling or 2,000 pounds of tobacco to "save the parish harmless"; Priscilla was to be given 30 lashes on her bare back (Document 926). Darby Danheny and Thomas Kehow, also servants of Pemberton, encountered problems as well. Danheny petitioned the court for his freedom and corn and clothes. Pemberton appealed to the General Court but did not appear; he still refused to pay Danheny his corn and clothes (Document 1259). On the same day, Thomas Kehow asked to be discharged from further service with Pemberton and also requested his corn and clothes. He met with the same results (Document 1260). Two months later Darby again complained to the court. Pemberton was ordered to pay Darby his corn and clothes with cost of court; Pemberton, however, appealed to the governor and council (Document 1265).

Robert Sibbalds, too, had difficulties with his servants. William Wier, having run away on two prior occasions, was ordered by the court to be sold by the sheriff after he ran away for the third time (Documents 1889, 1894, 1896). Patrick Malloy, a servant of Sibbalds, absented himself from his master's service for six months (Documents 1919, 1921). Jonathan Crooke was accused of stealing money from Sibbalds. The court, after hearing various witnesses and the prisoner himself, decided he should not be tried by the General Court but should be released (Document 1905). Mary Fitzgerells complained to the court of ill usage. She was ordered to "return to her service & that the s^d Robert use her better for the usuage" (Document 1928).

Problems between servants and their masters, Richard Cole and Peter Presly, have already been noted.

For most of the servants, the period of servitude was supposed to have been one of celibacy. Servants could not marry without the consent of their masters; as a result, there were few accounts of marriages taking place during the indented time. The master did not want the loss of labor from his women servants or the possibility of their death during childbirth. On 28 October 1651, John Kelly, in consideration of 2,000 pounds of tobacco and three barrels of corn, agreed to serve Hugh Lee one year on condition that he be allowed to marry Susan Watson, a servant of Lee. He and Susan would then be willing to serve Lee two and a half years (Document 29). David Lyndsay, a minister, was brought to court and fined 10,000 pounds of tobacco for marrying Richard Peirre, servant to Lee, and a woman servant belonging to Thomas Brewer. He did not have Lee's permission nor did he obtain or publish marriage banns. He pleaded ignorant of the law and was acquitted (Document 206). Peirre was ordered to serve John Lee, the son of Col. Richard Lee, one additional year. Peirre appealed to the General Court (Document 312). William Owen and Mary Harrison were willing to serve their master, John Hanks, an additional year on condition that he give permission to marry. If they had any children during their service, they were to serve an additional year (Document 1845).

It is not surprising that numerous women were brought to court for having illegitimate children or, as they were then called, base or bastard children. Jane Dolin, a servant to Richard Feilding, was to receive 20 stripes on her bare back until the blood came or pay 500 pounds of tobacco for the use of the parish for committing fornication with William Shepard. Although no child is mentioned, it is assumed there was one because of the reference to the use of the parish. Shepard paid his fine as well as Jane's (Document 402).

Phebe Cooke, servant to John Cockrell, was ordered to serve her master two additional years and be given 30 lashes on her bare back unless she paid a fine of £10. Cockrell agreed to pay her fine, and she was to serve him three years (Document 985). Phebe Whitter (Document 1356), Ellinor Reader (Document 1350), and Katherine Davis (Document 442) were each to receive 20 lashes on their bare backs.

During the mid-1700s, the whipping post is mentioned in reference to punishments. The court ordered that Ann Field, a servant belonging to Peter Presly, receive 25 lashes on her bare back at the common whipping post and serve her master one additional year (Document 1814).

The court was more concerned with the burden an illegitimate child would have on the parish, since the poor became the responsibility of the church, than with the welfare of the child or mother. Mary Morgan and Eleanor McDaniel agreed to serve their masters additional time provided they pay the parish fine (Documents 1755, 1811). John Nelmes, in 1708, agreed to pay the fine of Katherine Line and to make payment to the parish (Document 1357). On 22 March 1710/11, she was presented to the court again for having another child. This time she agreed to serve Elizabeth Walters, a widow, an additional three years for "paying her fine & saveing the Parrish of Wiccocomoco harmless from ye sd Child" (Document 1396). John Shaw and William Harding, fathers of children born out of wedlock, were ordered by the court to provide security "to save ye Parish of Wiccocomoco harmless" (Document 1354). Eleanor Bennett, a servant of Phillip Fisher, agreed to serve her master an additional year provided he would take care of her child (Document 1866).

In some cases, the women would refuse to name the father of the child (Documents 687, 1201, 1224). Martha Hunter, servant to James Nipper, after spending a day in jail, declared Timothy Riley was the father of her child (Document 1246).

A number of historians have stated that very often masters were the fathers of some of the illegitimate children. Northumberland records indicate only a few masters were the fathers of such children. Mathew Roles, servant to Richard Cox, declared in court that Cox was the father of her child. She was ordered to serve the parish two years and be whipped. Col. St. Leger Codd paid her fine, and she was acquitted of the punishment. Cox was ordered to pay a fine of 500 pounds of tobacco (Document 704). Elizabeth Philips was presented before a grand jury for having a bastard child. She swore the father was Robert Davis, her master. Davis and John Haynie Jr. entered into a recognizance "to keep the said child from being a charge to the Parrish and ordered that the said Elizabeth be sold as the law directs after her Indented time is expired" (Document 1531). Mary Rogers, as well, contended that her

master, Nicholas Liscome, was the father of her child (Document 1233).
  Although the masters may have lost the service of the women servants for a short period, at times they kept the children of the women servants until they were 21. By her own consent, Katherine Amery, servant to James Allen, permitted her son, William, to serve Allen until he was 21 (Document 503). For some reason, the child of Lucy Howard, servant to Mrs. Elizabeth Watts, was in "ye keeping of Onesiphorus Bennett." The child was to serve Bennett until she became 21 (Document 571).*

  Servant or not, white women giving birth to children fathered by African-Americans had to serve additional time, pay a fine, or be sold for a period of five years; their children had to serve until they were 31 years of age.[13] At a court held 14 October 1740, Ann Thomas, servant to Mrs. Clark Hobson, acknowledged that she had been delivered of a mulatto. She was ordered to serve her mistress one additional year and then be sold for five years (Document 1731). On 13 June 1743, she was in court again, having been delivered of another "mulatto bastard child." Unable to pay the fine, the court ordered the sheriff to sell her to the highest bidder and the money or tobacco to go to the use of the parish (Document 1756). Because it had not been five years since her first offense, one does not know what events may have occurred or for certain whether it is the same Ann Thomas. Martha Bryant also confessed in court that she had been delivered of a mulatto child. She agreed to serve Charles Betts Jr. one year after her other time of service on consideration of his buying her (Documents 1804, 1805). Mary Range, a servant of Winder Kenner, was in court on three occasions in reference to her having a mulatto child. On 11 August 1740, she was ordered, upon the expiration of her present time to her master, to pay to the churchwardens £15 current money or be sold for five years. Eight days later, she was ordered to serve Kenner an additional year for the trouble of the delivery of the child at his house. On 14 December 1741, Range, refusing to pay her fine, was ordered to be sold by the churchwardens for five years (Documents 1726, 1727, 1741).

  Because Elizabeth Turner was unable to pay her fine after giving birth to a mulatto, the court ordered that she be sold by the churchwardens to serve a term of five years. It is not certain that she was a servant, but because the child was born at the house of Lewis Lamkin, she was ordered to serve him one year "in recompence of the loss & trouble occasioned thereby" (Documents 1730, 1732).

  Winifred, daughter of Rachell Webb als Day, and Mary Kelly, mulattoes

---

  * Other documents in which children were to serve as servants: 202, 655, 816.
  13. Hening, *Statutes at Large*, vol. 3, 453.

born of white women, were ordered to serve until 31 years of age (Documents 1425, 1725). William, a mulatto, was ordered to serve Mary Price, a widow, according to law (Document 1384).

Joseph Ball, whose servant Milly Thomas, a mulatto who was to serve him until she was 31, motioned the court for Thomas to serve him an additional three years for having three children during her time of service. The court ruled that the "motion was illegal and contrary to Justice: therefore it is ordered to be dismissed" (Document 1969). In 1765, the General Assembly had ruled it was cruel and inhumane for bastards of women servants by a Negro to serve until 31. From that date, males were to serve until 21 and females until 18.[14]

Most of the women servants apparently were unmarried; however, we do not know how many husbands or wives may have been separated from their spouses. Unless there was a reason to go to court, there would be no indication of husband and wife. Edmund Maudley and his wife both were servants to Richard Hull. After the birth of their daughter, the child was ordered to serve Howell Williams until she was 21; thus, we see the separation of a child from her parents (Document 816). We know that George and Anne Nicholson, servants of William Johnstone, were husband and wife from a court order in which they petitioned the court for their freedom dues (Document 1876). Of course, there was always the fear of being separated as servants were sold like so many pots and pans. Thaddeus Dorgan and his wife, Joan, servants of Timothy Greenham, agreed to serve their master an additional year provided he would keep them together (Document 1484). Thomas Hicks, formerly a servant of Thomas Gill and then a servant to John Allgood, agreed to serve Allgood additional time provided his master would give Katherine, his wife, her board for four and a half years and provide him with a good suit upon demand besides what was due him by law when his term expired (Document 1621).

Husbands and wives with children must have felt a special concern for their young. John Symmons and his wife, servants of John Cockrell and the parents of three children, went to court concerning their children. Dorothy, the eldest child, and Joane were ordered to serve Cockrell according to act. John, when he received his freedom, was ordered to bring his youngest child, James, to court, and the court would decide what John should pay his master for his trouble of keeping the child. If John was able to pay, James would be free. If not, James would serve Cockrell (Document 346).

Even though there were numerous accounts of difficulties between

---

14. Ibid., vol. 8, 134.

masters and servants, wills of county residents support the fact that some masters felt a kindness for their servants. William Renalls, in his will, stated that his servant, William Danes, was to be delivered one cow calf when he became of age (Document 86). At this period in history, cows were very precious and usually an item left to children, grandchildren, or someone very close. Robert Lord, likewise, left to his servant, Sarah Pargater, one cow, as well as a breeding sow, at the time of her freedom (Document 275). John Barber in his will requested that at his death his servant, Mathew Cox, be set free and be given one large new chest, plus clothes (Document 595). John Spence, a mulatto belonging to Elizabeth Banks, was to be discharged from servitude at her death (Document 1498). William Fallin declared in his will that his Negro, Jamme Jamme, be free after his term of four years had expired (Document 1602). George Howell requested that Elizabeth Webster be given one cow, one calf, and a suit of clothes provided she remain in the service of his wife or child until she reached the age of 18 (Document 1609). Graciana Span wrote in her will that it was the desire of her husband, Richard, to acquit Jane Goare two full years of her service (Document 551).

By 1725, indentured servitude in Northumberland had passed its peak. Only six documents—1597, 1616, 1633, 1634, 1672, and 1788—concern themselves with young boys being brought before the court to have their ages judged. After 1725, neither order books nor record books contain certificates for land. One would have to check Nugent's *Cavaliers and Pioneers* and Gray's *Northern Neck Land Grants* for patents for land and headrights after this period. Most of the court records after 1725 involve disputes between servants and masters—servants running away, petitioning the court for freedom dues, or seeking the permission of the court to be bought by another master. Others agree to serve additional time beyond the terms of their contracts.

Indentured servitude was a system that robbed one of self-respect and human dignity. The servants had little or nothing to gain from their work. They had been lured, seduced, or forced to come to Virginia, often with promises that failed to materialize. The only thing they had to look forward to was their day of freedom. Hofstadter questions whether "freed servants, especially those from the tobacco fields were in any mental or physical condition to start vigorous new lives, or that long and ripe years of productivity lay ahead for them."[15]

One would have to do a careful study of the court records to determine whether a servant remained in the area. Deeds for land, estates that might

---

15. Hofstadter, *America at 1750*, 61.

include a person's name, and court orders could reveal the name of a former servant. Personal property taxes, beginning in 1782, include names both of those owning and of those not owning land; however, because of the late date, most of the servants would have been deceased by this time.

Some servants recognized the value of learning a trade and bound themselves apprentices after their indented time. Patrick Burne bound himself an apprentice to Henry Arther for a term of four years. The trade to be learned is not mentioned (Document 1240). Ann Conner agreed to serve Cary Keble for four years for his teaching her to sew, knit, and spin (Document 1580). Mary Jinkins, servant to Thomas Webster, agreed to serve her master two years beyond her indented time in consideration of his teaching her to read, write, knit, spin, and do household work (Document 1632).

Surely some servants, in search of better opportunities, moved west of Northumberland after their expired time. Thomas Hazelip, a servant to Col. John Mottrom, settled in Westmoreland County, where the name Hazelip can be found in the court records for several generations.

Arthur Marsh, although listed as a headright of Ambrose Fielding but first a bond servant to Thomas Gayner, remained in the area and, by the time of his death, acquired about 300 acres of land. Unfortunately, the record book in which the deed was recorded was destroyed in a fire of 1710. We learn of the land in a transaction of his sons at a later date.

Surely a study of court records pertaining to servants provides a more complete picture of colonial life in Virginia. "Their work not only increased the comfort and convenience of the family [of the planter] but provided it with income as well."[16] Without this picture, one's visual image of colonial life might be that only of the landed aristocracy. Such an image would fail to convey the hardships of the servants, their struggles and aspirations—their role in the colonial way of life.

---

16. Morgan, *Virginians at Home*, 51.

DOCUMENTS

1. 24 May 1650—These are to certifie that accordinge to sufficient proofe made before this Court there is due unto Capt Thomas Baldridge two hundred acres of land for the transportation of these severall persons into this Colony: Grace Bonam, Willm Baldridge, Sarah Bonam, Willm. Humphreys. *Deeds, Orders 1650–52, 41.*

2. 24 May 1650—These are to certifie that accordinge to sufficient proofe made before us there is due Francis Gray three hundred acres of land by assignment from Capt Francis Poythers for the transportation of these severall persons into this Colony, Viz^t John Tomlinson, Richard Willis, James Balerod, Daniell More, John Symson, Mary King. *Deeds, Orders 1650–52, 41.*

3. 24 May 1650—These are to certifie that according to sufficient proofe made before us, there is due unto Mr John Hollowes five hundred and fifty acres of land for the transportation of these severall persons into this Colony: John Hollowes, John Cone, Restitute Hollowes Sr., Willm Freake, John Knot, Restitute Hollowes Jr., Robert Street, Edward Frier, John Hanch, Willm Weathers, Andrew Quinborow. *Deeds, Orders 1650–52, 41.*

4. 24 May 1650—These are to Certifie that accordinge to sufficient proofe made before us there is due unto John Hillier by Assignment from Capt Francis Poythers two hundred acres of land for the transportation of these several persons into this Colony. Viz^t Edward Tovend [Corend ?], Elizabeth Bridges, Mary Hayes, Morris Oger, As also for his own adventure two persons, Edward Crowell, Robert Jones. *Deeds, Orders 1650–52, 41.*

5. 24 Aug. 1650—These are to certifie that according to sufficient proofe made before us, there is due to Mr John Rosier fifty acres of Land for the transportation of Elizabeth his Wife into this Colony. *Deeds, Orders 1650–52, 41.*

6. 24 Aug. 1650—These are to certifie that Robert Smyth is due Fifty acres of land for ye transportation of his wife Anne into this Colony. *Deeds, Orders 1650–52, 42.*

7. 24 Aug. 1650—Accordinge to sufficient proofe to this Court that there is due to William Spicer fifty acres of land for transportation of himselfe. *Deeds, Orders 1650–52, 42.*

8. 24 Aug. 1650—These are to certifie that accordinge to sufficient proofe made before us there is due unto George Colclough three hundred acres of Land for the transportation of these several persons into this Colony, Viz^t Mr Colclough twice, Henry Lane, James Ashton, Elizabeth Bedle, Mathew Skipper. *Deeds, Orders 1650–52, 42.*

9. 24 Aug. 1650—Accordinge to sufficient proofe to this Court that there is due to John Essex one hundred acres of land for transportation of himselfe and Elizabeth his wife. *Deeds, Orders 1650–52, 42.*

10. 24 May 1650—Accordinge to sufficient proofe to this Court that there is due to Mr Thomas Speke one hundred & fifty acres of land for transportation of these persons into this Colony, Viz^t John Nightingale, Alice White, James Gresall. *Deeds, Orders 1650–52, 43.*

11. 24 May 1650—According to sufficient proofe made to this Court, there is due to Mr Peter Knight One hundred & Fifty acres of Land for the transportation of these persons into this Colony, Viz^t his own transportation, Wm Knight, John Cloberry. *Deeds, Orders 1650–52, 43.*

12. 10 Jan. 1650—According to sufficient proofe made to this Court, there is due Rice Maddox Two hundred acres of land for transportation of these persons into this Collony, Viz^t Tho: Cockrill, Tho: Tillitt, Susan Cale, Rice Maddox. *Deeds, Orders 1650–52, 46.*

13. 10 Jan. 1650—According to sufficient proofe made to this Court, there is due to Edward Grymes eight hundred acres of land for the transportation of the s^d persons into this Collony. Viz^t Thos. Atwell, his first wife, Susan Scerry, Robt Elliott, Daniel Dollor, Martha Cottell, Wm Threader, Devorax Goreing, Edward Grymes, Eliza Milner, Wm Cravener [?], Wm Wood, Richard Squiren, Tho Greene, Rich Alford, Daniel Jones. *Deeds, Orders 1650–52, 46.*

14. 10 Jan. 1650—According to sufficient proofe made to this Court, there is due to Hugh Lee One hundred acres of Land for transportation of these persons into this Collony. Viz^t John Haies & Susan Watson. *Deeds, Orders 1650–52, 46.*

15. 10 Jan. 1650—According to sufficient proofe made to this Court, there is due to Walter Brodhurst Two hundred acres of land for the transportation of these persons into this Collony Viz^t Himselfe, Anne his Wife, Eliz: Brodhurst, Susan Brodhurst. *Deeds, Orders 1650–52, 46.*

16. 10 Jan. 1650—According to sufficient proofe made to this Court, there is due to John Bennett Fifty acres of Land for the transportation of his wife Elizabeth Bennett into this Collonyne. *Deeds, Orders 1650–52, 47.*

17. 10 Jan. 1650—According to sufficient proofe made to this Court, there is due to David Phillips one hundred acres for transportation into this Collony of himselfe and Anne his wife. *Deeds, Orders 1650–52, 47.*

18. 10 May 1650—According to sufficient proofe made to this Court, there is due to Thomas Phillipps one hundred acres of land for his owne transportation twice into this Collony. *Deeds, Orders 1650–52, 49.*

19. 20 Feb. 1650—According to sufficient proofe made to this Court, there is due to Gabriell Odyer one hundrd fifty acres of land for transportation of himselfe twice & Mary his wife into this Colony. *Deeds, Orders 1650–52, 49.*

20. 20 Feb. 1650—According to sufficient proofe made to this Court there is due to Richard Span one hundred acres of land due to him for the transportation of these persons into this Collony. Viz^t Himselfe, George Alderidge. *Deeds, Orders 1650–52, 49.*

21. 20 Feb. 1650—According to sufficient proofe made to this Court, there is due to Richard Hawkins Two hundred & fifty acres of Land for transportation of these persons following into this Colony, Viz^t Himselfe, Katherine Willowbye, Samuel Challienge, Margery Challienge, Edmund Larkin. *Deeds, Orders 1650–52, 49.*

22. 20 Feb. 1650—According to sufficient proof made to this Court, there is due to Alexander Baineham one hundred & fifty acres of land for transportation of these persons following into this Colony. Viz^t Himselfe, Ann his wife, Alexander Baineham. *Deeds, Orders 1650–52, 49.*

23. 20 Feb. 1650—According to sufficient proofe made to this Court, there is due to William Betts One hundred and fifty acres of Land for the transportation of these persons into this Colony, Viz^t Himselfe, Robert Casleton, Francis Roberts. *Deeds, Orders 1650–52, 49.*

24. 20 Feb. 1650—According to Sufficient proofe made to this Court, there is due to Arthur Terrell Two hundred acres of Land for the transportation of these persons into this Colony, Viz^t Himselfe, Elizabeth his wife, Arthur Terrell, Eliz: Terrell. *Deeds, Orders 1650–52, 49.*

25. 20 Feb. 1650—According to sufficient proofe made to this Court, there is due to Thomas Darrows one hundred acres of land for transportation of himselfe & Ann his wife into this Colony. *Deeds, Orders 1650–52, 49.*

26. 20 Feb. 1650—According to sufficient proofe made to this Court that there is due to Mr Richard Turney Six hundred acres of Land for the transportation of the following persons into this Colony, Viz^t Perry Hamon, Tho: Plackmett [?], Tho: Phillips, Tho: Griffith, John Blitto, Samu: Welding, Tho: Jones, John Quesenbery, Eliza: Wooton, Lyon the Turk, Manuel the Negro, Jorie the Negro. *Deeds, Orders 1650–52, 50.*

27. 20 Feb. 1650—According to sufficient proofe made to this Court, there is due to Nathaniel Hickman Two hundred acres of Land for transportation of these persons into this Colony, Viz^t Wm Smith, John Ensworth, Hannah Bittle, Jane Crowell. *Deeds, Orders 1650–52, 50.*

28. 20 Feb. 1650—According to sufficient proofe made to this Court, there is due to Mr Francis Clay Foure hundred acres of Land for transportation of these persons into this Collony, Viz^t Mary Edwards, Tho Olever, Edw Sampsoun, Wm Jones, Wm Bethell, Hen: Evans, John Cess, Eliza: Norman. *Deeds, Orders 1650–52, 51.*

29. 28 Oct. 1651—This Indenture made the 28 Day of October 1651 Between John Kelly of the one part and Hugh Lee of the other part Witness that the said John Kelly for ye consideration of two thousand pounds of merchantable Tobacco and three Barrells of corne to be paid the 20th of November 1652 shall live with & serve the said Hugh Lee from the first of November next till one yeare be fully and compleatly ended and upon condition that the said John Kelly shall at all the convenient speed he may marrie [marry] Susan Watson, the servant of the said Hugh Lee, and in consideration thereof the said John Kelly and Susan Watson shall serve the said Hugh Lee or his Assigns each of them two years an half beginning the first of November which shall be the year of our Lord 1652 till the said time be fully ended of two yeares and a halfe a peace and that the said John Kelly & Susan shall doe the said Lee good & faithfull service in Consideration whereof the said Hugh Lee shall find the said Kelly & Susan meate, drink, washing & lodging.... *Deeds, Orders 1650–52, 52.*

30. 20 Nov. 1651—According to sufficient proofe made before this Court, there is due to John Vaughan one hundred & fifty acres of Land for the transportation of these persons following into this Colony, Viz^t Richard King, Wm Thomas, Rich: Devill [?]. *Deeds, Orders 1650–52, 55.*

31. 20 Nov. 1651—According to sufficient proofe made before this Court there is due Mr Seth Foster one hundred & fifty Acres of Land for his owne transportation thrice into this Colony. *Deeds, Orders 1650–52, 56.*

32. 17 Jan. 1651—According to sufficient proofe made to this Court, there is due to Mr George Colclough one hundred acres of Land for the transportation of these persons following, Viz^t Ann Waller, Elizabeth Jeffery. *Deeds, Orders 1650–52, 58.*

33. 17 Jan. 1651—According to sufficient proofe made to this Court, there is due to Capt Gyles Brent Esqr. Nine hundred acres of Land for the transportation of these persons following into this Colony, Viz^t Capt Gyles Brent, Mrs Margaret Brent, Mrs Mary Brent, Mrs Mary Brent Wife to Capt Brent, Margaret Kendall, Thomas Foster, Wm Clarke, John Williams, Richard Tarling, Jane Gilpin, Mary Outris, John Fleete, Thomas Conepesarke, Ann White, Francis King, Francis Anketell, Richard Cotesford, John Rookwood. *Deeds, Orders 1650–52, 58.*

34. 23 April 1652—According to sufficient proofe made to this Court, there is due Mr Nicholas Morris two hundred acres of Land for transportation of these persons following into the Colony, Viz^t Katherine Madix, William Nicholls, John Warner, John Michem. *Deeds, Orders 1650–52, 59.*

35. 23 April 1652—According to sufficient proofe made to this Court, there is due to Capt John Smith Three hundred acres of land for transportation of these persons following into this Colony, Viz^t Himselfe, Mary his wife, John Prosser, Thomas Goodale, Bartho: Blome, Geo: West. *Deeds, Orders 1650–52, 61.*

36. 14 May 1652—This Indenture made ye first day of Novem: in ye yeare of our Sovereigne Lord ye King & in ye yeare 1649 Between me Edward Roberts of ye one party and Thomas Dunkington of ye other, It is agreed upon that ye said Dunkington doe by these presents binde my selfe to serve ye said Roberts or his heires or assignes from ye date hereof untill six yeares be fully accomplished in such service or imployment as ye said Edward or his assignes shall imploy him & in consideration of ye aforesaid service, ye said Roberts is to find ye said Dunkington meate, drinke & lodging dureing ye said terme & after ye said terme & after ye said terme to give him three barrells of Corne & clothes according to ye custome of ye Country As Witness our hands this first of Novem Ano Dom 1649

        Signed the mark of Tho: Dunkington

I edward Roberts doe assign over all my right & title of this Indenture to Richard Holden, As Witness my hand this 14th of May 1652

           Edward Roberts

RB 1652–58, 34.

37. 20 July 1652—According to sufficient proofe made to this Court, there is due Francis Bridges Two hundred & fifty acres of Land for the transportation of these persons following into this Colony, Viz^t John Sheapard, Matthew Nooth, Hercules Bridges, Rich: Peecox, Francis Bridges. *Deeds, Orders 1650–52, 64.*

38. 20 Sept. 1652—The Court doth order that Wm Linsey shall serve Wm Reynolds but fower yeares according to the Indenture and no longer though Thomas Hawkens hath sold him for five yeares. *OB 1652–65, 2.*

39. 20 Sept. 1652—According to sufficient proofe made before this Court there is due to Andrew Munroe one hundred acres of land for the transportation of these persons following into this Colony vizt

  John Wright   Andrew Edenborough

OB 1652–65, 2.

40. 20 Sept. 1652—According to sufficient proofe made before this Court, there is due to Thomas Youlle Two hundred Acres of Land for transportation of these persons following into this Colony:

  John Clenes   John Wilson
  John Cammell   Marga: Pes_cy U/I

OB 1652–65, 2.

41. 20 Sept. 1652—According to sufficient proofe made before this Court there is due to Wm Hardich Two hundred & fifty Acres of Land for transportation of these persons into this Colony vizt

  David May   Robert Anderson
  Makum Thomson   Henry Johnson

Henry Sheath
OB 1652–65, 3.

42. 20 Sept. 1652—According to sufficient proofe made before this Court, there is due to Mr George Colclough one hundred Acres of Land for the transportation of these persons following into this Colony vizt Tho: Brunton and Walter Donne. *OB 1652–65, 4.*

43. 20 Sept. 1652—According to sufficient proofe made to this Court, there is due to Mr Thomas Speke Three hundred Acres of Land for the transportation of these persons following into this Colony vizt

    Reynold Young   James Vallins
    John Thomson   James Colsorom
    John Marshall   Charles North

This cer^t was made in Wm Cocke's name & delivered unto him by Mr Speke's owne order. *OB 1652–65, 4.*

44. 20 Sept. 1652—According to sufficient proofe made before this Court, there is due to Mr Richard Turney Two hundred & fifty Acres of Land for the transportation of these persons following into this Colony vizt

    Tho: Roberts   Mary Griggs
    Tho: Jones   John Juice
    Nath: Hunt

OB 1652–65, 4.

45. 25 Nov. 1652—Whereas Mr Nathaniel Pope did produce in Court a letter of Attorney made by Mr Nicholas Hayward unto Richard Nicholas, his servant now deceased, as also a letter subscribed by the said Mr Hayward directed to the said Mr Pope. . . . *OB 1652–65, 6.*

46. 25 Nov. 1652—According to sufficient proofe made before this Court, there is due to Mr Walter Brodhurst One hundred Acres of Land for the transportation of these persons into the Colony vizt

    Francis Willis   Patricke Potts

OB 1652–65, 7.

47. 25 Nov. 1652—Whereas by bond given under the hand of Tho: Hawkins it appears that the said Hawkins sold a man servant unto Wm Reynolds for the time of five yeares, it being for longer time than ye said Hawkins had just power to dispose of the said serv^t right to serve as by Order of Court doth plainly appeare, wee doe therefor with a full consent allott that the said Hawkins shall performe & put unto Wm Reynolds (after the expiration of the fower yeares) as sufficient & able hand as that servant now in his custody is whether he live or dye to perform the compleate time of service as from bond from Hawkins is due unto the said Reynolds And wee doe allott Mr Hawkins to pay Court charges unto which wee have sett our hands. *OB 1652–65, 7.* [Unfortunately, the servant in question is not named.]

48. 25 Nov. 1652—According to sufficient proofe made before this Court, there is due to Mr Tho Speke one hundred & fifty Acres of land for the transportation of these persons into the Colony vizt
    David Cristom
    Wm Newberry
    Mary Wooldridge
OB 1652–65, 7.

49. 20 Jan. 1652/53—According to sufficient proofe made before this Court, there is due to John Bennett, carpenter, 50 Acres of Land for transportation of Mr Wm Spense into this Colony. *OB 1652–65, 8.*

50. 20 Jan. 1652/53—According to sufficient proofe made before this Court, there is due to Thomas Blagg one hundred Acres of Land for the transportation of himselfe & Judith Spencer into this Colony. *OB 1652–65, 11.*

51. 10 March 1652/53—According to sufficient proofe made before this Court, there is due to Mary Keene two hundred Acres of Land for the transportation of these persons into this Colony vizt

Tho: Keene	Wm Keene
herselfe	Susan Keene

OB 1652–65, 11.

52. 10 March 1652/53—According to sufficient proofe made before this Court, there is due to John Hull fower hundred Acres of land for the transportation of these persons into this Colony Viz^t

John Scriven	Ann Feild
Tho: Mecham	Judith Layton
Cha: Parker	Samuel Dunn
Walt: Moore	Marge: Clewer [or Clever]

The 5 first Serv^ts assigned over to Richd Smyth. Rich Hull heir of the s^d Jno Hull. *OB 1652–65, 12.*

53. 20 May 1653—According to sufficient proofe made before this Court, there is due Henry Rayner One hundred Acres of Land for the

transportation of these persons into this Colony vizt
           Archebald Reade   Thomas Watson
OB 1652–65, 13.

54. 20 May 1653—According to sufficient proofe made before this Court, there is due Thomas Orlye one hundred Acres of land for his own transportation twice into this Colony. *OB 1652–65, 13.*

55. 20 May 1653—According to sufficient proofe made before this Court, there is due to Clement Corbell five hundred & fifty Acres of land for ye transportation of these persons into this Colony vizt
           himselfe   Samuel Nicholls
           Angell his wife   Francs: Jones
           Gabriel Corbell   Henry Sentence
           John Corbell   James Peirce
           Anne Corbell   Marg: Barrow
           Angell Corbell
OB 1652–65, 13.

56. 20 Sept. 1653—According to sufficient proofe made to this Court, there is due to Robert Land One hundred Acres of Land for the transportation of these persons into this Colony vizt Francis Berry & Mary Dicks. *OB 1652–65, 15.*

57. 20 Sept. 1653—According to sufficient proofe made before this Court, there is due to Wm Reynolds one hundred Acres of Land for ye transportation of 2 persons into this Colony vizt Wm Linsey & Tho: Backster. *OB 1652–65, 15.*

58. 29 Oct. 1653—George Day 23 yeares or thereabouts being sworne & examined saith that this Depon^t came in ye ship with Mr Winter Chapman about 4 or 5 yeares agoe when ye said Mr Chapman brought in two boyes that were brothers, the Elder of them named Henry was to serve by Indenture for 5 yeares & ye younger named Thomas West was to serve for 7 yeares And this Depon^t heard ye said Thomas say that he was to serve 7 yeares in ye Country and that Colo. John Mottrom bought ye said Henry and Thomas of ye said Mr Chapman, And Further saith not.
                              George Day, his marke
RB 1652–58, 37.

59. 4 Nov. 1653—Thomas Speke, Gent. aged 30 yeares or thereabouts, being sworne & examined saith that Mr Winter Chapman brought into this

Country some servants 4 or 5 years agoe to sell & brought them to this Depon^ts house, amongst whom were two boys named Henry West and Thomas West, who were brothers.... *RB 1652–58, 37.*

60. 4 Nov. 1653—Anne ye wife of Tho: Speke, Gent., aged 42 yeares or thereabouts being sworne & examined saith that Mr Winter Chapman brought into this Country Servants about 4 or 5 yeares ago to sell & ... them to this Depon^ts husbands house among ... were two boys named Henry & Thomas, the boys were brothers, & ye older was bound by Indenture to serve 5 yeares and the other wch was ye younger, though no Indenture, was signed by ye said Boy, yet she this Depon^t heard ye said Boy say ... consent that he was to serve Colo. John Mottrom 7 yeares and for soe long time ye said Colo. Mottrom bought him. And farther this Depon^t saith not.

Ann Speke

RB 1652–58, 37.

61. 21 Nov. 1653—According to sufficient proof made to this Court, there is due Robert Sharpe ... acres of land for the transportation of ... into this Colony. *OB 1652–65, 18.* [Page badly damaged.]

62. 21 Nov. 1653—According to sufficient proofe made to this Court, there is due to John Haney One hundred Acres of Land for transportation of these persons into ye Colony vizt David, a Scotchman, and John Duglas. *OB 1652–65, 18.*

63. 21 Nov. 1653—According to sufficient proofe made to this Court, there is due to Hen: Rocke ... Acres of land for transportation of himself, John Squibb & John ... into this Colony. *OB 1652–65, 19.* [Parts of page torn.]

64. 21 Nov. 1653—According to sufficient proofe made to this Court, there is due to Wm Thomas two hundred Acres of Land for ye transportation of himselfe, Frances his wife, John Frissell & Ann Parry. *OB 1652–65, 20.*

65. 21 Nov. 1653—Whereas this cause is referred till ye next Court & if ye said Vincent Cox doe not then make appeare that ye shipp wch he came into this Country came to an Anchor in Virginia on ye 10th of Oct:, then he is to serve Mr Richard Cole according to assignm^t & make good ye time that he hath done out of Mr Coles his service. *OB 1652–65, 20.* [The names Vincent and Richard are in the margin of the page.]

66. 1 Dec. 1653—William Beesly, aged 22 yeares or thereabouts, being sworne & examined, saith that he this Depon^t came into this Colony of

Virginia on ye Shipp called y^e *Honor* in wch ship came one Vincent Cox servant to Mr Wm Bullocke & ye said Shipp came to Anchor in Virginia about the 8th or ye 10th day of October last was fower yeares. . . . *RB 1652–58, 42.*

67. 20 Feb. 1653/54—According to sufficient proofe made to this Court, there is due to Ann Moore 100 Acres of Land for ye transportation of herselfe & Ann her daughter into this Colony. *OB 1652–65, 22.*

68. 20 Feb. 1653/54—Whereas it doth appeare unto ye Court by ye Depositions of Wm Beesly & John Draper that Vincent Cox came into this Country ye 10th day of Octo: last was fower yeares & that ye said Cox was sold or Assigned by John Pettitt to Mr Richard Cole for ye serving him ye said Mr Cole ye remaind^r of fower yeares as by ye said Assignment may more at large appeare wth said time of service ye Court doth declare that ye said Cox hath served according to ye last Assignm^t. The Court doth order that he ye said Cox shall be free from ye said Mr Cole his service & that ye said Mr Cole shall pay ye charges of Court. . . . *OB 1652–65, 22.*

69. 20 Feb. 1653/54—According to sufficient proofe made to this Court, there is due to Mr Wm Nash 700 Acres of Land for the transportation of these persons following into this Colony

himself twice	Thomas Pearce
Ann his wife	John Marall
John Godfrey	Alex [?]
Robt Stafford	John Carter
James Morrey	Edw: Sedbery
Theodore Baker	Mary Mealey [?]
Mary Clurshene [?]	

OB 1652–65, 22.

70. 20 Feb. 1653/54—The Court doth order that Thomas Pearce shall serve his Master Mr Wm Nash for one yeare more to come since ye 28 of January last & then to be free, he coming in without an Indenture which is according to Act of Assembly. *OB 1652–65, 23.*

71. 20 Feb. 1653/54—Whereas it doth appeare unto ye Court by ye oathes of John Earle, John Walker & Ann Ball that Thomas Dankington doth belong to & is ye servant of Edward Roberts, the Court doth therefore order that Rich: Holden shall deliver up ye said Dankington forthwith to ye s^d Roberts & that ye said Holden shall pay charges of Court. . . . *OB 1652–65, 23.*

72. 20 July 1654—The Court doth order that Mr Richard Cole shall by ye 20th of October next pay unto Vincent Cox his late servant one cloth suite, one paire of shoes and stockings, one shirt, one hatt or capp & three barrells of Indian corne being due unto him at ye expiration of his service according to ye custom of ye Country with charges of Court. *OB 1652–65, 26.*

73. 20 July 1654—According to sufficient proofe made to this Court, there is due to Tho: Gerrard one hundred Acres of Land for transportation of Mary Wesson & Christopher . . . into this Country. *OB 1652–65, 26.* [Because of torn page, Christopher's surname is not on the page.]

74. 20 July 1654—According to sufficient proofe made to this Court, there is due to Matthew Rhodon three hundred Acres of Land for the transportation of these persons following

Himselfe	Daniel Glover
Geo: Carmickell	Sarah Read
Alex: Makewaler	Wm Wiles

OB 1652–65, 26.

75. 20 July 1654—According to sufficient proofe made to this Court, there is due unto Tho: Wilsford one hundred Acres of land for ye transportation of Sarah Southerne & Judeth Southerne into this Colony. *OB 1652–65, 28.*

76. 20 Nov. 1654— . . . grante unto Thomas Wilsford fower hundred & . . . acres of land lyeing scituate & being upon a Creek now known & called Perries Creeke beginning on a point on Perries Creek running east 1/2 east to a quarter marked tree at ye head branch . . . land from ye which divides this land from ye land now in ye possession of Richard White, carpenter, by marked trees, running down to ye head of a small Branch issueing out of Perries Creeke . . . the said land being due unto ye said Tho: Wilsford by purchase of Hugh Lee, overseer of ye Orphans of Jane Perrey deceased, as also of & for ye transportation of five persons into ye Colony all whose names are recorded under this Pattent & Dated ye 10th of Novem: 1651. . . . *RB 1652–58, 50.* [The five persons transported are not named.]

77. 20 Nov. 1654—According to sufficient proofe made to this Court, there is due to Tho: Hawkins one hundred Acres of Land for ye transportation of Mary Bayly & Wm Conger into this Country. *OB 1652–65, 29.*

78. 20 Nov. 1654—According to sufficient proofe made to this Court, there is due to Col. John Mottrom two hundred & fifty Acres of Land for ye transportation of 2 Scotts & 3 Irish bought out of Mr Warren's shipp & Capt Swanley's shipp. *OB 1652–65, 30.*

79. 20 Nov. 1654—According to sufficient proofe made to this Court, there is due to Mr Robert Newman six hundred & fifty Acres of land Assigned to him by John Branch & ye Cer^t was lost & no land ever taken up by virtue of ye former Cer^t at ye said Mr Newman deposed for ye transportation of these persons into ye Colony vizt

John Branch	Wm Wharwell
Mary his wife	Walt^r Prichard
Mary his daughter	Tho Parkes
Edw: Toogood	Rich Grigson
David Griffin	Rob Swaile
John Willis	John Clew
Wm Wade	

OB 1652–65, 30.

80. 20 Aug. 1655—Whereas it doth appeare unto the Court that Mr Hugh Lee is indebted unto Jno Kent a servant by condition from under the said Mr Lee his hand, the Court doth therefore order that the said Mr Hugh Lee shall by the tenth of November next make payment of one thousand five hundred and eighty pounds weight of good tobacco and caske in consideration of the s^d servant unto the s^d John Kent or his Attorney else execution. *OB 1652–65, 31.*

81. 20 Aug. 1655—According to sufficient proofe made to this Court, there is due to Richd Holden two hundred Acres of land for transportation of John Gibbins, Elizabeth Glisen, an Irish woman called Joan and June Brockett into this Colony. *OB 1652–65, 31.*

82. 20 Aug. 1655—According to sufficient proofe made to this Court there is due unto John Motteram 50 Acres of Land for transportation of himselfe into this Colony. *OB 1652–65, 31.*

83. 20 Aug. 1655—According to sufficient proofe made to this Court there is due unto Richd Gible fifty Acres of land for transportation of Wm Jones into this Colony. *OB 1652–65, 32.*

84. 20 Aug. 1655—According to sufficient proofe made to this Court there is due unto Robert Smyth two hundred and fifty Acres of Land for transportation of Ann Smyth, Sarah Smyth, Rose Gilbird, Wm Stratford, and Mary Stratford into this Collony. *OB 1652–65, 33.*

85. 20 Aug. 1655—According to sufficient proofe made to this Court there is due unto Wm Thomas two hundred Acres of Land (whoe hath assigned it unto John Mottram by the acknowledgment of the sd Mr Thomas in Court) for transportation of these persons following

    Lydia Sayer   Thomas Giouer
    Edward Giouer   Lyonell Britten

OB 1652–65, 33.

86. 20 Nov. 1655, Will of William Renalls—I give my Servt, William Danes, one Cowe Calfe to be delivered to him when he is of age.... *RB 1652–58, 56.*

87. 20 Nov. 1655—According to sufficient proofe made to this Court, there is due unto Major Samuel Smyth two hundred Acres of Land for transportation of these persons into this Colony (Viz^t)

    Elizabeth Reade   Tony, a Negro
    Bryand, an Irishman   Besse, a Negro

OB 1652–65, 36.

88. 20 Nov. 1655—These are testifie y^t Mr Sam Smyth hath had of me one mayde Servt ye last yeare and one man Servt this yeare for wch the Land due for their transportation belongs to him Witness my hand ye 20th of April 1654. Ri: Bennett *OB 1652–65, 36.*

89. 20 Nov. 1655—Whereas Jane Owen, being ye serv^t of Capt Richard Budd, made a complaint unto this Court of abuse by her M^{rs} & whereas it doth appear by the oathes of Mrs Morris & Mrs Hawley that ye sd Jane Owen had about twelve markes black & blew about her, the Court doth therefore order y^t the sd Capt Budd shall forthwth paye all charges of Court else Execution. *OB 1652–65, 36.*

90. 20 Jan. 1655/56—Memorandum. It is conditioned & agreed by & betwixt Thomas Kay on ye one part & Humfrey Higgenson on the other part that the sd Thomas Key hath put unto the sd Humfrey one Negroe girle by name of Elizabeth for & during the terme of nine yeares after the date hereof provided that the sd Humfrey doe finde & allowe the sd Elizabeth meate, drinke and apparell during the sd terme. And allsoe the sd Humfrey Higginson doth freely covenant & promise to & with the sd Thomas Key that if he the sd Humfrey doe dye before the end of the sd time above certified that then the sd Girle be free from the sd Humfrey Higginson & his assignes and if the sd Humfrey Higginson doe goe for England with an intention to live & remaine there that then he shall carry the sd girle with him & to pay for her passage & likewise that he put not of the girle to any man but to keepe her himselfe. In

Witness whereof I the sd Humfrey Higginson have hereunto sett my hand & seale the last day of Oct. 1656. Sealed & delivered in the presence of us

          Humfrey Higginson
          Robt. Routh
          Francis Meryman

RB 1652–58, 66.

91. 20 Jan. 1655/56—Whereas at a Court helden for this County of Northumberland the 22th daye of Nov. 1655 ye verdict of a Jury and Judgm^t did award & decree that whereas Mrs Eleanor Budd was arrested for the death of one Thomas Winn, her late servant.... *RB 1652–58, 67.* [The body of the victim was dug up, and Mrs. Budd was vindicated.]

92. 20 Jan. 1655/56—The Court doth order that Francis Roberts shall put in security for his appearance at ye next Co^{rt} to answer the complaint of Eliza: Essex, Servt to Mr Geo: Colclough before his departure from this Court. *OB 1652–65, 37.*

93. 20 Jan. 1655/56—According to sufficient proofe made to this Court, there is due unto James Allen fifty Acres of Land for transportation of Margaret Jones into this Colony. *OB 1652–65, 37.*

94. 20 Jan. 1655/56—According to sufficient proofe made to this Court, there is due unto Thomas Reade fifty Acres of Land for his own transportation into this Colony. *OB 1652–65, 37.*

95. 20 Jan. 1655/56—According to sufficient proofe made to this Court, there is due unto Capt John Rogers one hundred Acres of Land for transportation of Abraham Joyse & Roro Makatter into this Colony. *OB 1652–65, 39.*

96. 20 May 1656—According to sufficient proofe made to this Court, there is due unto Mr Hugh Lee 200 Acres of Land for transportation of these persons following into this Colony vizt

  Hannah Lee   Ann Murrall
  Mr David Lindsay   Joshua Esto

OB 1652–65, 45.

97. 20 May 1656—According to sufficient proofe made to this Court, there is due to Mr Nicholas Jurnew 200 acres of Land for the transportation of foure persons into this Colony Viz^t Thomas Williams, Gilbert Cooper, Ann Burton, Patrick Criss which said rights the said Mr Jurnew in open Court assigned unto William Thomas. *OB 1652–65, 46.*

98. 20 May 1656—According to sufficient proofe made to this Court, there is due to Mr Wm Presly 50 Acres of Land for transportation of John Dunnidge into this Colony. *OB 1652–65, 47.*

99. 20 May 1656—According to sufficient proofe made to this Court, there is due to Colonel John Trussell one hundred Acres of Land for transportation of Robert Hitchcocke & Abigall Bridge into this Colony. *OB 1652–65, 47.*

100. 21 July 1656—According to sufficient proofe made to this Court, there is due to Mr John Bardon one hundred & fifty acres of Land for the transportation of these persons into this Colony Viz^t himselfe, Hugh Addison, and Sarah Gomoyar. *OB 1652–65, 49.*

101. 20 Nov. 1656—These are to certifie y^t according to sufficient proofe made before the Court, there is due to Mr James Hawley, Ad^{tor} of the estate of Ralph Horsely dec^d, 300 Acres of Land for the transportation of these persons following into this Colony (Viz^t)

Andrew Cockerill	Wm Mundy
Wm Ballingall	Rich: Wall
Edward Meers	and one servant called Thomas

OB 1652–65, 52.

102. 20 Nov. 1656—According to sufficient proofe made before this Court, there is due to Richard Flynt 50 acres of Land for the transportation of Elizabeth James into this Colony. *OB 1652–65, 52.*

103. 20 Nov. 1656—Thomas Reade averreth in open Court that hee never did declare in any former oath by him taken that Mr Tho: Hopkins sold James Southward (Servant to Capt David Mansfield) unto Wm Chapman. *OB 1652–65, 53.*

104. 20 Jan. 1656/57—Will of William Presley... Item. I give Humphrey Fulfort at the end of the time he is to serve one Cow Calfe.... I give sonn W^m either the boy Jonathan or the servant wch Berry shall bring in.... *RB 1652–58, 95, 96.*

105. 20 Feb. 1656/57—There appearing to be due unto Thomas Hazelip, a late Servant unto Col. Jno Mottrom, his freedome Corne & Clothes. It is ordered with consent that Mr Wm Presly, Ador of the sd Col. Mottrom's estate, shall forthwith make paymt unto ye sd Hazelip three Barrells of Indian Corne, one sute of cloth clothes, one shirt, one paire of shoes & stockings, one Ax & a hoe out of the deceased's estate according to order else execution. *OB 1652–65, 54.*

106. 21 Feb. 1656/57—These are to certifie that according to sufficient proofe made before this Court there is due to John Howell 300 acres of Land for ye transportation of six persons into this Colony (Vizt)

  John Howell   Hannah Carpenter
  Francis Howell   Laurence Maurice
  Lancelot, a Scotchman Greene Abraham

OB 1652–65, 55.

107. 21 Feb. 1656/57—These are to Certifie yt according to sufficient proofe made before this Court, there is due unto Anthony Linton 100 acres of Land for transportation of two persons into this Colony Vizt Jane White & Elizabeth Pignett. *OB 1652–65, 56.*

108. 21 Feb. 1656/57—These are to Certifie that according to sufficient proofe made before this Court, there is due to Mr George Colclough six hundred acres of Land for transportation of these persons following into this Colony (Viz)

  Mr George Colclough   John Highland
  Mrs Ursula Colclough   George Cunny
  Sarah Thompson   Jno Ware
  Phillip Nutt   Amy Stevens
  Ralph Stevenson   Amy Yeomans
  Wm Osborne   Elizabeth Essex

OB 1652–65, 58.

109. 21 Feb. 1656/57—These are to certifie that according to sufficient proofe made before this Court, there is due to Capt Peter Lefevur 250 acres of Land for transportation of five persons into this Colony (Vizt)

  Peter Lefevur   Margaret Lefevur
  Abraham, Jane, & Jacob Lefevur

OB 1652–65, 59.

110. 23 March 1656/57—These are to Certify that according to sufficient proofe made before this Court, there is due to Tho: Philpott 150 acres of Land for the Transportation of these persons into this Colony (Vizt)

Jonathan Howe   Deborah Comey
Anthony Harris
OB 1652–65, 60.

111. 13 April 1657—These are to Certifie that according to sufficient proofe made before this Court, there is due unto Wm Warder two hundred & fifty acres of Land for the Transportation of these persons following into this Colony (Viz^t)
    Wm Warder   Hugh Forsett
    George Seeling   Ralph Stevens
    Noah Dance
OB 1652–65, 63.

112. 20 July 1657—These are to Certifie that according to sufficient proofe made before this Court, there is due unto Mr Wm Presly, the son of Mr Wm Presly dec^d, one thousand acres of Land Viz^t Certificate for 900 acres thereof being Attached in the hands of Thomas Orley of the estate of Mr Edward Moore in pt: of a debt due from the sd. Mr Moore to the sd Mr Presly dec^d & delivered to him by order of the County Court bearing date the 20th of July 1654 & the other hundred acres being due unto the sd Mr Presly Junior for the transportation of two persons into this Colony (Viz^t) Jno Camell & Richard Russell. *OB 1652–65, 69.*

113. 20 July 1657—These are to Certifie that according to sufficient proofe made to this Court, there is due to Thomas Kedby 100 acres of Land being assigned unto him from Mr John Mallett for his the sd Mr Mallett's transportation twice into this Colony. *OB 1652–65, 69.*

114. 26 July 1657, inventory of William Nash—one servant named Laurence Simons [Simmons] 2 yeares & 1/2 to serve. *RB 1652–58, 125.*

115. 21 Sept. 1657—These are to Certifie that according to sufficient proofe made before this Court, there is due to Jno Bennett 350 acres of Land for the transportation of seaven persons into this Colony (Viz^t)
    Wm Beasly   Saml Gosling
    Jno Draper   Robt Warner
    Elizabeth Russell   & Mabell ____
    Stephen Banbury
OB 1652–65, 69.

116. 21 Sept. 1657—These are to Certifie that according to sufficient proofe made before this Court, there is due to Jno Howett 200 acres of Land for the transportation of 4 persons into this Colony (Viz^t) Wm Angell, his wife, and two children. *OB 1652–65, 69.*

117. 21 Sept. 1657—These are to Certifie that according to sufficient proofe made before this Court, there is due to Mr Robt Clarke 1200 Acres of Land for the transportation of 24 persons into this Colony (Viz^t)

Elizabeth Neall	Wm Nonck [or Noncb]
Marga: Conalley	Hugh McFarther
Donough Ohunun	Owen McComer
Shellis Nishoe	Gillpatrick Obedine
Tigh Nulley	Jno Trower
Jno Namey	Joane Buttler
Jno Haluran	Ellen Ninars
Richd Coleman	Walt^r Webb
Richd Burrett	Phaelin Okoner
Beren Ohatonne	Edmund Gonogar
Cornelius Omney Corey	Diniogh Turner
Denish Sholauan	Dermot Dolien

OB 1652–65, 70.

118. 21 Sept. 1657—These are to Certifie y^t according to sufficient proofe made before this Court, there is due to Mr Wm Bacon 300 Acres of Land for transportation of himselfe thrice into this Colony & for transportation of three persons more (Viz^t) James Guy; Margery, a maide serv^t assigned by Mr Nichols Jernew; & Elizabeth, a maide Servt assigned by Tho: Philpott. *OB 1652–65, 70.*

119. 21 Sept. 1657—These are to Certifie y^t according to sufficient proofe made before this Court, there is due to Thomas Prickett 100 acres of Land for Transportation of himselfe & Bridgett his wife into this Colony. *OB 1652–65, 71.*

120. 21 Sept. 1657—These are to Certifie that according to sufficient proofe made before this Court, there is due to Richd Flynt 100 acres of Land for transportation of John Rodman & Anne Pomfrett into this Colony. *OB 1652–65, 71.*

121. 21 Sept. 1657—These are to Certifie y^t according to sufficient proofe made before this Court, there is due to Mr Wm Thomas 250 Acres of Land for the Transportation of two Negroes of his own, Elizabeth Johnson & one Negro woman assigned by Mr Tho: Hopkins & Mr James Gayland for his transportation assigned. *OB 1652–65, 72.*

122. 21 Sept. 1657—These are to Certifie y^t according to sufficient proofe made before this Court, there is due unto Jno Haynie 100 acres of Land for ye Transportation of Robt Stanton & Elizabeth Richmond into this Colony. *OB 1652–65, 72.*

123. 21 Sept. 1657—These are to Certifie that according to sufficient proofe made to this Court, there is due to Mr Jefferey Goche 50 acres of Land for his own Transportation into this Colony. *OB 1652–65, 72.*

124. 22 Sept. 1657, List of Servants belonging to the Estate of Col. John Mottrom—Thomas Hazellipp, Walter Owen, Jno Warren, Wm Taylor, George Slytham, Thomas Hammond. *RB 1652–58, 117.*

125. 22 Sept. 1657, Servants in the Estate of Col. John Mottrom—Walter Owen, 2 yeares next Octob.; Jno Warner, 2 yeares next Octob.; Wm Taylor, 5 yeares next January; George Slytham, 5 yeares March 21st 1655; Thomas Hammond, 11 yeares March 21, 1655. *RB 1652–58, 121.*

126. 22 Sept. 1657, Division of the Estate of Col. John Mottrom—Irish boy named Thomas Hamman, two English boys named George Slytham and John Warner, two English servants called Walter Owen and Wm Taylor. *RB 1652–58, 123, 124.*

127. 24 Nov. 1657—These are to Certifie that according to sufficient proofe made to this Court, there is due to Richd Nelmnes 200 acres of Land for the Transportation of 4 persons into this Colony (Viz^t)

    Richd Lansdell   Jno Philpott
    Richd Tadwell   Alice Merredith

OB 1652–65, 75.

128. 24 Nov. 1657—These are to Certifie that according to sufficient proofe made before this Court, there is due to Mr Peter Presly 450 Acres of Land for the Transportation of nine persons into this Colony (Viz^t)

    Himselfe   Anne Petit
    Wm Boswell   Margery White
    Elizab Smyth   Anne, a maide Servt
    James Hobart   Jonath: Parker
                               W$^{m.}$ Bradley

OB 1652–65, 76.

129. 20 Jan. 1657/58—These are to Certifie y^t according to sufficient proofe made before this Court, there is due to Tho: Orley 300 acres of Land

for the Transportation of six persons into this Colony (Viz^t)
    Susan & Rebecka his two wifes
    Jno Hill   Daniel Rylie
    Jno Benson   Sarah Rasee
OB 1652–65, 79.

130. 20 May 1658—These are to Certifie y^t according to sufficient proofe made before this Court, there is due to Jno Tingey 150 acres of Land for the transportation of three persons into this Colony (Viz^t)
    Sarah Jackson   Mauldin Van-Puck
    Dorothy Russell
OB 1652–65, 81.

131. 20 May 1658—These are to Certifie that according to sufficient proofe made before this Court, there is due to George Sutton 400 acres of Land for the transportation of eight persons into this Colony (Viz^t)
    George Sutton   Mary Sutton
    Sarah Sutton   Lidia Sutton
    Nath: Sutton   Sarah Sutton
    Joseph Sutton   Elizab: Sutton
OB 1652–65, 81.

132. 20 May 1658—These are to Certifie y^t according to sufficient proofe made before this Court, there is due to James Allen 50 acres of Land for the transportation of Jno Ashwin into this Colony. *OB 1652–65, 82.*

133. 20 May 1658—These are to Certifie y^t according to sufficient proofe made before this Court, there is due to Thomas Brewer 250 acres of Land for the Transportation of 5 persons into this Colony (Viz^t)
    Thomas Brewer   Jno Ounesse
    Sarah Brewer   Wm Furbush
    Nicholas Screver
OB 1652–65, 83.

134. 20 July 1658—Witnesseth that I Seth Foster doe bargaine & . . . presents have bargained & sold unto Francis . . . servant named William Coupter now in M^{rs}. . . . *RB 1658–66, 1.* [Most of document mutilated.]

135. 20 July 1658—These are to Certifie that according to sufficient proofe made before this Court, there is due to Mr Richard Wright 850 acres of Land for the transportation of 17 persons into this Colony by assignment from Mr Jno Bateman vizt

Jn⁰ Bateman
Simon Carpenter
Charles Winterne
Edward Sanders
Joseph Hary
Nich Smyth
John Knight
Wm Hanwell
Robt Wright

Miles Gray
Francis Acton
Tho: Winn
Mabell Jones
Jn⁰ Bateman
Mary Bateman
Charles Winterne
Mary Hewes

OB 1652–65, 89.

136. 24 Aug. 1658—These are to Certifie that according to sufficient proofe made before this Court there is due to Richard Cole gen^t 600 acres of Land for the transportation of 1 2 persons into this Collony vizt

Joane Agura
Mabell Joanes
Abraham Feild
Richard Coman
Elizabeth Coman
Manderford Kerby

Mary Edwards
Alice Plesington
Thomas Arpin
Thomas Watson
Sarah Bradford
Mary Dowry

OB 1652–65, 91.

137. 20 Sept. 1658—I Rice Maddocks of Nominy Chyrurgin for my selfe & assignes doe hereby assigne over unto Mrs Anna Cole, the wife of Richard Cole of Salisbury Parke in the County of Northumberland Merch^t by his own consent, an Irish girle named Mary Dowry about the age of seaven yeares for the term of fourteen yeares from the tenth day of November next.... *RB 1658–66, 11.*

138. 20 Sept. 1658—Certificate for 200 acres of Land is granted for Lt Col. Sam^{ll} Smyth for the transportation of foure persons into this Country Viz^t Joane Kitchinman, Mary Hutton, Ann Lewis and Thomas Harnesse. *OB 1652–65, 92.*

139. 20 Sept. 1658—These are to certifie that according to sufficient proofe made before this Court, there is due to Mr Jeffery Goche 50 acres of Land by assignment from Sam^{ll} Goche for his transportation into this Colony. *OB 1652–65, 93.*

140. 20 Sept. 1658—These are to Certifie y^t according to sufficient proofe made before this Court, there is due to Mr Tho: Broughton 100 acres of Land by assignment from Richard Wells for the transportation of two persons into

this Country (Viz^t)
    John Moises   Mary Gregory
OB 1652–65, 94.

141. 20 Sept. 1658—Certificate for 50 acres of Land is granted unto Richard Iland for his transportation into this Country. *OB 1652–65, 94.*

142. 20 Sept. 1658—These are to certifie that according to sufficient proofe made before this Court, there is due to Mr Peter Ashton 200 acres of Land for the transportation of 4 persons into this Country (Viz^t)
    Charles Hoyle   Edward Dyer
    Edward Rogers   Wm Florence
OB 1652–65, 94.

143. 20 Nov. 1658—These are to certifie that according to sufficient proofe made before this Court, there is due to Thomas Dorrell 50 acres of Land for the transportation of Anne Leech into this County. *OB 1652–65, 95.*

144. 20 Nov. 1658—These are to Certifie that Richard Flynt made his right appeare to 100 acres of Land for the transportation of two persons into this Collony vizt
    Robt Hudson   Thomas Money
OB 1652–65, 95.

145. 20 Nov. 1658—Whereas Walter Owen petitioned this Court for his freedom, It is ordered that the sd Owen forw^th returne to his Master Mr George Colclough's service & the matter referred till the next Court. *OB 1652–65, 96.*

146. 20 Nov. 1658—John Bailes confesseth judgement for the paym^t of sixteene hundred & seaven pounds of Tob^o & caske unto George Day for the use of Mrs Anne Temple within tenn days als execution. *OB 1652–65, 97.*

147. 20 Nov. 1658—It is ordered by this Court that Margarett Bashaw shall forthw^th be free from the service of Mr Hugh Lee & be at her own dispose & that the sd Lee shall upon lawfull demand deliver to the sd Margarett all such Cattle as are belonging to her in his custody or on keeping wth all their increase both male & female And whereas it doth appeare unto the Court by the oathes of Capt Jno Rogers & Mary Earle that the sd Mr Lee paid 150 pounds Tob^o out of the sd Margarett's or the Children's estate unto Wm Allenson in consideration of her Indenture, It is therefore further ordered that in regard her owne Tob^o purchased the Indenture that the sd Mr Lee shall forthw^th make paym^t of nine hundred pounds of Tob^o & caske unto the sd Margarett for three yeares service wch she hath served the sd Lee longer then of right she might to have done as alsoe three Barrells of Indian Corne & sufficient Clothing wth Costs of suite. *OB 1652–65, 97.*

148. 20 Jan. 1658/59—These are to Certifie that according to sufficient proofe made to this Court, there is due to Francis Carpenter 200 acres of Land for the transportation of himselfe twice, Thomas Wood & Jeffery Pedy into this Country. *OB 1652–65, 100.*

149. 21 Feb. 1658/59—These are to Certifie that Mr Laurence Dameron made his right appeare to 450 acres of Land for the transportation of Nine persons into this Country Viz^t

Himselfe	Joseph Jepson
his wife	Katherine Shawe
James Sibble	Richard Fenner
Joane Jones	Edward Stanford
Wm Rule	

OB 1652–65, 102.

150. 21 March 1658—These are to Certifie that George English made his right appeare to 450 acres of Land for ye transportation of these persons following into this Country vizt

Thomas Hurst	Jeffery Aston
Wm Sparkes	Falix Harling
Francis Hooper	Cornelius Wilton
Robt Stiles	Edward Sayle

OB 1652–65, 102.

151. 21 March 1658/59—These are to Certifie that Mary Raynor, widdow, made her right appeare to 500 acres of Land for the transportation of ten persons into this Country vizt

Thomas Sherly	Elizabeth Johnson
Henry Reade	Judith Palmer
Siscily Crowde	Wm Landrum
Henry Hapney	Robert Bridley
Henry Raynor	Domanew Gamber

OB 1652–65, 103.

152. 20 May 1659—These are to Certifie that Mr Hugh Lee made his right appeare to 450 acres of Land for the transportation of these persons following into this Country vizt

Himselfe	Sam^{ll} Cooper

Mr Sampson Cooper
William Smith
William Allen
Hannah Lee

Henry Smith
Elizabeth Francefois
Mary Brickfeild

OB 1652–65, 105.

153. 20 May 1659—These are to Certifie that Capt Richard Wright made his right appeare to 800 acres of Land for the transportation of these persons into this Country Viz^t

Himselfe twice
Mr Christopher Wright
Mr Nich: Spencer twice
John Mottrom Junior
Samuel Mills
Mr Robt Spencer
George Slightham

Jacob Willoughby
Thomas More
Robt Lawson
Mary Doughty
Mary Hughs
Sarah Bradford
Thomas Efford

OB 1652–65, 105.

154. 21 July 1659—I Capt Richard Wright administrator of ye estate of Col. Jno Mottrom doe assigne & transferr unto Wm Greensteed a maid servant formerly belonging unto the estate of the sd Coll. Mottrom commonly called Elizabeth Key being nowe wife unto the sd Greensteed and doe warrant the sd Elizabeth doe bind my selfe to serve her & the sd Greensteed from any molestation or trouble that shall or may futurely arise from or by any person or persons that shall pretend or claime any title or interest to any manner of service whatsoever from the sd Elizabeth   Richd Wright

RB 1658–66, 27.

155. 20 Sept. 1659—These are to Certifie that Jno Motley made his right appeare to 250 acres of Land for the Transportation of five persons into this Collony Viz^t

Nicholas Bulbrooke
John Ware
John Aires

Samuel Coxen
Thomas Tadwell

OB 1652–65, 111.

156. 20 Oct. 1659—These are to Certifie that Simon Richardson made his right appeare to 300 acres of Land for the transportation of 6 persons into this Colony Viz^t for his own transportation & for the transportation of 5 Negroes assigned him by Major George Colclough. *OB 1652–65, 113.*

157. 20 Oct. 1659—These are to Certify that John Bailes made his right appeare to 50 acres of Land for his own transportation into this Colony. *OB 1652–65, 113.*

158. 20 Oct. 1659—These are to Certify that Richard Flynt made his Right appeare to 100 acres of Land for the Transportation of two persons into this Collony (Viz^t)
        Edward Goodwyn   Anne Penning
OB 1652–65, 113.

159. 21 Nov. 1659, Will of Richard Budd— . . . my men vizt, John and Simon . . . service being faithfully fulfilled . . . & bequeath one cow calfe. . . . *RB 1658–66, 30.* [Portion of page mutilated.]

160. 20 Feb. 1659/60—This day Hezekiah Colledge appeared before this Court, hee being servant to Capt Wm Nutt and comeing into this Country without any Indenture, The Court Judgeth him to be of the age of twelve years, And it is ordered that hee the sd Hezekiah Colledge shall serve the sd Capt Nutt untill hee be of the age of 21 yeares. *OB 1652–65, 119.*

161. 20 Feb. 1659/60—This day Jonathan Saul appeared before this Court, hee being Servant to Mr Wilkes Maunder & coming into this Country without Indenture, the Court Judgeth him to be of the age of Fourteene yeares, And it is ordered that hee the sd Jonathan Saul shall serve the sd Wilkes Maunder untill hee be of the age of 21 yeares. *OB 1652–65, 119.*

162. 20 Feb. 1659/60—This day Beniamin [Benjamin] Williams (being servant to Mr Thomas Williams) appeared before this Court, hee coming into the Country without Indenture. The Court Judgeth him to be of the age of sixteene yeares, And it is ordered that hee the sd Beniamin Williams shall serve the sd Thomas Williams untill hee be of the age of 21 yeares. *OB 1652–65, 119.*

163. 20 Feb. 1659/60—This day Richard Ward appeared before this Court, hee being the Servant to Mr Isaac Foxcroft and coming into this Country without Indenture, the Court Judgeth him to be of the age of fourteen yeares, And it is ordered that he the sd Richard Ward shall serve the sd Mr Foxcroft untill hee be of the age of 21 yeares. *OB 1652–65, 119.*

164. 20 Feb. 1659/60—This day Compl^t [complaint] was made to ye Court y^t Susanna Milo, an orphan, was sold by Phillip Carpenter to Mr David Lindsay without the Courts knowledge. It is therefore ordered that the sd Susanna be warned to appeare at the next Court. *OB 1652–65, 120.*

165. 9 April 1660, Inventory of the Estate of Col. John Trussell—Abigail Bride serv^t having a yeare & 3 qtrs. to serve, 1000 lbs. tobacco. *RB 1658–66, 43.*

166. 20 April 1660—John Thomas, being servant to James Dasheild, appeared this day before the Court, hee coming into the Country without Indenture. The Court judgeth him to be of ye age of thirteene yeares. And whereas the sd James Dashield hath freely in the presence of this Court given him one yeare of his time, It is ordered that the sd John Thomas shall serve him the sd James Dashield from this day till seaven yeares be compleat & ended and then to be free. *OB 1652–65, 120.*

167. 20 April 1660—Bartholomew Yeomans, being servant to Andrew Cockron and Walter Dunn, was brought this day before the Court, hee coming into the Country without Indenture. The Court judgeth him to be of the age of thirteene yeares. It is therefore ordered that the sd Yeomans shall serve them the sd Andrew & Walter or their assigns untill hee be of the age of 21 years. *OB 1652–65, 120.*

168. 20 April 1660—William Owens, servant to James Magregor and Hugh Fouch, was this day brought before the Court, hee coming into this Country without Indenture. The Court judgeth him to be of the age of thirteen yeares. It is therefore ordered that the sd Wm Owen shall serve them the sd James & Hugh or their assigns untill hee be of the age of 21 yeares. *OB 1652–65, 121.*

169. 20 April 1660—This day Daniell Beacham being serv^t to Anthony Lenton was brought before the Court, hee coming into the Country without Indenture. The Court judgeth him to be of the age of fourteene yeares. It is therefore ordered that the sd Beacham shall serve him the sd Lenton or his assigns untill hee be of the age of 21 yeares. *OB 1652–65, 121.*

170. 20 April 1660—Edward Sherwood, being Servt to Richard Way, was this day brought before the Court, hee coming into the Country without Indenture. The Court judgeth him to be of the age of thirteen yeares. It is therefore ordered that the sd Edward Sherwood shall serve him the sd Richard Way or his assigns untill hee be of the age of 21 yeares. *OB 1652–65, 121.*

171. 3 May 1660—This day Sam^{ll} Webb, William Farlowe, John Hitchcock, & Thomas Warwick, being servants to Major George Colclough appeared before this Court, they coming into the Country without Indenture. The Court judgeth the sd Webb to be of the age of thirteene yeares, Farlowe twelve yeares, Hitchcock twelve yeares & Warwick ten yeares old. It is therefore ordered that each of them, the sd Sam^ll Webb, William Farlowe, John Hitchcock & Thomas Warwick shall serve him the sd Major George Colclough or his assignes untill they be of the age of one & twenty years. *OB 1652–65, 122.*

172. 3 May 1660—William Hood, servant to Major George Colclough, did this day appear before the Court, hee comeing into the Country without Indenture. The Court judgeth him to be of the age of fourteene yeares. And it is ordered that the sd W^m shall serve him the said Major Colclough or his assigns untill hee be of the age of one & twenty years. *OB 1652–65, 122.*

173. 21 May 1660—This day Robt Howe, being serv^t to Thomas Steed, appeared before the Court, hee coming into ye Country without Indenture. The Court judgeth him to be of the age between 15 & 16 yeares, & arrived the 17th of September last. It is therefore ordered that the sd Robt Howe shall serve the sd Thomas Steed or his assignes the full time & terme of six yeares to be accompted from his arrival aforesd according to an act of assembly made to that purpose. *OB 1652–65, 122.*

174. 21 May 1660—These are to Certify that Mr Thomas Broughton made his right appeare to 200 acres of Land for the transportation of 4 persons into this Collony vizt

    Susanna Blanck   Elizabeth Bets
    William Wandorill   Elizabeth James
OB 1652–65, 123.

175. 20 July 1660—These are to Certify that Thomas Phillpott made his right appeare to 150 acres of Land for the transportation of three persons into this Colony (Viz^t) Hannah Dyer, Thomas Parkes & Lydia Hoberry. *OB 1652–65, 127.*

176. 5 Sept. 1660—These are to Certify that there is due unto James Hill 500 acres of Land for the transportation of six persons into this Colony (Viz^t) Sarah Blumstone, Elizabeth Lovell, Katherine Southwell, John Wilson, Thomas Ploucer [?], Honorah Zwellawen. *OB 1652–65, 130.*

177. 5 Sept. 1660—These are to Certify that Mr Peter Presly made his right appeare to 300 acres of Land for the transportation of five persons into this Collony (Viz^t)

    Margaret Brasor   Wm Hubbart
    Richard Brasor   Jno Peney

Wm Head   Margaret Nicholls
OB 1652–65, 130.

178. deleted

179. 5 Sept. 1660—These are to Certify that Joseph Horsley made his right appeare to 250 acres of Land for the transportation of five persons into this Collony (vizt) Rose Horsley, William Hickson, Mary Smyth, George Noskes, Jone Auger. *OB 1652–65, 131.*

180. 5 Sept. 1660—These are to Certify that Major George Colclough made his right appeare to 1050 acres of Land for the transportation of 21 persons into this Collony (Viz:)

Phillip Biggs	Samuell Webb
Thomas Medcalfe	Charles Sparkes
Anne Gregory	William Moseley
Mary Hill	John Hitchcock
Alice ____ [no surname]	William Farlowe
John Sanders	Anne Wood
William Hood	Tho: Warwick
John Coningto	Fransisco, an Indian
Francis Stillingfleet	Maria, a Negro
Walker Howard	Richard, y^e Taylor
Peter Humphreys	

OB 1652–65, 131.

181. 8 Oct. 1660—These are to Certify that Mr Edward Sanders made his right appeare to 300 acres of Land for the transportation of 6 persons into this Collony (viz) Francis Ross, Mary Evans, Summer Adams, Richard Harword, William Wills & Edward Peterson. *OB 1652–65, 132.*

182. 14 Nov. 1660—George Durant standeth indebted unto Rice Maddocke by Bill a man servant for 4 years time & to be between the age of 16 & 30 Court ordered that the said Durant shall forthwith deliver a man servant unto Maddocke & shall also pay cost of suit. *OB 1652–65, 133.*

183. 14 Nov. 1660—These are to Certify that Robert Wilson made his right appeare to fifty acres of Land for the transportation of Anne Beavin into this Collony. *OB 1652–65, 133.*

184. 14 Nov. 1660—This day Robert Stiles (being servant to George English) appeared before the Court & comeing into the Country without

Indenture, The Court judgeth him to be of the age betweene 16 and 17 years or thereabouts. And it is ordered that the sd Robert Stiles shall serve him the sd George English or his assigns from the 10th of February next untill fower yeares be compleat & ended. *OB 1652–65, 134.*

185. 17 Dec. 1660, Will of Laurence Dameron—Item. I give unto Bartholomew, George and Thomas . . . men servants that have fower yeares or more to serve. *RB 1658–66, 49.* [Portion of page badly torn.]

186. 21 Jan. 1660/61—Jno Sirves, servant to George English, comeing into this Country without Indenture, is considered by this Court to be 13 yeares of age and ordered to serve him the sd English or his assigns eight yeares according to act of assembly. *OB 1652–65, 136.*

187. 21 Jan. 1660/61—William Pettus, Mathew Phillips and William Scott, Servants to Coll. Richard Lee, comeing into this Country without Indenture, their severall ages adjudged by this Court to be as followeth (viz) The sd Pettus & Phillips twelve yeares old a peice and the sd Scott thirteene yeares old. And it is ordered by the Court that the sd Wm Pettus, Mathew Phillips & Wm Scott shall serve the sd Coll Lee or his assigns untill each of them be of the age of 21 yeares according to act of assembly, that is to say Wm Pettus & Mathew Phillips to serve nine yeares a peice & Wm Scott to serve eight yeares. *OB 1652–65, 136.*

188. 21 Jan. 1660/61—It appearing unto the Court that Thomas Broughton is ingaged unto Walter English for the procuring him a Pattent for three hundred & fifty acres of land. . . .

Whereas it doth appeare unto this Court that Thomas Broughton is ingaged unto John Raven & John Clarke for the procuring them a Pattent for 450 Acres of Land in their own names, It is ordered that the sd Broughton shall deliver unto the sd Raven & Clarke a Pattent for the sd Land by March Court next or else to make good what damages they shall sustaine for the same. *OB 1652–65, 136.* [Although no one receives land in the above entries, they do reveal what went on behind the scenes in an effort to obtain land. One would have to do additional research to determine whether those persons named acquired land.]

189. 21 Jan. 1660/61—George Edmonds, servant to John Williams, comeing into ye Country without Indenture, is adjudged by this Court to be thirteene yeares of age and ordered to serve him the sd Jnn Williams or his assigns eight yeares according to act of assembly. *OB 1652–65, 136.*

190. 21 Jan. 1660/61—John Hine, servant to Mr Thomas Souley, comeing into ye Country without Indenture is adjudged by this Court to be foureteene yeares of age and ordered to serve him the s^d Mr Souley or his assigns seaven yeares according to act of assembly. *OB 1652–65, 136.*

191. 21 Jan. 1660/61—William Hartington, servant to Thomas Williams, comeing into this Country without Indenture, is adjudged by this Court to be sixteene yeares of age and ordered to serve him the s^d Tho: Williams or his assigns five yeares according to act of assembly. *OB 1652–65, 136.*

192. 21 Jan. 1660/61—Richard Jackson, servant to Mr Wm Willdey, comeing into this Country without Indenture, is adjudged by this Court to be fourteene yeares of age and ordered to serve him the s^d Mr Willdey or his assignes seaven yeares according to act of assembly. *OB 1652–65, 136.*

193. 21 Jan. 1660/61—These are to Certify that Mr William Presly made his right appeare to 450 acres of Land for the transportation of nine persons into this Collony (Viz^t)

       himselfe   Thomas Underhill
       Jone his wife   William Bancroft
       Joseph Beavan   William Boles
       John Lane   Hannah Newman
       Roger Lane
OB 1652–65, 136.

194. 26 Feb. 1660/61—Joseph Woodman, servant to Mr Henry Corbyn, comeing into this Country without Indenture, is adjudged by this Court to be fourteene yeares of age and ordered to serve him the s^d Mr Corbyn or his assigns seaven yeares according to act of Assembly. *OB 1652–65, 137.*

195. 26 Feb. 1660/61—Samuel Boxberry, servant to Mr Nicholas Jernew, comeing into this Country without Indenture, is adjudged by this Court to be fifteene yeares of age And ordered to serve him the s^d Mr Jernew or his assignes six yeares according to act of assembly. *OB 1652–65, 137.*

196. 26 Feb. 1660/61—William Vaughan (servant to Mr Thomas Brereton) comeing into this Country without Indenture, is adjudged by this Court to be thirteene yeares of age and ordered to serve him the s^d Mr Brereton or his assigns eight yeares according to act of Assembly. *OB 1652–65, 137.*

197. 26 Feb. 1660/61—Christopher Little (servant to William Downinge) comeing into this Country without Indenture is adjudged by this Court to be about the age of thirteene yeares And ordered to serve him the s^d Wm Downinge or his assignes eight yeares to be accompted from the thirtieth day of November last past. *OB 1652–65, 137.*

198. 7 March 1660/61—Thomas Dawes, servant to Coll. Richard Lee, comeing into ye Country without Indenture is adjudged by this Court to be 14 yeares of age And ordered to serve him the sd Coll. Lee or his assigns seaven yeares according to act of Assembly. *OB 1652–65, 139.*

199. 6 June 1661—John Holland, servant to Jonathan Parker, comeing into this Country without Indenture is adjudged by this Court to be of the age of 13 yeares or thereabouts And ordered to serve him the s^d Jonathan Parker or his assigns eight yeares to be accompted from the first day of December last past. *OB 1652–65, 142.*

200. 22 July 1661—Whereas William David, servant to James Allen, hath absented himselfe from his s^d Master's service the space of six weekes, the which hee confessed before the Court. It is therefore ordered that the s^d Wm David shall at the end of his time by Indenture his s^d Master three months according to Law & it is further ordered that the s^d Wm David shall serve his sd Master two months more in consideration of his Master's charge & trouble of getting his s^d servant home. *OB 1652–65, 143.*

201. 22 July 1661—In regard that Dennis, the wife of Jno Clarke, is not in a capacity (being now a servant to Daniell Holland) to continue the guardianship of Jane Medcalfe. . . . *OB 1652–65, 144.*

202. 22 Aug. 1661—This day Edward Sanders proffered a petition to this Court wherein hee setts forth that a woman servant of his named Jane Kitchingham have had a bastard child borne in the time of her servitude to his greate damage & charge & humbly prays that the s^d childe may be bound his apprentice untill hee attaines to the age of 21 yeares upon the s^d Sanders his petition. It is ordered that the s^d childe named John shall live & remaine with him ye said Edward Sanders as his apprentice until hee be of ye age of 21 yeares. *OB 1652–65, 146.*

203. 21 Oct. 1661—Whereas Phillip Browne, servant to Mr Richard Cole, came into this Country without Indenture & brought before this Court to have his age adjudged, hee is adjudged by this Court to be about the age of 16 yeares & ordered to serve his s^d Master or assignes the terme of five yeares from the first day of December next. *OB 1652–65, 147.*

204. 21 Jan. 1661/62—William Hughson, servant to Coll. Richard Lee, comeing into this Country without Indenture is Judged by the Court to be about the age of 14 yeares & ordered to serve his s^d Master seaven yeares from this day. *OB 1652–65, 149.*

205. 21 Jan. 1661/62—John Lewis, servant to Capt Peter Ashton, comeing into this Country without Indenture is Judged by this Court to be about the age of 11 yeares & ordered to serve his s^d Master ten yeares from this day. *OB 1652–65, 149.*

206. 21 Jan. 1661/62—Whereas Mr David Lyndsay, minister hath (contrary to ye Law in that case made & provided) celebrated a marriage between Richard Peirce Carpenter, servant to Coll. Richard Lee, & a woman servant belonging to Thomas Brewer without either the permission or allowance of the sd Coll. Lee or any licence obteyned or Publication of banes, It is therefore ordered by this Court that the sd Mr Lyndsay shall pay ten thousand pounds of Tobacco according to act of assembly for such his transgression together with all costs als execution. *OB 1652–65, 150.* [At a court held 20 November 1662, Mr. Lindsay was acquitted of the charges, he being ignorant of the law. Several persons, including the masters, informed the court that there weren't any reasons for not performing the marriage ceremony. *OB 1652–65, 167.*]

207. 21 Jan. 1661/62—These are to Certify that Robt Burrell made his right appeare to 50 acres of Land for the transportation of John Gibson into this Collony. *OB 1652–65, 152.*

208. 21 Jan. 1661/62—... do hereby signify that Elizabeth James, servant to Sam^{ll} Man of this same County haveing imputed a Bastard Childe to Mr Jno Haskins.... *OB 1652–65, 152.* [Haskins was acquitted of the charge, and Elizabeth James was to receive 30 stripes upon her naked back for the "false & scandallous imputation."]

209. 10 March 1661/62—Owen Fell, servant to Thomas Williams, comeing into the Country without Indenture is Judged by this Court to be about the age of nine yeares & ordered to serve his s^d Master twelve yeares to be accompted from the 25th day of Decemb^r last past. *OB 1652–65, 153.*

210. 10 March 1661/62—These are to Certify that Richard Nelmes made his right appeare to 200 acres of Land for the transportation of fower persons

into this Collony (viz)
        John Duggin   John Bound
        Joyce Mattux   Mary Floyd
OB 1652–65, 154.

211. 10 March 1661/62—These are to Certify that Mr Robt King made his right appeare to 400 acres of Land for the transportation of eight persons into this Collony (viz)
        Robt King Senior   Richard King
        Hannah King   Edward Jenings
        Robt King Junior   Thomas Stowe
        Daniell Nibbs   Eve, a maid servant
OB 1652–65, 154.

212. 10 March 1661/62—These are to Certify that Richard Flynt made his right appeare to 350 acres of Land for the transportation of seaven persons into this Collony (viz)
        Thomas Smith   Joanna Smith
        Henry Jorden   Richd Harrison
        David Carter   Elizabeth, a maid Servt
        James Barnes
OB 1652–65, 155.

213. 10 March 1661/62— ... then & there to answere to such matters as shall be alleadged ag^t them concerning the death & buriall of one Thomas Hughes who was servant to the said Daniell Holland. *OB 1652–65, 155.*

214. 21 April 1662—Whereas John Shenton, servant to Abraham Joyce, comeing into this Country without Indenture, he is Judged by this Court to be about the age of 15 yeares & ordered to serve his sd Master or his assigns the full terme of six yeares. ... *OB 1652–65, 156.*

215. 20 May 1662—These are to Certify that Richard Cole merch^t made his right appeare to 450 acres of Land for the transportation of nine persons into this Collony (viz)
        Himselfe   Katherine Mote
        William Skippe   Richard White
        James Oldum   Martha Passenger
        Mary Earle   Thomas Fetherstone
        Henry Harpin
OB 1652–65, 156.

216. 21 April 1662—Dan^ll Holland & Jno Clarke acquitted from the s^d suspected murder of Thomas Hughes. *OB 1652–65, 156.*

217. 20 May 1662—Whereas it doth appeare unto this Court that Henry Meese, merchant, standeth indebted unto John Kent (by obligation from under his hand) one male servant betweene 16 and 30 years of age with such clothing & lodging as belonge to him at his arrivall for wch servant Mr Daniell Hutt, attorney of the s^d Mr Meese, was arrested to this Court but failed in his appearance, It is therefore ordered that if neyther [neither] the s^d Mr Meese nor his attorney appeare the next Court held for this County then Judgment shall passe against the sherriffe according to Law. *OB 1652–65, 157.*

218. 20 May 1662—These are to Certify that John Aires made his right appeare to 100 acres of Land for the transportation of Sutton Quemy & Elizabeth Langley into this Collony. *OB 1652–65, 157.*

219. 20 May 1662—Sarah Oventon, servant to Christopher Garlington, comeing into this Country without Indenture is Judged by this Court to be about the age of 13 yeares & ordered to serve her s^d Master or assigns the full terme of eight yeares to be accompted from the 25th day of December last past. *OB 1652–65, 157.*

220. 20 May 1662—This is to Certify that Jonathan Parkes made his right appeare to 200 acres of Land for the transportation of fower persons into this Collony (viz)

    Himselfe   John Holland
    Nicholas Claughton   Francis Gilbert
OB 1652–65, 157.

221. 21 July 1662—Mary Earle, servant to Mr Richard Cole, haveing complained & made manifest to this Court that her master hath very much abused her by very unlawfull & causeless beatinge, now it is ordered that the s^d Mary Earle shall continue & remaine at the house of James Magregor where she now is untill the next Court at which time the said Mr Richard Cole is to make his personal appearance to answer the Complaint of the s^d Mary Earle. *OB 1652–65, 160.*

222. 7 Sept. 1662—Inventory of Major George Colclough . . . One man Servt named Charles Sparks haveinge 3 yeares 2 months, 1400 lbs.; Jno Sanders for 1 yeare & 4 months, 12000 lbs.; Wm Wood, a boy for 4 yeares 4 months, John Burchard, a boy [page worn]; Ab^r Wallis for 3 years 4 months, [page worn]; Tho: warreck, a small boy for about 8 yeares; Wm Mosely, a boy for 6 yeares 2 months, 1300 lbs.; Wm Tayler & his wife bigg wth child for 1 yeare, 600 lbs.; John Burchard, a boy [page worn], John Iland [Hand ?] for 1 yeare [page worn], John Pirson sickly [page worn], John Rogers, a sickly boy; Thomas Colton for 3 yeares; Franck Sisco, the Indian; John Hichcock, a small [page worn]; Mary Lennam to be [page worn]; Sarah Peirson for 4 yeares 6 months; Josias Blackwell to be bound at [page worn]; Constance Coles for 3 yeares, 14 lbs. tobacco; Peter Humphreys for 1 yeare, 800 lbs.; John Davis for 2 yeares, 1200 lbs. *RB 1658–66, 81, 82.* [Portion of page badly damaged.]

223. 8 Sept. 1662—Thomas Parkes, serv^t to Mr Thomas Phillpot, cominge into the Country without Indenture is adjudged by ye Court to serve eight yeares from the 20th day of November next. *OB 1652–65, 161.*

224. 8 Sept. 1662—Boaz Hollis, serv^t to Thomas Gaskins, cominge into the Country without Indenture is ordered by this Court to serve his s^d Master seaven yeares from the first of November next. *OB 1652–65, 161.*

225. 8 Sept. 1662—John Howell, serv^t to John Essex, havinge no indenture, is ordered by the Court to serve five yeares from the beginninge of October next, Always provided that if any indenture bee hereafter found or proved to have bin [been] y^t then the s^d Howell serve accordingly. *OB 1652–65, 161.*

226. 8 Sept. 1662—Edward Jennings, serv^t to Mr Thomas Phillpot, cominge into the Country without indenture is adjudged by the Court to serve eight yeares from the 20th of November next. *OB 1652–65, 161.*

227. 8 Sept. 1662—William Roobert, serv^t to Mr Francis Clay, cominge into the Country without indenture, is adjudged by the Court to serve seaven yeares from the 20th of October next. *OB 1652–65, 161.*

228. 8 Sept. 1662—These are to Certifie that Mr William Wildye made his right appeare for 650 acres of Land for the transportation of 13 persons into this Collony (viz)

Christopher Vaughan	Richd Jackson
Thomas Mash	Wm Smyth
Henery Clarck	Wm Boharry
____ Williams	Jane Fuller
Richd White	John Simpson
Samuell Webb	Joseph Harrington
	one mayde serv^t not named

OB 1652–65, 161.

229. 8 Sept. 1662—Certificate is at this Court granted unto Edward Coles for 350 acres of Land for transportation of seaven persons into this Collony (viz) Charles Mathews, Joseph Nudman, George Coote, Joane Jury, Mary Waters, Eliz: Hawkins, Jno Sheppard. *OB 1652–65, 162.*

230. 8 Sept. 1662—Whereas Mr Richard Cole was arrested to this Court at the suite of Capt Peeter Ashton & likewise of his serv^t Mary Earle & the s^d Cole not appearinge, the Sherr: is therefore fined the summe of 5000^{lbs} of Tob^o in Case the s^d Mr Cole doe not appeare at the next Court. *OB 1652–65, 162.*

231. 20 Nov. 1662—An Inventory of the Estate of Thomas Orley . . . 1 servant named Edward Whitby haveinge 2 yeares to serve, 1200 lbs. tobacco; 1 servant by name of Thomas Nash, 1000; 1 servant by name Thomas Miller, 1000; 1 servant by name Richard Vritt, 1000. *RB 1658–66, 82.*

232. 20 Nov. 1662—Robert Greene to serve Coll. Rich: Lee 6 yeares; Tho: Nash to serve William Holland 9 yeares; Jane Bateman to serve Mr Robt Jones 10 yeares; Henery Pickerill to serve Mr Nicholas Jurnew 9 yeares; Adam Kinge to serve Mr Nicholas Jurnew 6 yeares; Nathaniel Gardener to serve Rich: Nelmes 6 yeares; Jno Ducket to serve Rich: Nelmes 4 yeares. Ordered y^t the severall persons are to serve according to their times appointed by the Court. *OB 1652–65, 164.*

233. 20 Nov. 1662—Whereas John Heylen, Abraham Wallis, & Thomas Colton, serv^{ts} to Mrs Elizabeth Colclough, the relict & adm^{rix} of Major George Colclough dec^d absented themselves from the service of there s^d Mrs Colclough to the greate damadge of there s^d M^{rs} & charge in getting them againe amountinge to 3000^{lbs} of Tob^o And in regard the s^d serv^{ts} are at present incapable of makinge satisfaction & hazardable whether ever or not. It is therefore ordered that the s^d Heylin, Wallis, & Colton shall at the expiration of there time by Indenture each of them serve the s^d Mrs Colclough or her assigns one complete yeare. *OB 1652–65, 164.*

234. 29 Nov. 1662—Know all men by these presents that I Thomas Brewer have constituted, appointed & ordeyned James Gaylard my true & lawful Attorney for mee & in my name stead & place to acknowledge a certain writing (in Northumberland County Court) wherein I stand bound unto Coll. Richard Lee for the paym^t of three thousand eight hundred pounds of Tobacco & caske upon the tenth of October next & in case of my mortality & nonpayment then the s^d Coll. Lee to enjoy two of my Servants named Thomas

Lloyd & Thomas Smallpeice [?] as his own proper estate, ratifying & confirming what my s^d attorney shall act in the p:misses in as ample manner to all intents & purposes as if I my selfe were p:sonally present & did the same. Witness my hand & seale this 29th of November 1662.

                                       Thomas Brewer

RB 1658–66, 92.

235. 10 Feb. 1662/63—To all Xpian [Christian] people greeting know yee that I Thomas Treipe of great Wicocomico in Virginia planter doe hereby Covenant, bargaine & sell unto Capt Dan^ll Neale two men servants namely James Garnesey & Edward Lugg. *RB 1658–66, 86.*

236. 10 Feb. 1662/63, Will of Mary Broughton—... as for my cattle, my desire is that after my debts be satisfied that they may be shared betweene my sonnes, Thomas & Mathew, onely to my Sonne Mathew I give two cowes more then to Thomas, And I give to William Mouseley my God Child one Cow Calfe & likewise another to Elizabeth Perry & one to my Servant, Robert Brierie.... *RB 1658–66, 93.*

237. 10 Feb. 1662/63—The Court doth order that Dorothy Lockwitt, serv^t to Henry Winter, be forthwith free, it having bin [been] manifest to this Court that she hath served more than fower yeares. And it is further ordered that ye s^d Henry Winter doe forthwith pay unto the s^d Dorothy 3 Barrells of Corne, 2 paire of shoes & stockings, 2 shifts, one course cloth sute & canvas petticoat & 4 caps else execution. *OB 1652–65, 168.*

238. 10 Feb. 1662/63—John Smyth servant to Edward Humpston, comeing into this Country without Indenture is ordered by this Court to serve his s^d Master six yeares from this day. *OB 1652–65, 168.*

239. 10 Feb. 1662/63—Joseph Headnett, servant to Mr Thomas Bunbury, comeing into this Country without Indenture, is ordered by this Court to serve his s^d Master or assigns five yeares to be accompted from the 10th day of November last. *OB 1652–65, 168.*

240. 10 Feb. 1662/63—These are to Certify that Mr Edward Saunders made his right appeare to 300 acres of Land for the transportation of 6 persons into this Collony vizt

        Nicholas Ellery   William Kinneck
        Evan Davies   John Brigma
        Henry Mason   Anne Morgan

OB 1652–65, 168.

241. 10 Feb. 1662/63—These are to Certify that Mr Robert Jones made his right appeare to 400 acres of Land for the transportation of eight persons into this Collony vizt.

    Thomas Richman   James Mathews
    Jeffrey Chapman   Robert Jones
    Jane Thomas   William Kent [or Kirk]
    Jane Bateman   Jn° Smyth
OB 1652–65, 168.

242. 10 Feb. 1662/63—These are to certify that Christopher Garlington made his right appeare to 150 acres of Land for the transportation of 3 persons into this Collony vizt William Bennett, Robert Salisbury, Robt Hooper. *OB 1652–65, 168.*

243. 10 Feb. 1662/63—Whereas William Bennett, servant to Christopher Garlington, absented himselfe from his s^d Master's service upwards of fower months as is made manifest to this Court to his Master's great damage & charge in getting him againe, It is therefore ordered that the s^d Wm Bennett shall serve his s^d Master or assigns one compleat yeare after his time of service by custome or Indenture is expired. *OB 1652–65, 169.*

244. 10 Feb. 1662/63—These are to Certify that Jn° Tingey made his right appeare to 300 acres of Land for the transportation of 6 persons into this Collony vizt

    John Batman   Peter Richards
    Robert Mitchell   Mary Harwood
    Symon Walker   Alice Howell
OB 1652–65, 170.

245. 10 Feb. 1662/63—These are to Certify that Mr Wm Thomas made his right appeare to 1000 acres of Land for the transportation of 20 persons into this Collony vizt

    Sarah Williams   Tho: Allenson
    Mary Earle   Symon King
    Mary Waters   Christopher Bennett
    Frances Burinstone   John Taylor
    Ellenor Grimes   Sam^ll Bullock
    Rod Jones   Henry Lashly
    Richard Poulson   John White
    Thomas Dixon   John Butler
    Wm James   Sam^ll Stocks
    Wm Wilkinson   Joseph Hubburke

OB 1652–65, 170.

246. 10 Feb. 1662/63—It is ordered by this Court that Jane Makeile, an Irish woman, servant to Joseph Horsley shall be free from the 20th day of Octob^r next, the Court adjudging her to be upwards of twenty three yeares of age. *OB 1652–65, 172.*

247. 10 Feb. 1662/63—Judith Radforth, an orphan, have bin [been] under the guardianship of Walter Weekes & in his service severall yeares, shee haveing now attained to the age of 17 yeares, It is ordered that shee shall have the benefitt of her own labour & be at her owne dispose. *OB 1652–65, 172.*

248. 16 Feb. 1664/65, Deposition of Isabell Ashton— . . . whereupon I thought of making a Door ay ye end of ye Shedde wch I caused to be made & gave a pair of gloves to Walter Price, my hired Servt . . . My husband would need have about wth her at ye oven & . . . all her serv^t Fran: Price. . . . *RB 1658–66, 158, 159.* [Page badly mutilated.]

249. 8 March 1663, Inventory of Capt. Richard Wright— . . . five servants (Viz^t) Samuel Jewell, haveing three yeares to serve; William Grandee, haveing two yeares to serve; Edmund Holder, an Apothecary, two yeares to serve; Elizabeth Holmes, two yeares to serve; Margaret Richardson, three yeares to serve. . . . *RB 1658–66, 117.*

250. 12 March 1662/63—These are to Certify that Mr Peter Knight made his right appeare to 250 acres of land for the transportation of five persons into this Country (vizt) Richard Roberts, William Allcocke, Richard Phillips, Elizabeth Ward and Mary Pallas. *OB 1652–65, 173.*

251. 12 March 1662/63—William Thomas, servant to William Jollyns, is by Judgem^t of this Court to serve his s^d Master by the space of seaven yeares to commence from this day. *OB 1652–65, 173.*

252. 12 March 1662/63—William Batty, servant to Mr Richard Wright, is by Judgem^t of this Court to serve his s^d Master by the space of six yeares to commence from this day. *OB 1652–65, 173.*

253. 12 April 1663—Thomas Casterson, servant to Mr Wm Willdey, is by Judgem^t of this Court to serve his s^d Master the terme of seaven yeares from his arrivall. *OB 1652–65, 173.*

254. 12 April 1663—Sarah Hill & Elizabeth Tew, serv^{ts} to Richard Span, comeing into this Country without Indenture, their ages by this Court are adjudged as followeth (viz) Sarah her age thirteene yeares & Elizabeth twelve & are ordered to serve their s^d Masters from the time of their arrivall according to the Law in that case made & provided. *OB 1652–65, 173.*

255. 12 April 1663—These are to Certify that Mr Thomas Phillpott made his right appeare to 300 acres of land for the transportation of six persons into this Collony (viz)

John Miller	Richard White
George Brighton	William Skip
Frances Newman	Edward Jenings

OB 1652–65, 174.

256. 12 April 1663—These are to Certify that Mr Richard Coles made his right appeare to 350 acres of Land for the transportation of seven persons into this Collony (vizt)

Martha Passenger	Roger Morrer
Francis Gilbert	Peter Browne
Rose Parker	Grace Skinbark
Hannah Hawkins	

OB 1652–65, 174.

257. 12 April 1663—John Toby, servant to Thomas Williams, is Judgem^t of this Court adjudged to be Thirteene yeares of age & ordered to serve his s^d Master or assigns from ye time of his arrivall according to the Law in that case made & provided. *OB 1652–65, 174.*

258. 12 April 1663—Rowland Morgan, servant to Vincent Cox, is adjudged by this court to be nine yeares of age & ordered to serve his s^d Master or assignes from the time of his arrivall according to law in that case made & provided. *OB 1652–65, 174.*

259. 20 April 1663—Phillip Brisco, servant to John Williams, is by this Court adjudged to be fifteene yeares of age & ordered to serve his s^d Master or his assignes from the time of his arrivall according to the law in that case made & provided. *OB 1652–65, 175.*

260. 20 April 1663—John Watson, servant to James Jones, is adjudged to be twelve yeares of age & ordered to serve his s^d Master or his assignes according to law of this Country. *OB 1652–65, 175.*

261. 20 April 1663—Ralph Bishop, servant to Michaell Vanlandingham, is by this Court adjudged to be ten yeares of age & ordered to serve his s^d Master or his assignes according to the Law of this Country. *OB 1652–65, 175.*

262. 20 April 1663—William Kett, servant to Mr Robert Jones, is by this Court adjudged to be fifteene yeares of age & ordered to serve his s^d Master or his assignes according to the law of this Country, hee coming in without Indenture. *OB 1652–65, 175.*

263. 20 April 1663—It is ordered that Mary Earle, the daughter of John Earle, dec^d returne to the tuicon of Wm Clement & Elizabeth his wife untill good cause appeare for her removall & that present care be taken for the cure of her sore throat. *OB 1652–65, 176.*

264. 20 April 1663—Whereas M^r. Wm Presly bought a servant of Mr Richard Cole named Mary Earle when (in the time of her service with the s^d Mr Cole) had a bastard Child, the benefitt of the service thereby due being wholy assigned by the s^d Mr Cole to the s^d Mr Presly. It is therefore ordered that the s^d Mary Earle shall serve him the s^d Mr Wm Presly or assigns one compleat year after her time is expired by Custome or Indenture. *OB 1652–65, 176.*

265. 20 April 1663—These are to Certify that John Motley made his right appeare to 450 acres of land for the transportation of nine persons into this Collony (viz)

Richard Harkfoote	Anne Browne
Sarah George	John Steele
Anthony Rope	Henry Gilbert
William Browne	Thomas Smith
Elizabeth Harding	

OB 1652–65, 177.

266. 20 June 1663—John Smyth, serv^t to Mr Wilkes Maunder, coming into the Country without Indenture, is by this Court adjudged to be thirteene yeares of age & ordered to serve his s^d Master or assigns from the time of his arrivall according to act of assembly. *OB 1652–65, 178.*

267. 20 June 1663—Thomas Bridgeman, servant to Capt Wm Nutt, comeing into this Country without Indenture, is by the Court adjudged to be thirteene yeares of age & ordered to serve his s^d Master or assigns from time of his arrivall according to act of assembly. *OB 1652–65, 178.*

268. 20 June 1663—Whereas John Tillman, serv^t to Mr Wm Clement unlawfully killed a hog contrary to act of assembly by his own confession as also it appeares by the oath of Richard ___ [name not legible], It is therefore ordered that the s^d Wm Clement (being ... shall forthwith punish the s^d John Tillman by giving him twenty stripes upon his bare back. ... *OB 1652–65, 178.*

269. 20 June 1663—Whereas John Dew & Anne Givyer, servants to Daniell Holland came into this Country without Indenture, their ages by this Court are adjudged as followeth (viz) Jno is adjudged to be fifteene yeares of age & Anne Givyer sixteene & are ordered to serve their s^d Master or assigns from the times of their arrival according to act of assembly. *OB 1652–65, 178.*

270. 20 June 1663—Faith Cox, servant to John Gibson, comeing into this Country without Indenture, is by Judgement of this Court to serve her s^d Master or his assigns five yeares to commence from the time of her arrival. *OB 1652–65, 178.*

271. 20 June 1663—This may Certify that John Hughlett made his right appeare to 200 acres of Land for the transportation of fower persons into this Colony (viz)

John Butler	Sarah Grace
John Lewis	Faith Cocke

OB 1652–65, 178.

272. 20 June 1663—These are to Certify that Mr John Haynie made his right appeare to 250 acres of land for the transportation of five persons into this Collony (viz)

John Webb	Peter Bragg
Henry Clifford	Thomas Stevens
John Bater	

OB 1652–65, 178.

273. 20 June 1663—Whereas Esther Hayly, servant to John Coutanceau, had a bastard Child begott during the time of service about [page worn] yeares since, It is therefore ordered that the said Esther Hayly serve her s^d Master or his assigns one compleat year after her time is expired by custom or Indenture. *OB 1652–65, 179.*

274. 20 June 1663—These are to Certify that James Allen made his right appeare to 200 acres of land for the transportation of fower persons into this Collony (viz)

Thomas Licett	Elizabeth Bradberry

Jane Raynes   Anne Gwyn
OB 1652–65, 179.

275. 29 June 1663—Will of Robert Lord ... Item. I give unto my servant Sarah Pargater at the day of her freedom one Cowe within the age of five yeares & one breeding Sowe. ... *RB 1658–66, 72.*

276. 20 July 1663—Whereas Sarah Garnett, servant to Christopher Garlington, absented her selfe from her s^d Master's service ye space of eleven months or thereabouts & did carry away several goods of her s^d Master's to the values of one thousand three hundred eighty & five pounds tob^a all wch the s^d Sarah Garnett confessed in open Court, It is therefore ordered that shee, the s^d Sarah Garnett, shall serve her s^d Master or his assigns the full terme of three yeares & halfe after her time is expired by custome or Indenture in consideration of the time of her absence. ... *OB 1652–65, 180.*

277. 20 July 1663—Whereas Robert Howe, servant to Thomas Brewer, hath several times absented himselfe from his s^d Master's service to the great damage of his s^d Master's crop & charge in getting him againe, the damage & charge by computation is adjudged by this Court to be about 1200^{lbs} of tobacco besides his loss of time, It is therefore ordered that the s^d Robert Howe shall serve his s^d Master or assigns one compleate yeare after his time is expired by custome or Indenture. *OB 1652–65, 180.*

278. 20 July 1663—Whereas Elizabeth Lovell, servant to Symon Richardson, laid violent hands on her mistress by her own confession in open Court, It is therefore ordered that shee, th s^d Elizabeth Louell, shall serve her s^d Master or his assignes one compleat yeare after her time is expired by custome or Indenture. *OB 1652–65, 181.*

279. 20 Oct. 1663—Whereas Anne Mosse, servant to Daniell Holland, absented her selfe from the service of her s^d Master thirty seaven days at several times by her own confession before Mr Wm Presly who hath certificate the same to this Court from under his hand. ... *OB 1652–65, 182.*

280. 20 Oct. 1663—These may certify that Thomas Matthew, merch^t, made his right appeare to 600 acres of land for the transportation of himselfe into this Country three severall times, Thomas Mathew Junior five times & fower Negroes (viz) Plato, Tobey, Fryer & Jack. *OB 1652–65, 183.*

281. 20 Oct. 1663—These may certify that Walter Dunn made his right appeare to 150 acres of Land for the transportation of three persons into this

Collony (viz) Bartholomew Yeomans, Francis Hill & Charity Hayter. *OB 1652–65, 183.*

282. 20 Oct. 1663—These may certify that Thomas Roe made his right appeare to 50 acres of land for the transportation of William Archer into this Colony. *OB 1652–65, 183.*

283. 20 Oct. 1663—Whereas Anne Mosse, servant to Daniel Holland, since the last Court absented herselfe from her s^d Master's service nine dayes by her owne confession, It is therefore ordered that the s^d Anne Mosse shall serve her s^d Master eighteene dayes after her time is expired by custom, Indenture or any other former order. . . . *OB 1652–65, 183.*

284. 20 Oct. 1663—These may certify that Henry Watts made his right appeare to 250 acres of land for the transportation of five persons into this Collony (viz)

        William Anderson   Wm Rogers
        Christopher Seagreens   James Symmons
        Henry Dennis
OB 1652–65, 183.

285. 20 Oct. 1663—These may certify that William Cornish made his right appeare to 50 acres of land for the transportation of Mary Jones into this Collony. *OB 1652–65, 183.*

286. 10 Dec. 1663—Whereas Robert Bradley, servant to Mr Willes Maunder, absented himselfe from the service of his s^d Master the space of seaven months by his owne confession And whereas the s^d Mr Maunder hath bin [been] at five pounds short charge in getting his s^d servant as manifestly appeares to this Court, It is therefore ordered that the s^d Robert Bradley shall serve his s^d Master or assigns two compleat yeares after his time of service is expired by custome or Indenture in consideration of the damage the s^d Mr Maunder hath sustained by his absence & the charge hee hath bin [been] in getting his s^d servant againe. *OB 1652–65, 184.*

287. 10 Dec. 1663—Whereas it manifestly appeareth to this Court by good & sufficient evidence that William Buckley, servant to Coll Richard Lee, hath unlawfully killed a hogg belonging to Mr Robert Jones. . . . It is therefore ordered that the s^d Wm Buckley shall serve him the s^d Mr Robert Jones two compleat yeares after his time of service. . . . *OB 1652–65, 184.*

288. 10 Dec. 1663—These may certify that Mr John Coutanceau made his right appeare to 200 acres of land for the transportation of fower persons into this Collony (viz)

   David Davis   Thomas Briars
   John Bowles   Hesther Hayley
OB 1652–65, 184.

289. 10 Dec. 1663—These may certify that Jno Raven made his right appeare to one hundred acres of land for the transportation of two persons into this Collony (viz)

   Jane Bolt   Richard Golo
OB 1652–65, 185.

290. 10 Dec. 1663—Whereas Hesther Hayley, servant to Mr John Coutanceau hath lately (in his service) had a bastard child, It is therefore ordered that the s^d Hester Hayley shall serve her s^d Master or assigns two compleat yeares after her time of service is expired by law, or Indenture according to act of assembly. *OB 1652–65, 185.*

291. 10 Dec. 1663—Whereas Frances Newman, servant to Mr Richard Cole, hath this day made complaint to the Court of her s^d master's cruelly & barbarism towards her in giveing her unreasonable blowes & very hard usage as is made evident to this Court by sufficient Witnesses, It is therefore ordered that the said Frances Newman shall be & remaine in the sheriffs custody untill the next Court in wch meane time the s^d Mr Cole hath liberty to sell the s^d servant & in case hee shall not in that time make sale of her that then the sherriff bring her to the next Court where further order will be taken about her. *OB 1652–65, 185.*

292. 10 Dec. 1663—Whereas it doth appeare to this Court by Certificate from Mr Wm Presly that Robert Pinnell absented himselfe from the service of his master Daniell Holland the space of thirty three dayes, It is therefore ordered that the s^d Robert Pinnell shall serve his s^d Master sixty six dayes after his time of service is expired by custom, Indenture or otherwise. *OB 1652–65, 186.*

293. 20 Jan. 1663/64—Whereas Sarah Richardson, a woman servant belonging to William Betts, had a bastard Child borne in the time of her service as evidently appeares, It is therefore ordered that the s^d Sarah Richardson shall serve her s^d Master Wm Betts or assigns two compleat yeares after her time is expired by custome or Indenture. *OB 1652–65, 187.*

294. 20 Jan. 1663/64—These may certify that Capt Peter Ashton made his right appear to eleven hundred acres of land for the transportation of 22 persons into this Collony (viz)

John Cawsey	Robert Atkins
Katherine Ayres	Mary Wilkinson
John Gage	John Whitcrost
Elizabeth Mallard	William Aldridge
Richard Harvey	Elizabeth Bundy
John Bradley	Elizabeth Pride
Peter La-pero	Robert ap-Thomas
John Simpson	Margaret Phillips
John Brigsby	Thomas Corbett
William Barker	Jane Cubb
John Lewis	William Wheeler

OB 1652–65, 187.

295. 20 Jan. 1663/64—Whereas Anne Pond, servant to Abraham Byram, came into this Country without Indenture, The Court adjudged her to be about the age of fowerteene yeares & is ordered to serve her s^d Master or assigns untill she bee of the age of twenty fower yeares according to act of assembly. *OB 1652–65, 187.*

296. 20 Jan. 1663/64—Thomas Caulker, servant to Capt Peter Ashton, comeing into the Country without Indenture, is by the Court adjudged to be under the age of sixteen yeares & the law of this Court obligeth all those who come servants hither without Indenture the s^d age of 16 yeares to serve untill they be 21 & whereas the s^d Capt Ashton hath freely & voluntarily remitted one yeares service, It is ordered that the s^d Tho: Caulber shall serve him the s^d Capt Peter Ashton or his assigns seaven compleat yeares from this day. *OB 1652–65, 188.*

297. 20 Jan. 1663/64—Charles Cane, servant to John Motley, comeing into this Country without Indenture is by this Court adjudged to be about thirteen yeares of age & ordered to serve his s^d master or his assignes until hee bee 24 yeares of age. *OB 1652–65, 188.*

298. 4 Feb. 1663/64—Whereas Richard Boyer, servant to Mr Robert Jones, came into this Country without Indenture & being brought before this Court his age is adjudged to be about Fowerteene yeares and ordered by the Court to serve his s^d Master or assignes ten yeares to commence from his arrivall. *OB 1652–65, 190.*

299. 4 Feb. 1663/64—Whereas Charles Mew & Thomas Terry, servants to Coll. Richard Lee, came into this Country without Indenture & being brought before this Court, their ages are adjudged to be about fourteene yeares each and are ordered by the Court to serve their s^d Master or assignes ten yeares a peice to commence from their arrivall. *OB 1652–65, 190.*

300. 4 Feb. 1663/64—John Gardner, servant to Coll. Richard Lee, comeing into this Country without Indenture is by the Court adjudged to be about 14 yeares of age & ordered to serve his s^d Master or assignes ten yeares to commence from his arrivall. *OB 1652–65, 190.*

301. 4 Feb. 1663/64—James Gray, servant to Mr George Wale, comeing into this Country without Indenture is by this Court adjudged to be under the age of sixteene yeares & ordered to serve his s^d Master or assignes eight yeares to commence from his arrival. *OB 1652–65, 190.*

302. 4 Feb. 1663/64—These are to certify that James Johnson made his right appeare to 150 acres of land for the transportation of three persons into this Country (viz)

Samuell Glyn	Anne Middleton
Prudence Edwards	

OB 1652–65, 190.

303. 4 Feb. 1663/64—These are to certify that James Claughton made his right to 400 acres of Land for the transportation of eight persons into this Country

Samuell Churrell	Mathew Corvell
Hugh Harris	Sarah Francis
Richard Johnson	Thomas Simmons
Mary Jones	June [or Jone] Middleton

OB 1652–65, 190.

304. 4 Feb. 1663/64—Thomas Tayler, servant to James Austen, comeing into this Country without Indenture & being brought before this Court, is adjudged to be about 13 yeares of age & ordered to serve his s^d Master or assigns eleven yeares to commence from his arrivall. *OB 1652–65, 190.*

305. 4 Feb. 1663/64—Joseph Dickson, servant to Richard Peirce, comeing into this Country without Indenture, by consent of both parties is ordered to serve his s^d Master or assigns seaven yeares from this day. *OB 1652–65, 190.*

306. 4 Feb. 1663/64—These are to certify that Capt Jno Rogers made his right appeare to 600 acres of Land for the transportation of twelve persons into this Country (viz)

  Mary Hooper   Isaac Amorite
  Daniell Wilmore   John Ashe
  Martin Browne   Robert Spencer
  Hugh Statham   Edward Gatinge
  Thomas West   Sarah Williams
  Emlin Banning   William Crabb

OB 1652–65, 191.

307. 8 March 1663/64—These are to certify that Robert Sech made his right appeare to 200 acres of land for the transportation of fower persons into this Country (viz)

  George Monday   Benjamin Bushell
  Phillip Evans   Jane Wiggin

OB 1652–65, 192.

308. 8 March 1663/64—Thomas Phelps, servant to William Flower, comeing into this country without Indenture & being brought before this Court is adjudged to be under the age of sixteene yeares & with the consent of his Master is ordered to serve him or his assigns the terme of eight yeares to commence from the thirteenth day of November last past. *OB 1652–65, 193.*

309. 20 April 1664—Whereas William Corker, servant to Mr Peter Presly, came into this Country without Indenture, hee is by this Court adjudged to be about 14 yeares of age & ordered to serve his s^d Master or assignes ten yeares, which time is to commence from the 18th of January last past. *OB 1652–65, 193.*

310. 20 April 1664—Whereas Richard Ormond, servant to Mr Nicholas Journew, came into the Country this last shipping without Indenture, hee is by this Court adjudged to bee about fifteene yeares of age, & is ordered to serve his s^d Master or assigns untill hee be of the age of 24 yeares according to act. *OB 1652–65, 193.*

311. 20 April 1664—Whereas Piles Collins, Robert Lucas, & Thomas Lord, serv^{ts} to Mr Wilkes Maunder, came into this Country without Indenture, they are each of them adjudged by this Court to be about the age of 15 yeares & ordered to serve their s^d Master or his assignes each of them seaven yeares, their time to commence from the 30th of November last past, it being consented to by their s^d Master. *OB 1652–65, 193.*

312. 20 April 1664—Whereas it manifestly appeares to this Court that

Richd Peirre, in the time of his being a servant to Coll. Richard Lee now dec^d, married contrary to the law in that case made & provided, It is therefore ordered that the s^d Richard Peirre shall serve Mr Jno Lee, the son & executor of the s^d Coll. Richd Lee one compleate yeare according to act of assembly. *OB 1652–65, 194*. [Richard Peirre appealed the judgment to the next General Court. *OB 1652–65, 194*.]

313. 20 April 1664—These may certify that Mr John Lee made his right appear to 4700 acres of Land for the transportation of ninety fower persons into this Collony by his father Coll. Richd Lee who is now dec^d (viz)

Timothy Freeman	Jno Askwith
William Bell	William Segar
John Way	William Hancock
Richard Sharpe	Peter Colvin
Thomas Sparrow	Edward Knight
Thomas Woodard	Thomas Arshridge
Stephen Aday	John Mophats
Gawen Kennady	Thomas Browne
John Wilson	Francis Wood
Jnkins Thomas	William Wilson
Henry Maunders	Elizabeth Gilbert
Alexander Fleming	Richard Smith
Christopher Sangbail	Thomas Kickly
Richard Williams	William Scott
Thomas Forsithe	Edward Peckett
Lewis Beard	Hugh Lewis
William Osmotherly	Edward Staller
Peter Waterson	Edward Russell
Thomas Gregson	Margaret Butcher
Thomas Hutchinson	Elizabeth Fowke
John Butcher	John Barnes
William Battin	James Soile
John Griffith	William Fitzherbert
John Hemmerson	Richard Samwell
Richard Lentail	William Buckler
William Morris	Thomas Hayward
William Hill	William Howson
Richd Chapman	Evan Jones
John Fish	William Brocke
John Buxton	Thomas Das
John Thompson	John Smith
Robert Thickes	Ten Negroes in Green's ship

Thomas Price	Ten Negroes in the *Elizabeth*
Matthew Merriockes	George Creedwell
Matthew Bently	Robert Greene
Richard Fortice	Thomas Swan
John Oliver	Elizabeth Stafford
John Bell	Edward Sampson

OB 1652–65, 195.

314. 20 April 1664—These may Certify that Jn° Hull made his right appear to 450 acres of land by the transportation of nine persons into this Collony (viz)

William Pigler	Cesar Pere-de boutre
James Tibergine	Mary Wadmore
Thomas Stevens	Mathew Elliot
Mary Askew	Hannah Churchell
Mary Fisher	

OB 1652–65, 195.

315. 20 April 1664—These may certify that Mr Leonard Howson made his right appear to 500 acres of land for the transportation of ten persons into this Collony (viz)

himselfe	Charles Hughson
Robert Howson	Symon Thompson
Thomas Dawson	Alice Thornley
Richard Hartley	Thomas Peake
William Smallcole	James Tenant

OB 1652–65, 195.

316. 20 April 1664—These may Certify that James Pope made his right appear to 100 acres of land by the transportation of Dorcas Horton & Jn° Rosse into this Collony. *OB 1652–65, 195.*

317. 20 April 1664—These may Certify that Mr David Lyndsay made his right appeare to 650 acres of land for the transportation of thirteen persons into this Collony (vizt)

himselfe	Thomas Quick
Susanna his wife	Henry Waldon
John Simpson	John Thomas
William Thomas	John Lane
Beniamin Johnson	Anthony Lancaster
Robert Oldage	Jane Symms
Samuell Symms	

OB 1652–65, 195.

318. 20 April 1664—These may Certify that Jno Kent made his right appear to 150 acres of land by the importation of three persons into this Collony (viz)

    Thomas Dyer   Hester Poole
    Joseph Fisher
OB 1652–65, 195.

319. 20 April 1664—These may Certify that Richard Rice made his right appeare to 50 acres of land by the importation of John Mills into this Collony. *OB 1652–65, 195.*

320. 11 May 1664—It is ordered by this Court that the sherriffe forthwith summon the Jury of inquest who were sworne to inquire of the death of one Rose Parker, late servant to Mr Richard Cole . . . to make further inquirey thereof. . . . *OB 1652–65, 196.*

321. ___ June 1664—Know all men by these presents y^t I Anne Williams doe here bind my selfe truly & justley to serve Jno Raven, his heyres or assignes y^e full terme & time of 3 yeares wch is from Oct. 1664 to Oct. 1667. . . .

                         Y^e mark of Anne Williams
                         Y^e mark of John Raven
RB 1658–66, 154.

322. 20 June 1664—These may certify that Mr Wm Jallion made his right appeare to 200 acres of Land by the importation of fower persons into this Collony viz John Dawson, Wm Thomas, Thomas Svirton & Prudence Hughes. *OB 1652–65, 196.*

323. 20 June 1664—Whereas Anne Morgan, serv^t to Mr Nich: Morris, hath lately been delivered of a Bastard child in the time of her service, It is therefore ordered that the sd Anne Morgan shall serve her s^d Master or assigns 2 years after her time is expired by custome, Indenture, or otherwise . . . the sd Anne Morgan chargeth one Evan Davis, serv^t to Edw: Saunders, to be the father of her sd child, It is further ordered y^t if the sd Mr Morris & the sd Evan Davis, when a freeman, do not agree concerning the dammage sustained by the sd Morris y^t then ye same to be determined by the Court. *OB 1652–65, 196.*

324. 20 June 1664—These may Certify that Mr Tho: Mathews made his right appeare to 200 acres of Land by ye importation of John Houghton & Nath:

Brale into this Collony. *OB 1652–65, 197.*

325. 20 June 1664—John Jencken, serv^t to John Bowen, is adjudged to be 13 years of age, & to serve according to act. *OB 1652–65, 197.* [In the margin the name is Jeckell.]

326. 20 June 1664—Wm Quinborow, serv^t to Mr Wm Thomas, is censured by the Court to be 13 yeares of age & ordered to serve his M^r until he be 24 yeares of age to commence the 25 of December last. *OB 1652–65, 197.*

327. 20 June 1664—James Pomray, serv^t to And: Bowyer, is adjudged to be 15 yeares of age & to serve according to act. *OB 1652–65, 197.*

328. 20 June 1664—Whereas Rich: Gold, serv^t to John Raven, absented himselfe from his sd Master . . . , It is therefore ordered y^t ye s^d Rich: Gold shall serve his sd Master fower months after his time is by custom, Indenture. . . . *OB 1652–65, 197.*

329. 20 June 1664—Whereas severall charges hath occurred by a coroners Inquest of the death of one Rose Parker late serv^t to Mr Rich: Cole. . . . *OB 1652–65, 197.*

330. 21 June 1664, Inventory of the estate of Elizabeth Symmons— . . . 1 man Servt named James Guy, about 2 yeares & a halfe to serve; 1 mayd Servt named Eliz: Betts, about 20 months to serve. . . . *RB 1658–66, 123.*

331. 21 June 1664—John Tayler deposeth y^t during ye time of his beinge Mr Garlington's serv^t there came home 2 or 3 wild shoats wch were kild & ye eares nayled up likewise there were some lesser pigs wch were in the house wch pigs were caught & kild; this was done 5 yeares agoe. . . . *RB 1658–66, 136.*

332. 6 Sept. 1664—It is ordered y^t Alice English, serv^t to Mr Rich: Cole, remaine in Mr Knight's custody unto the next Court. *OB 1652–65, 199.*

333. 20 Oct. 1664—Certificate is granted unto Anth: Lynton for 250 Acres of Land due 5 persons imported into this Collony (vizt) Dan Becham, Anne Thorton, Hester Small, Hugh Harris & Dennis Swetever. *OB 1652–65, 199.*

334. 20 Oct. 1664—Whereas John Davis, serv^t to Maj. Geo: Colclough dec^d, absented himselfe from his Master, Mr Isaac Allerton who maryed the relict & Adm^r of ye sd Maj. Geo: Colclough, the full terme of one yeare & a quarter by his own confession, It is ordered y^t ye sd Davis serve his sd Master according to Act of Assembly after the tyme that his service of custome, or Indenture is expired. *OB 1652–65, 200.*

335. 20 Oct. 1664—The deposition of Franc: Christmas, aged 23 yeares or thereabouts, sworne & examined sayeth y^t March last was 2 yeare Wm Hartington, the serv^t of Tho: W^{ms}, told yor depontent y^t his master had killed a great sow of Mr Christopher Garlington. . . . *OB 1652–65, 201.*

336. 29 Sept. 1664 (At a Court held for James City)—Whereas Duglasse Watts, serv^t to Tho: W^{ms}, hath by her false information occasioned great disturbance in this county & scandelized her master, It is ordered that the sherr: take her into his custody & that he give her 20 stripes on her bare back & y^t she ask her sd Master forgiveness. *OB 1652–65, 202.*

337. 29 Sept. 1664 (At a Court held for James City)—Whereas Alice English, serv^t to Mr Rich: Cole, came to Capt Rogers to complain of the abuses y^t he had made from her Master & was by him committed unto Mr Knight (the sherr:) his custody till the next Court & she appearing to make good her complaint notwithstanding many many summons Mr Cole appeared not & by reason of the sickness of the sd Alice & her child Mr Knight was exposed to very great charge & trouble, this Court hath ordered y^t the sd Mr Rich: Cole pay unto ye sd Mr Pet: Knight in consideration of his troubles & charge one hundred pounds of tob & cask a month wth costs else execution & the sd serv^t to remain in Mr Knight's Custody till further order. *OB 1652–65, 202.*

338. 20 Dec. 1664—It is ordered y^t Dan: Holland & his wife enter into Bond for their good behaviour, & y^t they appear ye next Court to show cause why they deteyne Dennis Clark their servant. *OB 1652–65, 203.*

339. 3 Jan. 1664/65—Know all men by these presents y^t I Den: Clark, widdow, doe appoint Jon: Roston my true & lawfull attorney to acknowledge for me before ye Worshipfull ye Commissioners for ye County of Northumberland an Indenture wch I sealed & signed ye 3^d day of Jan^{ry} 1664 to serve Master Dan: Holland for y^r terme of two full yeares & eleven months. . . . *RB 1658–66, 154.*

340. 20 Jan. 1664/65—Tho: Cooper, serv^t to John Cossens, is adjudged by this Court to be 15 yeares of age & to serve his sd Master accordinge to Act. *OB 1652–65, 204.*

341. 20 Jan. 1664/65—Wm Hartington, serv^t to Tho: Williams, declareth y^t what he hath formerly sworne ag^t his Master were unthruthes & y^t he knows nothinge of his Master killinge of Christopher Garlington's hogs, but by ye words of Franc: Christmas & by y^e . . . of bad neighbors. *OB 1652–65, 204.*

342. 20 Jan. 1664/65—Whereupon It is ordered by ye Court y^t ye sd Hartington be forthwith taken into ye sherrif's custody & receive 20 stripes upon his bare back till ye blood runs. *OB 1652–65, 204.*

343. 20 Jan. 1664/65—Whereas by reason of ye misdemeanor of Mr Rich: Cole . . . and there beinge in Mr Knight's hands a woman serv^t of ye sd Cole, It is ordered y^t ye sd servant be appraised by fower sufficient men & forthwth sold by Mr Pet: Knight & y^t he give an account thereof ye next Court. *OB 1652–65, 204.*

344. 20 Jan. 1664/65—It is ordered y^t Dan: Holland make his appearance ye next Court & bringe Dennis Clark wth him & then to give an account how she comes to be & remaine his servant. *OB 1652–65, 205.*

345. 20 Jan. 1664/65—Whereas Tho: W^{ms} was arrested to this Court by Jno Waddy for satisfaction for a monthes service of his serv^t Fran: Christmas, who was forced to go to James Towne to answer ye appeale of Mr Tho: W^{ms}, ye sd Williams producinge a discharge from ye sd Christmas. *OB 1652–65, 205.*

346. 20 Jan. 1664/65—It is ordered by this Court y^t ye sd John Symmons & his wife serve accordinge to ye custome of ye country & y^t Dorothy Symmons, ye oldest daughter of ye sd John (who is adjudged by this Court to be 15 yeares of age) serve according to act & y^t Joane, daughter of ye sd John (who is adjudged to be 5 yeares old) serve accordinge & y^t James, son to ye sd John who is 2 yeares of age next April, by ye consent of his Master John Cockrill & ye father of ye sd child, when ye sd John Symmons is free ye sd child shall be brought into ye Court & ye Court shall Judge what ye sd John shall pay his Master for his trouble & charge wth his child, wth if ye sd John then will pay, ye sd James shall be free & goe wth his father if not, then ye sd James shall serve his aforesd Master John Cockrill according to act. *OB 1652–65, 206.*

347. 20 Jan. 1664/65, Inventory of the estate of Jon: Parker—Wm Archer to serve one yeare & 7 months; Nich: Clayton to serve 4 yeares. *RB 1658–66, 140.*

348. 20 Jan. 1664/65— . . . I Joane Henly of Cherry Poynt in Northumberland County in Virginia, widow, for diverse good causes &

considerations me thereby movinge, but more especially out of ye naturall love & affection I bear my children, Viz^t Anne, Susanna, Sarah, & Edward Henly, & for their livelyhood & maintenance have given, granted . . . unto my sd children two Serv^{ts}, the one named Rich: Jones, ye other named Eliz: Harman. . . . *RB 1658–66, 150.*

349. 20 Jan. 1664/65—These are to certify all whome it may concerne y^t whereas I Dennis Clark of the County of Northumberland made a complaynt on ye 20th day of Nov. last ay ye Co^{rt} house before ye Wors^{ful} Com^{rs} Mr Rogers, Mr Allerton & Mr Jones y^t I was beaten & abused by my master Dan: Holland & his wife, these are therefore to certify y^t what I did say was untruth & lyes forged by my selfe as witness my hand this 3^d Jany 1664. *RB 1658–66, 153.*

350. 20 Jan. 1664/65—This Indenture made ye 3^d of Jan^{ry} in ye yeare of our Lord 1664 between Dennis Clark of ye one part & Dan: Holland on ye other part Witnesseth y^t ye s^d Dennis doth covenant & grant to ye s^d Dan: Holland his heyres or assigns from ye day of ye date hereof & after for & . . . to serve in such service & imploym^{ts} as ye s^d Holland & his Wife shall imploy her; in consideration whereof ye s^d Dan: doth grant wth ye s^d Dennis to find & allow her meat, drink and apparrell wth other necessaryes duringe ye time & to release ye s^d Dennis of Country Levy & Pish [Parish] Dutyes & alsoe ye s^d Dennis is not to beate at ye Nor   unless it be in case of necessity. . . .
                                    the mark of Dennis Clark
RB 1658–66, 153, 154.

351. 20 Feb. 1664/65—A Certificate is granted unto Mr Wm Presly for 600 acres of Land for ye importation of 12 persons into this Collony (viz)

John Freman	Sarah Wakely
Robt Izard	Jeremiah Robins
Char: Pursline	Jacob Stevens
Eliz: Horton	Dan: Robinson
Wm Corker	Wm Deadman
Roberta Stembridge	Jno Harris

OB 1652–65, 207.

352. 20 Feb. 1664/65—John Hawes, serv^t to Christopher Garlington, is adjudged by this Court to be eleaven yeares of age & to serve his sd Master according to Act. *OB 1652–65, 207.*

353. 20 Feb. 1664/65—James Teuxbury, serv^t to James Austin, is adjudged to be eleaven yeares of age & to serve according to Act. *OB 1652–65,*

208.

354. 20 Feb. 1664/65—Charles Paule, serv^t to James Austin, is adjudged by this Court to be thirteen yeares of age & to serve his sd Master according to Act. *OB 1652–65, 208.*

355. 20 Feb. 1664/65—A Certificate is granted unto John Gardner for 450 Acres of Land for ye Inportation of 5 persons into this Colony Viz

      Tho: Jones   Eliz: Hall
      Hugh Gayner   Polonia Crow
      Jno Cooper

OB 1652–65, 208.

356. 20 March 1665, Phebe Kent's Bill of Sale—I doe warrant to him ye s^d Henry Rocke from any clayme of any manner of persons what soever and also one man Servt named Joseph Fisher, for & dureinge ye full terme he hath to serve according to ye custome of ye country. . . . *RB 1658–66, 146.*

357. 1 May 1665—Robt Barrow, serv^t to John Mottourne, is judged by this Court to be 14 yeares of age & to serve his sd Master according to Act. *OB 1652–65, 209.*

358. 1 May 1665—Steven Hubbard, serv^t to And: Pettegrea, is judged by this Court to be 15 yeares of age & to serve his sd Master according to act. *OB 1652–65, 209.*

359. 1 May 1665—Tho: Moore, serv^t to John Mottrom, is adjudged by this Court to serve his sd Master 4 yeares & as much as since ye twentieth of September. *OB 1652–65, 209.*

360. 1 May 1665—Mary Lennam, serv^t to Mr Isaac Morton, is judged by this Court to serve her sd Master 5 yeares to commence from ye 10th of September next. *OB 1652–65, 209.*

361. 1 May 1665—Josias Blackwell, serv^t to Mr Isaac Allerton, is judged by this Court to serve his sd Master six years to commence from the 10th of September last. *OB 1652–65, 209.*

362. 1 May 1665—Isaac Hudson, serv^t to Mr Hopkins, is judged by this Court to be 16 yeares of age & to serve his said Master according to act vizt until he be 24 yeares of age. *OB 1652–65, 209.*

363. 20 June 1665—Will of John Kent . . . Item. I give to Hugh Man [page worn] Tho: Daniell, his serv^t my left handed gunne. . . . *RB 1658–66, 151.*

364. 20 June 1665—Rebecca Chaberline, serv^t to Mr Pet: Presly, is ajudged by this Co^{rt} to be 15 yeares of age & to serve her sd Master accordinge to Act her time of service to commence from ye 23^d of January last. *OB 1652–65, 209.*

365. 20 June 1665—It is ordered by this Court y^t Wm Moy, an orphant, serve Mr Tho: Hopkins untill ye first of February in ye year 1666 & y^t ye sd Hopkins then deliver unto ye sd W^m one suit of good cloathes & 2 heifers of 2 yeares old. . . . *OB 1652–65, 210.*

366. 7 Aug. 1665—The Deposition of Wm Fourobush aged 28 yeares or thereabouts sworne & examined sayth y^t formerly when Mr Dav: Lindsay did live at Thos: Brewers yor Depontent was servant there . . .
         Sign Wm: Forroughbush
RB 1658–66, 161.

367. __ Aug. 1665—The Deposition of Eliz: Morris aged 22 yeares or thereabouts sworne & examined sayeth y^t when yor Dep^t was Servt to Mr. David Lindsay. . . . *RB 1658–66, 164.*

368. 6 Sept. 1665—A Certificate is granted James Austin for 500 Acres of Land for ye importation of ten persons into this Colony (vizt)

   Morditay Evans   Sam: Tirkbury
   Nich: Brookes   Eliz: Miles
   John Terry   An: England
   Tho: Harwood   John [no surname]
   Charles Paule   James Austin
OB 1652–65, 211.

369. 6 Sept. 1665—Whereas Eliz: Michell, serv^t to Mr Peter Knight, hath brought a Bastard Child in ye time of her service, It is ordered y^t ye sd Elizabeth serve her sd M^r according to Act. *OB 1652–65, 211.*

370. 6 Sept. 1665—Whereas Benj: Johnson, serv^t to Mr David Lyndsay, hath in Court sworne y^t he is in feare of loosinge his life by Mr Tho: Mathew, It is therefore ordered y^t ye sd Mr Tho: Mathew give Bond wth security for ye peace else ye sherr: to take him into safe Custody. *OB 1652–65, 212.*

371. 6 Sept. 1665—Certificate is granted unto Mr John Lee for 300 Acres of Land for ye Importation of 6 persons into this colony vizt.

    Robt Sesly   John Hughes
    Dav Dansy   Tho: Leyton
    Rog: Arney   Wm Rowland
OB 1652–65, 212.

372. 6 Sept. 1665—A Certificate is granted unto Mr Wm Nutt for 100 Acres of Land for ye Importation of 2 persons into this Colony (vizt) Tho: Philips and Robt Logge. *OB 1652–65, 212.*

373. 14 Sept. 1665—Inventory of Richard Flynt . . . One serv^t named James Barn haveing 14 months to serve, 1000 lbs. tobacco; one mayd serv^t Fran: Newman 14 months to serve, 700 lbs. tobacco. . . . *RB 1658–66, 171.*

374. 20 Nov. 1665—Mary Lamkin, an orphant of Tho: Lamkin dec^d, is ordered to serve John Motley & Eliz: his wife until she be 17 yeares of age, or untill she be maryed [married], they no ways abusing ye sd Child & providinge necessaryes for her duringe ye sd terme. *OB 1652–65, 213.*

375. 20 Nov. 1665—Whereas Summar Adams hath got a woman Servt of Mr Peter Knight wth Child, It is ordered by this Court y^t ye sd Adams give security for ye keepinge of ye sd Child & y^t he be fined accordinge to Act for his default. *OB 1652–65, 213.*

376. 20 Nov. 1665—John Franklin, serv^t to Mr John Motrom, coming into this Country wthout Indenture, is ordered to serve his sd Master 5 yeares according to Act. *OB 1652–65, 214.*

377. 20 Nov. 1665—Whereas Sarah Garnet, serv^t to Mr Christopher Garlington, hath had a base child in ye time of her service, It is ordered y^t ye sd Child serve ye sd Garlington untill he be one & twenty years old, unless ye father of ye sd Child appeare in ye meanetime & give Bond to provide for it & y^t ye sd Servt serve her sd Master according to Act. *OB 1652–65, 214.*

378. 20 Jan. 1665/66—Certificate is granted unto John Tayler for 500 Acres of Land for ye Importation of 10 persons (vizt)

    Henry Thomas   Morgan Dorll
    Ed: Nolt   Edw: Kelly
    Edw: Hardinge   James Greene
    Rich: Lee   Fran: Cole

Rich: Dell   Anne Olford
OB 1652–65, 215.

379. 20 Jan. 1665/66—Certificate is granted unto James Hill for 100 acres of Land for ye Importation of himselfe & James Lucson into this Colony. *OB 1652–65, 215.*

380. 20 Jan. 1665/66—Certificate is granted unto Hen: Mayes for 400 Acres of Land for ye Importation of 8 persons into this Colony (Viz^t)
    Henry Mayes   Wm Copppage
    James White   Steven Sadler
    Wm Evans   Mary Perry
    Rich: Symmons   Elino^r Day
OB 1652–65, 215.

381. 20 Jan. 1665/66—Sar: Pearson, serv^t to Maj^r Isaac Allerton, is adjudged to serve her sd Master accordinge to Act for her haveing two Bastard Children in ye time of her service & John Birch, serv^t to ye sd Maj^r Allerton, is putatived father of y^e sd Sarah's last Child is ordered to make satisfaction for his sd default according to Law & to give Bond. . . . *OB 1652–65, 216.*

382. 20 Jan. 1665/66—Certificate is granted unto Henry Bradley for y^e Importation of two persons into this Colony (vizt) Mary Bradley & ____ Benbow. *OB 1652–65, 217.* [No first name for Benbow.]

383. 20 Jan. 1665/66—Ordered y^t Dennis Clarke be free from Dan: Holland & y^t she have her Cloathes & what goods she shall make appeare to belonge unto her from him. *OB 1652–65, 217.*

384. 7 Feb. 1665/66—Whereas it appears to this Court y^t John Squire, Christopher, ye Taylor, Black Harry, black Dick, & black Jack, serv^{ts} to Mr John Lee, did go into Wicocomako Towne in ye night & did kill a hog of Edw: King & did rudely & riotously beat & abuse . . . of ye Indians, It is ordered y^t ye sd King for ye sd hog & y^t ye sd John, Christopher, black Dick, black Jack & black Harry have 20 stripes upon their backs. . . . *OB 1652–65, 217.*

385. 5 March 1665/66—Dan: Crabtree, serv^t to John Tyngey, is adjudged by this Court to be 15 yeares of age & to serve his sd Master according to Act. *OB 1652–65, 220.*

386. 5 March 1665/66—Edw: Brittaine, serv^t to Col. Pet: Ashton, is adjudged by this Court to serve his sd Master eight yeares but his sd Master late declared himselfe satisfied y[t] he shall serve him but 7 yeares to commence from y[e] 10th of November next. *OB 1652–65, 220.*

387. 5 March 1665/66—Certificate is granted unto Tho: Salisbury for 100 Acres of Land for y[e] importation of Rob[t] Lee, James Martyn. *OB 1652–65, 220.*

388. 5 March 1665/66—Certificate is granted unto W[m] Griffin for 300 Acres of Land for y[e] importation of 6 persons into this Colony.

    Anne Lawson   Edw: Rattle
    John Lawson   Alexander Griffin
    Eliz: Lawson   Arth: Kevie

OB 1652–65, 220.

389. 5 March 1665/66—Certificate is granted unto Tho: Towers for 150 Acres of Land for y[e] importation of 3 persons (viz[t]) Tho: Towers, John Bryan, Ann Bryan. *OB 1652–65, 221.*

390. 5 March 1665/66—Certificate is granted to M[r] John Saffin for 400 acres of Land by y[e] importation of 8 persons into this Colony

    John Saffin   John Saffin
    George Elliston   Sam Woolsteed
    Sam: Woolsteed   John [page worn]
    Jeffery, a Negro   Geo: Elliston

OB 1652–65, 222.

391. 5 March 1665/66—Whereas John Houghton, serv[t] to M[r] Tho: Mathew, did run away from his said Master wth fower of his Negroes 15 dayes to y[e] great charge & loss of y[e] sd M[r] Mathew, It is ordered y[t] y[e] sd John serve his sd Master two yeares & six monthes after y[e] expiration of his time of service by Indenture, Custome or otherwise. *OB 1652–65, 222.*

392. 16 April 1666—Geo: Ellistone aged 21 yeares sworne sayeth y[t] Tho: Barrat did commonly harbor & intertaine Jerimiah Canady, one of my Master's Serv[ts] at Exet[rs] Lodge.... *RB 1666–72, 9.* [Other entries in reference to Canady on pages 9 and 10. At times he is referred to as Jeremy Cannady.]

393. 16 April 1666—Henry Hartley, aged 26 yeares or thereabouts, saith that in y[e] month of April 1665 Thomas Barrett finding mee, this Depon[t] at Maryland told mee that he had bought mee of my Master for five hundred pds of Tob[o] but when he said Barrett perceived I would not beleave him, he said if thy Master when thou comest home doe not come fairly off with thee, come to mee & Ile write thee a discharge, for I know two Commissioners hands wch I will sett thereto & soe Ile write a Letter to a man y^t lives at ye Clifts to signify thay you are a free man soe you may goe clear away & further this Deponent saith not.

Henry Hartley his marke

RB 1666–72, 10.

394. 16 April 1666—... he saw ye s^d Barrett wth his fist beat Miles Miller, another serv^t of Mr Saffin at Exeter Lodge. *RB 1666–72, 10.*

395. 16 April 1666—... I, this Depon^t, saw Tho: Barrett beat Michael Miller, servant to Jno: Saffin at Exeter Lodge.... *RB 1666–72, 10.*

396. 16 April 1666—... Another time in ye night ye sd Cannady tooke a brand of fire & being askt where he was going, he said he was going to Mr Barretts, and several times both him, ye s^d Cannady & also Tho: Young, another Servt of Mr Saffins, when they had been absent from their business at Exeter Lodge would say they had been at Barretts.... *RB 1666–72, 10.*

397. 16 April 1666—... & that Thomas Young sometime servant to Mr Saffin should then have been free also.... *RB 1666–72, 11.*

398. 16 April 1666—Wm Dowlane aged 19 yeares or thereabouts being examined & sworne sayth this Depon^t being set to keep James Philips (his Masters) Cowes & loosing them feared to go home & thereupon went to Mr Flynts plantation at Cherry Poynte.... *RB 1666–72, 9.*

399. 10 May 1666—Certificate is granted unto Josias Draper for 500 Acres of Land for ye importation of 10 persons (viz)

Edw: White	Wm Fowle
Tho: White	Jos: Draper
Anne White	Hanna White
Joane White	Tho: Draper
	Tho: White & his wife

OB 1652–65, 223.

400. 20 Aug. 1666—Whereas Mary Perry, serv^t to Henry Mayes, hath had a bastard Child in ye time of her service, It is ordered y^t she serve her said Master for her said default according to Law. *OB 1652–65, 226.*

401. 20 Aug. 1666—Whereas Jane Dolin, serv^t to Mr Rich: Feilding, hath committed fornication ye Co^{rt} doth therefore order y^t she shall forthwith receive twenty stripes on her bare back untill ye blood comes or pay 500^{lbs} tobacco to ye use of ye parish besides what ye law shall require to be paid to her Master. *OB 1652–65, 227.*

402. 20 Aug. 1666—It is ordered that ye sher: take Wm Shepard into safe custody until he gives bond wth sufficient security for his good behaviour for committing fornication wth Jane Dolin & for y^e present paym^t of one thousand pounds of Tobacco & cask for y^e use of y^e parish, 500^{lbs} for his owne default & 500^{lbs} for y^e said Jane wch he hath undertaken to pay. *OB 1652–65, 227.*

403. _____—Certificate is granted unto Jno Graham for 100 Acres of Land for the importation of these persons into this Colony (vizt) Wm Chadborne, Rich Fasshoe & Roseland Bushell. *OB 1666–78, 1.*

404. _____—Certificate is granted unto Tho: Brerton for thirteen hundred Acres of Land for the transportation of twenty six persons into this Colony (vizt)

Wm Brereton	Jno ___ [no surname]
Tho Brereton	Sam: Hull
Henry Reading	Wm Gunfrie
Margaret Balterman	Benj Hunt
Joseph Bayly	Wm Perriman
Rice Jones	Anne Frigham
Anne Luxmeeze	Gilbert James
Anna Whitehook	Joane, his wife
Isaac Cooke	Edw: Souse
Tho: Alford	Tho: Harrison
Jno Evans	W^m & Mitchall, Frenchman
Wm Vaughan	Jno Atkins
Abell Williams	

OB 1666–78, 1.

405. _____—Rich: Smyth, serv^t to Mr Jno Mottrom, is adjudged by this Court to be thirteen yeares of age & ordered to serve his said Master according to Act. *OB 1666–78, 1.* [Name of Smyth determined by checking Index.]

406. 20 Dec. 1666—Certificate is granted unto Tho: Lane for 500 Acres of Land for the importation of ten persons into this Colony vizt

Himself	Jane Le Bay
Eliza: his wife	Jno Barbar
Wm Molin	Jno Howell

Val: Monsloe Edw: Morris
[not legible] Morgan Mary Cloud
OB 1666–78, 2.

407. 20 Dec. 1666—Whereas Wm Ballingall hath gott Mary Jones wth Child & is departing ye County, ye Co^{rt} doth order y^t ye sher: take ye said Ballingall into safe Custody untill he give bond wth sufficient security to keep ye parish harmless from ye said Child. *OB 1666–78, 3.*

408. 20 Dec. 1666—Whereas Wm Jones, serv^t to Mr Rich: Feilding dec^d, did by ye oaths of Franc: Brittain & Mary Flowers made appeare to this Court y^t Mr Rich: Feilding did promise to remitt two yeares of his fower yeares service by Indenture in consideration of fower serv^{ts} . . . by ye sd Jones for ye said Feilding when in England & having made appear y^t what . . . served two years to ye sd Feilding ye Court order y^t he be now free. *OB 1666–78, 3.*

409. 8 April 1667—Certificate is granted unto Mr Edw: Saunders for two hundred & fifty Acres of Land for ye Importation of 5 persons into this Colony (vizt) Marg: Walker, Marg: Morgan, John Brookes, Leon^d Southerly, Tho: Butler. *OB 1666–78, 7.*

410. 8 April 1667—Margaret Scull, serv^t to Mrs Helena Lyndsay, Judged by this Court to be 16 yeares of age & ordered to serve her sd M^{rs} according to Act. *OB 1666–78, 7.*

411. 20 May 1667—Jane Gore, serv^t to Rich: Span, is adjudged by ye Court to be nine yeares of age & ordered to serve her sd Master according to Act. *OB 1666–78, 7.*

412. 20 May 1667—It is ordered wth ye mutual consent of both parties y^t Wm Coppage, serv^t to Henry Mayes, serve his sd Master untill ye 20th of October next & y^t his sd Master then pay him his Corne & Cloathes furtherwth deliver him a yearling Heyfer. *OB 1666–78, 8.*

413. 20 June 1667—Susan Philips, serv^t to Mr Hen: Watts, is adjudged by this Court to be 15 yeares of age & ordered to serve her said Master according to Act. *OB 1666–78, 9.*

414. 20 June 1667—Geo: Read, serv^t to Mrs Dorothy Dameron, is adjudged by this Court to be fowerteen yeares of age & ordered to serve her sd Master according to Act. *OB 1666–78, 9.*

415. 20 June 1667—Whereas Mr Christopher Garlington did make his complaynt to this Court y^t his serv^t [the name William Bennet is in the margin of the page] hath absented himself from his service by running away one yeare & ten days at severall tymes, It is therefore ordered y^t Bennet serve his sd Master for his sd default according to Act double ye sd time. *OB 1666–78, 10.*

416. 20 June 1667—Whereas Eliz: Jones, serv^t to Mr Pet: Presly, hath been delivered of a Bastard Child in ye time of her service, It is ordered y^t ye sd Eliz: make satisfaction unto her sd Master according to Act & it is further ordered y^t ye sherr: take ye sd Eliz: into safe Custody & give her 20 stripes on her bare back untill ye blood come unless she give caution for her future good behaviour & for ye paym^t of ye fine of 500^{lbs} Tobacco according to Act. *OB 1666–78, 10.*

417. 20 June 1667—Certificate is granted Tho: Gaskoyne for 150 acres of Land for ye importation of 3 persons into this Colony (vizt) John Goozy, Boaz Hollis, Anne Owens. *OB 1666–78, 10.*

418. 20 June 1667—Pet: Maunding, serv^t to Jno Waddy, declaring himself in Court to be eight yeares of age, is ordered to serve his sd Master according to Act. *OB 1666–78, 10.*

419. 20 June 1667—Certificate is granted to Wm Downinge for 400 Acres of Land for the Importation of 8 persons into this Colony (vizt)

Anne Ailiff   Wm Richards
Edw: Lugge   himselfe twice
Wm Benes   Marg: Lewis
Eliz: Howard [or Hobart]

OB 1666–78, 11.

420. 20 Aug. 1667—Elizabeth Taylor sworne saith y^t she had heard Arthur Stevens, ye Servt of Bennett Madrin, say (after ye sd Servt had run away) y^t he had ye writings y^t his s^d master said he had lost & y^t he had putt them under a tree & further saith not. *RB 1666–72, 27.* [Additional depositions in reference to Arthur Stevens continue for several pages.]

421. 20 Oct. 1667—Whereas by ye Complynt of Philip Peyton & ye Testamony of some of ye neighbors, It appears y^t Phil: Peyton & Nath: Garner, serv^{ts} to Rich: Nelmes, have grivous sores on his legges & are very much neglected by their sd Master who taketh nor care to see ye sd sores Cured, It is ordered y^t ye sd Nelmes forth endeavour to get ye sd Serv^{ts} Cured & if y^e

next Vestry held for this parish Mr Wm Wildey & Mr Wm Downing (who are by ye Court desired to inquire into ye sd business) shall then give their report y^t ye sd Nelmes hath been remiss in ye effectual performance of what here ordered y^t then ye Court to be further . . . therein. *OB 1666–78, 12.*

422. 20 Dec. 1667—Whereas Mr Rich: Span did make his complaynt unto this Court y^t Lewis Harris & Thomas Willon, his serv^{ts}, did run away fower months in y^e . . . tyme of his crop, It is ordered y^t ye sd serv^{ts} doe both of them serve their Master double ye time y^t they were for absent & also seaven monthes a piece in consideration of ye sd . . . charge & damage when y^t their time of servitude by Indenture, Custome or otherwise is expired. *OB 1666–78, 14.*

423. 20 Dec. 1667—Certificate is granted Jno Donoway for fifty Acres of Land for ye importation of himself into this Colony. *OB 1666–78, 14.*

424. 20 Dec. 1667—Whereas And: Pettegrew complaynth to this Court y^t Joanna Mopsons, his serv^t, hath run away one month, It is ordered y^t ye sd Joanna serve her sd Master five months for her sd Default & his damage after her time of service by Indenture, Custome, or otherwise be expired. *OB 1666–78, 14.*

425. 20 Dec. 1667—Whereas Joanna Mopsons, serv^t to And: Pettegrew, hath had a Bastard child in ye time of her service, It is ordered y^t she make her sd Master satisfaction for his trouble & losse according to Act. . . . *OB 1666–78, 14.*

426. 20 Jan. 1667/68—Upon ye petition of Anne Harwood, serv^t to Mr Franc: Clay, she having served her sd Master five yeares, & come into this Country without Indenture, It is ordered y^t ye sd Anne be free. *OB 1666–78, 14.*

427. 20 Jan. 1667/68—Certificate is granted Tho: Hobson for 500 Acres of Land for the Importation of 10 persons.

Wm Blake	Wm Croft
James Jackson	Kate Danvers
Evan Johnson	Tho: Whitley
Wm Colyar	Hen: Davis
Sar: Swift	Wm Leech

OB 1666–78, 15.

428. 20 Jan. 1667/68—Certificate is granted Wm Wildey for 100 acres of

Land for ye Importation of Tho: Spilman & Mary Spilman assigned to Tho: Hobson. *OB 1666–78, 15.*

429. 27 Jan. 1667/68—Know all men by these presents that I George Courtnell have by these presents granted, bargained and sold and by these presents doe grant, bargaine & sell unto Mr Leonard Howson two men servants named Lewis Jenkin & Nicholas Allgrove.... *RB 1666–72, 69.*

430. 27 Feb. 1667/68—Robt Pinnar, serv^t to James Houghton, Judged to be twelve yeares of age & ordered to serve his sd Master according to Act. *OB 1666–78, 16.*

431. 27 Feb. 1667/68—Tho: Tucker, serv^t to Mr Edw: Coles, is adjudged by this Court to be twelve yeares of age & ordered to serve his sd Master according to Act. *OB 1666–78, 16.*

432. 27 Feb. 1667/68—Certificate is granted Mr Leonard Howson for two hundred & fifty Acres of Land for the Importation of Wm Hobson, Rowland Lawson, Cyrus ___ [no surname], Philip Boulton, Jno Parkes. *OB 1666–78, 17.*

433. 27 Feb. 1667/68—Certificate is granted Mr Ambrose Fielding for 600 Acres of Land for y^e Importation of

    Rich: Browne   Tho: Izeberris
    Dav: Jennings   Jno P___ [not legible]
    Wm Drinkwater   Mary Shewter
    Wm Jones   Jane Dollin
    Rich: Tipton   Geo: Philips
    Fran: Britton   Arth: March

OB 1666–78, 17.

434. 27 Feb. 1667/68—Ediff Symms, serv^t to Geo: Clark, is adjudged to be 12 yeares of age & Joane Ailey, serv^t to y^e sd Clark to be tenne yeares of age & both ordered to serve their sd Master according to Act. *OB 1666–78, 17.*

435. 27 Feb. 1667/68—Whereas Alic Arnoll, serv^t to Fran: Robts, hath had a Bastard Child in ye tyme of her service, It is ordered y^t she make her sd Master satisfaction by service according to Act. *OB 1666–78, 17.*

436. 7 April 1668—Alexander Gemball, serv^t to ye estate of Mr Rich: Flynt, is adjudged to be 15 yeares of age & ordered to serve y^e Ex^s of y^e sd Flynt according to Act. *OB 1666–78, 18.*

437. 7 April 1668—Certificate is granted James Claughton for 200 Acres of Land for y^e Importation of 4 persons (vizt) Robert Pinnar, Edw: Fanning, Elinor ___ [no surname given], Hugh Mongomery, all in 4. *OB 1666–78, 18.*

438. 7 Aprill 1668—Capt. Tho: Smyth doth in Co^{rt} declare y^t in y^e yeare 1662 he did sell a serv^t to Lt. Col. Sam: Smyth for 7 yeares & y^t he had no Indenture wch serv^t was named John Parsons. *OB 1666–78, 18.*

439. 7 April 1668—Kath: Emery, serv^t to James Allen, hath had a Bastard child in ye tyme of her service, wherefore it is ordered y^t she make her sd Master satisfaction according to Act, & pay ye fine imposed by Law for sd default, James Allen undertaking to pay ye sd fine, it is ordered y^t ye sd Catherine serve her sd Master half a yeare for this sd disbursem^t. *OB 1666–78, 18.*

440. 7 April 1668—Joseph Elvis, serv^t to Mr Pet: Presly, is adjudged by this Court to be nine years of age & ordered to serve his sd Master according to Act. *OB 1666–78, 18.*

441. 20 June 1668—Jno Amie, serv^t to Col. Pet^r Ashton, is adjudged by this Court to be 15 years of age; Philip, a French boy servant to Tho: Roe, is adjudged to be 10 yeares of age; John Wolford, serv^t to Nich: Nichols, is adjudged to be 15 yeares of age; John, a French boy serv^t to Dan: Neale, is adjudged to be 12 yeares of age; Nich:, a French boy servant to Geo: Countnall, is adjudged to be 12 yeares of age; Luke, a French boy servant to Christopher Neale, is adjudged to be 13 yeares of age; Edward Jacob, serv^t to Mr Saunders, is adjudged to be 9 yeares of age; Oliver Coutanshaw, serv^t to Mr Saunders, is adjudged to be 10 yeares of age; Elizabeth, a French wench serv^t to Tho: Hobson, is adjudged to be 15 yeares of age; Abraham, a French boy serv^t to Wm Wildey, is adjudged to be 12 yeares of age; Andr:, a French boy serv^t to Charles Ashton, is adjudged to be 12 yeares of age; ordered y^t these above sd serv^{ts} serve their respective Masters according to Act. *OB 1666–78, 19.*

442. 20 June 1668—Kath: Davis, having committed ye sin of fornication & having lately had a bastard Child, it is ordered y^t ye sherr: take ye sd Katherine into safe Custody & give her 20 stripes on her bare back untill ye blood come. *OB 1666–78, 19.*

443. 20 June 1668—Whereas Kath: Davis, serv^t to Capt John Rogers, hath lately had a Bastard child, It is ordered y^t ye sd Kath: make her sd Master satisfaction according to Act. *OB 1666–78, 19*.

444. 20 June 1668—Whereas Jno Seaman hath comitted ye filthy sin of fornication & gott Kath: Davis wth Child, It is ordered y^t ye sherr: take ye sd Thomas [Order Book here states Thomas, but the name John is in the margin of the page as well as at the beginning of this court order] into safe Custody untill he gives bond wth good security for his failure good behaviour to pay ye fine of 500^{lbs} tobacco for his sd default & to for ye keeping of ye sd Child. *OB 1666–78, 19*.

445. 22 July 1668, Mary Million's Indenture—Mary Million of or from ye Parish or place of Drury Lane in ye County of Middx spinister . . . also to serve Thomas Smith for four years. . . . *RB 1666–72, 86*.

446. 22 July 1668, Christopher Wade's Indenture—I doe hereby certifie all whom it doth or may concerne y^t ye 22 day of July in ye yeare of our Lord 1668 Christopher Wade of & from ye Parish & place of Cumberland & of London, able Taylor, came before me & declared y^t being free & neither Servt nor Apprentice but at his own dispose & desirous to goe to some of his Master's Plantations in America was willing & did voluntarily without any deceitful or sinister practice whatsoever . . . And then did also promise & agree from ye day of ye date hereof untill his first & next arrivall ye sd Land of Virginia and after for & during ye Terme of fower yeares to serve in such service & imployment as ye sd Thomas Smith or his assignes shall there appoint & imploy him. . . . *RB 1666–72, 86*.

447. 8 Sept. 1668—John Pelke, serv^t to Tho: Perym [or Peryn] is adjudged to be 15 yeares of age & ordered to serve his Master according to Act. *OB 1666–78, 20*.

448. 8 Sept. 1668—Mr Mathew, having a French boy who being sick is incapable to come to ye Court to have ye Court's Judgm^t & whereas ye Act injoynes Masters to bring their serv^{ts} within such a limited tyme, It is ordered y^t if y^e sd Wm Mathew bring hie serv^t to y^e Court as soon as he is well y^t he have y^e benefit of y^e Act. *OB 1666–78, 20*.

449. 8 Sept. 1668—Certificate is granted Mr Pet: Presly for 50 Acres of Land for y^e Importation of Sarah _____ [no surname given] assigned to Wm Cornish. *OB 1666–78, 20*.

450. 8 Sept. 1668—John Russell, serv^t to Mr Wm Brereton, is adjudged by this Court to be thirteen yeares of age & ordered to serve his Master according to Act. *OB 1666–78, 20.*

451. 8 Sept. 1668—Charles Shelly, serv^t to Capt Edm: Lyster, is adjudged by ye Court to be 16 yeares of age & ordered to serve his sd Master according to Act. *OB 1666–78, 20.*

452. 8 Sept. 1668—James, a French boy serv^t to Mr Rich: Span, is adjudged to be 14 yeares of age & Joseph Omer, serv^t to ye sd Span 15 yeares & both ordered to serve their sd Master according to Act. *OB 1666–78, 20.*

453. 8 Sept. 1668—Certificate is granted Dan: Holland for 250 Acres of Land for ye importation of Robt Pennell, Anne Mosse, Wm Goff, Wm Harbert, John Dew. *OB 1666–78, 21.*

454. 8 Sept. 1668—Wm Nichols, serv^t to Mr Leon: Howson, is adjudged by this Court to be eighteen years of age & ordered to serve according to Act. *OB 1666–78, 21.*

455. 8 Sept. 1668—Certificate is granted Rich: Nelmes for 300 Acres of Land for ye Importation of Erasmus Whithall, Philip Payton, Geo: Whitehorne, Mary Peirse, An: Higgham, Mary Vizard. *OB 1666–78, 22.*

456. 2 Oct. 1668—Know all men by these presents y^t I Edw: Williams of ye County of Rappahannock doe appoint & ordaine my well beloved friend Jno Rotheram to be my true & lawfull attorney for me & in my name & steed & in my use to ask, demand, record & receive satisfaction from Walter Price of ye County of Northumberland or any other person or persons y^t hath entertayned my Servant by name Jno: Sherry. . . . *RB 1666–72, 59.*

457. 20 Oct. 1668—Maudlin Plessee, serv^t to Tho: Lane, is adjudged by this Co^{rt} to be 15 yeares of age & ordered to serve her sd Master according to act. *OB 1666–78, 22.*

458. 20 Oct. 1668—Mary Levistone, serv^t to Mr Leonrd Howson, is adjudged by this Co^{rt} to be 17 yeares of age & ordered to serve her said Master according to Act. *OB 1666–78, 22.*

459. 5 Nov. 1668—Sam: Ortland, serv^t to Mr Peter Knight, adjudged by this Court to be 18 yeares of age & ordered to serve his sd Master according to Act. *OB 1666–78, 23.*

460. 20 Nov. 1668—Jos: Atkins, serv^t to James Robinson, is adjudged by this Court to be fifteen yeares of age & ordered to serve his sd Master according to Act. *OB 1666–78, 24.*

461. 20 Nov. 1668—Joell Stripling is by this Court adjudged to be 17 yeares of age & ordered to serve his sd Master [the name of Col. Ashton is in the margin] according to Act. *OB 1666–78, 25.*

462. 11 Jan. 1668/69—Anne Duncombe is adjudged by this Court to be fifteen yeares of age & ordered to serve her said Master [Wm Griffin] according to Act. *OB 1666–78, 25.*

463. 11 Jan. 1668/69—Whereas Mr Nich: Hale petitioned this Court for satisfaction of Walter Price for his illegal entertainment of a serv^t of ye sd Hale who had run away from him three months, It is ordered y^t ye sd Price make ye sd Hale satisfaction according to Act. *OB 1666–78, 25.*

464. 27 Jan. 1668/69—Eliz: Evans & Isaac Hudson, serv^{ts} to Mrs Grace Hopkins, having run away without their sd Mistress's Lycense, it is ordered y^t ye sherr: take them into safe Custody & give them 20 stripes a peice on their bare backs untill ye blood come, & y^t then he deliver them unto ye next Constables to be conveyed to their sd Mistress's house. *OB 1666–78, 26.*

465. 5 Feb. 1668/69—This Indenture . . . between Jno Carey of ye one party & Rich: Voss on ye other party Witnesseth y^t ye sd Rich: Voss doth hereby Coven^t, promise & grant to & with ye said Jno Carey . . . from ye day of ye date hereof untill ye first & next arrivall in Virginia and after for & during ye terme of fower yeares to serve in such service & imploym^t as he ye said Jno Carey shall there employ him according to ye Custome of the Country wherof ye said Jno Carey doth hereby grant to ye s^d Rich: Voss to pay for his passing & to find & allow him meat drinke apparell & lodging. . . . *RB 1666–72, 87.*

466. 10 March 1668/69—Wm Sparkes, serv^t to Tho: Hobson, having run away three weekes, is ordered to double ye sd tyme & be whipt. *OB 1666–78, 29.*

467. 10 March 1668/69—Wm Jeffs, serv^t to Wm Shoare, being by this Court Judged to be 13 yeares of age, was ordered to serve his sd Master according to Act, but his sd Master hath in Court acquitted him of one year of his sd service. *OB 1666–78, 29.*

468. 10 March 1668/69—Whereas Geo: Guesse, serv^t to Mr John Coutanceau, hath run away from his said Master one month & his sd Master hath expended seaven hundred & fifty pounds of tobacco & cask in ye getting of him again, it is ordered y^t ye sd George serve his sd Master ten monthes after his tyme of service by Custom or Indenture is expired & y^t he receive 20 stripes on his bare back. *OB 1666–78, 29.*

469. 10 March 1668/69—Wm Sparkes, having run away from his Master Tho: Hobson's service and cost him 400^{lbs} pounds Tobacco & cask to procure him agayne, it is ordered y^t he serve his sd Master ten monthes for his sd default & be whipt. *OB 1666–78, 29.*

470. 6 April 1669—Tho: Meiny, serv^t to Mr Rhodon, adjudged by this Court to be 14 yeares of age & ordered to serve his sd Master according to Act. *OB 1666–78, 30.*

471. 6 April 1669—Charles Harry, serv^t to Wm Tignall, adjudged to be twelve yeares of age & ordered to serve his sd Master according to Act. *OB 1666–78, 30.*

472. 6 April 1669—John Whitney, serv^t to Mr Rhodon, adjudged by this Court to be 17 yeares of age & ordered to serve his sd Master according to Act. *OB 1666–78, 30.*

473. 6 April 1669—Walter Jenkins, serv^t to John Cockrell, is adjudged by ye Court to be ten yeares of age & ordered to serve his sd Master according to Act. *OB 1666–78, 30.*

474. 6 April 1669—Whereas Anne, serv^t to John Motley, hath had a Bastard Child in ye tyme of her service, It is ordered y^t she make her sd Master satisfaction for his trouble, Charge & losse of tyme, & be fined according to Act.

Mr John Motley ingageth to pay ye fine of five hundred pounds of tobacco & Cask in ye behalf of ye Delinquent. *OB 1666–78, 31.*

475. 6 April 1669—Alice Arnold, serv^t to Fran: Roberts, having had a bastard in ye tyme of her service, is ordered to make her sd Master satisfaction for his trouble, paynes, & loss of tyme by service according to Act & y^t ye sherr: take ye sd Alice into safe Custody & give her 20 stripes on her bare back untill ye blood come unless she give caution for her future good behaviour & for ye paym^t of ye fine imposed by ye Law for sd default. *OB 1666–78, 31.*

476. 6 April 1669—Mr James Austen ingageth to pay ye fine above sd.

OB 1666–78, 31.

477. 6 April 1669—Alice Dryer, serv^t to Tho: Williams, having run away from her sd Master ten weekes & three dayes, It is ordered y^t ye sd Alice serve her sd Master for her sd default according to Act.

Tho: Swift, serv^t to John Motley, is adjudged by this Court to be 14 yeares of age & ordered to serve his sd Master according to Act. *OB 1666–78, 31.*

478. 23 May 1669, Inventory of Mr. Thomas Hopkins—... Isaac Hudson 4 yeares to serve, 1500 lbs. tobacco; Jno Heales 7 yeares to serve, 1800 lbs. tobacco; Wm Bevin 4 yeares 8 months to serve, 1500 lbs. tobacco; Humfry Taylor 8 months to serve, 800 lbs. tobacco; Elizab: Evans 14 months to serve, 800 lbs. tobacco.... *RB 1666–72, 90.*

479. 22 June 1669—Jno Rumley, serv^t to Mr Tho: Mathew, is adjudged to be 16 yeares of age & ordered to serve his sd Master according to Act to commence from this day. *OB 1666–78, 32.*

480. 22 June 1669—Certificate is granted Mr Edw: Sanders for six hundred Acres of Land for y^e Importation of 12 persons (vizt)

Jno Reynolds	Rich: Otter
Jno Brookes	James Allen
Sus: Wherrett	Tho: Waterman
Edw: Jacob	Tho: Harris
Oliv^r Coutansheau	Sar ____
Wm Petts	Eliz: Jermin

OB 1666–78, 33.

481. 22 June 1669—Certificate is granted Hugh Fouch for 150 Acres of Land for y^e importation of James Hadwell, Joyce How & Jane Baley. *OB 1666–78, 33.*

482. 22 June 1669—Whereas it appears to this Court y^t Tho: Crosse, serv^t to Richard Kenner, hath run away from his master one month & three dayes, & cost his master two hundred thirty one pounds of Tobacco & cask to recover him, it is ordered y^t ye sd Crosse serve his sd Master five months & 6 dayes after y^t ye tyme of his service by Indenture, Custome or otherwise is expired. *OB 1666–78, 33.*

483. 22 June 1669—Guillian, an Irish wench, serv^t to Mr Mathew Rhodon, is adjudged by this Co^rt to be 14 yeares of age & ordered to serve her sd Master according to Act. *OB 1666–78, 33.*

484. 22 June 1669—James Hickley, serv^t to Geo: Clark, is adjudged to be 14 yeares of age & ordered to serve his sd Master according to Act. *OB 1666–78, 33.*

485. 22 June 1669—Certificate is granted Tho: Lane for 100 Acres of Land for ye Importation of Rog: Thomas & Maudlin Rulpey. *OB 1666–78, 33.*

486. 22 June 1669—Whereas John Roach did exhibit a Complaynt against Mr Tho: Mathew, his Master, Mr Mathew being absent, it is ordered y^t he appeare ye next Court to answer ye sd Complaynt & y^t he have notice hereof. *OB 1666–78, 33.*

487. 24 Aug. 1669—Geo: Harris, serv^t to Sym: Richardson, is adjudged by this Court to be 17 yeares of age & ordered to serve his sd Master according to Act. *OB 1666–78, 35.*

488. 24 Aug. 1669—Whereas it appears to this Court y^t Wm Bennet, serv^t to Mr Christopher Garlington, hath run away from his sd Master's service from ye 20th of August untill ye 7th of Christmas following, it is ordered y^t he serve his sd Master double ye time.... *OB 1666–78, 35.*

489. 24 Aug. 1669—Whereas Michaell Waterland, serv^t to Dan: Holland, hath absented himself from his sd Master's service thirty dayes & cost his Master ... four hundred pounds of Tobacco to recover him, it is ordered y^t ye sd Mich: serve his sd Master fower monthes for his sd default after y^t his tyme of service by Indenture, Custome, or otherwise is expired. *OB 1666–78, 36.*

490. 24 Aug. 1669—Whereas Dan: Scott, serv^t to Rich: Hull hath absented himself from his sd Master nigh fower monthes & cost his sd Master 300^lbs Tobacco in looking of him & procuring him agayne, It is ordered y^t ye sd Scott (wth ye consent of his sd Master) serve for his sd default fifteen monthes after y^t his tyme of service to his sd Master or assigns is expired by Custome, Indenture, or otherwise. *OB 1666–78, 37.*

491. 24 Aug. 1669—Certificate is granted Tho: Roe for 50 Acres of Land for ye Importation of Phi: Nephew assigned to one Wm Thomas. *OB 1666–78, 37.*

492. 24 Aug. 1669—Certificate is granted Tho: Holbrooke for 50 Acres of Land for ye importation of himself assigned to one Wm Thomas. *OB 1666–78, 37.*

493. 5 Oct. 1669—Certificate is granted Mr Wm Thomas for 400 Acres of Land for ye Importation of

Wm Quinbourough	Tho: Hobs
Eliz: Palmer	Math: Roberts
John and Thomas bought	Tho: Holbrook
of Capt Smith	Wm Archer

OB 1666–78, 37.

494. 5 Oct. 1669—Whereas certificate was granted Tho: Roe for 50 Acres of land 8^{ber} [October] 20th 1663 for ye Importation of Wm Archer, he doth in Co^{rt} assign ye sd right to Mr Wm Thomas. *OB 1666–78, 37.*

495. 5 Oct. 1669—Certificate is granted Mr Robt Jones for 200 Acres of Land for ye Importation of Robt Jones, Dan: Lynch, Isabell Fynney, a Dutch man taken from him by ye Dutch fleet. *OB 1666–78, 37.*

496. 20 Nov. 1669—Whereas Geo: Hill, serv^t to Rich: Hull, did absent himselfe from his sd Master's service 4 months in ye choice time of ye Crop & Cost his Master 115^{lbs} Tobacco & Cask to procure him, It is ordered y^t ye sd Geo: Hill serve his Master two yeares & an halfe after ye time of his service is expired by Indenture, Custom or otherwise. *OB 1666–78, 38.*

497. 20 Nov. 1669—Hen: Player, serv^t to Mr Dan: Neale, adjudged to be 15 years of age & ordered to serve his sd Master according to Act. *OB 1666–78, 39.*

498. 20 Nov. 1669—Morgan Evans, serv^t to Mr Rhodon, is adjudged by this Court to be seaventeene yeares of age & ordered to serve according to Act. *OB 1666–78, 39.*

499. 20 Nov. 1669—Jno Pett, serv^t to Mr Rhodon, is adjudged by this Court to be thirteene yeares of age & ordered to serve according to Act. *OB 1666–78, 39.*

500. 23 Nov. 1669—Whereas Jno Roach hath complayned in this Court y^t his Master, Mr Tho: Mathew, hath employed him in base service imploym^t, It is ordered y^t ye said Roach continue wth his sd Master during the terme y^t he is to serve by his Indenture and y^t ye sd Mr Mathew only imploy him as a merchant & not in any base service imploym^t. *OB 1666–78, 41.*

501. 9 Dec. 1669—This Indenture made ye 9th day of December 1669 sheweth that whereas Capt. Tho: Brereton Attor: of Mr. Wm Wathen did this day bring before me Nich Owen, Gent., one of his Maties [Majesty's] Justices of ye peace for ye County of Northumberland in ye Colony of Virg^a one Elizabeth Robbins, an orphant, left when very young to ye tutele [tutelage] & oversight of ye sd Mr Wm Wathen & his predecessors, I doe hereby order ye sd Eliz: to serve ye sd Mr Wm Wathen & his assignes for ye full terme of seaven yeares in such work & imploym^t as becometh a household Servt, not to work in ye ground, beat ay ye morter or ye like, the sd Wathen or his assignes to provide for ye sd Eliz: during the sd terme sufficient dyett, cloaths & lodging & at the expiration thereof to cloath her decently. Witness my hand.
                                                        Nicholas Owen
RB 1666–72, 141.

502. 20 Dec. 1669—John Hanies, serv^t to Mr Peter Presly, adjudged to be fourteen years of age; John Walker, serv^t to Mr Wm Presly, adjudged to be fowerteen years of age; Sam: Ball, serv^t to Mr Wm Presly, adjudged to be fowerteen years of age; Jervas Ellistone, serv^t to Rich: Hull, adjudged to be eleaven years of age. *OB 1666–78, 41.*

503. 20 Dec. 1669—Whereas Kath: Amery, serv^t to Jam: Allen, hath had a bastard Child named William, wth ye consent of ye sd Katherine ye Court doth order in . . . of ye sd Allen's charge in keeping & being . . . ye sd child, y^t he serve ye sd Allen untill he be one & twenty yeares of age. *OB 1666–78, 41.*

504. 20 Dec. 1669—Whereas Loveday Philips, serv^t to Dan: Holland, hath had a Bastard Child, It is ordered y^t she make her sd Master satisfaction by service according to Law & y^t she pay ye fine of 500^{lbs} tobacco for her sd default or be whipt. *OB 1666–78, 41.*

505. 20 Dec. 1669—Wm James, serv^t to Jno Bearmore, adjudged to be fifteen yeares of age & ordered to serve his said Master according to Act. *OB 1666–78, 42.*

506. 20 Jan. 1669/70—Robt Fouch, serv^t to Rich: Kenner, adjudged to be 18 years. *OB 1666–78, 43.*

507. 20 Jan. 1669/70—John Williams, serv^t to Mr Jno Cuttanceau, adjudged to be 16 yeares but at ye motion of ye s^d Mr Cuttanceau to serve 7 yeares. *OB 1666–78, 43.*

508. 20 Jan. 1669/70—Margaret Payne, serv^t to Mr Christopher Garlington, wth child & having sworne in Court y^t Tho: Peirce is ye father thereof, It is ordered y^t ye sherr: take ye sd Thomas into safe Custody untill he give bond wth sufficient security for his future good behaviour and to discharge what damages her said Master shall sustaine thereby. *OB 1666–78, 43.*

509. 5 Feb. 1669/70—This Indenture ... between Jno Cary ... and Wm Batts ... Witnesseth y^t ye sd Wm Batts doth hereby covenant, promise & grant to & wth ye sd John Cary ... from ye date of ye date hereof untill ye first & next arrivall in Virginia, and after for & during ye terme of fower yeares to serve in such service & imploym^t as ye sd Jno Cary or his Assigns shall there imploy him according to ye Custom of ye country.... *RB 1666–72, 87.* [The page is badly worn.]

510. 20 Aug. 1670, Will of Henry Lambert—Item. All ye rest of my goods & chattles in Virginia & Maryland I leave it to my Servt John Boy who I make Executor of this my Last Will & Testament.... *RB 1666–72, 119.*

511. 26 April 1670—Know all men by these presents y^t I Jno Boy of Chopnam in ye County of Wilts, Adm^r of ye estate of Hen: Lambert deced have nominated & constituted & in my stead appointed Capt Tho: Brereton of ye County of Northumberland in Virginia my lawfull Attorney ... to receive all such monies ... goods Tobaccos or what else shall ... be due unto ye estate of ye sd Lambert from any person or persons whatsoever wthin Virg^a or province of Maryland ... hereby confirming w^t my sd Attorney shall lawfully doe or cause to be done in ye p:mises as if I were personally present. In Witness whereof I have hereunto sett my hand & seales this 26th. day of April 1670.
             John Boye ye Seale
RB 1666–72, 142.

512. 21 March 1669/70—Edward Price, serv^t to Mr Wm Brereton, is adjudged by this Court to be 6 yeares of age & ordered to serve his sd Master according to Act. *OB 1666–78, 46.*

513. 20 April 1670—Whereas Wm Crue, serv^t to Mr John Motley, hath beaten his overseer and threatened his master, It is ordered that the Sherriffe take him into custody & give him 20 stripes on his bare back untill blood come, but upon ye desire of his said Master & ye said Crues, it is ordered y^t at present he be acquitted from ye said punishment. *OB 1666–78, 47.*

514. 20 April 1670—Whereas Alice Arnold, serv^t to Wm Betts, had a Bastard child wch upon her oath she hath layd to Francis Roberts, It is ordered y^t the said Francis Roberts take care to keep his said child. *OB 1666–78, 47.*

515. 20 May 1670—Tho: Bowyer, serv^t to Mr Dan: Neale, judged to be fifteen yeares of age & ordered to serve his sd Master according to Act. *OB 1666–78, 48.*

516. 20 May 1670—Whereas Franc: Hill, serv^t to Dan: Holland, hath absented himselfe from his sd Master's service from ye second of February to ye twelfth of Aprill last & cost his sd Master a thousand pounds of tobacco to procure him againe, It is ordered y^t ye sd Francis serve ye sd Holland double ye tyme he hath soe absented himself according to Act & y^t he give ye sd Holland good caution for ye repaym^t of ye sd 1000^{lbs} Tobacco & cask or in default thereof serve ye sd Holland ten monthes in lieu of his charge as aforesd. *OB 1666–78, 48.*

517. 20 May 1670—Certificate is granted James Pope for 150 Acres of Land for ye Importation of Rich: Harvey, Grace Cole & Kath: Mayes. *OB 1666–78, 48.*

518. 20 May 1670—Whereas Sabrina Parker, serv^t to John Wood, is with child & pretends Paul Winbourough to be ye father thereof, it is ordered y^t ye sd Paul give bond for his future good abearing. . . . *OB 1666–78, 48.*

519. 20 July 1670—Pet: Gallee, serv^t to Col. Smyth, is adjudged to be eleaven yeares of age; Ad: Gardee, serv^t to Mr Wm Brereton, fourteen yeares of age; Pet: LaFolly, serv^t to John Bonum, seaven yeares; Pet: Gardee, serv^t to John White, thirteen yeares; Nich: Lee-how, serv^t to Mr Leonard Howson, fourteen yeares; Ellis Merret, serv^t to Tho: Hobson, fifteen yeares; John, a French boy serv^t to Tho: Howson, fourteen yeares; Robert Barbar, serv^t to Mr Edw: Coles, fourteen yeares; Rachell Grandee, serv^t to Fran: Roberts, sixteen yeares; Jane Servee, serv^t to Wm Wildy, fourteen yeares; Jno Hamlin, serv^t to John Swanson, eleaven yeares; Pet: Hocar, serv^t to Hugh Baker, eleaven yeares; Mary Servee, serv^t to Tho: Gaskin, sixteen yeares; Franc: Jude, serv^t to Mr Edw: Sanders, twelve yeares; Julian Gillen, serv^t to Mr Edw: Sanders, twelve yeares; Pet: Cartwright, serv^t to Mr Rho: Lane, eleaven yeares; Clem^t Cheksheir, serv^t to John Motley, twelve yeares; Math: Swath, serv^t to Ralph Waddington, twelve yeares; Colen Severin, serv^t to Ralph Waddington, twelve yeares; John Atkins, serv^t to Tho: Williams, nine yeares & all adjudged to serve their respective masters according to Act. *OB 1666–78, 49.*

520. 20 July 1670—Certificate is granted Tho: Lane for 350 Acres of Land for ye importation of 7 persons into this Colony (vizt)

        Dan: Lane   Jno Russell J^r
        Hester Lane   Stephen Cotroy

John Russell   Mary Russell
Hannah Russell
OB 1666–78, 49.

521. 20 July 1670—Whereas Sabrina Parker, serv^t to John Wood, hath absented herself from her sd Master's service in ye tyme of ye Crop ye Court doth order y^t she serve her sd Master twenty five dayes for his trouble & her default after her tyme of service is expired by Indenture, custome or otherwise. *OB 1666–78, 49.*

522. 15 Sept. 1670—Whereas Jno Thorton, serv^t to Miles Martin of Boston in New England mariner, did leave his sd Master upon pretence of greivious abuses rec^d by him & now lives with Anth: Lynton, It is ordered y^t ye sd John continue with ye sd Anth: Lynton unless ye sd Miles Martin doth come & lay claime to ye sd servant. *OB 1666–78, 51.*

523. 15 Sept. 1670—James Thompson, serv^t to Azariam Parker, is adjudged to be eighteen yeares of age & ordered to serve his sd Master according to Act. *OB 1666–78, 51.*

524. 15 Sept. 1670—Tho: Coutancheau, servant to one Robt Jones, is adjudged to be sixteen yeares of age & ordered to serve his sd Master according to Act. *OB 1666–78, 51.*

525. 20 Dec. 1670—John Wilcox, serv^t to Mr Wm Presly, is adjudged to be fifteen yeares of age & Tho: Ryder fourteen yeares of age & ordered to serve ye sd Mr Presly according to Act. *OB 1666–78, 53.*

526. 20 Dec. 1670—Whereas Michaell Waterland, serv^t to Dan: Holland, hath run away from his sd Master 4 monthes in ye choice tyme of his Crop, he is adjudged to serve his sd Master for his sd default one yeare after his tyme of service by Custome, Indenture or otherwise is expired. *OB 1666–78, 54.*

527. __ Jan. 1670/71—Hannah Bently, serv^t to Robt Sech, is adjudged to be 16 yeares of age; Tho: Newman, serv^t to Rich: Kenner, twelve yeares; Math: Scanbrook, serv^t to Rich: Thompson, fifteen yeares; Fran: Moor, serv^t to John Warner, eleaven yeares and each ordered to serve their respective Masters according to Act. *OB 1666–78, 55.*

528. __ Jan. 1670/71—Jos: Fielding did complayne to this Court y^t Robt Wilson, his serv^t, run away forty five dayes & did him great damage by suffering his house to be burned through his neglect, It is ordered y^t y^e sd

Wilson for his sd default & negligence serve his sd Master one full yeare after his tyme by Indenture, Custome, or otherwise is expired. *OB 1666–78, 55.*

529. ___ Jan. 1670/71—Whereas Sabr: Parker, serv^t to Jno Wood, hath absented her self from her sd Master's service 46 dayes, It is ordered y^t she serve her sd master for her sd default double y^e sd tyme, and whereas y^e sd Sabr: hath had a Bastard child, It is ordered y^t she serve her Master two yeares according to Act & also half a yeare for ye fine wth ye sd Jno Wood engaged to pay, to acquitt her from punishment she was judged to suffer. *OB 1666–78, 55.*

530. 5 Jan. 1670/71, Mr Francis Lee his discharge to Jno Squire—These are to Certify whom it shall concerne y^t ye Bearer of Jno Squire hath served his full tyme to ye estate of Col. Rich: Lee & my selfe, as witness my hand this 5th of January 1670/71.   Francis Lee
RB 1666–72, 149.

531. 21 Feb. 1670/71—Certificate is granted Mr Pet: Knight for 200 acres of Land for ye Importation of 4 persons (vizt)

    John Stephens   Sam: Oakland
    Geo: Browne   Elin^r Price
OB 1666–78, 58.

532. 21 Feb. 1670/71—Whereas a French boy named Phil: Hocar, now serv^t to Hugh Baker, was July ye 20th last judged to be eleaven yeares of age & ordered to serve his sd Master according to Act by ye name of Pet: Hocar And when a Mr Tho: Bandenall hath made oath in Court y^t he bound ye sd boy by Indenture to serve but eight yeares & Mr Edw: Lebreton hath made oath y^t he sold ye sd boy unto ye sd Baker but for eight yeares, It is ordered y^t ye former order by voyd and y^t ye sd Philip Hocar serve his sd Master Hugh Baker only eight yeares to commence from ye first day of ye arrivall of ye ship y^e *Nicholaus* into great Wicomoco River. *OB 1666–78, 59.*

533. 28 March 1670/71—Whereas ye 11th of November last it was ordered y^t John Richards should serve his Master Mr Edw: Sanders according to Act for having layd violent hands upon his sd Master, It is ordered y^t ye sd order be confirmed & y^t ye sd Richards serve his sd Master for his sd default one full yeare according to Act. *OB 1666–78, 61.*

534. 28 March 1670/71—It is ordered y^t Sabrina Parker serve John Wood two full yeares according to a Condition under her hand dated ye 10th of March 1669 ye sd Sabrina consenting to this order. *OB 1666–78, 61.*

535. 11 April 1671—I Thomas Steed doe authorize Jno Trimell not to suffer any of my goods or chattles moveable or immoveable to goe off my plantation till you have order from mee, nor my Servant, Matthew Harris, to goe without your consent & his owne for ye use of any man but my owne selfe. . . .   Sign   Thomas Steed
RB 1666–72, 130.

536. 20 May 1671—Jno Worthingham, serv^t to Andr: Pettegrew, fowerteen yeares of age; Geo: King, serv^t to Mr Jones, ten yeares of age & ordered to serve their Master according to Act. *OB 1666–78, 61.*

537. 20 May 1671—Jeremiah Nelson, serv^t to Jno Waddy, adjudged to be twelve yeares of age & ordered to serve his sd Master according to Act. *OB 1666–78, 61.*

538. 19 July 1671—Edw: Woldridge, serv^t to James Claughton, is adjudged by the Court to be fifteen yeares of age & ordered to serve his sd Master according to Act. *OB 1666–78, 63.*

539. 19 July 1671—Whereas last Court John Worthingham, serv^t to Andr: Pettegrew, was judged to be fourteen yeares of age & ordered to serve his sd Master according to Act and whereas it appeares to this Court y^t he was not at his first arrivall sold unto Tho: Buckley but for 6 yeares & by ye sd Buckley assigned for ye sd tyme unto James Hill, It is ordered y^t ye former order be voyd & y^t ye sd serv^t serve according to ye aforesd assignment. *OB 1666–78, 63.*

540. 19 July 1671—Whereas it appears to this Court y^t John Tayler, serv^t to Mr Wm Thomas, did run away from his sd Master's service eleaven weekes in ye choice tyme of his crop & put his master to ye charge of . . . [not legible] hundred pounds of tobacco besides ye trouble of his serv^{ts} to get him agayne, It is ordered y^t ye sd serv^t serve his sd Master two yeares (for ye damages & charges y^t his master hath susteyned as aforesd) after ye tyme of his service by custome or Indenture is expired. *OB 1666–78, 64.*

541. 19 July 1671—Whereas William Merriman by an Indenture under his hand dated ye 20th of January 1670 did ingage himself to serve Robt Prichard ye full terme of five yeares, It is ordered y^t ye sd Meriman serve ye sd Prichard according to ye tenure of ye sd Indenture. *OB 1666–78, 65.*

542. 29 July 1671—Will: Garnett saith y^t hee heard George, ye Servant of Richard Nelmes, say y^t hee the Boy & Phillip Peyton, killed two of his Masters hoggs. . . . *RB 1666–72, 130.* [The next six entries relate to George killing his master's hogs. In these entries we learn that his surname is Whitthorne.]

543. 18 Oct. 1671—Ordered y^t ye sherriff bring Edw: Scuse, the reputed father of a bastard child borne by Lucy Howard unto ye next Court. *OB 1666–78, 66.*

544. 18 Oct. 1671—Whereas Lucy Howard, serv^t to Mrs Eliz: Watts, hath had a bastard Child in ye time of her service, It is ordered y^t ye said Lucy serve her sd Mistress according to Act unless the next Court she produce good evidence y^t her Mistress had satisfaction for ye trouble y^t she should susteyne by reason of her having sd bastard. *OB 1666–78, 66.*

545. 18 Oct. 1671—Whereas Martha Carre, serv^t to Phil: Drake, hath had a bastard child in ye time of her service, It is ordered y^t ye sd Martha serve according to Act. *OB 1666–78, 66.*

546. 18 Oct. 1671—Anne Seaman, serv^t to Mr Gaylord, to serve one year for running away by her owne consent. *OB 1666–78, 66.*

547. 15 Nov. 1671—Jno James, serv^t to Rich: Kenner, is adjudged to be fifteen yeares of age; Tho: Plankett, serv^t to John Bearmore, thirteen yeares & both ordered to serve their respective masters untill they be twenty fower yeares of age according to Act. *OB 1666–78, 67.*

548. 15 Nov. 1671—Certificate is granted Henry Mayse for one hundred Acres of Land for ye Importation for Rich: Bushell & Jane Thompson. *OB 1666–78, 68.*

549. 15 Nov. 1671—Certificate is granted Mr Ambr: Fielding for 600 Acres of Land for ye importation of 12 persons vizt

    Arth: Mash   John Jenkins
    Henry Conoway   Geo: Philips
    Rich: Sweetland   Char: Morgan
    Jno Hall   Jno Lewis
    Jno Williams   Tho: How
    Geo: Brett   Jno Hancock

OB 1666–78, 68.

550. 15 Nov. 1671, A Deed of Gift from Graciana Span to her sons Richard and Cuthbert Span—Six servants, Viz^t Tony, a Negro; Edward Harvey; Eliz: Tew; Richard Stephens; Edward Bennet; Joseph Humphry. *RB 1666–72, 206.*

551. 29 Nov. 1671—Know all men by these presents y^t I Graciana Span for divers good reasons mee thereto movinge, but more especially to performe the desire of Richard Span my late deceased husband, have acquitted, discharged & released & do hereby acquitt, discharge & release my servant Jane Goare from two full yeares of ye time y^t she was & adjudged at ye Co^{r}t to serve my sd deceased husband. *RB 1666–72, 211.*

552. 20 Dec. 1671—Whereas Susan Wherret, serv^t to John Hudnall, hath had a Bastard Child in ye tyme of her service, It is ordered y^t she make her sd Master satisfaction for his losse & charge & trouble by service according to Act & pay ye fine imposed by Law or recieve twenty stripes on her bare back. *OB 1666–78, 69.*

553. 20 Dec. 1671—Certificate is granted Sam: Jewell for ye bringing home of a serv^t of Col. Codds named Tho: Burnell who was run away from his sd Master his service as farre as Rhapahannock River. *OB 1666–78, 69.*

554. 20 Dec. 1671—Pet: Lehoot, serv^t to Capt Jno Rogers, is adjudged to be nine yeares of age & ordered to serve his sd Master according to Act. *OB 1666–78, 69.*

555. 20 Dec. 1671—Ordered y^t Elino^r, ye bastard child of Francis Roberts serve Edw: Jones or his assigns untill she be eighteen yeares of age. *OB 1666–78, 70.* [The name is spelled Francis.]

556. 17 Jan. 1671/72—Tho: Fuse, serv^t to Mr Rich: Kenner, judged to be fourteen yeares of age & ordered to serve his sd Master according to Act. *OB 1666–78, 70.*

557. 17 Jan. 1671/72—Joanne Cox, serv^t to Mr Wm Brereton, judged to be eighteen yeares of age & ordered to serve her sd Master according to Act; Edw: Peirce, serv^t to Joseph Fielding judged to be ten yeares of age & ordered to serve his sd Master according to Act. *OB 1666–78, 70.*

558. 23 Jan. 1671/72—I Thomas Brereton for divers good reasons . . . have given, granted and bargained & sold to Eliz: Tew one heifer of a black pyed colour of two yeares of age & of ye proper mark of Rich: Span decd. To have & to hold ye sd Heifer wth all her future increase. . . . *RB 1666–72, 216.*

559. __ Feb. 1671/72—Jno Cope, serv^t to Mr Pet: Chivanne, is adjudged to be thirteen yeares of age; Mary Widsey, serv^t to Mr Tho: Mathew, thirteen yeares of age: Wm Crosthead, serv^t Mr Leonrd Howson, fourteen yeares of age; Wm Sack, serv^t to Wm Jallon, ten yeares of age & all ordered to serve their respective Masters or their assigns according to Act. *OB 1666–78, 71.*

560. _ Feb. 1671/72—Whereas John Wilson, serv^t to John Coutansheau, did absent himself nine dayes from his sd Master's service by running away, It is ordered y^t ye sd John serve his sd Master for his sd default & for his trouble & charge in procuring him agayne five monthes after ye tyme of his service by Indenture, Custome, or otherwise is expired. *OB 1666–78, 71.*

561. _ Feb. 1671/72—Whereas Mich: Melton serv^t to John Coutanceau did pray this Court y^t he might not be imployed at any other work but at his trade of a taylor, ye Court doe order, according to ye tenure of ye sd Melton's Indenture, y^t his master hath not Imploym^t for him at his sd trades he sett him to work in any lawfull & necessary work he thinks fit to imploy him about. *OB 1666–78, 71.*

562. 12 March 1671/72—I Josias Gaskins do hereby ingage my heyres y^t Patrick Brunaugh, a man servant y^t I bought of Mr Edw: Lappage merch^t of ye Ship ye Indeavor of Bristoll shall not serve me or my assigns above the terme of fower yeares to commence from ye first day of ye arrivall of ye said ship into ye River of great Wicocomoco this yeare unless by runing away or other misdemeanor he shall be by ye Court adjudged to serve longer. *RB 1666–72, 225.*

563. 28 March 1671/72—These presents witness y^t I Sibbry Parker doe bind my selfe a Coven^t Servt unto Jno Wood of great Wicomico in ye County of Northumberland from the date hereof untill the tenth of January next come two years. I the sd Sibbry Parker engaging my selfe to serve ye sd Jno Wood, his heirs in such service & imploym^t as hee ye sd Jno Wood shall employ mee. In consideration of my service of ye sd Sibbry Parker I ye sd John Wood doe bind my selfe my heirs for to find ye sd Sibbry Parker convenient clothing, lodging, washing & dyett and at ye expiration of the sd terme of time to make paym^t unto ye sd Sibbry Parker one suit of cloth given under my hand this 10th of March 1669. *RB 1666–72, 165.*

564. 28 March 1671/72—Sibbery Parker, aged thirty yeares or thereabouts sworne & examined, saith that Daniel Neale senior upon the exchange betwixt mee & man servant of John Wood did agree with ye sd Wood to pay him six hundred pounds of Tobacco a yeare for three yeares & to finde yor Depon^t clothes for the year past & further yor Depon^t saith not.

Sign. Sibbere Parker

RB 1666–72, 184.

565. 28 March 1671/72—Florence Driscoll sworne & examin^d saith y^t when yor Depon^t was servant to Capt Dan: Neale heard Jno Wood say y^t he was willing to give a man servant named Rowland Lawson for a mayd servant y^t Capt Dan: Neale had if y^t sd mayd was willing to serve ye sd Jno Wood ye time y^t ye sd Rowland Lawson had to serve; further yor Depon^t heard ye sd mayd say y^t she had rather serve Jno Wood ye time ye sd Lawson had to serve & a year longer rather than to serve her owne time to her aforesd master; further yor Depon^t heard Jno Wood & his wife say y^t they would & willinge change because they could not understand what the sd Lawson sayd, being an outlandish man & he would doe nothing for them. . . . *RB 1666–72, 185.*

566. 4 April 1672—Cornelius Macguire, serv^t to Mr Edward Coles, adjudged to be 15 yeares of age & to serve his sd M^r till twenty fower according to Act. *OB 1666–78, 73.*

567. 4 April 1672—Upon petition of Timothy Tracy, formerly serv^t to Mr Edw: Coles, declaring he hath served the tyme for which he was first sold & y^t same appearing by severall orders . . . ye Court do therefore order ye sd Tymothy Tracy be free accordingly & that his sd M^r pay him his corne according to Custom. *OB 1666–78, 73.*

568. 17 April 1672—Cornelius Haley, serv^t to Mr Wm Downinge, adjudged to be 15 yeares of age; John Kelly, serv^t to Capt Edm: Lyster, adjudged to be thirteen yeares of age; Thomas Lyliesse, serv^t to Capt Edw: Lyster, fourteen yeares of age; Cornelius Monohery, serv^t to Joyce Holland, seaventeen yeares; James Russell, serv^t to Mr Wm Presly, fifteen yeares & all ordered to serve their respective masters according to Act. *OB 1666–78, 73.*

569. 17 April 1672—Whereas John Philpott, serv^t to Mr Pet: Presly, hath run away from his sd Master's service from ye 20th of March unto ye 12th of April & cost his sd Master 1220^{lbs} of tob^o & cask to procure him agayne, It is ordered y^t ye sd serv^t take ye sd John into safe Custody & give him twenty stripes on ye bare back untill ye blood comes. . . . *OB 1666–78, 73.*

570. 17 April 1672—Whereas Joyce Holland complayned to this Court y^t Mich: Waterland, her serv^t, had run away three weekes from her service & whereas per an order of this Court dated ye 20th of Dec. 1670, It was ordered y^t ye sd Michael should serve one yeare for running away four monthes, y^e

Court y^t ye 3 weekes now demanded was involved in ye former order. It is ordered y^t ye 28th of March next ye sd Mich: be free & y^t then his sd Mistress pay him his Corne & Cloathes according to Custome. *OB 1666–78, 73.*

571. deleted

572. 17 April 1672—Whereas Lucy Howard, late serv^t to Mrs Eliz: Watts, hath had a Bastard child in ye tyme of her service wch she layed to Edw: Scuse wch child is now in ye keeping of Onosepheous Bennett, it is ordered y^t ye sd Lucy serve for her trouble & charge given her sd M^{rs} according to Act & y^t ye sd child serve ye sd Bennett untill she be one & twenty yeares of age, ye sd Onos: Bennett, Wm Hartland & John White obliging themselves in ye penall sume of 40£ sterl: to save ye parish harmless. *OB 1666–78, 73.*

573. 17 April 1672—Whereas Margarett Payne, serv^t to Mr Christopher Garlington, hath had two bastard children in ye tyme of her service, It is ordered y^t she serve her sd Master according to Act. . . . *OB 1666–78, 73.*

574. 17 April 1672—Whereas Jeremiah Robins, did by covenant oblige himself to serve Dan: Holland & his assigns from ye 2^d of March 1670 untill ye 25th of October following for four hundred pounds of Tobacco & whereas Jeremiah aforesd did run away seaventeen monthes & put his sd Master to expenses to procure him, It is ordered y^t ye sd Jere: Robins serve Joyce Holland, ye relict of ye sd Dan: Holland, or his assigns untill ye last of October next. . . . *OB 1666–78, 73.*

575. 17 April 1672—Whereas John Moseley, serv^t to Mr Thomas Opy, hath absented himself from his sd Master's service by running away three weeks in ye choicest tyme of ye Crop & cost a thousand pounds of Tob^o to procure him agayne, It is ordered y^t in case he remayne on ye plantation as a faithfull serv^t y^t then he shall serve one yeare for his sd default & his Master's charge as aforesd but if otherwise y^t he serve one full yeare & a half after y^t his tyme by Custome, Indenture, or otherwise is expired. *OB 1666–78, 74.*

576. 17 April 1672—Jos: Fielding confesseth Judgm^t for ye present paym^t of five hundred pounds of Tobacco & Cask, being ye fine imposed by Law for ye aforesd Honora her fault & ingaged to keep ye parish harmless from ye sd child. *OB 1666–78, 75.*

577. 17 April 1672—Whereas Honara Carter, serv^t to Jos: Fielding, hath had a Bastard Child in ye tyme of his service, It is ordered y^t she make her sd Master satisfaction for his trouble, payment, & loss of tyme by service according to Act. *OB 1666–78, 75.*

578. 19 June 1672—Whereas ye last Court it was ordered y^t Geo: Brereton, formerly serv^t to John Champion & by him sold to Mr Ambr: Fielding who (as it then appeared) had fully compleated his tyme of service should be free & y^t ye sd Mr Fielding, who was his last Master, should pay him his Corne & cloathes wch order (by reason of other business interposing) was by ye Clark omitted to be entered, It is ordered y^t it be now entered & y^t ye sd Mr Fielding pay ye sd Brereton his corne & cloathes accordingly. *OB 1666–78, 75.*

579. 19 June 1672—Tho: Horton, serv^t to Mr John Farnefold, is adjudged to be fifteen yeares of age; Jack Black, serv^t to John Cockrell, sixteen yeares; Mary Wright, serv^t to Wm Jallons, eight yeares & judged to serve their respective Masters according to Act. *OB 1666–78, 75.*

580. 19 June 1672—Whereas John Williams, serv^t to Ambr: Fielding, hath absented himself from his sd Master's service by running away thirteen months and put his Master aforesd to great trouble & Charge to procure him agayne, it is ordered ye sd Williams, for his sd default & lieu of his Master's charge as aforesd, shall serve his sd Master or his assigns four yeares after y^t his tyme by Custome, Indenture, or otherwise is expired. *OB 1666–78, 75.*

581. 19 June 1672—Whereas it appeares to this Court by ye information of Mr Wm Presly & ye confession of John Chin, serv^t to Capt John Mottrom, y^t ye sd John Chin hath unlawfully killed a hog belonging unto ye sd Mr Wm Presly.... *OB 1666–78, 76.*

582. 19 June 1672—Whereas it appeares to this Court y^t Roger Thomas hath fully served his tyme wth his Master Anth: Morris, It is ordered y^t ye sd Roger be free & y^t his sd Master Anth: Morris be acquitt from ye paym^t of ye sd Roger his Corne & cloathes in lieu of seaven hundred pounds of Tobacco payd by ye sd Morris unto Tho: Lane on ye acc^t of ye sd Rog: Thomas. *OB 1666–78, 76.*

583. 19 June 1672—Whereas it appeares to this Court y^t John Coutanceau took up a run away serv^t named Anne Geate belonging unto Mr Wm Wildey above ten miles from her sd Master's house, It is ordered y^t he have a Certificate thereof unto ye Assembly according to Act. *OB 1666–78, 76.*

584. 21 Aug. 1672—Whereas Anne Graves, serv^t to Mr Math: Rhodon, hath had a Bastard child in ye tyme of her service, it is ordered y^t ye sd Anne make her sd Master satisfaction for his charge, trouble, & loss of tyme according & y^t she be whipt for her sd default. *OB 1666–78, 77.*

585. 21 Aug. 1672—Upon ye petition of Joseph Fielding, ye Court doe order y^t ye sd Fielding be discharged from ye fine wch was imposed upon him per ye Court (wth his own consent) for his serv^t Honora's default in having a Bastard child in consideration of his great charge & loss in ye death of his sd servant. *OB 1666–78, 79.*

586. 21 Aug. 1672—Whereas it appeares to this Court by an Indenture under ye hand of Humphrey Mould, y^t ye sd Humphrey doth oblige himself to serve John Bryan fower yeares, The Court doth order, wth ye consent of ye sd Bryan, y^t if ye sd Mould doe give ye sd Bryan security for ye paym^t of fifteen hundred pounds of Tobacco & cask, y^t he be free or otherwise serve his sd Master or his assigns according to ye tenure of ye sd Indenture. *OB 1666–78, 79.*

587. 16 Sept. 1672—Certificate is granted Francis Roberts for ye taking up three run away serv^{ts} belonging unto Capt Lightfoot according to Act. *OB 1666–78, 81.*

588. 16 Sept. 1672—Whereas it appeares to this Court y^t Eliz: Fammer, serv^t to Mr Wm Thomas, came into this Country wthout Indenture & had not her age adjudged by ye Court according to Act & hath served her sd Master eight yeares, It is ordered y^t ye sd Elizabeth be free & y^t ye sd Mr Thomas pay her her Corne & cloathes according to Act. *OB 1666–78, 81.*

589. 18 Dec. 1672—Whereas Wm Cornish petitioned the Court for Judgm^t against Mich: de Contee for ye deteyning a mayd serv^t named Faith Cox & whereas it appeares y^t ye sd Contee did enterteyne ye said Faith by order from Mr Leonard Howson, one of his Majesty's Justices of this County, to cure her of some sores she had on her legs, It is ordered y^t ye said Contee forthwith pay unto ye sd Cornish Three hundred pounds of Tobacco in lieu of part of ye said Fayth her wages paid by ye sd Cornish and y^t she serve ye said Contee ye full terme of a year for ye Cure of her legs. *OB 1666–78, 83.*

590. 19 Feb. 1672/73—Marmaduke Thompson, serv^t to Mr Wm Downing, is adjudged by this Court to be eleaven yeares of age. John Ager, serv^t to Richard Nutt, nine yeares of age. John Davis, serv^t to Thomas Towers, ten yeares of age & all judged to serve their respective masters according to Act. *OB 1666–78, 84.*

591. 19 Feb. 1672/73—Robt Barbar, serv^t to Edw: Coles, being brought to this Court to have his age adjudged of ye 20th of July 1670 & being then adjudged to be fowerteen yeares of age, The sd Robt now in Court having declaring & Mich: Furshaw swearing y^t he heard the sd Robt his father say y^t he was not but fowerteen yeares of age, it is ordered y^t he yet serve his sd Master ten yeares any thing in ye former order to ye contrary not withstanding. *OB 1666–78, 84.*

592. 19 Feb. 1672/73—It is ordered y^t Wm Tempteer returne to his Master, Master Tho: Brereton his service, untill ye next Court & if then it shall appeare y^t he ought to be free, y^t his sd Master give him satisfaction for ye tyme he hath served more then by his Indenture he ought to doe. *OB 1666–78, 85.*

593. 19 March 1672/73—Whereas Wm Davis, serv^t to Jno Robinson, hath absented himself from his sd Master one month & foure dayes, It is ordered y^t ye sd W^m serve his sd Master double ye tyme he hath soe absented himself, according to Act, after ye tyme of his service per Indenture or Custome is expired. *OB 1666–78, 87.*

594. 19 March 1672/73—Jno Magrillus, serv^t to Major Tho: Brereton, judged to be fowerteen yeares of age & ordered to serve his master according to Act. *OB 1666–78, 87.*

595. 26 March 1672/73, Will of John Barber— ... Item First my will y^t if it please God to take me out of this world y^t then my man Mathew Cox shall then be free. Mr Leon^d Howson haveing his Indenture in Keeping. I give him one large new Chest & w^t [what] clothes I have. *RB 1666–72, 230.*

596. 21 April 1673—Whereas Josias Long, serv^t to Mr Alexander Watts, who was apprehended for being a confederate wth his sd Master in bringing a serv^t of Robt Goffes out of Caroline, wth Long petitioned this Court for his release, pretending serv^t to ye sd Watts & noe confederate & presenting ye sd petition.... This Court doe judge y^t ye sd Long's allegations is true & therefore order y^t he be released from his restraints. *OB 1666–78, 88.*

597. 21 May 1673—Eliz: Wetheull, serv^t to Mr Jno Cossens, confessing her self to be sixteen yeares of age ye next Michaelmas, It is ordered y^t she serve her sd Master according to Act to commence from ye tyme aforesd. *OB 1666–78, 89.*

598. 21 May 1673—Valent: Vaughan, serv^t to Mr Fran: Lee, is adjudged to be fourteen yeares of age & ordered to serve his sd Master according to Act. *OB 1666–78, 89.*

599. 21 May 1673—Eliz: Roberts . . . to be free. *OB 1666–78, 89.*

600. 21 May 1673—Whereas Jane Thompson, serv^t to Hen: Mayse, hath had a Bastard child in ye tyme of her service, it is ordered y^t ye sd Jane make her sd Master satisfaction for his charge, trouble, or loss of tyme according to Act. *OB 1666–78, 90.* [The court ordered that the sheriff take her into custody and give her 20 stripes on her bare back.]

601. 16 July 1673—John Parnell, serv^t to Wm Keyne coming into this Country without Indenture is adjudged to be sixteen yeares of age. Thomas Wilkinson, serv^t to Mr Hancock Lee, fourteen yeares of age. Wm Rutter, serv^t to Tho: White, fifteen yeares & each of them ordered to serve their respective masters according to Act. *OB 1666–78, 90.*

602. 16 July 1673—Whereas Richard Buzzell, serv^t to Henry Mayes, hath absented himself by running away sixty nine dayes & given his Master great trouble & charge to get him againe, It is ordered y^t ye sd Rich: Buzzell serve his sd Master for his sd default & his Master's charges a whole year after his tyme per Indenture, Custome, or otherwise is expired. *OB 1666–78, 91.*

603. 16 July 1673—Mary Smyth, serv^t to Wm Hartland, complaining to this Court y^t her sd Master intends to send her to Accomack & sett her there for more yeares then she hath to serve, It is ordered y^t ye sd Hartland appeare ye next Court to answere her said complaint. *OB 1666–78, 91.*

604. 16 July 1673—David Lindsey, having fully compleated his tyme of service to Wm Keyne, petitioned this Court for Judgm^t ag^t ye sd Wm Keyne, his Master, for his corne & cloathes according to Custom. Judgm^t is granted ye sd Lindsey ag^t sd Keyne for his corne & cloathes with Costs. *OB 1666–78, 91.*

605. 16 July 1673—Elizabeth Kitchingham, being an orphant y^t hath from an infant lived wth Andrew Pettigrew & his wife & hath nothing of an estate left her, It is ordered y^t she serve ye sd Andr: Pettigrew or his assigns untill she be one & twenty yeares of age. *OB 1666–78, 91.*

606. 17 Sept. 1673—Whereas Elizabeth Jones, serv^t to Mr Jno Hughlett, hath absented herself forty days by running away & given her master trouble to get her againe, It is ordered y^t ye said Elizabeth Jones serve her sd Master for her sd default & her master's charges in procuring [her] againe as aforesd fower months after her time per Indenture or custome is expired. *OB 1666–78, 92.*

607. 17 Sept. 1673—Whereas Jn° Warner petitioned the Court for satisfaction from Sarah Hill, his serv^t, for having a bastard child, It is ordered y^t she serve her sd Master according to Act of Assembly, ye sd Warner ingaging himself in Court to pay ye fine. *OB 1666–78, 92.*

608. 17 Sept. 1673—Whereas Richard Smyth, who was formerly bound to Mr Thomas White and then sold to Capt Jn° Mottrom, is to be free. *OB 1666–78, 93.*

609. 1 Oct. 1673—That whereas Mary Smyth per a condition under her hand bearing date ye 17th of February 1672 hath engaged herself to serve Wm Hartland seaven yeares conditionally y^t he cause her to be cured of her distemper.... *OB 1666–78, 93.*

610. 19 Nov. 1673—Whereas George Ellet, serv^t to Mr Garlington, did run away from his Master's service forty five days, It is ordered y^t ye sd George serve his sd Master three months after y^t ye time of his service is expired either by Custome or Indenture. *OB 1666–78, 94.*

611. 19 Nov. 1673—Whereas Joane Jasper, serv^t to M^r Jn° Farnefold, doth say she is wth child by Rich: Bryant, It is ordered y^t ye sherr: take ye sd Rich: into safe custody untill he gives bond for his future good behaviour. ... *OB 1666–78, 94.*

612. 18 Feb. 1673/74—Wm Provish, serv^t to James Johnson, is adjudged by this Court to be fourteen yeares of age & to serve his Master according to Act. *OB 1666–78, 97.*

613. 19 Feb. 1673/74—Whereas it appears to the Court y^t Eliz^a Tew, serv^t to Major Tho: Brereton, hath had a Bastard Child in ye tyme of her service, It is ordered y^t ye sd Pew serve her sd Master (for his charge & trouble) according to Act. *OB 1666–78, 97.*

614. 19 Feb. 1673/74—Whereas Josias Harrison, serv^t to Mr Ambros: Feilding, hath absented himself from his sd Master by his owne confession three months & cost his master three thousand pounds of Tobacco in caske to procure him againe, It is ordered y^t ye said Josias serve his said Master for his said default & master's charge as aforesd three yeares of his ye time of his service by custome, Indenture, or otherwise is expired. *OB 1666–78, 98.*

615. 19 Feb. 1673/74—Wm Forbus, having served Sam^{ll} Gouche five yeares, It is ordered y^t ye sd Forbus be free according to Act. *OB 1666–78, 98.*

616. 19 Feb. 1673/74—Whereas it appears to this Court y^t Dan^{ll} & Hugh, two Irishmen, serv^{ts} of Tho: Hobson, did unlawfully absent & abuse their overseer, It is ordered y^t ye sd serv^{ts} make their said master satisfaction for their said default according to Act. *OB 1666–78, 98.*

617. 18 March 1673/74—Whereas it appeares to the Court y^t Sam^{ll} Ockland, serv^t to Capt Peter Knight, did beat & abuse his master, It is ordered y^t ye said Ockland make his sd master satisfaction for his said default according to Law. *OB 1666–78, 99.* [The name is Okland in the Index.)

618. 18 March 1673/74—Whereas Julius Thurston did serve Henry Wicker & his children ye full tyme of service, It is ordered y^t Mr Jno Haynie, Sam^{ll} Goche, Exer^s of ye sd Wicker pay ye said Thurston his cloathes according to custome. *OB 1666–78, 100.*

619. 15 April 1674—Leah Riscott, serv^t to Mr Wm Keyne, having had a bastard child in ye tyme of her service, It is ordered y^t ye said Leah make satisfaction unto her said master according to Act. *OB 1666–78, 101.*

620. 15 April 1674—Whereas Leah Riscott hath lately had a bastard Child wch in Court she did sweare was begott by Jno Ramsey, It is ordered y^t ye sherr: take ye sd Ramsey in safe custody untill he give . . . wth security save ye parish harmless & pay ye fine for his sd default imposed by Law. *OB 1666–78, 101.*

621. 17 June 1674—Whereas George Elliot, serv^t to Mr Christopher Garlington, coming into this Country without Indenture & hath fully served ye terme of five yeares, It is ordered y^t ye said George be free & y^t his master pay him corne & cloathes according to custome. *OB 1666–78, 102.*

622. 17 June 1674—A Certificate is granted Wm Tigner unto ye Assembly for ye taking up a runaway serv^t of Lt. Col. Christopher Wormley's named Anthony. *OB 1666–78, 103.*

623. 19 Aug. 1674—Jno Terry, serv^t to Mr Nich: Owen, adjudged to be sixteen yeares of age; Marbe Mott, serv^t to Mr Jno Cotanchew, fourteen; George Harward, serv^t to Wm Hancock, sixteen; Robert More, serv^t to Mr Francis Lee, fifteen; Rich: Wright, serv^t to Col. St Leger Codd, thirteen & ordered to serve their respective masters according to Act. *OB 1666–78, 104.*

624. 19 Aug. 1674—Thomas Cutler, servant to Mr George Bledsoe, judged to be nineteen yeares of age and ordered to serve according to custom. *OB 1666–78, 104.*

625. 19 Aug. 1674—Whereas Joan Jasper, serv^t to Mr Jno Farnefold, hath had a bastard child in ye time of her service wth child on her oath she hath declared to be begotten by Rich: Bryan. . . . *OB 1666–78, 104.*

626. 19 Aug. 1674—Upon ye petition of Mr Francis Lee, a certificate is granted him for two hundred Acres of Land being for ye transportation of Elizabeth Brookes, Valentine Vaughan, Robt. Moor & W^m [no surname given]. *OB 1666–78, 104.*

627. 21 Oct. 1674—John Gambles, servant to Mr Hancock Lee, is adjudged to be eighteene yeares of age and ordered to serve his said master according to Act. *OB 1666–78, 105.*

628. 21 Oct. 1674—Whereas Ann Sprage, servant to Capt John Rogers, hath had a bastard Child in the time of her service, It is ordered that shee make her sd master satisfaction for the charge and trouble according to Act, Capt Rogers engaging to pay her fine. *OB 1666–78, 105.*

629. 21 Oct. 1674—Whereas William Crabe hath got Ann Sprage with a base child, It is ordered that the sherr: take the said William into safe custody untill he give bond for his future good behaviour and for the payment of the fine imposed by Law for his sd default. *OB 1666–78, 105.*

630. 21 Oct. 1674—Whereas Joseph Seers, a hired servant to Phillip Drake, hath absented himself seaventeen dayes by running away and in regard of the said Drake's trouble and charge in getting him againe, It is ordered that the sd Seers doe serve his said master one halfe yeare for his sd default after the time of his service by contract is expired. *OB 1666–78, 105.*

631. 21 Oct. 1674—John Craven, servant to George Bletsoe, is adjudged to be fourteen yeares of age and ordered to serve his said Master according to Act. *OB 1666–78, 106.*

632. 21 Oct. 1674—To Mr James Austin for John Davis, servant to Thomas Towers, 200^{lbs}. *OB 1666–78, 107.*

633. 18 Nov. 1674—Whereas Richard Bryan was bound to keep the parish harmless from maintaining a bastard child & since the child is dead, It is ordered the said Bryan have in his bond the fine in Law imposed being first satisfied. *OB 1666–78, 108.*

634. 16 Dec. 1674—Cornelius Everson, servant to Mr Richard Pemberton, is adjudged to be fowerteen yeares of age & ordered to serve his said master according to Act. *OB 1666–78, 108.*

635. 3 Feb. 1674/75—Phillip Matthews, servant to Jno Muttone, is adjudged to be seventeene yeares of age & ordered to serve his sd master according to Act. *OB 1666–78, 109.*

636. 3 Feb. 1674/75—Whereas James Matthewes did petition the Court for Corne & Cloathes due to him from Mr Jno Haynie according to Custome wth whome he served his tyme, It is ordered y^t ye said Mr Haynie pay ye said James Matthew his Corne & cloathes. *OB 1666–78, 110.*

637. 17 March 1674/75—Robert Reeves, serv^t to Mr Peter Presly Junr, is adjudged to be nine yeares of age; Ignatius Oliver, serv^t to Mr Thomas Matthewes, ten yeares of age; Dan^{ll} Thomas, serv^t to Mr Tho: Matthew, fowerteen yeares of age; Michaell Griffin, serv^t to Wm Keyne, eighteen yeares of age; Benjamin Browne, serv^t to Robert Bryerly, sixteen yeares of age are ordered to serve their respective masters according to Act. *OB 1666–78, 113.*

638. 17 March 1674/75—Whereas Jno Williams, serv^t to Mich: Vanlandingham, hath run away from his said master & did forge a passe or discharge from his master whom he said was Cloud Tellus & put Capt Rogers name to it, It is ordered that the sd Jno williams serve his said Master for his said default six months after his tyme by Indenture, Custome, or otherwise is expired & that ye sherriff take ye said Jno Williams into safe custody & give him twenty stripes on his bare back untill his blood comes. *OB 1666–78, 113.*

639. 17 March 1674/75—Whereas Philip Dymsey, serv^t to Tho: Towers, did absent himself from his master by running away twenty dayes & Cost his master besides his own trouble & loss fower hundred & thirteen pounds of Tobacco. . . . *OB 1666–78, 113.*

640. 19 May 1675—Jane Graham, serv^t to Elizabeth Richardson, is adjudged by this Court to be sixteene yeares of age & ordered to serve her sd mistress according to Act. *OB 1666–78, 113.*

641. 19 May 1675—George Matthew, servant to Mr Wm Downinge, cominge into this country wthout Indenture, the Court doth order wth ye consent both of master & servant y^t he serve his sd master seaven yeares. *OB 1666–78, 113.*

642. 16 June 1675—Whereas Leah Rishcott, serv^t to Mr Wm Keyne, hath had a bastard child in the tyme of her service & sworne y^t Jno Chafee is ye father of it, It is ordered y^t she make her said master satisfaction for his paines & charge according to Act & ordered y^t ye sherriffe take ye sd Leah & give her twenty stripes on her bare back untill ye blood comes. *OB 1666–78, 116*. [In one place the name is spelled Riscott.]

643. 16 June 1675—Whereas Richard Pouzell [the name is Poushell in the margin of the page], serv^t to Mr Henry Mayes hath run away two months in ye tyme of his Crop, It is ordered y^t ye said Richard serve his sd Master for his said default one full yeare after ye time of his service by Custome, Indenture or otherwise is expired. *OB 1666–78, 117*.

644. 16 June 1675—Nicholas Hewes, serv^t to Col St Roger Codd, is adjudged per this Court to be sixteene yeares of age & ordered to serve his said master according to Act. *OB 1666–78, 117*.

645. 18 Aug. 1675—Samuel Roe, serv^t to Col. St Leger Codd, is adjudged by the Court to be eighteene yeares of age & ordered to serve his sd Master according to Act. *OB 1666–78, 117*.

646. 18 Aug. 1675—George Marsh, serv^t to Tho: Gascoynes, is judged by this Court to be eighteen yeares of age & ordered to serve his said master according to Law. *OB 1666–78, 118*.

647. 15 Sept. 1675—Whereas Rose Morris hath had a base child in ye tyme of her service wch she hath upon her oath layd unto Jno Allon, It is ordered y^t ye sherriff take ye sd Jno Allon into safe custody untill he give bond for his future good behaviour & ordered that ye said Rose serve Angell Jacobus, her master, two yeares for his paines & charge in child bed after her tyme of service is expired. . . . *OB 1666–78, 119*.

648. 18 Nov. 1675—Whereas by Act of Assembly, It is ordered y^t ye respective Courts should take care to put out ye children of indigent persons apprentices according to their directions, & whereas Sabrina Parker, serv^t to Mr Wm Wildey hath a little younger daughter, wch she is not capable to provide for, but ye Child hath beene kept at ye charge of ye sd Mr Wildey, It is therefore ordered y^t Rose, ye Daughter of ye sd Sabrina serve ye sd Mr Wildey or his assignes untill she is eighteen yeares of age. *OB 1666–78, 122*. [Rose Parker could have been indeed an apprentice and not a servant as the word apprentice is used; however, nothing is mentioned about her learning a trade such as weaving or sewing, or learning to read and write. Also, in the margin of the page the word servant is used.]

649. 19 Jan. 1675/76—John Williams, serv^t to M^r ___ Jones [no first name given], adjudged to be nine yeares of age & ordered to serve his said Mr According to Act. *OB 1666–78, 125.*

650. 19 Jan. 1675/76—Edward Killpatrick, serv^t to Mr Jno Farnefold, adjudged to be twelve yeares of age and ordered to serve his sd Mr According to Act. Dan^{ll} MacKarty, serv^t to Tho Deuvenant, adjudged to be fifteene yeares of age & ordered to serve his sd M^{sr} According to Act. Neale O Dorhoty, serv^t to James Napor, adjudged to be fifteene yeares of age & ordered to serve his sd Mr According to Act. Sam^{ll} Cammell, serv^t to Dennis Eyse, adjudged to be twelve yeares of Age & ordered to serve his sd M^r according to Act. William Macktire, serv^t to Mr Wm Coutanceau, adjudged to be fourteen yeares of age & ordered to serve his M^r according to Act. John Brookes, serv^t to John Corbell, adjudged to be eighteene yeares of age & ordered to serve his sd M^r according to Act. Jeremiah Thomas, serv^t to Walter Dunne, Adjudged to be seaventeen yeares of age & ordered to serve his sd M^r according to Act. Turner Muckle, serv^t to Mr Pet: Presly, Adjudged to be thirteen yeares of age & ordered to serve his sd M^r according to Act. Cormeck Castide, serv^t to Mr Pet: Presly, Adjudged to be thirteene yeares of age & ordered to serve his sd M^r according to Act. George Browne, serv^t to Mr Presly, Adjudged to be twelve yeares of Age & ordered to serve his sd M^r according to Act. Jane Macklangha, serv^t to Rich: Hill, Adjudged to be fourteene yeares of Age & ordered to serve her sd M^r according to Act. Mannas Macklangha, serv^t to Tho: Sadler, Adjudged to be thirteen yeares of Age & ordered to serve his sd M^r according to Act. Arthur O Neal, serv^t to Rich: Hill, Adjudged to be fifteen yeares of Age & ordered to serve his sd M^r according to Act. Dan^{ll} O Muddy, serv^t to Mr Pet: Presly Junr, Adjudged to be seaventeen yeares of Age & ordered to serve his sd M^r according to Act. John Crage, serv^t to Mr Edw: Coles, Adjudged to be fifteen yeares of Age & ordered to serve his sd Mr According to Act. Charles Blackwell, serv^t to Downing [no first name given], Adjudged to be eleaven yeares of Age & ordered to serve his sd Mr According to Act. Laurence Keire, serv^t to Mr Phill: Shaply, Adjudged to be thirteen yeares of Age & ordered to serve his sd M^r according to Act. Dan^{ll} a [O ?] Loth, serv^t to Mr Phill: Shaply, Adjudged to be sixteen yeares of Age & ordered to serve his sd Mr According to Act. Humphrey Ereale, serv^t to Mr Phill: Shaply, Adjudged to be fourteen yeares of Age & ordered to serve his sd Mr According to Act. Dax: [?] Mag=Jone, serv^t to Wm Downing Junr, Adjudged to be twelve yeares of age & ordered to serve his sd Mr According to Act. James Guttery, serv^t to Den: Conway, Adjudged to be seaventeen yeares of Age & ordered to serve his sd M^r according to Act. James Lyn, serv^t to Major Brereton, Adjudged to be thirteen yeares of age & ordered to serve according to Act. James Davis, serv^t to Maj^r Brereton, adjudged to be seaventeen yeares of Age & ordered to serve according to Act. John Harrar, serv^t to John Motley, Adjudged to be thirteene yeares of Age & ordered to serve according to Act. Alexander Cammell, serv^t to Tho: Hobson, adjudged to be sixteen yeares of Age & ordered to serve according to Act. *OB 1666–78, 125, 126.*

651. 19 Jan. 1675/76—Jno Macklanhan, serv^t to Mr Dan^{ll} Neale Junr, adjudged to be thirteene yeares of Age & ordered to serve his said Mr According to Act. *OB 1666–78, 127.*

652. 1 March 1675/76—David Griffith, serv^t to Wm Downing, adjudged to be eighteene yeares of Age & ordered to serve his said Master according to Act. *OB 1666–78, 130.*

653. 1 March 1675/76—Edw: A. Dinney, serv^t to Col. St Leger Codd, adjudged to be fourteen yeares of Age, & ordered to serve his sd Mr According to Act. *OB 1666–78, 130.*

654. 1 March 1675/76—Whereas 2 Runaways were brought to this Court who, being by ye Court examined, did confess y^t they were serv^{ts} and ye one called Alexander Duglas, belonging unto Tho: Bright of ye Isle of Kent, ye other called Jno Parsons, belonging unto Mathew Read of the aforesd Isle, It is ordered y^t ye sherriffe take them into safe Custody & cause them to have 30 Stripes a peice on their bare backs . . . And to convey them unto ye house of Wm Calvert Esquire, Secretary of the province of Maryland from thence to be sent to their respective masters. *OB 1666–78, 131.*

655. 19 April 1676—Whereas Capt Jno Rogers hath kept Jno Goreham, sonne to Miles Goreham sometyme & the father of the said Child hath absented himselfe out of this Country wth the Consent of the said John: The Court doth order y^t the said John serve the said Capt Jno Rogers untill he attaine to the Age of one & twenty yeares. *OB 1666–78, 134.*

656. 19 Aprill 1676—Whereas Thomas Watts did petition this Court for his Corne & Cloathes agt the estate of Mr Ambroase Feilding, Judgm^t is granted the sd Watts agt the sd Mr Feilding's estate according to custom for his Corn & Cloathes als execution. *OB 1666–78, 134.*

657. 19 April 1676—Susana Robinson, servant to Mr Christopher Garlington, is adjudged to be fifteen yeares of Age & ordered to serve her said

Mr According to Act. *OB 1666–78, 134.*

658. 19 April 1676—Mary James, servant to Jno Champion, being adjudged by this Court to be fowerteene yeares of Age, is ordered to serve her sd Mr According to Act. *OB 1666–78, 135.*

659. 17 May 1676—William Davis, servant to Mr John Cotanceau, is adjudged to be tenn yeares of Age & ordered to serve his said master According to Act. *OB 1666–78, 137.*

660. 17 July 1676—Henry Chackly [Chalkley in the Index], serv^t to Capt Mottrom, is adjudged to be tenn yeares of Age & ordered to serve his said Master According to Act. *OB 1666–78, 139.*

661. 19 July 1676—Whereas Eliz: Jones, late serv^t to Jno Hughlett, for runing away and other charges, was ordered to make her said master satisfaction by service, the said Eliz: Jones did in this Court in lieu of the service aforesd and to be exempted from punishment declare y^t she was willing to serve Richard Rice the Assignees of the sd John Hughlett three yeares. . . . *OB 1666–78, 139.*

662. 19 July 1676—Whereas the Act of Assembly doth provide y^t ye Children of Indigent parents should be put out by the Court, This Court wth ye Consent of the parents of James Hawkins doe order y^t the said James serve Richd Hull untill he be one and twenty yeares of Age. *OB 1666–78, 139.*

663. 19 July 1676—Whereas Jno Machall, William Machall & John Machelvey, servants to Mr Christopher Garlington, hath run away from their sd M^r 12 dayes, stole several goods from him and put him to great Charge to procure them againe, It is ordered y^t John Machall and Wm Machall serve their sd M^r for their sd default, each of them six monthes after their tyme of service is expired And y^t John Mathelvey (whom the Court doe Judge to be less culpable) serve his sd M^r two monthes. . . . *OB 1666–78, 139.*

664. 19 July 1676—Whereas it appeares to this Court by the oath of Mr Dan^{ll} Neale senior and the attestation of Mr Phillip Shapleigh that Anne Colloughcor came into this Country but fower yeares, It is ordered y^t the said woman be free and y^t William Cornish (who was her last Master) pay her her Corne & Clothes according to Custome. *OB 1666–78, 140.*

665. 19 July 1676—Whereas John Griffith was arrested to this Court at the suite of Mr Peter Presly for certaine damages which allegeth y^t he had sustained and the said Griffith not appearing a nonsuite is granted ye sd Mr Presly agt the sd Griffith according to Act. *OB 1666–78, 141*.

666. 19 July 1676—Whereas it appeares to this Court by a Covenant under ye hands of Robert Berry dated ye 12th of Jany 1675, y^t ye sd Berry was to serve Robt Hughlett from the day of the date thereof untill the 20th of December 1677, It is ordered y^t he ye sd Berry serve according to Covenant. *OB 1666–78, 141*.

667. 21 March 1676/77—James Macklanhan, serv^t to Jno Bowen, Judged to be thirteen yeares of Age & ordered to serve his sd master According to Act of [Assembly]. Jane Younge, serv^t to Jno Bowen, judged to be seaven yeares of Age & ordered to serve his sd master According to Act. Robert Low, serv^t to Geo: Dameron, judged to be eleven yeares of Age and ordered to serve his sd Mr According to Act. Phillip Mackmartin, serv^t to George Dameron, judged to be seaven yeares of Age and ordered to serve his sd master According to Act. *OB 1666–78, 142*.

668. 21 March 1676/77—Whereas Mary Evans, serv^t to Tho: Hobson, hath had a bastard Child in ye tyme of her service, It is ordered y^t she serve her said master two yeares after ye tyme of her service by Indenture, Custome, or otherwise is expired for her sd master's paines, charge and trouble in ye tyme of her lyeing inn. *OB 1666–78, 143*.

669. 18 April 1677—Henry Price, serv^t to Mrs Martha Jones, is adjudged to be twelve yeares of Age & ordered to serve his said Mistress according to Act. *OB 1666–78, 143*.

670. 18 April 1677—Geo: Hancock, serv^t to Walter Dunne, is adjudged to be fourteen yeares of Age & ordered to serve his sd Master according to Act. *OB 1666–78, 143*.

671. 20 June 1677—Tho: Jrock [or Jcock], serv^t to Capt Jno Rogers, adjudged to be seaventeen yeares of age; Wm White, serv^t to Christopher Neale, adjudged to be nine yeares of age; Edmon Weston, serv^t to Hugh Harris, adjudged to be thirteene yeares of age and ordered y^t they all serve their respective Masters according to Act. *OB 1666–78, 146*.

672. 20 June 1677—Whereas Edmond Maclinshaw was by his master when he came into this Country sould [sold] to the said John Symmons for only six yeares as he hath made out by good Testimony, It is ordered y^t he shall serve his sd terme to commence from the tyme of ye last Arrivall of the ship the

George into Wicomico River. *OB 1666–78, 146.*

673. 20 June 1677—Whereas it appeares to this Court yt Robt Berry, servt to Robt Hewes, absented himselfe from his sd Master's service seaven months & sixteene dayes by a Certificate from Capt Pet: Knight, Judgm{t} is granted Mrs Martha Jones the execution of the sd Hughes agt the sd Berry for double the sd tyme according to Act. *OB 1666–78, 147.* [The above is a good example of a surname being spelled two different ways in the same document.]

674. 20 June 1677—Mrs Martha Jones confesseth Judgm{t} for the present payment of three Barrells of Indian Corne & a sow into Robt Berry. . . . *OB 1666–78, 147.*

675. 20 June 1677—Whereas Katherine Ingram, Attorney for Tho: Ingram, did petition this Court for further service of John Dabbs, pretending ye sd Dabbs, his Indenture to be false, which doth appeare to this Court to be true, It is ordered yt ye sd Dabbs be free and yt ye sd Ingram pay him his Corne and Cloathes According to Custome. *OB 1666–78, 148.*

676. 18 July 1677—Whereas it appeares to this Court yt Roger Oneale did serve Mr Ambrose Feilding . . . ye full terme of tyme which he came into this country for, Judgm{t} is granted ye said Roger agt ye estate of ye sd Feilding for his Corne & cloathes according to ye Custome. *OB 1666–78, 149.*

677. 18 July 1677—Whereas Eliz: Robinson, late servt to Capt Jno Mottrom, hath fully served her tyme . . ., It is ordered yt the said Mottrom pay unto Tho: Robinson, husband to ye sd Elizabeth, her Corne & Cloathes according to Custome. . . . *OB 1666–78, 149.*

678. 19 Sept. 1677—Upon ye petition of Richd Cox wherein he complaineth that he hath kept a Child of Mary Mankins three yeares, It is ordered that the sherriffe summon ye sd Mary to the next Court when if she appeare not that then Richd Cox keep the said Child untill he come to age. *OB 1666–78, 153.*

679. 19 Sept. 1677—A Certificate is granted Andrew Pettigrew for fower hundred fifty Acres of Land for ye transportation of

   James Martin   Robt Wright
   Marke Lafeazsone [?]   John Younge
   Jno Worthingham   Wm Seneger
   Stephen Hubbert   Anne Williams
   Jno Oasling

OB 1666–78, 154.

680. 21 Nov. 1677—Sam^{ll} Hickson, serv^t to Jno Reason, comeing into this Country without Indenture, wth the consent of both parties is adjudged to serve his said Master nine yeares. *OB 1666–78, 155.*

681. 21 Nov. 1677—Ellin^r Mackenell, servant to James Napper, is adjudged to be two & twenty yeares of Age & ordered to serve her sd master According to Act. *OB 1666–78, 156.*

682. 22 Nov. 1677—Whereas Mary Herbert hath in Court put her child Mary to serve Thomas Gill untill she come to the age of one & twenty yeares and the sd Gill doth oblige himselfe to give the sd Mary when she attaines to the age of seventeen yeares a Cow wth a cow calfe by her side and to keep the increase of the sd Cattle until she comes to the age of one & twenty yeares. *OB 1666–78, 157.*

683. 22 Nov. 1677—Whereas Mrs Martha Jones petitioned this Court for satisfaction for a Bastard child borne by her servant Anne Ramies in the time of her service, the Court upon examination finding that the sd Child was not borne in the time that the said servant had first to serve but during the time thereforesd for a former default in having a Bastard and of opinion that the sd servant ought not to come for her second default and ordered y^t Mrs Jones's suite therein be dismissed. *OB 1666–78, 158.*

684. 8 Dec. 1677—Debts to ye charges of Runawayes: Richd Hill for taking up two servants, John & William Mackaules, belonging to Mr Christopher Garlington; Mr Edw: Osbourne for taking up John Davies, servant to Mr Richd Kenner; to John Johnson for taking up John Ewes & Thomas Butler, servants to Mr Thomas Brewer; To William Tigner for taking up Anth: Greening, servant to Col. Wormley; to Nich^o Wrenn for taking up Geo: Every, servant to Mrs Paine of Rappahannock; to Phillip Shapleigh for taking up Tho: Morgan, servant to Major Walker; to Col. Sam^{ll} Smyth for taking up Nath: Bridgeman, servant to Mrs Miles, and John Bryant, serv^t to Walter Heard; to Willm Cornish for taking up Hen: Compton, servant to Thomas Spelman; to John Taylor for taking up John Harrison, servant to Mr Davenport; to Francis Brittaine for taking up Thomas, servant to Col. Austeene; to William Flowers for taking up William Marttin, servant to the orphants of Hugh Brent; to Francis Cursom for taking up Margarett, serv^t unto Richd Way; to John Moses for taking up a wench of Capt David Fox; to John Knott for taking up John Branch, serv^t to Mr Giles Brent; to Tymothy Green for taking up Millie White, serv^t to Capt Apleton; to Col Smyth for Hen: Simson, Tho: Walker, Edw: Baker, Christopher Smyth, Jno Williams (a Mulatto), three belonging to Mr James [?], & two to Mr George Pendexter. Sent Col. Sam^{ll} Smyth for Tho:

Morgan, serv^t to Tho: Walker; Abraham Joyce, a hired serv^t referred to ye House. *OB 1666–78, 162, 163.*

685. 19 Dec. 1677—Whereas per Act of Assembly ye County Courts are injoyned to take Care to provide for the Children of indigent persons, This Court does therefore order that Rachell Hassell, Daughter of William Hassell, serve Adam Yarratt ye full terme of eight yeares from this day, ye sd Adam Yarrett during the said terme allowing the said Rachell sufficient meat, drink, Clothing, Washing and Lodging. *OB 1666–78, 164.*

686. 19 Dec. 1677—Joseph Taylor, servant to Mrs Joane Garlington, is adjudged to be seaventeen yeares of Age and ordered to serve his said Mrs According to Act. *OB 1666–78, 164.*

687. 19 Dec. 1677—Whereas Leah Riscott, servant to William Keen, hath had a bastard child, & will not confess to the father of the sd Child, the Court does therefore order that the sherriffe take the sd Leah & give her twenty stripes on her bare back, and that the sherriffe take the sd Leah & keep her in safe Custody untill she confess the father of her sd Child; by reason ye sd Leah is now sick, It is ordered y^t her punishment be referred untill the next Court. *OB 1666–78, 165.*

688. 19 Dec. 1677—Whereas Ann Beauchamp hath had a Bastard Child in the tyme of her service, It is ordered y^t she serve her Master Thomas Davies or Assigns two full yeares after her tyme by Custom or Indenture is expired for her sd Master's trouble & charges in the tyme of her service.... *OB 1666–78, 166.*

689. 19 Dec. 1677—Whereas Mr William Presly did petition this Court y^t he had one servant woman named Susanna Jacobs which had a Bastard Child in ye time of her service, who by reason of sickness and weakness of this Child, is incapable of being brought to Court to have ye benefitt of the Act ag^t her his sd servant and the reputed father of her sd Child, Josias Harris, The Court doe order y^t ye sd serv^t shall have no benefitt by any ... of tyme for their not being brought to Court. *OB 1666–78, 166.*

690. 19 Dec. 1677—Whereas Francis Cursome hath arrested to this Court Mr Hancock Lee for a mare killed upon ye sd Mr Lee's land by one Willm: Browne, servant to Mr Thomas Laurence & hath demanded reparation by Virtue of ye 77th Act of Assembly. ... *OB 1666–78, 166.*

691. 5 March 1677/78—Whereas per Act of Assembly ye sd ... County

Courts are impowered to provide for the Children of Indigent persons with the consent of Elizabeth Pickring the mother of Rosamond Pickering is ordered that the said Rosamond Pickering serve Mr Thomas Matthew his heires or assignes the full terme of fowerteen yeares from ye day of the date of this Court. *OB 1666–78, 171.*

692. __ March 1677/78—[?] Mackness servant to Mr William Presly, is adjudged to be nine years of Age and ordered to serve his said Master According to Act. *OB 1666–78, 172.* [First name not legible.]

693. __ March 1677/78—Whereas per Act of Assembly ye County Courts are impowered to place out orphans y^t have not estates to keep __ [page worn], It is ordered y^t Peter Russell, an orphan, at his own request be placed with Adam Yarrett & serve him untill he be one & twenty yeares of age. *OB 1666–78, 172.*

694. __ March 1677/78—Ordered y^t Richd West, son to Joane West, being in Court by ye sd Joane given to John Tayler and Anne his wife untill he come to one and twenty. *OB 1666–78, 172.*

695. __ March 1677/78—Elizabeth Green, servant to Mr Thomas Winter, adjudged to be eighteen yeares of Age and ordered to serve her sd Master According to Act. *OB 1666–78, 174.*

696. 17 April 1678—Solomon Mason adjudged to be fifteene yeares of age & ordered to serve his Master Mr William Presly according to Act. Thomas Flattman, servant to Mr Pet: Presly, adjudged to be thirteen yeares of Age & ordered to serve his sd Master according to Act. John Lukas, servant to John Corbell, adjudged to be fowerteen yeares of age & ordered to serve his sd Master According to Act. Daniell Neale, servant to Mr Thomas Matthew, adjudged to be thirteen yeares of age & ordered to serve his sd Master according to Act. Susanna Oldfield, servant to Mr Thomas Matthew, adjudged to be fifteene yeares of age but upon ye confession of ye sd Matthew y^t he bought ye sd Sarah for six yeares & no longer, It is ordered y^t she serve her sd Master ye sd terme of six yeares. Hester Jess, servant to Richard Bradly, adjudged to be thirteen yeares of age & ordered to serve her sd master According to Act. Sarah Piles, serv^t to Mr Daniell Neale, adjudged to be thirteen yeares of age & ordered to serve her sd master according to Act. *OB 1666–78, 175.*

697. _____ —A Certificate is granted James Claughton for two hundred & fifty Acres of Land being for the Importation of five persons (vizt)

Tho: Merrifield   Seileife Alverton
Edw Woolridge   Anth: Nash
Henry Gubboy
OB 1666–78, 177.

698. 21 Aug. 1678—Severall Serv^ts Bound: James Gosse, servant unto Sam^ll Mahen, is adjudged to be thirteen years of age; Teage Hogan, servant to Thomas Fowne, tenn yeares; John Travers, servant to John Swanson, tenn yeares; Edmund Magray, servant to John Dennis, eleven yeares and all are ordered to serve their respective Masters according to Act. *OB 1678–98, Part 1, 1.*

699. 21 Aug. 1678—Edward Smyth, servant unto William Shoares, coming into this Country wth Capt Thomas Smyth & having lost his Indenture, It is ordered wth ye Consent of both parties that he serve his sd Master nine yeares from the tyme of the last Arrivall of the said Capt Smith. *OB 1678–98, Part 1, 1.*

700. 21 Aug. 1678—Patrick Mallin, servant unto Mr Thomas Matthew, is adjudged to be fifteen yeares of age and ordered to serve his sd Master According to Act. *OB 1678–98, Part 1, 2.*

701. 21 Aug. 1678—Several Serv^ts bound to Mr Winter: Christopher Varley, servant to Thomas Winter, Adjudged to be eight yeares of Age; John Varley, serv^t to Thomas Winter, tenn yeares of Age; James Varley, serv^t to Thomas Winter, six yeares of Age; Jennett Varley, servant to Thomas Winter, fowerteen yeares; Elizabeth Varley, servant to Thomas Winter, twelve yeares and ordered to serve their said Master According to Act. *OB 1678–98, Part 1, 3.*

702. 21 Aug. 1678—Whereas John Marshall & William Laurence, servants to Barth: Dameron, and Edward Chilton, servant to Christopher Garlington, have absented themselves from their sd Masters's service from the 13th of May to the 14th of June & Cost their sd Master for getting of them againe three thousand pounds of Tobacco.... *OB 1678–98, Part 1, 4.*

703. 21 Aug. 1678—A Certificate is granted William Sheares for six hundred Acres of Land being due to him for the Importation of twelve persons (vizt)

Kathein Cadamy   Robt Michaell
Sam^ll Wills   William East
Pet: Richards   John Cowt

Symon Walker   Morris Jenkins
Walter Davey   Elizabeth Thomas
Tho: Duke   Eward Smyth
OB 1678–98, Part 1, 4.

704. 6 Oct. 1678—Whereas it appeares to the Court y^t Matthew Roles, serv^t to Richd Cox of the parish of Chickacone in this County, hath had a bastard child in the time of service, which on her oath she hath layd unto her sd Master, It is ordered that the sd Matthew, for her sd default, serve the parish two yeares according to Act of Assembly in that Case made & ordered y^t ye sd Matthew be whipt, Col. St Leger Codd ingaging to pay ye fine layd on the sd Matthew by law. It is ordered y^t she be acquitted from the sd punishment and ordered that the sherriff take the sd Richd Cox into safe Custody untill he hath given bond wth security for his good behaviour & the payment of his fine of five hundred pounds of Tobacco. *OB 1678–98, Part 1, 5.* [In the Index the name is Rolles.]

705. 16 Oct. 1678—Whereas it appeares to this Court y^t Benjamin Adington, John Gyles & John Sawter, servants to Mr Thomas Opye, did unlawfully kill a hogg, It is ordered y^t the sherriffe take the sd Adington, Giles & Sawter into Custody & give each of them twenty stripes. *OB 1678–98, Part 1, 6.*

706. 16 Oct. 1678—Whereas Henry Howard, serv^t to Thomas Webb, did petition this Court for his freedom, he having presented a copie of his Indenture from y^e ... in Bristoll & an attestation from ye Majo^r of the sd Citty under the Seale of ye office of the Mayorally of the same wherein he was bound to serve John Woolvin or his Assignes fower yeares after his arrivall into this Country, and whereas the sd Howard hath fully served the sd terme. . . . *OB 1678–98, Part 1, 6.*

707. 20 Nov. 1678—Whereas Abraham Ford, servant to William Hartland run away from his sd master fower dayes & gave his master some charge to procure him, It is ordered y^t the sd Abraham serve his sd master for his sd default & Charges two monthes after that his tyme of service by Indenture Custome or otherwise is expired. *OB 1678–98, Part 1, 13.*

708. 20 Nov. 1678—Certificate is granted Jno Roach to the next Assembly for taking up Runaway servants of William Hartland's run from his sd Master into Westmoreland County. *OB 1678–98, Part 1, 14.*

709. 21 Nov. 1678—Certificate is granted Mr John Harris for seaver hundred Acres of Land for the Importation of fowerteen persons into this Colony (vizt)

        John Harris   Jennett Taylor
        Isaac Hudson   Eliz: Munrow
        Wm Brissin   Alex: Grant
        Eliz: Wright   John Hill
        Ann Paine   Sam^{ll} Oakeley
        John Mordey   Alex: Lloyd
        John Burdman   Lucy Howard

OB 1678–98, Part 1, 15.

710. 15 Jan. 1678/79—Susan Hall, servant to William Downing, Junior, nine yeares of age; Daniell Hall, serv^t to Will: Downing senior, eight yeares of age; John Williams, serv^t to John Hughlett, to be nine yeares of age & are all ordered to serve their respective masters According to Act. *OB 1678–98, Part 1, 18.*

711. 19 Feb. 1678/79—Whereas Hester Smyth, serv^t to Mr William Jones, hath had in the tyme of her service a Bastard Child wch under oath she layd to a Negro belonging to Mr Thomas Haines, It is ordered that ye sd Hester make her master satisfaction for his losse of tyme According to Act and that the sher: take ye sd Hester into safe Custody & give her twenty stripes on her bare back for her sd default. *OB 1678–98, Part 1, 21.*

712. 19 March 1678/79—Certificate is granted Capt John Haynie for three hundred Acres of Land for ye Importation of six persons into this Colony (vizt)

        Luke de Marratt   Abigall Mayfield
        Richard Burgess   a Negro woman
        Tho: Hawley   a Negro child

OB 1678–98, Part 1, 28.

713. 19 March 1678/79—Several Servants Bound: William Carpenter, servant to Henry Mayse, adjudged to be sixteen yeares of Age; William Jones, serv^t to James Johnson, fowerteen yeares of Age; John Harris, servant to Mr William Presly, eleaven yeares of age; Mathew Winsborough, serv^t to Mr Richd Kenner, sixteen yeares of age; John Hicks, servant to Robt Seth, seaventeen yeares of age; Joseph Harmestone, serv^t to Mr Christopher Neale, eighteen yeares of Age and are ordered to serve their respective masters according to Act. *OB 1678–98, Part 1, 28.*

714. 19 March 1678/79—Certificate is granted Mr Christopher Neale for twelve hundred Acres of Land for the Importation of fower & twenty persons (vizt).

Tho: Haverfeild	Steph: Salloes
Jn⁰ Hutton	James Jersey
Luke Marrow	Geo: Pedley
Pet: Blackley	Eliz: Hawkins
Joan Francis	Ann Brooks
Joan Sanders	Thomas Saddler
Mich: McGennis	Henry Saddler
Patrick McGennis	Robert Saddler
Jn⁰ Itrey	Fran: Discoll
Ann Reinon	Jn⁰ Powell
Will:, a Negro	Eliz: Musgraine
Diano, a Negro	Mingo, a Negro

OB 1678–98, Part 1, 32.

715. 19 March 1678/79—Certificate is granted John Downing for one hundred Acres of Land for ye Importation of two persons into this Colony (vizt)

    Charles Blackwell   Margarett Harley
OB 1678–98, Part 1, 29.

716. 21 May 1679—Certificate is granted Richard Bradley for one hundred Acres of Land for ye Importation of two persons into this Collony (vizt) Hugh Mony & Hester Jesse: Sworne. *OB 1678–98, Part 1, 33.*

717. 21 May 1679—Certificate is granted Dennis Carty for three hundred & fifty Acres of Land for the Importation of seaven persons into this Colony (vizt).

Dennis Carty	Margaret May
Jn⁰ Woolard	Mary Olliver
Teage Adannough	Gilbert O Hart
Tho: Oldwill	

OB 1678–98, Part 1, 33.

718. 21 May 1679—William Spence, servant to Mr Thomas Banks, adjudged to be eighteen yeares of Age, and Martha Venner, servant to Mr William Keen, adjudged to be eighteen yeares of Age & are both ordered to serve their said masters According to Act. *OB 1678–98, Part 1, 34.*

719. 21 May 1679—John Macalle & Wm Macalle, servants to Mr Christopher Garlington, having run away from their Master's service fifteen dayes are ordered to serve their sd Master one month after their tyme of service by

Indenture, Custome, or otherwise is expired. *OB 1678–98, Part 1, 35.*

720. 21 May 1679—Whereas on Sunday last John Ford, servant to M[r] John Harris, did run away from his sd Master to the house of Cap[t] Peter Knight. ... *OB 1678–98, Part 1, 36.*

721. 18 June 1679—Certificate is granted Jn[o] Robinson for one hundred Acres of Land for the Importation of Thurlow Jewell & Annie Robinson. *OB 1678–98, Part 1, 40.*

722. 18 June 1679—Certificate is granted Thomas Hobson for twelve hundred Acres of Land for the Importation of twenty fower persons into this Collony (viz[t])

Tho: Rowland	Alice Argile
W[m] Sharts	Alexand[r] Cammell
Rich[d] Baule	Phill: Pitts
W[m] Betts	Mary Evans
Ellias Merritt	Hugh Cannon
Jn[o] Butler	Pet: Platt
Eliz: Salmon	Mary Pledjoell
Eliz: Doggett	Joseph Holt
Marg[t] Taypett	Fra: Wares
Dan[ll] Linch	Tho: Jeanes
Hugh Broughton	W[m] Clay
Henry Sanders	Mary Hortman [?]

The first 9 assigned to Samuel Mahane; the next 6 assigned to Peter Hack. *OB 1678–98, Part 1, 42.*

723. 15 Oct. 1679—Certificate is granted Sam[ll] Mahen for two hundred & fifty Acres of Land for y[e] Importation of John Dodd & Thomas Howard, James Gilbert, James Pope & ___ [no first name given] Blewfeild. *OB 1678–98, Part 1, 45.*

724. 22 Oct. 1679—Certificate is granted Rich[d] Cox to y[e] Assembly for taking up a runaway servant of Cap[t] Jn[o] Rogers in Westmoreland County named Tho: J Cocke. *OB 1678–98, Part 1, 49.*

725. 22 Oct. 1679—Certificate is granted Maj[r] Tho: Brereton for the taking up Tho: Robinson & Rich[d] Hayes who run away out of Maryland. *OB 1678–98, Part 1, 49.*

726. 22 Oct. 1679—Certificate is granted W[m] Downing Jun[r] unto the

Assembly for taking up Henry Parker, serv^t to Robt Young of Morattico in Rapp^a. *OB 1678–98, Part 1, 49.*

727. 22 Oct. 1679—Certificate is granted Thomas Hopper for taking up a runaway Servant of Mr Thomas Wilks of Rapp^a named John Holder. *OB 1678–98, Part 1, 49.*

728. 22 Oct. 1679—Certificate is granted Richd Cox to Assembly for taking up a Runaway serv^t of Mr Wm Wildey named John Conoway. *OB 1678–98, Part 1, 49.*

729. 22 Oct. 1679—Certificate is granted Richd Lamprey to the Assembly for the taking up two Runaway Servants, one named Timothy Norton belonging to Maj^r Robt Beverly, the other named Thomas Russell belonging to Mr Charles Morgan. *OB 1678–98, Part 1, 49.*

730. 3 Dec. 1679—Whereas James Hickson, Servant to Dan^{ll} Neale, hath runaway from his sd Master, as (he sayeth fifteen dayes), It is ordered y^t ye sd James go home & serve his sd Master untill ye next Court, and y^t then, if the sd Neale make his sd allegation appeare true, that ye Court proceed ag^t the said James according to Act. *OB 1678–98, Part 1, 51.*

731. 21 Jan. 1679/80—Certificate is granted Richd Rice for three hundred Acres of Land for ye Importation of six persons into this Collony (vizt)

Dan^{ll} Hay	Rog^r Hayes
Jno Butler	Ann Hay
Jno Lewis	Eliz: Lovell

OB 1678–98, Part 1, 54.

732. 21 Jan. 1679/80—Whereas Christopher Bryerley petitioned this Court & did therein declare that he had served Mr Thomas Matthew five yeares, and (whereas per the deposition of Mr Tho: Penry) who sold the sd Byerley to Mr Tho: Matthew but for fower yeares & no longer tyme, the Cour^t that the sd Mr Tho: Matthew pay unto ye sd Byerley for his last yeares service one thousand pounds of Tob^a & Caske wth Costs. *OB 1678–98, Part 1, 54.*

733. 21 Jan. 1679/80—Whereas Frances Lewis did by her petition complained unto this Court that Abraham Morris, servant to Clem^t Lattimore, had violently assaulted her & broke her head so grievously that the sd wound cost her for the Cure five hundred pounds of Tobacco & Caske besides ye damage of loss of time & great pain thereby suffered while she lay under ye sd Cure the Court doth order y^t the said Morris, after his tyme of service is expired, pa^y

unto the sd Frances Lewis the sum of twelve hundred pounds of Tobacco and Caske with Costs. *OB 1678–98, Part 1, 54.*

734. 18 Feb. 1679/80—Certificate is granted Mr Tho: Mathew for three thousand eight hundred Acres of Land for y^e Transportation of seaventy six persons into this Colony (vizt)

Mr Thomas Mathew & ten Negroes from Barbados
Mr Tho: Matthew from London
three Negroes from New England

Steph: Sallowes	Robt House
Jno Haughton	Tho: Curtis
Matt: Neale	Jno Cope
Steph: Proctor	Mary Cooper
Mary ___	James Seabury
Jno Hendy	Edw: Owsman
Jno Rumley	Tho: Morris
Lau: Fulbrook	Jno Turraine
Sarah Statham	Jno Bamfold
Robt Mundy	Pet: de Jerzey
Anth: Paw	Miles Crawley
Geo: Lyle	Hawett Ignatious
Jos: Beeton	Oliver & Mary ___
Arthur Rickett	Turner ___
Mich: Domundy	Henry Burke
Christopher Byerley	Jno Whittington
Jno Daulson	Tho: Dew
Dan^{ll} Kneton	James Jenn
Christopher Clarke	Ann Cleaves
Mary Packman	Thomas ___
Edw: Watts	Matt: Peterson
Mary Downes	Dan^{ll} Neale
Tho: Holley	Wm Woggan
Susanna Ofile	Patr: Maly
Wm Parker	Robt Dunn
Wm Sage	Tho: Owen
Steph: Walton	Tho: Hea
David Hughes	Phill: Welsh
Dan^{ll} Shea	Ja: Alexander & Mary ___
Mary Cavernaugh	Sam^{ll} Bankley

OB 1678–98, Part 1, 56.

735. 18 Feb. 1679/80—Sarah Moore, wth the Consent of Walter Moore her father, doth in Court bind herself to serve Thomas Hobson untill she shall be seaventeen yeares of Age. *OB 1678–98, Part 1, 57*. [She may have been an apprentice.]

736. 17 March 1679/80—Whereas Mary Webb, who as servant of Tho: Coppage, was attached for eight hundred ninety pounds of Tobacco & Caske due unto Tho: Webb from ye sd Coppage, petitioned y^t she was free. *OB 1678–98, Part 1, 62*. [Mary Webb could not prove that she should be free, and as a result four men were appointed to determine how long she was to serve Coppage. After deliberation, they concluded she was to serve one year and a quarter.]

737. 14 April 1680—Certificate is granted John Hughlett for three hundred & fifty Acres of Land for ye Importation of seaven persons into this Colony, vizt.

John Williams	Rich: Banister
John Porkey	Jam: Gearding
Sar: Stuck	Edw: Ellis
Jno Church	

Assigned to Wm Coppage. *OB 1678–98, Part 1, 64*.

738. 19 May 1680—Certificate is granted Phil: Evans for three hundred & fifty Acres of land for ye Importation of seaven persons into this Colony

Hann: Macguire	Mary Whitebread
Owen Maley	Wm Tresteale
Prissilla Day	More Hart
Dam: Flamagon	

OB 1678–98, Part 1, 68.

739. 19 May 1680—... John Church, serv^t to ye sd [John] Hughlett.... *OB 1678–98, Part 1, 68*.

740. 19 May 1680—The whole Jury doe conclude ye Robt Barklett is serv^t unto Jno Webb. *OB 1678–98, Part 1, 68*.

741. 21 July 1680—Whereas Mary Mackastelly, serv^t to Jam: Napar, hath had a base Child in ye time of her service, It is ordered y^t ye sd Mary serve her sd Master for his troubles & Charge according to Act & also for her sd default, her Master having engaged to pay her fine. *OB 1678–98, Part 1, 70*.

742. 21 July 1680—Whereas Joane Merrick, serv^t to Mr Jam: Claughton, hath had a Bastard Child in ye time of her service, It is ordered y^t she serve her sd Master for his loss of time & charge. . . . *OB 1678–98, Part 1, 70.*

743. 21 July 1680—Jeffery Reynolds, serv^t to Mr James Claughton, judged to be thirteen yeares of age, but by his Master's concession is ordered to serve his sd Master but ten yeares. *OB 1678–98, Part 1, 70.*

744. 21 July 1680—Eliz: Smyth, serv^t to Mr Nick: Owen, is judged to be 12 yeares of age but by her Master's confession, ordered to serve but her sd Master but ten yeares. *OB 1678–98, Part 1, 70.*

745. 21 July 1680—Tho: Williams, serv^t to Mr Rich: Kenner, is judged to be fifteen yeares of age & ordered to serve his sd Master According to Act. *OB 1678–98, Part 1, 70.*

746. 21 July 1680—Whereas Robt Bryery, Constable for Cherry Poynt, had a serv^t named Jno Moody. . . . *OB 1678–98, Part 1, 70.*

747. 21 July 1680—Jno Mosse, serv^t to Capt Tho: Mathew, is judged to be fifteen yeares of age & ordered to serve his sd Master according to Act. *OB 1678–98, Part 1, 70.*

748. 21 July 1680—Whereas Robt Barbar, serv^t to Mr Edw: Coles, was ye 20th July 1670 by ye Court judged to be fowerteen yeares of age & ordered to serve his sd Master according to Act . . . & ordered y^t his sd Master forthwth pay him his Corne & Cloathes according to Custome. *OB 1678–98, Part 1, 72.*

749. 16 Aug. 1680—Whereas Nicholas, a French boy formerly serv^t to George Courtnell & by Rich Cox Adm^r of ye said Courtnell sold to Tho: Hayes, hath fully served ye time, wch by an order of Court dated ye 20th June 1668, he was adjudged to serve, I doe therefore order Augustine Kireton [?] (who marryed ye relict of ye said Tho: Hayes) forthwith to deliver to ye said Nicholas his Corne & Cloathes wth Costs. *OB 1678–98, Part 1, 74.*

750. 15 Sept. 1680—Whereas Mildright Rew, serv^t to James Johnson, hath had a bastard Child in the time of his service wch she sweares was gott by Wm Lambert, it is ordered y^t she serve her master for his losse of time & charge according to Act. . . . *OB 1678–98, Part 1, 74.*

751. 15 Sept. 1680—Several Slaves of Mr Thomas Judged: Thomas, an Indian boy, Saray, an Indian girl, Susan, a Negro girl, is judged to be eight yeares of age; Harry, a Negro boy, Jane a Indian girl 5 yeares of age; George, an Indian boy, 4 yeares of age; Anne, a mulatto girl 2 yeares of age all serv^{ts} to Mr Thomas. *OB 1678–98, Part 1, 74.*

752. 2 March 1680/81—Thomas Davis, servant to Mr John Farnefold, is adjudged to be eleaven yeares of Age, And ordered to serve his said Master according to Act. *OB 1678–98, Part 1, 83.*

753. 2 March 1680/81—Whereas Hannah Ware, lately to Henry Mayse, prayed that she might be freed, And that her master might pay her Corne and Cloathes, It is ordered (It appearing by the oathes of Edward Washbury and John Lewis that the said Hannah Ware came into this Country by Indenture for foure yeares) that the said Hannah be free, And that her said master pay her, her Corne and Cloathes according to Custome of this Country wth Costs. *OB 1678–98, Part 1, 84.*

754. 2 March 1680/81—Certificate is granted Tho: Waddy for three hundred Acres of Land for the Importation of six persons into this Collony vizt

Amos Jeffard	Anne Smythergill
John Raney	Adam Howkar
Peter Morning	Peter Damisson

OB 1678–98, Part 1, 85.

755. 3 March 1680/81—Whereas Richard Pemberton was arrested to this Court at the suite of John Harris for Corne and other goods and not appearing Judgment is granted the said Harris against the sherriff for the said goods according to Law. *OB 1678–98, Part 1, 88.*

756. 15 June 1681—James Southerne, servant to Mr Richard Flynt, is adjudged to be tenn yeares of Age, and ordered to serve his said Master according to Law. *OB 1678–98, Part 1, 95.* [In the Index the name is John Southerne.]

757. 15 June 1681—Joseph Walker, servant to Mr Peter Presly, is adjudged to be seaventeene yeares of Age, and ordered to serve his said Master according to Act. *OB 1678–98, Part 1, 95.* [In the Index the name is Peter Presly Junior.]

758. 17 Aug. 1681—Certificate is granted William and Charles Betts for foure hundred Acres of Land for the Importation of eight persons vizt,

Tho: Treit	Sarah Anderson
James Dunelay	Elisha Howell
Edwd Feilds	Tho: Barbar

Mary Williams   Lydia ____
OB 1678–98, Part 1, 99.

759. 17 Aug. 1681—Henry Charles, servant to Mrs Elizabeth Tipton, is adjudged to be six yeares of Age and ordered to serve his said M^{rs} according to Act. *OB 1678–98, Part 1, 99.*

760. 17 Aug. 1681—James Crosse, servant to Mr Richard Kenner, is adjudged to be eleaven yeares of age and order[ed] to serve his said Master according to Act. *OB 1678–98, Part 1, 100.*

761. 17 Aug. 1681—Whereas Capt Thomas Mathew obteyned Judgment against his servant, Mary Griffin, for her having a Bastard, the Court being dissatisfied wth the order, It is ordered that Capt Mathew bring the said Mary to the next Court, and then on a rehearing of the said matter the Court may proceed to Judgm^t against the said Mary. *OB 1678–98, Part 1, 100.*

762. 19 Oct. 1681—Whereas Pet: Diamond, serv^t to Mr Wm Presly, John Harding & Thurlo Micklehome, serv^{ts} to Mr Pet: Presly, have been runaway from their sd Masters service ever since ye 18th of July last & after a long, chargable pursuit of ye sd serv^{ts} Thurlo Micklehouse, one of ye sd serv^{ts} of Mr Pet: Presly, was brought home ye 16th Instant. . . . *OB 1678–98, Part 1, 104.* [A lengthy court entry.]

763. 19 Oct. 1681—Deborah Adams hath in Court bound herself to serve Anth: Morris & his wife in case he useth all ye means he possibly can procure to make a perfect cure of her soare legs. *OB 1678–98, Part 1, 105.* [She could have been an apprentice.]

764. 19 Oct. 1681—Certificate is granted Mrs Jane Wildey for two hundred & fifty Acres of Land for ye Importation of 5 persons, vizt:

    Tho: Spilman   Jno Cunny
    Mary Spilman   Owen Macgaaine
    Benj: Ricketts
OB 1678–98, Part 1, 105.

765. 20 Oct. 1681—Whereas Mr John Eustace was arrested to this Cour at ye suit of Eliz: Witherall for her Corne & Cloathes & satisfaction for a yeare service & not appearing Judgm^t is granted ye sd Eliz: ag^t ye sher: according to Law. *OB 1678–98, Part 1, 107.*

766. 18 Jan. 1681/82—Whereas it appears to this Court y^t Eliz: William hath fully served her Master, Christopher Kirk, ye time for wch she was bound by Indenture, It is ordered y^t she be free & her sd Master pay her her Corne & Cloathes according to Custome. *OB 1678–98, Part 1, 118.*

767. 18 Jan. 1681/82—Whereas Edm: Watts, serv^t to Capt Tho: Mathew, moved this Court for his freedom & produced an Indenture wch ye Court having proved find to be forged doe order ye sd serv^t to go home to his Master's house & serve him ye full time y^t he came into this Country for. *OB 1678–98, Part 1, 119.*

768. 15 March 1681/82—Whereas a woman serv^t wth child belonging to John Champion did complayne to this Court y^t she had been much abused by her Master & Mistress, It is ordered y^t ye sd Champion & his wife make their personall appearance ye next Court to answer ye sd Complaynt & y^t in ye mean tyme they refrayne from doing ye sd serv^t or his [her] child any further wrong. *OB 1678–98, Part 1, 127.*

769. 17 May 1682—Anth: Manby, serv^t to Mr Tho: Opye, is adjudged to be fourteen yeares of age & ordered to serve his sd Master according to Act. *OB 1678–98, Part 1, 129.*

770. 19 July 1682—Rich: Marrow, serv^t to Robert Sech, is judged to be 18 yeares of age; Robt Harrison, serv^t to Mr Wm Presly, 11 yeares. Tho: Jackson, servt to Mr Wm Presly, 14 yeares. Rich: Booth, serv^t to Mr Pet: Presly, Junr, 11 yeares, and Mac Marrey, serv^t to Rich: Hull, 11 yeares of age & ordered y^t ye sd serv^{ts} serve their respective Masters according to Act. *OB 1678–98, Part 1, 135.* [In the Index the name is Murry.]

771. 19 July 1682—It is ordered y^t Margarett Crane, serv^t to Tho: Williams, serve her sd Master two yeares for keeping her in ye time of her lying in wth a Bastard wch she had by Tho: Taylor on her oath & his loss of time & also half a yeare, he ingaging to pay ye fine for her default after her time by Custome or otherwise is expired. *OB 1678–98, Part 1, 135.*

772. 19 July 1682—John Davis, formly serv^t to Tho: Towers, by him assigned to Mr Rich: Kenner & Mr Kenner assigned to Mr Rich: Flynt, did in this Court produce an Indenture under ye hands of ye sd Towers wherein he ye sd John was to serve ye sd Towers but ten yeares wch being expired, It is ordered y^t ye sd Davis be free & y^t his last Master pay him his Corne & Cloathes according to Custome wth Costs. *OB 1678–98, Part 1, 136.*

773. 19 July 1682—Certificate is granted John Walters for three hundred

& fifty Acres of Land for ye Importation of seaven persons into this Colony vizt

John Walters	Mary Walters
Hester Walters	Easter Walters
Phoebe Walters	Jno Walters
Diana Walters	

OB 1678–98, Part 1, 138.

774. 16 Aug. 1682—Tho: Childermasse, serv^t to Hen: Gaskoyne, is adjudged to be thirteen yeares of age. Daniell Powers, serv^t to Henry Mayse, twelve yeares of age & ordered to serve their respective masters according to Act. *OB 1678–98, Part 1, 139.*

775. 17 Aug. 1682—Certificate is granted Tho: Winter for 1500 Acres of Land for ye Importation of 30 persons into this Colony vizt

Robt Maursh	Jno Lee
Robt Ash	Robt Berry
Jno White	Rich: Cook
Jno Moor	Jno Tipto
Mary Godding	Anne Lee
Jno Thomas	Jam: Edney
Rob Chilcock	Wm Wood
Tho: Tap	Eliz: Green
Tho: Camplaime	Christopher Varley Senr
Wm Tozar	Mary Varley
Jno Pithard	Jane Varley
Edm Wheaden	Eliz: Varley
Tho: Williams	Jno Varley
Sam: Miller	Christopher Varley Junr
Jno Dabbs	Jam: Varley

OB 1678–98, Part 1, 144.

776. 17 Aug. 1682—Whereas John White sold a serv^t boy named John Davies unto Tho: Towers & both buyer & seller did give an oath ye sd boy an obligation under their respective hands & seales y^t ye sd boy should serve ye sd Towers or his assigns but ten yeares. *OB 1678–98, Part 1, 144.* [A lengthy court order in which the reader learns John Davies was later sold to Richard Kenner, who in turn sold him to Richard Flynt.]

777. 17 Aug. 1682—Whereas Mr Rich: Flynt by Capt Mathews his Certificate did prove y^t John Davies, lately his serv^t had run away. . . . *OB 1678–98, Part 1, 144.*

778. 18 Oct. 1682—Whereas Edw: Payne, serv^t to Mr Wm Keyne, hath run away from his sd Master's service five monthes, in ye choice time of ye Crop & given his Master an extra ordinary charge in procuring him agayne, It is ordered y^t ye sd Payne serve his sd Master for his loss of time & charges two yeares after his time of service by Indenture, Custome, or otherwise is expired. *OB 1678–98, Part 1, 145.*

779. 18 Oct. 1682—Whereas John Davies, serv^t to Mr Rich: Flynt by assignment from Mr Richard Kenner, hath run away from his sd Master's service ten weekes in ye time of his Crop & given his Master trouble & Charge to procure him agayne, It is ordered y^t he serve his sd Master for his loss of service & charge eight monthes after his time of service by Indenture, Custome, or otherwise is expired. *OB 1678–98, Part 1, 145.*

780. 6 Dec. 1682—Whereas Emuell Newland, serv^t to Mr Christopher Garlington, hath had a Bastard Child in ye time of her service, It is ordered y^t she serve her sd Master for his trouble charge to loss of time & for her fine wch her sd Master hath ingaged to pay for her sd default according to Act. *OB 1678–98, Part 1, 150.*

781. 17 Jan. 1682/83—Certificate is granted Mr Leonrd Howson for three hundred acres of Land for ye importation of six persons into this Colony vizt

Wm Chanler	Jane Smyth
Jane Groves	Alex: Brodie
Ed: Stockten	Wm Nichols

OB 1678–98, Part 1, 156.

782. 17 Jan. 1682/83—Certificate is granted Mr Wm Harcum for three hundred Acres of Land for ye importation of six persons into this Colony:

Wm Harcum	Th: Chandler
Lidia Harcum	Th: Smyth
Jam: Harcum	Mary Webb
Wm Harcum	Wilf Williams
Mary Harcum	Abigall Harcum

OB 1678–98, Part 1, 156.

783. 17 Jan. 1682/83—Mary James, serv^t to John Champion, petitioning this Court y^t she might [be] free though formly judged to serve according to Act, It is ordered y^t she serve her sd Master according to ye purport of ye former order. *OB 1678–98, Part 1, 156.*

784. 21 Feb. 1682/83—Certificate is granted Rich: Kenner for thirteen hundred & fifty Acres of Land for ye Importation of twenty seaven persons into this Colony

    Th: Crosse   Benj: Johnson
    Dor: Hust   Anne Gill
    Eliz: White   Tho: Jones
    Jone Francis   Jam: Croass
    Th: Winstone   Math: Winberry
    Christopher Wade   More Moughley
    Mary Wade   Sus: Tinoth
    Th: Newman   Rawl: Oslen
    Robt Chewes   Samb: a Negro
    Th Chewes   Lawr: a Negro
    Jno James   Toney: a Negro
    Jno Osborne   Maddam: a Negro
    Mar: Sparhalt   Rachell: a Negro
    Jone Maghley

OB 1678–98, Part 1, 162.

785. 21 March 1682/83—Whereas Tho: Barnes gave information to this Court y^t Rich: Cox hath concealed diverse persons out of ye list given in one of his tithables (vizt) one a miller, his serv^t named Tho: Surtherin, & made good his sd information. . . . *OB 1678–98, Part 1, 170.*

786. 18 April 1683—Whereas it appears to this Court y^t Hugh Callon, serv^t to Coll Tho: Brereton, did run away from his sd Master's service ten dayes and took with him a lusty Negroe and cost his master to procure them again two thousand three hundred & fifty pounds of Tobacco & Caske, It is ordered y^t ye sd Hugh serve his sd Master for his sd Default & his great Charges two yeares & a halfe after his time of service by Indenture, Custome or otherwise is expired. *OB 1678–98, Part 1, 176.*

787. 18 April 1683—Jno Harris, serv^t to Robt Bryery, judged to be fourteen yeares of Age and ordered to serve his sd Master according to Act. *OB 1678–98, Part 1, 176.*

788. 18 April 1683—Whereas Allice Baker, serv^t to Jno Tayler, hath had a bastard Child by a Negro man in ye time of her service, It is ordered y^t ye sd Allice make her sd Master satisfaction from his loss of service & trouble according to Act and ordered y^t ye sherriff take her into safe Custody & give her twenty stripes on her bare back for her sd Default. *OB 1678–98, Part 1, 176.*

789. 19 April 1683—Whereas Edwd Watts, servant to Capt Tho: Mathew, moved ye Court to have his freedom, producing an Indenture under ye hand & seale of Jno Harris, his first master, for four yeares, The Court finding ye expressed time in ye Indenture raised & interlined doe judge ye sd Indenture to be voyd and ye sd Edwd lyable to serve five yeares according to Custome wch time allsoe he having fully served, It is ordered y^t he be free An [and] y^t his sd master Capt Tho: Mathew pay him his Corne & clothes according to Custome wth Costs. *OB 1678–98, Part 1, 182.*

790. 20 June 1683—Jenny, a Negro of Mr Pet: Presly Junr, is judged to be ten yeares of age: Jack, a native Negro of Mr Rich: Kenner, eleaven years of age; Jno Walters, serv^t to Mr Coutanceau Junr, thirteen yeares of age. *OB 1678–98, Part 1, 184.*

791. 20 June 1683—Whereas Sarah Medcalf had a Bastard child after her time of service was expired but became bound to serve some yeares for a Cure wc^h was made on her wth time she having served, It is ordered y^t she be free & y^t she have her Child wth her, Mr Jam: Claughton ingaging to save ye parish harmless from ye sd child. *OB 1678–98, Part 1, 186.*

792. 20 June 1683—Ordered y^t Rebecca Thomas, serv^t to Mrs Jane Wildey, being a runaway serv^t & noe way beneficial to her, be freed from ye levy. *OB 1678–98, Part 1, 186.*

793. 18 July 1683—Mary Chambers, serv^t to Rich: Hull, having a bastard Child, did this day on her oath declare y^t Mr Wm Pitchard was the father thereof. *OB 1678–98, Part 1, 189.*

794. 19 Dec. 1683—Whereas Eliz: Hobson, serv^t to Lt Coll. Sam^{ll} Smyth, hath had a bastard child in ye time of her service, It is ordered y^t ye sd Eliz: serve her sd Master for his charge & loss of time two yeares after ye time of her service by Indenture, Custome or otherwise is expired and ye punishment acquitted, Coll. Smyth paying ye fine. *OB 1678–98, Part 1, 207.*

795. 16 Jan. 1683/84—Certificate is granted Jno Downing for three hundred & fifty [acres] of land for ye importation of seaven persons into this Colony vizt

    Jer: Harris   Dor: Howard
    Jno Charigon   Mary Morris
    Hen: Charles   two slaves
OB 1678–98, Part 1, 212.

796. 19 March 1683/84—Anne Royla, serv^t to Wm Keyne, is by this Court adjudged to be twelve yeares of age & ordered to serve her Master according to Act of wch time her Master hath in Court abated four yeares. *OB 1678–98, Part 1, 217.*

797. 4 June 1684—Whereas Fran: Jones, serv^t to Mr Daniell Neale, was by his said Master brought to this Court to have their Judgm^t of his age, ye Court doe judge him to be twelve yeares of age, but being sold to ye sd Neale by Mr Sam: Hartnell for but for seaven yeares time, It is ordered y^t he ye sd Fran: shall serve his sd Master or his assigns ye sd terme of seaven yeares & noe longer. *OB 1678–98, Part 1, 227.*

798. 20 Aug. 1684—Mary James, serv^t to Cuthbert Span, haveing had a bastard Child in the time of her servitude, It is ordered y^t she serve her sd master for her sd default according to Act. *OB 1678–98, Part 1, 235.*

799. 19 Nov. 1684—Whereas Mary James, serv^t to Cuthbert Span hath had a Bastard child in ye time of her service, It is ordered y^t she serve her sd Master according to Act, y^t ye sherr: give her twenty stripes on her bare back & summon in Humphrey Veale, ye father of ye sd child to ye next Court to give security for his good behaviour & to save ye parish harmless from ye sd child. *OB 1678–98, Part 1, 248.*

800. 19 Nov. 1684—Certificate is granted Mr Wm Rogers for five hundred Acres of Land for ye Importation of ten persons (vizt)

Jno Althorp	Phil Gammonds
Hen: Tayler	Anne Sprag
Tho: Ecock	Israell Berry
Dan: A Dooly	Judith Kanne
Kath: Bryant	Dominick Rice

OB 1678–98, Part 1, 251.

801. 21 Jan. 1684/85—Jam: Cox, serv^t to John Bowen, is judged to be ten yeares of age. John Frost, serv^t to Peter Maxwell, twelve yeares. Anth: Cotoone, serv^t to Clem: Latemore, seventeen yeares of age, & all ordered to serve their respective Masters according to Act. *OB 1678–98, Part 1, 252.*

802. 18 March 1684/85—Hen: Hudson, serv^t to Mr Jno Coutansheau Junr, ordered, with ye consent of both parties, y^t he serve his sd Master six yeares & noe longer. *OB 1678–98, Part 1, 256.*

803. 18 March 1684/85—Jam: Mortemore, serv^t to Mr Coutansheau sen^r,

is judged to be sixteen yeares of age & ordered to serve his sd Master according to Act. *OB 1678–98, Part 1, 256.*

804. 18 March 1684/85—Thomas Higgins, serv^t to Jno Hull, is judged to be seaventeen yeares of age & ordered to serve his sd Master according to Act. *OB 1678–98, Part 1, 256.*

805. 18 March 1684/85—Anne Greenstone, daughter of Jno Greenstone, being nine yeares of age, is ordered, wth ye consent of her father, to serve Wm Yarratt & Jane his wife untill she be seaventeen yeares of age but not to serve any other person but them or ye survivors of them. *OB 1678–98, Part 1, 256.* [Anne may have been an apprentice.]

806. 18 March 1684/85—Tho: Grimstead, seaven years old, & Jno Grimstead, four yeares, wth ye consent of Wm Grimstead their father, are ordered to serve Wm Tayler untill they be one & twenty yeares of age, but if it should happen y^t Wm Tayler, his wife & son should depart this life before ye sd Children attaine ye age of one & twenty that then they be free. *OB 1678–98, Part 1, 256.*

807. 20 May 1685—Cha: Nowland, serv^t to Mr Robt Sech, is judged to be ten yeares of age; Ellin^r Morclay, serv^t to Jno Corbell, is judged to be thirteen yeares of age and ordered y^t they serve their sd masters according to Act. *OB 1678–98, Part 1, 268.*

808. 20 May 1685—Sarah, an Indian serv^t to Richd Hull, is adjudged to be twelve yeares of age. *OB 1678–98, Part 1, 269.*

809. 20 May 1685—Whereas Margaret Crane, serv^t to Thomas Williams, had a bastard Child and her sd master having in Court engaged to pay ye fine imposed by law, It is ordered y^t she be acquitted from her punishment serving her sd master halfe a year. *OB 1678–98, Part 1, 269.*

810. 15 July 1685—Whereas Eliz^a Steward complained to this Court y^t whereas one Symon Crouch sold her to Capt Thomas Mathew for ye term of four yeares wch was out in December last & she still deteiyned [detained] in ye sd Capt Mathew's house as a servant and prayed satisfaction for ye time she hath been detained there since ye expiration of ye sd term, And whereas ye sd Steward hath produced ye sd Crouch his deposition who sweareth that he sold her ye sd Steward unto ye sd Capt Mathew for ye sd terme of four yeares & noe longer & y^t ye sd time was expired ye last Christmas, It's ordered y^t she be free & y^t ye sd Mathew pay her two hundred & fifty pounds of Tobacco and Cask for wch time she hath been there since ye sd expired time wth Corne & Cloathes accustomed & Costs of suit. *OB 1678–98, Part 1, 276.*

811. 15 July 1685—Nicho: Rhodes, a poor Child being three yeares of age in October next & given by his mother unto John Freeman, It's ordered y^t he serve ye sd Freeman untill he is one & twenty yeares old, he paying ye sd Child at ye expiration of ye sd time his Corne & Cloathes accustomed. *OB 1678–98, Part 1, 277.*

812. 16 July 1685—Whereas Mr Geo: Knight complained to this Court y^t he hyred [hired] one Wm Besouth alias Woodamore for seaven hundred pounds of Tob: & a p^r of shoes to live w^th & serve him from March last untill Christmas not wth standing the sd Besouth alias Woodamore from his service did depart & absent himselfe from ye sd Knight to ye loss of his Cornfield.... *OB 1678–98, Part 1, 288.* [The jury found Besouth guilty, and he was ordered to serve the remainder of his time and pay three hundred pounds of tobacco for the loss of Knight's cornfield. *OB 1678–98, Part 1, 289.*]

813. 17 Sept. 1685—Whereas Jam: Waddy complained to this Court y^t he did (in January last) hire a woman named Mary Tutt for one yeare for to doe him such service as he should imploy her in but not wth standing her Agreement she hath departed.... *OB 1678–98, Part 1, 297.*

814. 18 Nov. 1685—Coezar, a negro boy belonging to Mr John Coles, is adjudged to be nine yeares of age. *OB 1678–98, Part 1, 306.*

815. 18 Nov. 1685—John Foster, serv^t to Henry Metcalfe, is adjudged to be fourteen yeares of age and ordered y^t he serve his sd Master according to Act. *OB 1678–98, Part 1, 306.*

816. 18 Nov. 1685—Edmund Maudley & his wife, serv^ts to Richd Hull, having an infant lately borne, are willing (with ye Consent of their sd master) y^t ye sd Child shall serve Howell Williams & his wife untill she be one and twenty yeares old. It's therefore ordered y^t ye sd Child serve ye sd Howell & his wife ye sd term, they paying at ye expiration thereof Corne & Clothes accustomed always provided y^t if ye sd Howell & his wife should dye before ye end of ye sd terme y^t ye sd Child shall be free immediately after their decease. *OB 1678–98, Part 1, 306.*

817. 18 Nov. 1685—Will, a negro boy belonging to Mr Jno Downing, is adjudged to be nine yeares of age. *OB 1678–98, Part 1, 307.*

818. 16 Dec. 1685—Tho: Wheeler, serv^t to Tho: Brewer, is adjudged to be fourteen yeares of age; Robt Wilks, serv^t to John Bowen, is adjudged to be ten yeares of age and ordered y^t they serve their sd masters according to Law. *OB 1678–98, Part 1, 316.*

819. 20 Jan. 1685/86—Jane Shirley, serv^t to Mr Peter Presley Junr, having had a bastard child in ye time of her service, It's s ordered y^t she serve her sd master for her offence according to act & her punishment remitted, her sd master paying ye fine, and alsoe ordered y^t ye sd Mr Presley bring Joseph Walker (who ye sd wench hath sworne is ye father of ye sd Child) to ye next Court. *OB 1678–98, Part 1, 322.*

820. 24 Feb. 1685/86—Whereas Margarett Smyth, serv^t to Mr Robert Sech, was brought to this Court for having a bastard child and hath sworne y^t it was gotten at sea by Symon Pickmore, chirurgion, and whereas ye sd Sech hath in court assumed to pay ye fine, It's ordered y^t her punishment be remitted. *OB 1678–98, Part 1, 328.*

821. 17 March 1685/86—Mary Aubourne, serv^t to Mrs Anne Farmer, is adjudged to be eleaven yeares of age. Eliz^a Price, serv^t to Thomas Flynt, is adjudged to be seaventeen yeares of age. Robt Phillips, serv^t to Mr Jno Cralle, is adjudged to be eight yeares of age. David Roberts, serv^t to W^m & Jno Keen, is adjudged to be fifteen yeares of age. Jno Aro, serv^t to Peter Coutanceau, is adjudged to be thirteen yeares of age and all ordered to serve their respective masters according to Act. *OB 1678–98, Part 1, 337.*

822. 17 March 1685/86—Certificate is granted Mr Phillip Shapleigh for three hundred acres of Land for ye transportation of six persons into this Collony (vizt)

    Mathew Benham   Dan^{ll} Leloge
    Katherine Longham   Laurence Okeane
    Stephen Chaukerett   Humphrey Veale

OB 1678–98, Part 1, 337.

823. 17 March 1685/86—Certificate is granted Jno Davis to ye Assembly for two hundred acres of Land for ye transportation of four persons into this Collony.

    Jno Davis Senr Hester Davis
    Jno Davis Junr Mathew Davis

OB 1678–98, Part 1, 337.

824. 17 March 1685/86—Whereas Susanna Kettle, serv^t to M^r Jno

Coutanceau, petitioned this Court y^t she might be free, she having served her full time out, it being four yeares, and whereas Richard Tidwell, upon oath in Court declare y^t he heard Mr Mich: Chin (who was ye person y^t sold ye said Susanna unto ye said Coutanceau) say y^t ye said Susanna hath but four yeares to serve, and Rach^{ll} Yarrett having likewise upon oath declared y^t she heard Mr Thomas Friend say y^t ye said Susanna had but four yeares to serve, It's ordered that she be free, & y^t ye sd Coutanceau forthwth pay her Corne & Clothes accustomed to wth Costs of suit. *OB 1678–98, Part 1, 338.*

825. 19 May 1686—Whereas Anne Pitts, serv^t to Mary Maxwell, hath had a base child in ye time of her service, it's ordered y^t she serve her sd mistress for her sd Default according to act after ye expiration of her time by indenture, Custome or otherwise & y^t her punishment be remitted, her sd mistress having in Court assumed to pay ye fine. *OB 1678–98, Part 1, 339.*

826. 19 May 1686—Moses Sheffeild, serv^t to Tho: Winter, is adjudged to be fifteen yeares of age and ye said Winter haveing in Court promised to give him two yeares of his service, it's ordered y^t he serve his sd master untill he comes to the age of two and twenty yeares & noe longer. John Dyer, serv^t to Josias Gaskoyne, is adjudged to be twelve yeares old and ordered y^t he serve his sd master according to act. *OB 1678–98, Part 1, 339.*

827. 19 May 1686—Tom, a negro boy belonging to Mr Richd Hull, is by ye Court adjudged to be six yeares old. *OB 1678–98, Part 1, 342.*

828. 21 July 1686—Whereas Mrs Anne Farmer brought a serv^t boy named Cha: Hunt into this Court and declared y^t Mr Jno Crumpton of whom she bought ye sd servant did sell him to her for eight yeares and ye sd serv^t haveing declared y^t he had an Indenture for five yeares and noe longer but (by some means or other destroyed) could not produce ye same, It's ordered y^t he serve ye sd Mrs Anne Farmer ye sd terme of eight yeares unless ye next shiping by Mr Crumpton it shall appeare otherwise. *OB 1678–98, Part 1, 347.*

829. 21 July 1686—Wm Bennett, serv^t to James Jones, is adjudged to be sixteen yeares of age and ordered to serve his said master according to act. *OB 1678–98, Part 1, 348.*

830. 21 July 1686—Whereas Christian Rich, serv^t to Mr Anthony Lynton, hath had a base child by a negroe in ye time of her service, it's ordered y^t she serve her sd master for her said Default according to act & that ye sherr: take her into Custody and give her twenty stripes on her bare back untill ye blood come. *OB 1678–98, Part 1, 348.* [On the same page of the Order Book is an entry stating that Christian Rich escaped before she received her punishment.]

831. 21 July 1686—Peter Williams, serv^t to Jno Downing, is adjudged to be eight yeares old. *OB 1678–98, Part 1, 350.*

832. 17 Nov. 1686—Whereas Robt Baker, serv^t to Mrs Eliz^a Keen, hath absented himself... ye full terme of ninety five dayes from his sd mistress's service.... *OB 1678–98, Part 1, 358.*

833. 17 Nov. 1686—Certificate is granted Mr Cuthbert Span for eight hundred & fifty acres of Land for y^e Importation of seventeen persons into this Collony Viz^t

    Edward Harvey   Rich: Stephens
    Joseph Amee   Edmund Powell
    Edward Bennett   Andr: a Scotchman
    Eliz^a Bennett   Thomas, ____ [a Scotchman ?]
    Thomas Hilman   Sam^{ll} Bateson
    David Davis   Tony, a negro
    Howell Propert   Judith, a negro
    Kath: Hughlett   Naple, a negro
    Owen Brady
OB 1678–98, Part 1, 358.

834. 17 Nov. 1686—Certificate is granted Richa: Hull for six hundred acres of Land for y^e importation of twelve persons into this Collony (vizt)

    George Hill   Grace Warnars
    Doro Sabrice   Andr^w Mackey
    Gerv. Ellistone   Edm^d Maudley
    Arthur Oneale   Jane Maudley
    Jam Maclowghla   Sarah, an Indian
    John Hilley   Tom, a negro
OB 1678–98, Part 1, 359.

835. 26 Feb. 1686/87—This day Jno (ye son of Benjamin) Wall did in Court wth ye Consent of his mother Ruth (ye relict and widow of ye sd Benjamin) Wall bind himself, being about ye age of six yeares, unto Wm Yarrett for to serve him and his wife or either of them or their heirs until he attaine ye age of one & twenty yeares paying his Corne & Clothes accustomed, always provided y^t if it should happen y^t they shall both dye wthout issue y^t ye sd Jno to be free. *OB 1678–98, Part 1, 375.*

836. 16 March 1686/87—Edward Clark, serv^t to Sam^{ll} Mahen Senr, is adjudged to be eleaven yeares of age. Mary Harrox, serv^t to James Ednee, is adjudged to be twelve yeares of age. Margarett Moor, serv^t to Walter Jenkins, is adjudged to be nine yeares of age. Fenley Morris, serv^t to James Nipper, is adjudged to be fifteen yeares of age and all ordered to serve their aforesaid masters according to Law. *OB 1678–98, Part 1, 379.*

837. 16 March 1686/87—Whereas Tho: Tayler brought his serv^t, Jno Adams, to this Court for to have ye Court's Judgm^t of his age and prayed that ye sd Adams might serve him according to act. . . . *OB 1678–98, Part 1, 379.*

838. 16 March 1686/87—James Montgomerie, serv^t to Jno Corbin, is adjudged to be seventeen yeares of age and ordered to serve his sd master according to act and ye sd Corbin hath given him one year of his time. *OB 1678–98, Part 1, 379.*

839. 16 March 1686/87—Henry Fisher, serv^t to Dan^{ll} Neale, is adjudged to be thirteen yeares of age and ordered to serve his said master according to act only ye sd Neale hath in Court released him from one yeare of his service. *OB 1678–98, Part 1, 379.*

840. 20 April 1687—Sam^{ll} Havliss, servant to Richard Nutt, is adjudged to be ten years of age. Hugh Maconald, serv^t to Jno Eustace, is adjudged to be sixteen yeares of age. Tho: Armstrong, serv^t to Jno Eustace, is adjudged to be fifteen yeares of age. Evan Frances, serv^t to Mr Phill Shapleigh, is adjudged to be fourteen yeares of age and all ordered to serve their sd masters according to Act. *OB 1678–98, Part 1, 388.*

841. 20 April 1687—Whereas Jno Parris, serv^t to Joseph Palmer, hath burned his sd Master's Cornfield and Pasture and hath likewise absented himself from his sd master's service sometime, It's ordered (ye sd Jno having in Court consented thereto) y^t he serve for his sd default after ye expiration of his time by custome or otherwise one whole year. *OB 1678–98, Part 1, 389.*

842. 20 April 1687—Jno Joyce, serv^t to Jno Bayley, is adjudged to be eleaven yeares of age. *OB 1678–98, Part 1, 389.*

843. 18 May 1687—James James, serv^t to Mr Peter Hack, is adjudged to be six yeares & 1/2 old. *OB 1678–98, Part 2, 393.*

844. 18 May 1687—Wm Hazlas, serv^t to Tho: Waddy, is adjudged to be thirteen yeares of age and ordered to serve his sd master according to act. *OB 1678–98, Part 2, 393.*

845. 18 May 1687—Whereas Richa: Ayrie, serv^t to Walter Dunne, hath absented himself from his sd master's service ye term of twenty five days and whereas ye sd Walter hath been at ye charge of seaven hundred and seaventy pounds of Tobacco and cask in procuring his sd serv^t againe, It's ordered y^t he serve for his sd default and his master's expenses aforesd ye full term of one whole yeare after ye expiration of his time by Indenture, custome, otherwise. *OB 1678–98, Part 2, 394.*

846. 20 July 1687—Henry Pearce, serv^t to Edwd Sanders, is adjudged to be fifteen yeares of age and ordered to serve his said master according to act. *OB 1678–98, Part 2, 397.*

847. 20 July 1687—Thomas Childermas, serv^t to Henry Gaskins, having absented himselfe from his sd master's service ten dayes in the height of his crop..., It's ordered y^t he serve his sd master three monthes after ye expiration of his time by custome or otherwise and whereas ye sd Thomas did carry away a canoe belonging to Joseph Palmer and left her adrift, It's ordered y^t he pay ye sume of two hundred pounds of tobacco & cask unto the said Joseph Palmer for ye same after his times expired. *OB 1678–98, Part 2, 399.*

848. 20 July 1687—Whereas at a Court held for this County ye 18 day of November 1685 Eliz^a, an infant daughter of Edmund Maudley, servant to Richard Hull, was ordered to serve Howell Williams & Ellin^r his wife, wth ye consent of ye sd Hull & ye sd Edmund, father to ye sd child as aforesd, untill she should attaine the age of one and twenty yeares and if it should so happen y^t the said Howell and Ellin^r, his wife, should dye before ye expiration of ye sd term, then ye sd Eliz^a to be immediately free and whereas the sd Howell and his wife are both deced. and some difference hath happened between ye parish of Fairfeilds and ye sd Hull concerning ye charge of keeping ye sd child, It's ordered y^t ye sd Hull who hath ye father of ye sd child, still in his service, keep and maintenance or cause to be kept and maintained ye sd child at his own cost untill her said father's time shall be expired. *OB 1678–98, Part 2, 399.*

849. 20 July 1687—Whereas Margett Crane, serv^t to Thomas Williams, hath run away from her said master's service and hath been absent eighteen dayes and whereas ye sd Williams hath upon his oath declared y^t himselfe or someone by his procurement was fourteen dayes in search of her during her absence, It's ordered y^t she serve half a yeare after her time by Custome, Indenture or otherwise is expired. *OB 1678–98, Part 2, 401.*

850. 5 Oct. 1687—Whereas Jane Liggate, serv^t to Jno Eustace, hath had a bastard Child in the time of her service, it's ordered that she serve her said master two yeares (after her time of indenture, custome or otherwise is expired) according to Law and whereas her sayd master hath in Court engaged to pay the fine imposed by Law, it's ordered that she serve him halfe a yeare for ye same and y^t her punishment be remitted. *OB 1678–98, Part 2, 403.*

851. 5 Oct. 1687—Whereas Dan^{ll} Webb, a mulatto son of an English woman serv^t to ye orph^{ts} of Maj^r Jno Mottrom deced, petitioned this Court (haveing attained the age of one and twenty yeares) he might be free, It's ordered that if the said Dan^{ll} make appeare that he hath attained the age aforesd and no reasons appeares to the Contrary from ye Honorable Nicho: Spencer who manages the estate of the sd orphts, he the said Dan^{ll} be immediately free the next Court. Richard Haynie Atorney of Dan^{ll} Webb. *OB 1678–98, Part 2, 405.*

852. 16 Nov. 1687—Zachariah Coynia, serv^t to Mr Jno Scott, is adjudged to be fourteen yeares of age and ordered to serve his said master according to act. But ye sd Scott hath this day in Court given ye sd Zach: Coynia three full yeares of his time wch by the above executed act is sett forth. *OB 1678–98, Part 2, 410.*

853. 16 Nov. 1687—Tom, a negro boy belonging to George Berrett, is adjudged to be eight yeares of age. *OB 1678–98, Part 2, 410.*

854. 16 Nov. 1687—Jack, a negro boy belonging to Tho: Ferne, is adjudged to be six yeares of age. *OB 1678–98, Part 2, 410.*

855. 17 Nov. 1687—Whereas several persons Viz^t Elizabeth Oldis, Alice Hudnall, Eliz^a Gerrard, a woman servant of Jno Boaz's named Mary, were presented to this Court by Mr Richa Rogers and Dan^{ll} Neale for Bastardizing. . . . *OB 1678–98, Part 2, 411.*

856. 17 Nov. 1687—Laurence Roach, serv^t to Mrs Kath: Coutanceau, is adjudged to be eleven yeares of age and ordered to serve his said mistress according to act. *OB 1678–98, Part 2, 412.*

857. 28 Dec. 1687—Patrick Omullion, serv^t to Jane Wildey, is adjudged to be thirteen yeares of age and ordered to serve his sd mistress according to act. *OB 1678–98, Part 2, 416.*

858. 28 Dec. 1687—Jno Fagan, servant to Phill Norgate, is adjudged to be twelve yeares of age and ordered to serve his said master according to act. *OB 1678–98, Part 2, 416.*

859. 21 March 1687/88—Whereas Mary Stephens, serv^t to Richard Cundiffe, hath had a bastard child in the time of his service, it's ordered that she serve her said master for her said default according to Act and that the sherriff take her into his Custody and give her fifteen lashes on her bare back to be well layd on. *OB 1678–98, Part 2, 424.*

860. 28 March 1687/88—Certificate is granted Mr Jno Haynie for one hundred acres of Land for the importation of two persons into this Collony vizt Jno Magrill and Joseph Bland. *OB 1678–98, Part 2, 428.*

861. 20 June 1688—Harry, a negro boy, belonging to Mr Peter Presley Senr is adjudged to be eight yeares of age. *OB 1678–98, Part 2, 429.*

862. 20 June 1688—James, a negro boy belonging to Tho: Webb, is adjudged to be six year old. *OB 1678–98, Part 2, 429.*

863. 20 June 1688—Jno Wilson, serv^t to Tho: Baker, is adjudged to be seaventeen yeares of age and ordered to serve his sd master according to act. *OB 1678–98, Part 2, 429.*

864. 20 June 1688—Primus, a negro boy belonging to Capt Tho: Jones, is adjudged to be eleaven yeares of age. *OB 1678–98, Part 2, 430.*

865. 20 June 1688—John Malpus (being a native of this country), serv^t to Christopher Garlington, is adjudged to be fourteen yeares of age. *OB 1678–98, Part 2, 430.*

866. 20 June 1688—Whereas Anne Pitts, serv^t to Joseph Hoult, hath had a bastard child in the time of her service by a Negro, it's ordered that she serve her said master for her sd default according to act and ordered that the sherr: take her into Custody & well lay on thirty lashes on her bare back. *OB 1678–98, Part 2, 430.*

867. 20 June 1688—Jack, a negro boy belonging to Cuthbert Span, is adjudged to be six yeares of age. *OB 1678–98, Part 2, 432.*

868. 21 Nov. 1688—Richard Ayry, serv^t to Capt Richard Kenner, having absented his sd Master's service and taken an able negro man belonging to ye sd Capt Kenner wth him. . . . *OB 1678–98, Part 2, 443.*

869. 21 Nov. 1688—Tho: Sims, serv^t to Mr James Johnson, having petitioned this court for his freedom and produced a firm indenture, under the hand and seale of Jno Burrage merch^t dated Augt the 6, 1684, to serve him the sd Burrage or his assigns but four years and noe longer wch time being fully ended and completed in the service of the sd Johnson, It's ordered that he be immediately free and that the sd Johnson pay costs of suit. *OB 1678–98, Part 2, 443.*

870. 19 Dec. 1688—Jno Ogen, serv^t to Dennis Eyes, is adjudged to be fourteen years of age and ordered to serve his sd Master according to act. *OB 1678–98, Part 2, 447.*

871. 19 Dec. 1688—William Smyth, serv^t to Mr Nicholas Owen, haveing absented himselfe from his master's service fourteen months. . . . *OB 1678–98, Part 2, 447.*

872. 19 Dec. 1688—Edmund Maudley, serv^t to Mr Richard Hull, having produced an Indenture to this Court under his hand and seale of Thomas Witter wherein he was obliged to serve the sd Witter or his assigns four years and no longer, and it appearing by a Certificate under the hand of Mr Andrew Gregg, master of the ship which transported the sd Edmund into this Collony, that the sd Edmund hath arrived here December the 18th 1684 wch sd term of four years doth thereby appear on the 18th of this was expired, It's therefore ordered on the petition of the sd Edmund that he be immediately free and y^t the sd Richard Hull pay him his Corne & Clothes accustomed wth Costs of suit. *OB 1678–98, Part 2, 447.*

873. 20 Dec. 1688—Jno Nuball, serv^t of Ebenezer Sanders, is adjudged to be fifteen years of age and ordered to serve his sd master according to act provided he produce noe legall Indenture ye next Court. *OB 1678–98, Part 2, 449.* [Surname determined by checking the Index. At a court held 17 April 1689, John Nuball presented an Indenture in court, but it was declared void because Nicholas Ley, master of the vessel that brought Nuball to the country, did not have the authority to indent him. *OB 1678–98, Part 2, 461.*]

874. 20 Feb. 1688/89—Margery Worsly, serv^t to Mr Dan^{ll} Neale, haeving made her complaint to this Court that her mistress, wife to ye sd Mr Dan^{ll} Neale, had been too rigid and severe to her, and it appearing to this Court by oath of ye sd Margery and Testimony of some of the members of ye Court (to whom she had before Complained) y^t her sd mistress hath been unreasonably and unlawfully severe to her, It's therefore ordered y^t she be free and y^t her sd mistress be henceforth debarred from keeping any Christian woman serv^t under her service unless she give caution for her better behaviour. *OB 1678–98, Part 2, 454.*

875. 20 Feb. 1688/89—Jn° Hinds, serv^t to Mr Peter Presly Junr, moveing this Court y^t he might be free & alledging y^t he, coming a small boy into ye Country, had served Mr Wm Presly, father to ye sd Peter Presly Junr, and him severall years more then what is allowable by Law in that Case, haveing never been judged for his age as he ought to be at the County Court, And whereas it appears to this Court y^t the sd Jn° Hinds was adjudged to serve Mr Wm Presly according to act by the name of Jn° Harris, Jn° Wilkins, Tho: Ryder, and Charles Moo , haveing been all serv^{t}s to ye sd Mr Wm Presly & upon oath declared y^t there had not been any other serv^t at that time nor since ye arrivall of ye sd Hinds (bound at Court to serve ye sd Mr Wm Presly) whose name was Jn°, It's therefore ordered y^t he serve his sd master untill he attaine ye age twenty four years according to act. *OB 1678–98, Part 2, 454.*

876. 17 April 1689—Thomas Northage, serv^t to Antho: Steptoe, is adjudged to be ten years old; Kester Woodworth, serv^t to Lazarus Tayler, is adjudged to be twelve years old & ordered to serve their said masters according to act. *OB 1678–98, Part 2, 460.*

877. 17 April 1689—Margrett Murrow, servant to Mr Charles Lee, having had a bastard Child by a negro during her service, it's ordered that she serve her said Master for her sd Default according to act & her sd Master haveing in Court engaged to pay the fine imposed by law, it's ordered y^t her punishment be remitted. . . . *OB 1678–98, Part 2, 460.*

878. 17 April 1689—Anne Thompson, serv^t to Abra: Sheers, is adjudged to be eighteen yeares of age & ordered to serve her sd master according to act. *OB 1678–98, Part 2, 460.*

879. 17 April 1689—Mary Young, serv^t to Mrs Ann Farmer, haveing had a bastard child in the time of her service by a negro, It's ordered y^t she serve her sd mistress for her sd default according to act, and whereas the sd Mrs Anne Farmer hath in Court assumed to pay the fine imposed by law, it's therefore ordered y^t her punishment be remitted. *OB 1678–98, Part 2, 461.*

880. 15 May 1689—James Courtney, serv^t to Patrick Pollick, is adjudged to be fifteen years of age & ordered to serve his sd master according to act. *OB 1678–98, Part 2, 462.*

881. 15 May 1689—Margrett Lawson, serv^t to Jn° Jones, petitioning this Court y^t she might be free, and it appearing by the Testimony of Mrs Anne Farmer (whose husband Mr Wm Farmer deced brought ye sd Marg^t into the Country. . . . *OB 1678–98, Part 2, 463.* [The court ordered that Margrett

Lawson be set free.]

882. 22 May 1689—Jane Crane, serv^t to Mr Richard Rogers, being adjudged to be fifteen years of age and the said Rogers declaring that he bought the said Jane to serve him six yeares and noe longer, it's ordered that she serve her sd master or his assigns untill the sd terme be expired. *OB 1678–98, Part 2, 466.*

883. 17 July 1689—William Wallis, servant to Mr Christopher Garlington, is adjudged to be thirteen years of age and ordered to serve his sd master according to act. *OB 1678–98, Part 2, 471.*

884. 17 July 1689—Jno Coleman, servant to Thomas Berry, haveing runaway from his sd master into Lancaster County where, being absent four days in June last, ye sd Coleman was brought home to his sd master by an inhabitant of that County, to whom the sd Berry haveing affirmed y^t he posted his obligation for two hundred pounds of tobacco for taking & bringing home ye sd Coleman & prayed that ye sd Coleman might serve him for his sd absented time according to law and also serve him for his sd tobacco engaged for as above sd, It's therefore ordered y^t ye sd Coleman serve ye sd Berry after his time by Indenture, Custome, or otherwise shall be expired the full terme of four monthes and a half. *OB 1678–98, Part 2, 471.*

885. 6 Nov. 1689—Christian Rich, servt to Mrs Jane Lynton, haveing had a bastard Child by a negro in the time of her service, It's ordered that she serve her sd mistress or her assigns for her sd Default according to act & ordered that ye sherr: take ye sd Christian into safe Custody and give her twenty lashes upon ye bare back. *OB 1678–98, Part 2, 478.*

886. 6 Nov. 1689—Whereas Jno Fipps, servant to Alexander Weatherstone, hath absented himselfe from his sd master's service twenty four days. ... *OB 1678–98, Part 2, 478.*

887. 20 Nov. 1689—Mary Gridly, serv^t to Mr Phill Shapleigh, having had a bastard Child in ye time of her service declared upon her oath to be begotten by Henry Evans. ... *OB 1678–98, Part 2, 484.*

888. 22 Nov. 1689—The Churchwardens of the parish haveing presented to the Court Mary Day for haveing a bastard Child, Eliz^a Gerrard for two bastard Children, Allice Hudnall, Jno Haynie Jun^{rs} servant woman, Robt Sech's serv^t Woman, Thomas Adams's servant woman, Jno Hughlett Sen$^{r's}$ serv^t woman, Jno Cole's servant woman for haveing each of them had bastard children, It's ordered y^t y^e sherr: bring each of y^e sd women to y^e next Court to answer for their sd Default. *OB 1678–98, Part 2, 494.*

889. 19 March 1689/90—Mary Court, serv^t to Mr Jno Coutanceau, haveing had a bastard Child in the time of her service by Thomas Saddon as she hath made oath in Court, It's ordered y^t she serve her sd master for her sd default according to act.... *OB 1678–98, Part 2, 501.* [In the next court entry, Thomas Saddon is ordered to pay five thousand pounds of tobacco and casks to the parish of Fairfields by reason of a bastard child begotten on the body of Mary Court.]

890. 21 May 1690—Marmaduke Smitton, serv^t to Stephen Weels, haveing absented himself from his sd master's service forty five dayes, part thereof being in ye hight of ye Crop.... *OB 1678–98, Part 2, 504.*

891. 21 May 1690—Evan Roberts, serv^t to Mr Jno Coutanceau, is adjudged to be eighteen yeares of age & ordered to serve his sd master according to Act. *OB 1678–98, Part 2, 504.*

892. 21 May 1690—Whereas it appears to this Court that Jno MacDaniell & Mary MacDaniell, serv^{ts} to Mr George Cooper, have falsely & scandalously abused their sd master, by giving out ill reports of him & ... the same in open Court the positive proofe appears to the Contrary, It's therefore ordered y^t ye sherr: immediately take the sd Jno MacDaniell into safe Custody & give him one and thirty lashes upon ye bare back well layd on & whereas the sd Mary MacDaniell is now big wth child in wch case her punishment is too grievous to be inflicted upon her at present, It's therefore ordered y^t she have the life punishment wthin a Convenient time after she shall be delivered. *OB 1678–98, Part 2, 505.*

893. 21 May 1690—Joan MacMaghagn, serv^t to Richard Lewis, haveing had a bastard Child in the time of her service.... *OB 1678–98, Part 2, 506.*

894. 18 June 1690—Henry Bragg, serv^t to Mr Rhodon Kenner, is adjudged to be fourteen yeares of age & ordered to serve his said master according to act. *OB 1678–98, Part 2, 507.*

895. 18 June 1690—Sampson Helps, servant to Mr Jno Downing, is adjudged to be twelve yeares of age & ordered to serve his sd master according to act. *OB 1678–98, Part 2, 507.* [In one place the name is spelled Hellps.]

896. 18 June 1690—Jno Fipps, serv^t to Alexander Weatherstone, haveing run away from his sd master's service thirty four days.... *OB 1678–98, Part 2, 508.* [Figgs was ordered to serve an additional year and a half.]

897. 16 July 1690—Mary Phillips, serv^t to Mr Thomas Banks, haveing had a bastard Child by a negro of ye sd Banks named Wm Smyth who ye sd Mary hath made oath begott ye same.... *OB 1678–98, Part 2, 511.* [Thomas Banks paid her fine, and she was ordered to serve an additional time according to law.]

898. 17 Sept. 1690—Jno Simkins, serv^t to Mr Chr: Neale, is adjudged to be twelve years of age and ordered to serve his sd master according to act. *OB 1678–98, Part 2, 519.* [The name is indexed as Simkins; in the court order it is spelled Simpkins.]

899. 17 Sept. 1690—Alice Thompson, serv^t to Joseph Palmer, haveing had a bastard Child in ye time of her service begotten by Tho: James as she hath made oath in Court.... *OB 1678–98, Part 2, 519.* [Her punishment was remitted because Joseph Palmer paid the fine; however, she was ordered to serve an additional six months.]

900. 17 Sept. 1690—Bridgett Richardson, serv^t to Mr Richard Hull, haveing had a bastard child (as she hath made oath begotten by Edm^d Maudley) in ye time of her service and ye sd Edm^d having in Court assumed to pay ye fine imposed by law.... *OB 1678–98, Part 2, 519.* [Her punishment was remitted, but she was to serve her master for her default unless Maudley paid 2,000 pounds of tobacco.]

901. 19 Nov. 1690—Thomazine Lackey, serv^t to Thomas Bearcroft, haveing had a bastard Child (as she hath in Court confessed) borne wthin her indented time.... *OB 1678–98, Part 2, 520.* [Her master paid the fine. Richard Kenner stated that Thomazine made oath that Andrew Edee was the father of the child.]

902. 19 Nov. 1690—Katherine Smyth, haveing in Court declared (being serv^t to Mr Dennis Eyes) y^t she is wth Child by Jno MaGill, it's ordered y^t ye sd MaGill forthwth give good caution to save parish harmless & to pay ye fine imposed by law in ye like cause provided. *OB 1678–98, Part 2, 521.*

903. 19 Nov. 1690—Whereas Mary Stephens, serv^t to Tho: Foulks, hath been most basely & inhumanly beaten and abused by her sd master as appears by the reports of divers women appointed by ye court to ... ye sd servant is therefore ordered y^t she be released from one year's service in violation of y^e

injury received and y^t ye sherr: forthwth take ye sd Foulks into safe Custody till he give good caution for his good behaviour. *OB 1678–98, Part 2, 521.* [Foulks is spelled as Fulkes in the Index.]

904. 19 Nov. 1690—Mary Little John, serv^t to Richard Pemberton, haveing had a bastard Child in ye time of her service, it's ordered y^t she serve for her sd default according to act & y^t her punishment be remitted, her sd master paying ye fine & she serving six monthes for ye same according to act. *OB 1678–98, Part 2, 522.*

905. 18 Feb. 1690/91—Mary May, serv^t to Mr Jno Hughlett Senr, having had a bastard child in the time of her service, It's ordered y^t she serve her said master or his assigns for her sd Default two years and a halfe according to Law, her sd master haveing in Court engaged to pay ye fine. *OB 1678–98, Part 2, 538.*

906. 20 May 1691—Eliz^a Horedome, serv^t to Mr Jno Downing, haveing had a bastard child in the time of her service as she hath made oath begotten by one Jacob Williams, It's ordered y^t she serve her sd master for her sd default. . . . *OB 1678–98, Part 2, 550.* [In the Index the name is spelled Horedum.]

907. 20 May 1691—Upon ye petition of Jno Guy, late serv^t to Adam Yarratt who complained his sd master (though he had justly served his time out) refused to pay his accustomed Corne, two howes [hoes] & an axe, It's ordered that ye sd Adam Yarrett pay ye sd Jno Guy three barrells of Corne accustomed in ye sd Cases & one hoe and one axe wth Costs of suit. *OB 1678–98, Part 2, 552.*

908. 20 May 1691—Upon ye petition of Priscilla Dixon, late serv^t to Mr Richd Pemberton, It's ordered y^t ye sd Pemberton forthwth pay unto ye sd Dixon her accustomed Clothes in y^e . . . [page worn] and also one axe & one hoe. *OB 1678–98, Part 2, 552.*

909. 1 July 1691—Whereas Jno Hayes, serv^t to Mr Tho: Jones, hath absented himselfe from his sd master's service eight dayes, it is ordered that he serve for his sd Default according to act. *OB 1678–98, Part 2, 560.*

910. 1 July 1691—Memorand^m—Clem^t Lattemore, Churchwarden of Wicomico parish, this day in Court present Jno Flowers for begetting a bastard on y^e [body] of a serv^t woman belonging to Mr Jno Eustace. *OB 1678–98, Part 2, 566.*

911. 16 Sept. 1691—Jn⁰ Evans petitioned this Court against his serv^t, James Anderson, for running away & prayed service according to act for his sd default.... *OB 1678–98, Part 2, 567.*

912. 16 Sept. 1691—Jn⁰ MacDan^{ll} and Mary his wife . . . serv^{ts} to Mr Denis Eyes petitioning this Court, that haveing served the sd Eyes their full time as by discharge may appear, they may have order for their freedom Corne & Clothes accustomed & ye sd Mr Eyes not being present, It's ordered he appeare next Court to answer the sd Complaint. *OB 1678–98, Part 2, 567.*

913. 18 Nov. 1691—Francis [Frances] Whilliard, serv^t to Mr Peter Presly, haveing had a bastard child in ye time of her service begotten (as she hath made oath) by Robt Reeves, It's ordered y^t she serve her sd master for her sd default according to act & ordered y^t her punishment be remitted, her sd master haveing ingaged in Court to pay ye fine imposed by act, she serving halfe a yeare for ye same. *OB 1678–98, Part 2, 570.*

914. 18 Nov. 1691—Wm Steward, serv^t to Thomas Maize, is by the Court adjudged to be ten yeares old. *OB 1678–98, Part 2, 570.*

915. 16 Dec. 1691—James Camnwell, serv^t to Patrick Pollick, is by the Court adjudged to be eleaven yeares of age. Francis Dun, serv^t to Thomas Knight, is by the Court adjudged to be twelve yeares old. ____ [page worn] Brady, serv^t to Clement Lattimore is by the Court adjudged to be eleaven yeares old, the sd servants being brought to Court by their severall masters to know when they are tytheable [tithable]. *OB 1678–98, Part 2, 573.*

916. 16 Dec. 1691—Jn⁰ MacDaniell, serv^t to Mr Denis MacCarty, haveing petitioned this Court that he might be free and also his sd master might be ordered to pay him his Corne & Clothes accustomed, ye sd MacDaniell affirming in his sd petition that he had served his full time out and whereas an order of this County Court was produced dated ye 21 day of May 1690 wherein ye sd MacDaniell wth his wife by their own consents were ordered to serve the sd M^r MaCarty from that date ye full terme of three years wch not being expired upon ye petition of the sd MaCarty, it's ordered y^t ye sd MacDaniell forthwth returne to his sd master's service till ye sd terme be expired. *OB 1678–98, Part 2, 576.*

917. 20 Jan. 1691/92—James Anderson, serv^t to Jn⁰ Evans, haveing absented himselfe several dayes from his sd master's service . . . , it is ordered that he serve Sam^{ll} Mahen Junr (who purchased him of ye sd Evans) the term of halfe a yeare for his sd default.... *OB 1678–98, Part 2, 577.*

918. 20 Jan. 1691/92—Charles Nowland, serv^t to Mr Robt Seth, haveing absented himselfe from his sd master's service.... *OB 1678–98, Part 2, 577.*

919. 20 Jan. 1691/92—Mathew Troth, serv^t to Mr Jno Hughlett Senr, haveing confesseth in Court y^t he did unlawfully kill a hogg belonging to his sd master, upon the petition of his sd master, it's ordered that ye sd Mathew serve him or his assigns the full terme of two yeares according to act in ye like cases provided after his time by Custome, Indenture, or otherwise be expired. *OB 1678–98, Part 2, 577.*

920. 19 Feb. 1691/92—Joan Harbott als Murfien, serv^t to James Edney, & haveing had a base Child in the time of her service, It's ordered that she serve her sd master for her sd default two yeares & a halfe after her time by Indenture. ... *OB 1678–98, Part 2, 584.* [Her master paid the fine imposed by law.]

921. 19 May 1692—Joseph Austen, haveing complained to this Court against Mr James Austen y^t he did and doth unlawfully deteign [detain] him as his serv^t.... *OB 1678–98, Part 2, 591.* [At the next court on June 15, 1692, the court declared that whereas James Austen produced no reasons why Joseph should become his servant, he was to be set free immediately. *OB 1678–98, Part 2, 593.*]

922. 20 July 1692—Frances Clarke, serv^t to Mr Barth: Damiron [Dameron], did this day in Court engage to serve Mr Jno Nickless the full terme of five yeares besides her time of service due to ye said Dameron in consideration that the sd Nicklesse would release her from her sd master Dameron. The sd Frances therefore ordered to serve the sd Nicklesse the full terme of time due to the sd Mr Dameron and five yeares after the expiration thereof, the sd Nicholls at ye expiration of her sd time paying her Corne & Clothes accustomed. *OB 1678–98, Part 2, 595.*

923. 20 July 1692—Charles Nowland, now serv^t to Mr Peter Flynt, being formerly ordered by the Court to serve Mr Robert Seth his then master for running away wch happening in the month of June when the time of giving in the list of tithables by law was required wch had not the sd serv^t runaway he had been free before & his master not lyable to pay his levy wch sd ..., It's therefore ordered that the sd Charles Nowland serve in consideration for his levy the full terme of two monthes after his service shall be expired. *OB 1678–98, Part 2, 598.*

924. 21 Sept. 1692—Mary Stephens, serv^t to Mr Richd Haynie, haveing had a bastard Child in the time of her service due for such former crime but not by Indenture, Custom, etc, And the said Haynie moveing the Court that he might be allowed for the sd Default two yeares service as he considered the law in such cases directs, the Court are of opinion y^t her indented time being expired before the sd default was committed that her service ought to be remitted but not withstanding doe order that the sherr: take the sd Mary into Custody (she not being capable to pay her fine) & give her thirty lashes on the bare back according to Act. *OB 1678–98, Part 2, 600.*

925. 10 Oct. 1692—Eliz^a Price, serv^t to Mr Thomas Flynt, haveing had a Bastard Child in the time of her service as she hath made oath begotten of William Harding, It is ordered that she serve for her sd default (her sd master paying the fine imposed by Law) the full terme of two yeares & a halfe after her time by Custome, Indenture or otherwise shall be expired according to act. *OB 1678–98, Part 2, 603.*

926. 16 Nov. 1692—Priscilla Dixon, having had a base child as she hath under oath by Doctor Richard Pemberton, whereby they both lye lyable to the penalty of an act of Assembly imposing a fine on each party of ten pounds of Sterl[ing], three monthes imprisonment or thirty lashes, It's ordered that the sd Pemberton pay the sd fine of ten pounds sterl or two thousand pounds of tobacco in lieu thereof to the uses by the sd Law prescribed wth Costs else exec & y^t he enter into bond wth surety for the same and save the parish harmless by reason of the sd Child & ordered the sherr take her the sd Priscilla into Custody and give her thirty lashes on the bare back according to act. *OB 1678–98, Part 2, 604.*

927. 21 Dec. 1692—Elizabeth Tate, servant to John Paine, being this day presented to ye grand inquest for fornication, It is ordered the sherr: take her into Custody untill she shall give Caution for her appearance next Court to answer for her sd default. *OB 1678–98, Part 2, 607.*

928. 21 Dec. 1692—Jno and Rachell, two mulatto children twins being born ye 17 February last, begotten basely on the body of Mary Day, serv^t to John Webb, are bound by the Court to serve the said John Webb or his assigns untill they attaine the age of thirty years according to ye prescription of ye law in that case provided. *OB 1678–98, Part 2, 607.*

929. 11 Feb. 1692/93—Tho: Davis, serv^t to Mr Jno Farnefold, haveing absented himselfe sometime from his sd master's service. . . . *OB 1678–98, Part 2, 613.*

930. 15 Feb. 1692/93—Jno Phipps, serv^t to Alex^r Weatherstone, haveing absented himself from his said master's service for some considerable time. *OB 1678–98, Part 2, 613.*

931. 15 Feb. 1692/93—Whereas Kath: Rutter, serv^t to Mr Thomas Jones, hath absented herselfe 22 dayes from her sd master's service. . . . *OB 1678–98, Part 2, 613.*

932. 19 April 1693—Jno Haynie Junr, having been at considerable charge and trouble & expences wth Hester Smyth, a dissolute person who was delivered of a bastard child at the house of the sd Haynie, the said Hester in consideration thereof did this day come into Court and oblige herselfe to serve the sd John or his assigns untill the term of five yeares shall be expired. *OB 1678–98, Part 2, 620.* [On the same day, Hester Smith bound her son an apprentice to John Haynie Jr.]

933. 18 May 1693—John Laland, serv^t to Mr Richard Nutt, is adjudged by the Court to be eleaven yeares old. Laurence Fox, serv^t to Mr Rawleigh Travers, is by ye Court adjudged to be eleaven years old. *OB 1678–98, Part 2, 622.*

934. 21 June 1693—Thomas Lishman, serv^t to Tho: Salsbury, is adjudged to be sixteen yeares of age and ordered to serve his sd master according to Act. *OB 1678–98, Part 2, 623.*

935. 21 June 1693—Henry Hopkins, serv^t to Tho: Baker, is adjudged to be fourteen yeares of age and ordered to serve his said master according to act. *OB 1678–98, Part 2, 623.*

936. 22 June 1693—Wm Fitzgerrad, serv^t to Charles Vallen, having made complaint against his sd master for detaining him. . . . *OB 1678–98, Part 2, 628.* [A trial by jury was held and Richard Smyth, foreman, reported that William Fitzgerrad was to return to his master's service. *OB 1678–98, Part 2, 628.*]

937. 20 Sept. 1693—Susanna Unthanke, serv^t to Mr James Johnson, haveing had a base child by Jno Thomas as appeares by the confession of both parties, and her sd master having in Court assumed to pay the fine, It is ordered she serve her said master or his assigns (after her time by Indenture, Custome or otherwise shall be expired) two yeares & a halfe for her said default according to act. *OB 1678–98, Part 2, 630.*

938. 15 Nov. 1693—Frances Clarke, serv^t to Mr Jno Nicklesse, haveing had a bastard Child as she made oath by Neale MaKenny and the sd Nicklesse haveing assumed in Court to pay the fine imposed by Law, It is ordered she serve her said master for same according to Act. *OB 1678–98, Part 2, 632.*

939. 15 Nov. 1693—Margret Gerrard, serv^t to Mr Peter Flynt, having attended four dayes . . . on behalfe of William Dawson against Capt Rodham Kenner, It is ordered y^t Wm Dawson pay forty pounds tobacco per diem for the same. . . . *OB 1678–98, Part 2, 636.*

940. 20 Dec. 1693—Edward Clarke, serv^t to Samuel Mahen, haveing absented himselfe from his said Master's service at least three hundred dayes as appeares by Certificate under the hand of Mr John Turbervile . . . , It is therefore ordered that the said Edward Clarke serve his said master or assigns after his time by Custome, Indenture or otherwise expired six hundred dayes for his said default according to Law. *OB 1678–98, Part 2, 637.*

941. 4 April 1694—James Mullagan, serv^t to Mr John Harris, is by ye Court adjudged to be sixteen yeares of age. Henry Armstrong, serv^t to Mr Jno Harris, is by ye Court adjudged to be sixteen yeares of age. George Ringken, serv^t to Mr Jno Harris, is by ye Court adjudged to be thirteen yeares of age. Charles Calvin, serv^t to James Waddy, is by the Court adjudged to be fourteen yeares of age. Christopher Wilson, serv^t to Abraham Sheeres, is adjudged by ye Court to be eleaven years of age. John Beazles, serv^t to Capt Thomas Opie, is adjudged by ye Court to be seaventeen years of age. William Wilson, serv^t to Thomas Gaskins, is adjudged by ye Court to be eleaven yeares of age. Edward Grimes, serv^t to Bartho: Schreever, is by ye Court adjudged to be thirteen yeares of age. David Boyd, serv^t to John Nicklesse, is adjudged to be twelve yeares of age. Edmund Jones, serv^t to Lazarus Tayler, is by the Court adjudged to be sixteen years of age and ordered that all and every the sd servants serve their several respective masters or their assigns untill they attaine the age of twenty four yeares according to Act. *OB 1678–98, Part 2, 648.*

942. 4 April 1694—Margrett Peters, serv^t to Mrs Jane Wildey, is by the Court adjudged to be sixteen yeares of age, and ordered she serve her sd mistress or assigns untill she shall attaine the age of four and twenty years according to act. *OB 1678–98, Part 2, 648.*

943. 21 March 1693/94—Eliz^a Wilson, serv^t to the estate of Mr Peter Presly deced, having had a bastard Child (as she hath made oath) by James Russell. . . . *OB 1678–98, Part 2, 651.* [Her master paid the fine, and she was ordered to serve an additional two and one half years.]

944. 21 March 1693/94—Margrett Garrard, serv^t to Mr Peter Flynt, having had a bastard child (as she hath made oath) by Peter Howell. . . . *OB 1678–98, Part 2, 651.*

945. 21 March 1693/94—John Smyth, serv^t to Thomas Tayler, is adjudged by the Court to be eleaven years of age and ordered that . . . serve his sd master . . . untill he attaines the age of twenty four yeares according to Act. *OB 1678–98, Part 2, 651.*

946. 21 March 1693/94—Elizabeth Sloen, serv^t to Thomas Maize, is by the Court adjudged to be fourteen yeares of age . . . and ordered she serve her sd Master . . . untill she shall attain to four and twenty yeares of age according to act. *OB 1678–98, Part 2, 652.* [In the Index the name is Sloan.]

947. 16 March 1693/94—Daniel MacDennis, serv^t to Patrick Pollick, is by the Court adjudged to be sixteen years of age. . . . *OB 1678–98, Part 2, 652.* [Surname of Daniel determined by checking the Index.]

948. 16 March 1693/94—Christian Rich, serv^t to Mr Antho: Lynton, having had a base Child since her indented or accustomed time expired as she hath made oath by Jno Elson, It is ordered the sherr: take the sd Christian into Custody & give her thirty lashes on the bare back of her sd default according to act & y^t ye sd Elson enter into bond wth good caution to save the parish harmless. *OB 1678–98, Part 2, 652.*

949. 16 March 1693/94—Peter Waterson, serv^t to Mr Jno Eustace, is adjudged by the Court to be eighteen yeares of age. . . . *OB 1678–98, Part 2, 652.*

950. 16 March 1693/94—John Thomas, serv^t to Mr James Johnson, by recognizance, stood bound to his good behaviour & his master his security wch said Jno having since behaved himself well, It is therefore together with his sd master hereby released from the sd recognizance. *OB 1678–98, Part 2, 653.*

951. 16 March 1693/94—Elizabeth Claveron, serv^t to Thomas Knight, haveing had a bastard Child in the time of her service by Denis Doyle as she hath in Court made oath. . . . *OB 1678–98, Part 2, 661.* [Thomas Knight paid her fine of 500 pounds of tobacco, and Elizabeth was ordered to serve an additional two and one half years.]

952. 16 March 1693/94—Elizabeth Wilcox, serv^t to Capt Rodham Kenner, is by the Court adjudged . . . to be fifteen yeares & a half old. . . . *OB 1678-98, Part 2, 661.*

953. 16 March 1693/94—Margrett Rheine, serv^t to Capt Wm Jones, having had a bastard Child in the time of her service and not being capable to pay her fine, upon ye motion of ye sd Capt Jones, It is ordered that ye sherriffe take ye sd Marg^t into Custody & give her twenty lashes on her bare back according to law. *OB 1678-98, Part 2, 662.*

954. 16 March 1693/94—John Wornom and Wm Yarratt, Churchwardens of Fairfeilds parish, having in Court this day presented Susana Jackson, Jno Houghton's serv^t woman & Joseph Hoult's serv^t woman for fornication as may appear by bastard Children borne of their bodies. . . . *OB 1678-98, Part 2, 662.*

955. 20 June 1694—Margrett Rheine, a native of this Country, serv^t to Capt Wm Jones, bound by the Vestry of Christ Church parish to serve him according to law, having this day been whipped for having a bastard Child, & the sd Jones having moved for satisfaction according to ye directions of the Hundreth Act provided ag^t [against] fornication, The Court are of opinion that ye sd Act doth not extend to those persons natives of this Country & doe therefore order (notwithstanding the sd act) she be acquitted from service or other satisfaction for her sd default. From which order Capt Wm Jones appeals to a hearing before his Excellency, the governor & Councill the fifth day of the next Gen^{ll} Court for the prosecution whereof Thomas Hobson enters himselfe security. *OB 1678-98, Part 2, 663.*

956. 15 Aug. 1694—Marg^t Garrard, having formerly made oath y^t Peter Howell had begotten a bastard Child of her body. . . . *OB 1678-98, Part 2, 670.* [Howell was fined 500 pounds of tobacco and cask and to pay the same to the use of the parish.]

957. 21 Nov. 1694—Sarah Pendrill, orp^t daughter of Jno Pendrill deced, ten yeares old ye first day of March last, is bound by the Court to serve Christopher Garlington or his assigns untill she shall attaine to such age as the law in such cases provides. *OB 1678-98, Part 2, 673.*

958. 21 Nov. 1694—Henry Cople, serv^t to Wm Coppedge, is by the Court adjudged to be twelve yeares of age & ordered y^t he serve according to act. *OB 1678-98, Part 2, 673.*

959. 21 Nov. 1694—Frances Wheeler, serv^t to Mr Peter Presly, haveing had a bastard Child (as she hath made oath) by Mich^l Hurst. . . . *OB 1678–98, Part 2, 673.* [Her master paid the fine, and she was to serve Presly an additional two years.]

960. 23 Nov. 1694—Phoebe Witter als Cook, serv^t to ye estate of Mr Ebenezer Sanders deced, haveing had a bastard Child as she hath made oath in Court by Tom, an Indian slave belonging to ye sd estate. . . . It's ordered y^t ye sd Phoebe serve ye sd [John] Cockrell [the administrator of the estate of Sanders] . . . two yeares and a half. . . . *OB 1678–98, Part 2, 680.* [Cockrell paid the fine of 500 pounds of tobacco.]

961. 23 Nov. 1694—Anne Witter als Cook, base child of Phoebe Witter als Cook as she hath made oath begotten by Tom, an Indian slave belonging to ye estate of Mr Ebenezer Sanders deced, is bound by this Court to serve Jno Cockrell. . . . *OB 1678–98, Part 2, 681.*

962. 17 Jan. 1694/95—Jno Wornom & Willm Yarratt, Churchwardens of Fairfeilds parish against Michael Hurst continued to ye next Court. *OB 1678–98, Part 2, 684.*

963. 20 Feb. 1694/95—Jane Rich (bastard child of Christian Rich, servant to Jane Lynton) being about a yeare old is bound hereby to serve Anthony Lynton or his assigns untill she shall attaine to eighteen yeares of age. . . . *OB 1678–98, Part 2, 686.*

964. 20 Feb. 1694/95—Jno East, serv^t formerly to Martha Norris now to James Edney . . . having absented himselfe from ye sd Norris her service six monthes as appeares by certificate from Coll. Jno Carter and Capt Jno Pinckard dated in June & December before such assignment, It's therefore ordered y^t ye sd Jno East service his sd master or his assigns (after his indented or accustomed time expired) twelve monthes for his sd default. *OB 1678–98, Part 2, 686.*

965. 20 Feb. 1694/95—Richard Staples, having exhibited a complaint ag^t Capt. Jno Haynie y^t he hath been contrary to ye law of this Country continueingly drawn into service by the sd Capt. Haynie and hath served his full time, yet is still detained as a serv^t & refuseth to sett him free or allow necessaryes fitting for a Christian . . . and Richd Haynie appearing in defense & on behalfe of ye sd Capt Haynie (being absent) . . . It's therefore ordered y^t ye sherriff take ye sd Richd Haynie into Custody and remove him from ye Barr & ordered y^t y^e

sd Capt Haynie appeare ye next Court and answer ye Complaint of ye sd Staples. *OB 1678–98, Part 2, 687.*

966. 20 Feb. 1694/95—Jno Webb brings suit against Wm Muckleteer for four years service wch he declared due to him ye plt. from ye Defend^t for valluable consideration reced . . . ye Defend^t by Richd Haynie his Atorney. . . . *OB 1678–98, Part 2, 686.* [Portions of the document are badly worn. Another entry of John Webb and William Muckleteer is on page 689.]

967. 20 June 1695—Richd Staples, haveing absented himselfe from his master, Mr Jno Haynie Senr, his service under pretence of some complaint he had to make to this Court ag^t him and he ye sd Staples not showing any just cause for such Complaint, It's therefore ordered y^t he forthwith returne to his sd Master's service. *OB 1678–98, Part 2, 698.*

968. 22 Aug. 1695—Jno Webb brought suit ag^t Wm Muckleteer and not appearing to prosecute a nonsuit is granted ye sd Muckleteer ag^t ye sd Webb & ordered ye sd Webb pay damages according to law wth Costs or else exuction. *OB 1678–98, Part 2, 705.*

969. 22 Aug. 1695—. . . on ye Complaint of Mrs Anne Ladner y^t her serv^t named Rach^{ll} Freebone had feloniously taken from her certain goods, To witt a canvas sheet, three plates & a cupp & suspected divers persons for receiving & concealing ye sd goods. . . . *OB 1678–98, Part 2, 706.* [The items were found in the possession of certain persons and Rachel was to receive 20 lashes; however, Mrs. Ladner requested that Rachel be acquitted of such punishment.]

970. 18 Sept. 1695—Margrett Chapman, serv^t to Mr Jno Hughlett Senr, haveing had a bastard child by Tho: Thompson (as she hath made oath) in the time of her service, It is ordered she serve her sd master for her sd default two yeares (after her time by Indenture, Custome or otherwise shall be expired according to Law. *OB 1678–98, Part 2, 709.* [Charles Harris paid 500 pounds of tobacco, and Chapman's punishment was remitted.]

971. 17 Oct. 1695—Jno Fipps, now serv^t to Mr Richd Haynie & formerly to others, petitioned this Court that having served out his time by Custome, Indenture or otherwise for wch he came into this Country to serve, he might be free, And ye sd Mr Haynie haveing produced an agreem^t under ye sd Fipps his hand made before Capt. Wm Jones . . . obligeing ye said Fipps to serve his then master Alexander Weatherstone, his heires, or assigns from ye 25th of December 1693 untill four yeares would be expired. It's therefore ordered y^t

ye sd Fipps accordingly serve until the sd term be fully ended. *OB 1678–98, Part 2, 713.*

972. 18 Dec. 1695—Katherine Rutter, haveing had a bastard Child in ye time of service begotten on her as she hath made oath in Court by Tho: Hughes, It's ordered on ye motion by her master Mr Thomas Hughlett y^t she serve him or his assigns for her sd default according to act & y^t she be excused from punishment, her sd master haveing assumed to pay ye fine, And further ordered that ye sherriffe take ye sd Hughes into Custody untill he enter bond wth security to save ye parrish harmless. *OB 1678–98, Part 2, 714.*

973. 19 Dec. 1695—Jno Phips, having run away and been absent from his master Mr Richard Haynie for whose recover his sd master haveing been at charge & expence besides the want of his services. . . . *OB 1678–98, Part 2, 716.* [Phips was to serve an additional one year and pay cost of court for having run away. In the margin of the page the name is spelled Phipps.]

974. 19 Dec. 1695—John Webb ag^t William Mackleteer in Chancery continued. *OB 1678–98, Part 2, 716.*

975. 15 Jan. 1695/96—William Stott, serv^t to Mr John Taylor, being brought to this Court to be adjudged to be fourteen yeares of age and ordered that he serve his said master. *OB 1678–98, Part 2, 719.*

976. 20 May 1696—Thomas MacDovett, Servt to Mr Jno Farnefold, is by ye Court adjudged to be eleven yeares of age & ordered he serve his said Master or his assignes according to Law. Charles Macgee, serv^t to Edward Saunders, is adjudged by the Court to be seventeen yeares of age & ordered that he serve his said Master or his assigns according to Law. Alexander Adire, serv^t to Tho: Baker, is adjudged by the Court to be twelve yeares old and ordered that he serve his said master or his assignes according to Law. John Cammell, serv^t to Mr Edwd Feilding, is by the Court adjudged to be sixteene yeares of age and ordered that he serve his said master or his assigns according to Law. *OB 1678–98, Part 2, 722.*

977. 20 May 1696—Owen Jones, serv^t to Mr Richard Rogers, is by the Court adjudged to be eleven yeares of age & ordered that he serve his said Master or his assignes according to Law. *OB 1678–98, Part 2, 723.*

978. 15 July 1696—William Thompson, serv^t to Richard Nutt, is by the Court adjudged fourteene yeares of age & ordered he serve his said master according to Law. *OB 1678–98, Part 2, 732.*

979. 15 July 1696—James Macgee, serv^t to Charles Nelms, is by the Court adjudged thirteene yeares of age & ordered he serve his said Master according to Law. *OB 1678–98, Part 2, 732.*

980. 15 July 1696—Certificate is granted Mr Denis Eyes for five hundred & fifty acres of Land for the Importation of eleven persons into this Colony the said Eyes haveing made oath in Court he never made use of any of the said Rights.

    Tho: Aldwell   Marg^t May
    Barbara Jackson   Isabell Mason
    Jane Thompson   Wm Twison
    Teige Mackdanell   Kath Smith
    Gillicrest Oheart   Jno Ogan
    Sam^{ll} Camell

OB 1678–98, Part 2, 733.

981. 15 July 1696—Certificate is granted Mr John Hanye Senr for four hundred and fifty acres of land for the Importation of nine persons into this Colony, the said Mr Haynie haveing made oath in Court he never made use of the Rights vizt

    Richard Burgess   Jane Peterson
    John Beard   John Macgill
    Joseph Bland   Luke Demeratt
    Thomas Harley   Tho: Hope
    Abigaile ___

OB 1678–98, Part 2, 733. [The name is spelled Haynie in the margin of the page.]

982. 15 July 1696—Certificate is granted Mr Richard Haynie for two hundred acres of Land for the Importation of four persons into this Colony, the said Mr Haynie haveing made oath in Court he never made use of any of the said Rights vizt

    Morris Brassill   John Gurrill
    Mary Stephens   Elinor Ormsby

OB 1678–98, Part 2, 733.

983. 15 July 1696—Certificate is granted Mr John Harris for two hundred & fifty acres of Land for the Importation of five persons into this Colony, the said Harris haveing made oath in Court he never made use of any of the said Rights.

    James Ward   Jamose Milligin
    Neal MaCarty   George Runkin

Henry Armstrong
OB 1678–98, Part 2, 733.

984. 16 Sept. 1696—Benjn Soape, serv^t to Capt Wm Jones, is by the Court adjudged seventeen yeares of age and ordered to serve his said master according to Law. *OB 1678–98, Part 2, 740.*

985. 16 Sept. 1696—Phebe Cooke, servant to Mr John Cockrell, haveing had a bastard child as she hath made oath by Robert Cliford in the time of her service, It's ordered she serve her said master for her said default two yeares according to Law and ordered the sheriffe take her into Custody and give her thirty lashes on her bare back according to Law unless she give good caution to pay the fine of ten pounds according to Law and ordered the sheriff summon the said Reputed father to the next Court to give caution to save the parish harmless. *OB 1678–98, Part 2, 741.* [In the next entry, John Cockrell agrees to pay Cooke's fine of 2,000 pounds of tobacco, and Cooke was to serve him three years.]

986. 5 March 1696/97—Nathaniell Walker, servant to Mr Cuthbert Spann, is by the Court adjudged thirteene yeares old and ordered that he serve his said master according to Law. Andrew Wright, servant to Mr Cuthbert Spann, is by the Court adjudged twelve yeares of age and ordered that he serve his said master according to Law. John Meath, servant to Mr John Downing, is by the Court adjudged fifteene yeares of age and ordered that he serve his said master according to Law. Joseph Gately, servant to Mr John Coles estate, is by the Court adjudged twelve yeares of age and ordered that he serve those who are intrusted with the said estate according to Law. John Johnson, servant to Mr Wm Nutt, is by the Court adjudged fifteene yeares of age and ordered he serve his said master according to Law. Robert Mitchell, servant to Mr Thomas Bushrod, is by the Court adjudged eleven yeares of age and ordered that he serve his said master according to Law. John Maxfield, servant to Henry Franklin, is by the Court adjudged twelve yeares old and ordered that he serve his said master according to Law. John Cammell, serv^t to Mr James Waddy, is by the Court adjudged thirteene yeares old and ordered that he serve his said master according to Law. James Macmend, serv^t to Mr James Waddy, is by the Court adjudged twelve yeares of age and ordered that he serve his said master according to Law. James Moore, serv^t to Mr Thomas Taylor, is by the Court adjudged fourteene yeares of age and ordered that he serve his said master according to Law. James Doak, serv^t to Mr John Harris, is by the Court adjudged sixteene yeares old and ordered that he serve his said master according to Law. Joseph Oliver, serv^t to Mr John Harris, is by the Court adjudged twelve yeares of age and ordered he serve his said master according to Law. *OB 1678–98, Part 2, 758, 759.*

987. 22 April 1697—John Webb brings suit ag^t William Wood for that the said Wood being a servant to one John Lenham by covenant as assignee of William Hill in or about November 1694 the said Webb bought the said William of the said Lenham for which he was to give two thousand pounds of tobacco and caske but the said William haveing sometime runaway from the said Lenham for which he was at five hundred pounds of tobacco charge for his retakeing which the said William ought to satisfie the said William did then promise & assume to the said Webb that if he would pay the said Lenham the five hundred pounds of tobacco he would serve him halfe a yeare after his time by Covenant ended which five hundred pounds of tobacco the said Webb hath paid to the said Lenham yett the said William refuseth to comply with his promise the said covenanted time being ended. *OB 1678–98, Part 2, 768.* [John Webb brought suit against Wood for performance of the said covenant. The case was referred to a jury, and Wood was ordered to serve half a year or pay Webb 500 pounds of tobacco and cost of court.]

988. 25 July 1697—John Dalton, servant to Walter Dunne, haveing been brought by his master to Court to be adjudged for his age whom the Court doth esteeme to be at least nineteene yeares old but the said Dalton affirmeing that he hath Indentures which were to come into this Country in another ship. It's ordered that he have hereby for one month according to Law to enquire for such Indentures and in Case none appeares the next Court that he serve his said master according to the Custome of the Country. *OB 1678–98, Part 2, 779.*

989. 25 July 1697—Thomas Cavenah, serv^t to Mr Thomas Banks, being brought to this Court to be adjudged is by the Court adjudged sixteene yeares of age and ordered to serve his said Master according to Law. *OB 1678–98, Part 2, 780.*

990. 25 July 1697—Nicholas Hutchinson, servant to William Keene, being brought to this Court to be adjudged is by the Court adjudged thirteene years of age and ordered he serve his said Master according to Law. *OB 1678–98, Part 2, 780.*

991. 25 July 1697—Manns Handling, serv^t to Anthony Steptoe, being brought to this Court to be adjudged is by the Court adjudged sixteene yeares of age and ordered he serve his said master according to Law. *OB 1678–98, Part 2, 780.*

992. 25 July 1697—John Burke, serv^t to Richard Pemberton, haveing been brought by his said master to be adjudged for his age & the said John haveing produced an Indenture wherein he is bound an apprentice to serve Aaron Whitson or his assignes seaven yeares and the said Pemberton haveing ... that he purchased the said John for seven yeares service & noe more, It's ordered the said John serve the said terme of seven yeares & noe longer the said Pemberton haveing owned he bought him but for that terme. *OB 1678–98, Part 2, 780.* [Burke may have been an apprentice; however, there isn't any mention of a trade to be learned or any schooling.]

993. 25 July 1697—Ignatius Oliver & Catho: MacDonnell haveing both attended this Court two days for ye proofe of the nuncupative will of Tho: Austen deced, It's ordered they be allowed each forty pounds of tobacco p day according to Law out of the sd deced estate als Ex.

18 Aug. 1697—William Covenah, servant to Mr Wm Wildy, being brought to this Court to be adjudged is by the Court adjudged sixteen yeares of age and ordered he serve his said Master according to Law. *OB 1678–98, Part 2, 782.* [In the margin the name is spelled Cavenah.]

994. 18 Aug. 1697—Edward Peters, serv^t to Mr Rawl: Travers, being brought to Court to be judged is by the Court adjudged thirteen yeares of age and ordered he serve his said Master according to Law. *OB 1678–98, Part 2, 784.*

995. 16 Feb. 1697/98—Peter Suillivant, servant to Walter Jenkins, being brought to this Court to be adjudged is by the Court adjudged to be seventeene yeares old and ordered he serve his said Master according to Law. *OB 1678–98, Part 2, 801.*

996. 16 Feb. 1697/98—Robert Hughs, servant to Mr Richard Hanieye [Haynie], being brought to this Court to be adjudged is by the Court adjudged twelve yeares of age and ordered he serve his said Master according to Law. *OB 1678–98, Part 2, 801.*

997. 16 Feb. 1697/98—Mary Farrel, serv^t to Mr John Downing, haveing had a bastard Child in the time of her service by Tho: Blach [or Biach] as she hath made oath, It's ordered she serve her said Master for her said default twelve monthes according to Law and also ordered her punishment be remitted, the said Mr Downing haveing in Court assumed the payment of her fine. *OB 1678–98, Part 2, 801.*

998. 16 Feb. 1697/98—Sam^{ll} Witherton, serv^t to John Baily, being brought to this Court to be adjudged is by the Court adjudged to be nine yeares of age and ordered he serve his said Master according to Law. *OB 1678–98, Part 2, 801*.

999. 16 Feb. 1697/98—Thomas Williams, servant to Mr Christopher Neale, being brought to this Court to be adjudged is by the Court adjudged to be sixteene yeares of age and ordered he serve his said master according to Law. *OB 1678–98, Part 2, 801*.

1000. 16 Feb. 1697/98—Margarett Chapman, servant to Mr Peter Coutanceau, haveing had a bastard Child in the time of his service as she hath made oath by Richard Calphew, It's ordered she serve her said Master for her said Default twelve monthes according to Law and also ordered that her punishment be remitted, the said Mr Coutanceau haveing in Court assumed the payment of her fine. *OB 1678–98, Part 2, 801*.

1001. 16 Feb. 1697/98—Christopher King, servant to Mr Thomas Hughlett, being brought to this Court to be adjudged is by the Court adjudged to be fifteene yeares of age and ordered he serve his said master according to Law. *OB 1678–98, Part 2, 801*.

1002. 20 Aprill 1698—William Macarty, servant to Richard Swanson, being brought to the Court to be adjudged, is by the Court adjudged to be fourteene yeares and a halfe old but the Richard by his wife Elizabeth Swanson in Court haveing the advantage of the Law in such cases doth acknowledge himselfe with six yeares service and order to serve his said master six yeares and noe longer. *OB 1678–98, Part 2, 815*.

1003. 20 Aprill 1698—William Wilson, serv^t to John Bryant, being brought to this Court to be adjudged, is by the Court adjudged to be fifteene yeares old and a halfe but the said Bryant by his wife in Court declaring he would be satisfied with six yeares service from the said Wilson. It's ordered he serve his said master six yeares & noe longer. *OB 1678–98, Part 2, 815*.

1004. 20 Aprill 1698—Edmond Murrow, serv^t to Mr John Bayly, being brought to the Court to be adjudged, is by the Court adjudged eleven yeares old but by the Consent of his Master in Court, It's ordered he serve his said Master nine yeares and noe longer. *OB 1678–98, Part 2, 815*.

1005. 20 Aprill 1698—Matthias Chetwood, serv^t to Mrs Elizabeth Banks, being brought to this Court to be adjudged is by the Court adjudged to be fourteene yeares of age and ordered he serve his said Master according to Law. *OB 1678–98, Part 2, 815*.

1006. 20 April 1698—Raley Turloraldy, servant to Ignatius Oliver, being brought to this Court to be adjudged is by the Court adjudged to be fifteene yeares of age and ordered he serve his said master according to Law. *OB 1678–98, Part 2, 815.*

1007. 20 April 1698—John Loynes, serv^t to John Cockrell, being brought to this Court to be adjudged, is by the Court adjudged to be thirteene yeares of age and ordered he serve his said master according to Law. *OB 1678–98, Part 2, 815.*

1008. 20 Aprill 1698—Alexander Browne, serv^t to Thomas Brewer, being brought to this Court to be adjudged, is by the Court adjudged eighteene yeares of age and ordered he serve his said Master according to Law. *OB 1678–98 Part 2, 815.*

1009. 20 Aprill 1698—Robert Merrill, serv^t to Lazarus Taylor, being brought to this Court to be adjudged, is by the Court adjudged to be nineteene yeares of age and ordered he serve his said master according to Law. *OB 1678–98, Part 2, 815.*

1010. 20 Aprill 1698—Edward Forrester, serv^t to Capt Spencer Motrom being brought to this Court to be adjudged, is by the Court adjudged to be fourteene yeares of age and ordered he serve his said Master according to Law *OB 1678–98, Part 2, 815.*

1011. 20 Aprill 1698—Andrew Gallaway, serv^t to Pitts Curtis, being brought to this Court to be adjudged, is by the Court adjudged to be fourteene yeares of age and ordered he serve his said master according to Law. *OB 1678–98, Part 2, 816.*

1012. 20 Aprill 1698—Henry Gallion, serv^t to John Haynie, is by the Cour adjudged to be twelve yeares old and noe more for the paym^t [payment] of hi Levy. *OB 1678–98, Part 2, 816.*

1013. 20 Aprill 1698—John Henry, servant to Mrs Jane Yarrat, being brought to this Court to be adjudged, is by the Court adjudged to be thirteene yeares of age and ordered to serve his said master according to Law. *OB 1678– 98, Part 2, 817.*

1014. 20 Aprill 1698—George Marsh, serv^t to Anthony Hanye, being brought to this Court to be adjudged, is by the Court adjudged to be fifteen yeares of age and ordered to serve his said Master according to Law. *OB 1678-*

98, Part 2, 817. [The name is spelled Haynie in the margin of the page.]

1015. 21 April 1698—Jane Muckfannon, serv^t to Mr Christopher Neale, haveing had a bastard Child in the time of her service, It's ordered she serve her said Master one yeare for her said Default according to Law and ordered that the sheriffe take the said Jane into Custody & give her twenty lashes on the bare back for her sd default. *OB 1678–98, Part 2, 820.*

1016. 21 April 1698—John Purney & Katherine his wife, serv^{ts} to Tho: Hughlett, haveing made oath they attended this Court each eleven dayes, being summoned on the behalfe of Edwd Watkins concerning a horse in difference between John Bush & John Turner, It's ordered the said Hughlett be allowed forty pounds of tobacco p[er] day for each of his said servants according to Law and ordered the said Watkins pay the same with Costs als ex. *OB 1678–98, Part 2, 820.*

1017. 18 May 1698—Morgan Price, serv^t to Mr Thomas Wynter, being brought to this Court to be adjudged, is by the Court adjudged to be sixteen yeares of age and ordered that he serve his said Master according to Law. *OB 1678–98, Part 2, 822.*

1018. 18 May 1698—William Calfew, base child of Richard Calfew and Margaret Chapman, is bound apprentice to serve Mr Peter Coutanceau or his assigns untill he arrives to twenty one years of age. *OB 1678–98, Part 2, 822.*

1019. 18 May 1698—John Murrow, serv^t to John Ingram, being brought to this Court to be adjudged, is by the Court adjudged to be fifteene yeares of age and ordered that he serve his said Master according to Law. *OB 1678–98, Part 2, 822.*

1020. 18 May 1698—John Poore, serv^t to Coll. Sam^{ll} Griffin, being brought to this Court to be adjudged, is by the Court adjudged to be seventeene yeares of age and ordered he serve his said Master according to Law. *OB 1678–98, Part 2, 823.*

1021. 19 May 1698—Matthew Jackman, serv^t to Capt Rodham Kenner, being brought to this Court to be adjudged, is by the Court adjudged to be twelve yeares of age and ordered he serve his said Master according to Law. *OB 1678–98, Part 2, 824.*

1022. 19 May 1698—Denis Macarty, servant to Mr Peter Coutanceau, being brought to this Court to be adjudged, is by this Court adjudged to be fifteene yeares of age and ordered he serve his said Master according to Law. *OB 1678–98, Part 2, 824.*

1023. 19 May 1698—Tho: Smith, servant to Capt Rodham Kenner, being brought to this Court to be adjudged, is by the Court adjudged to be seventeene yeares of age and ordered he serve his said Master according to Law. *OB 1678–98, Part 2, 824.*

1024. 19 May 1698—Richard Burk, serv^t to Capt Rodham Kenner, being brought to this Court to be adjudged, is by the Court adjudged to be ten yeares of age and ordered he serve his said Master according to Law. *OB 1678–98, Part 2, 824.*

1025. 19 May 1698—Phil Sennett, servant to Capt Rodham Kenner, being brought to this Court to be adjudged, is by the Court adjudged to be ten yeares of age and ordered he serve his said Master according to Law. *OB 1678–98, Part 2, 824.*

1026. 19 May 1698—Dan^{ll} Bryant, serv^t to Mrs Elizabeth Kenner, being brought to this Court to be adjudged, is by the Court adjudged to be fourteene yeares of age and ordered he serve his said M^{rs} or her assignes according to Law. *OB 1678–98, Part 2, 824.*

1027. 15 June 1698—Edward Williams, servant to Mr Hancock Lee, being brought to this Court to be adjudged, is by the Court adjudged to be ten yeares old and ordered he serve his said master or his assignes according to Law. *OB 1678–98, Part 2, 826.*

1028. 20 July 1698—Thomas Abraham, servant to Josias Gaskins, being brought to this Court to be adjudged, is by the Court adjudged to be twelve yeares of age and ordered he serve his said Master according to Law. *OB 1678–98, Part 2, 828.*

1029. 20 July 1698—Thomas Walcupp, servant to Joseph Venables, being brought to this Court to be adjudged, is by the Court adjudged to be nine yeares of age and ordered he serve his said Master according to Law. *OB 1678–98, Part 2, 828.*

1030. 17 Aug. 1698—Andrew Grey, serv^t of Thomas Hayes, being brought to this Court to be adjudged, is by the Court adjudged to be twelve yeares of age and ordered he serve his said Master according to Law. *OB 1678–98, Part 2, 836.*

1031. 21 Sept. 1698—Owen Oneale, serv^t to Capt Wm Jones, being brought to this Court to be adjudged, is by the Court adjudged to be seventeene yeares of age and ordered he serve his said Master according to Law. *OB 1678–98, Part 2, 837.*

1032. 21 Sept. 1698—James Smyth, serv^t to Jno Ingram, being brought to this Court to be adjudged, is by the Court adjudged to be fourteene yeares of age but his said Master haveing in Court remitted a year's service, It's ordered he serve his sd Master Rem^r [remainder] of the said term according to Law. *OB 1678–98, Part 2, 837.*

1033. 16 Nov. 1698—John Birk, servant to Mr James Waddy, being brought to this Court to be adjudged, is by the Court adjudged to be thirteene yeares of age and ordered to serve his said Master according to Law. *OB 1678–98, Part 2, 841.*

1034. 16 Nov. 1698—Symon Holland, serv^t to Mr James Waddy, being brought to this Court to be adjudged, is by the Court adjudged to be fourteene yeares of age but his said master abateing him two yeares of service which he ought to serve by Law, It's ordered he serve his said Master the Remainder according to Law. *OB 1678–98, Part 2, 841.*

1035. 16 Nov. 1698—Terrence Bourne, servant to Elizabeth Sheeres widow, being brought to this Court to be adjudged, is by the Court adjudged to be eighteene yeares of age and ordered he serve his said Mistress according to Law. *OB 1678–98, Part 2, 841.*

1036. 16 Nov. 1698—Andrew Harrison, serv^t to Charles Moorehead, being brought to this Court to be adjudged, is by the Court adjudged to be eleven yeares of age but his said Master in Court abateing him one yeare's service of his time he ought to serve by Law, It's ordered he serve his said Master the Remainder according to Law. *OB 1678–98, Part 2, 842.*

1037. 16 Nov. 1698—Jacob Keley, servant to John Lewis, being brought to this Court to be adjudged, is by the Court adjudged to be fifteene yeares of age and ordered he serve his said Master according to Law. *OB 1678–98, Part 2, 842.*

1038. 16 Nov. 1698—Charles Mulloy, servant to Mr Thomas Gaskins, being brought to this Court to be adjudged, is by the Court adjudged to be fourteene yeares of age and ordered to serve his said Master according to Law.

OB 1678–98, Part 2, 842.

1039. 16 Nov. 1698—David Cavenah, servant to Thomas Baker, being brought to this Court to be adjudged, is by the Court adjudged to be fourteene yeares of age and ordered to serve his said Master according to Law. *OB 1678–98, Part 2, 842.*

1040. 16 Nov. 1698—Richard Casey, servant to James Symmons, being brought to this Court to be adjudged, is by the Court adjudged to be fifteene yeares of age and ordered he serve his said Master according to Law. *OB 1678–98, Part 2, 842.*

1041. 16 Nov. 1698—James Bourne, servant to Joseph Humphryes, being brought to this Court to be adjudged, is by the Court adjudged to be fourteene yeares of age and ordered he serve his said Master according to Law. *OB 1678–98, Part 2, 842.*

1042. 16 Nov. 1698—Elizabeth Burke, servant to James Hill, being brought to this Court to be adjudged, is by the Court adjudged to be fifteene yeares of age and ordered he serve his said Master according to Law. *OB 1678–98, Part 2, 842.*

1043. 16 Nov. 1698—William Burke, servant to Mr John Curtis, being brought to this Court to be adjudged, is by the Court adjudged to be sixteene yeares of age and ordered he serve his said Master according to Law. *OB 1678–98, Part 2, 842.*

1044. 16 Nov. 1698—Timothy Bird, servant to Mr John Curtis, being brought to this Court to be adjudged, is by the Court adjudged to be fifteene yeares of age and ordered he serve his said Master according to Law. *OB 1678–98, Part 2, 842.*

1045. 16 Nov. 1698—Katherine Redman, servant to John Webb, haveing had a Bastard Child as she hath made oath in Court by Thomas Petty, It's ordered she serve for her said default one yeare according to Law. *OB 1678–98, Part 2, 843.*

1046. 17 Nov. 1698—John Emerson, servant to William Nelmes, being brought to this Court to be adjudged, is by the Court adjudged to be fifteene yeares of age and ordered he serve his said Master according to Law. *OB 1678–98, Part 2, 843.*

1047. 21 Dec. 1698—Richard Archer, servant to John Moore, being brought to this Court to be adjudged, is by the Court adjudged fourteene yeares old and ordered to serve his said Master according to Law. *OB 1678–98, Part 2, 847.*

1048. 21 Dec. 1698—John Hayes, servant to John Cockrell, being brought to this Court to be adjudged, is by the Court adjudged to be fourteene yeares of age & ordered he serve his said Master according to Law. *OB 1678–98, Part 2, 847.*

1049. 21 Dec. 1698—James Welch, servant to Mr Henry Brereton, being brought to this Court to be adjudged, is by the Court adjudged to be thirteene yeares of age and ordered that he serve his said Master according to Law. *OB 1678–98, Part 2, 847.*

1050. 21 Dec. 1698—Ralph Allen, servant to Theodore Baker, being brought to this Court to be adjudged, is by the Court adjudged to be fourteene yeares of age and ordered he serve his said Master according to Law. *OB 1678–98, Part 2, 847.*

1051. 21 Dec. 1698—William Deawy, serv^t to John Howton, being brought to this Court to be adjudged, is by the Court adjudged to be fourteene yeares of age and ordered that he serve his said Master according to Law. *OB 1678–98, Part 2, 847.*

1052. 21 Dec. 1698—Henry Davis, serv^t to Thomas Downing, being brought to this Court to be adjudged, is by the Court adjudged to be seventeene yeares of age & ordered he serve his said Master according to Law. *OB 1678–98, Part 2, 847.*

1053. 21 Dec. 1698—Matthew Simmons, serv^t to Mr Dan^{ll} Neale, being brought to this Court to be adjudged, is by the Court adjudged to be eleven yeares of age and ordered he serve his said Master according to Law. *OB 1678–98, Part 2, 847.*

1054. 21 Dec. 1698—James Beorane, serv^t to Thomas Berry, being brought to this Court to be adjudged, is by the Court adjudged to be fifteene yeares of age and ordered he serve his said Master according to Law. *OB 1678–98, Part 2, 847.*

1055. 21 Dec. 1698—Richard Nornitt, serv^t to Joseph Hudnall, being brought to this Court to be adjudged, is by the Court adjudged to be eleven yeares old and ordered he serve his said Master according to Law. *OB 1678–*

98, Part 2, 847.

1056. 21 Dec. 1698—Matthew Welch, serv^t to Mr William Harcum, being brought to this Court to be adjudged, is by the Court adjudged to be fifteene yeares of age and ordered he serve his said Master according to Law. *OB 1678–98, Part 2, 847.*

1057. 21 Dec. 1698—John Seaham, serv^t to Mr Peter Coutanceau, being brought to this Court to be adjudged, is by the Court adjudged to be fifteene yeares of age and ordered he serve his said Master according to Law. *OB 1678–98, Part 2, 847.*

1058. 21 Dec. 1698—John Bryan, servant to Mr Peter Coutanceau, being brought before this Court to be adjudged, is by the Court adjudged to be twelve yeares old and ordered he serve his said Master according to Law. *OB 1678–98, Part 2, 847.*

1059. 21 Dec. 1698—Francis Macarmick, serv^t to Tho: Gill, being brought before this Court to be adjudged, is by the Court adjudged to be thirteene yeares of age and ordered he serve his said Master according to Law. *OB 1678–98, Part 2, 848.*

1060. 21 Dec. 1698—Phillip Clissen, servant to Charles Nelms, being brought before this Court to be adjudged, is by the Court adjudged to be fifteene yeares of age and ordered he serve his said Master according to Law. *OB 1678–98, Part 2, 848.* [The name could be Cussen; Richard Cussion is in Document 1062.]

1061. 21 Dec. 1698—Loughlin Ryan, servant to Edward Sanders, being brought before this Court to be adjudged, is by the Court adjudged to be eighteene yeares of age and ordered he serve his said master according to Law. *OB 1678–98, Part 2, 848.*

1062. 21 Dec. 1698—Richard Cussion, servant to Mrs Eliza: Kenner, being brought before this Court to be adjudged, is by the Court adjudged to be thirteene yeares of age and ordered he serve his said M^rs according to Law. *OB 1678–98, Part 2, 848.*

1063. 21 Dec. 1698—Robt Tearney & Dan^ll Hogan, serv^ts to Capt Rodham Kenner, were by him this Day brought to Court to be adjudged of their age and there being but three Justices besides himselfe at the Court the said servants therefore could not be adjudged. *OB 1678–98, Part 2, 848.*

1064. 21 Dec. 1698—William Wooll, serv^t to Mr John Cralle, being this day brought to Court, his said Master who informed the Court that the said William had an Indenture for five yeares as alsoe affirmed by Capt Tho: Pretty John who sold the sd servant to the said Mr Cralle but that the said servant gave up his Indenture provided the said Pretty John would dispose of him to the said Cralle and caused therefore to serve the said Cralle eight yeares & the said servant haveing in Court owned the said Confession & affirmed that he is willing to serve the said terme of eight yeares, It's therefore ordered he serve the said terme to the said Mr Cralle according to his said Consents. *OB 1678–98, Part 2, 848.*

1065. 19 Jan. 1698/99—Morris Brassell, serv^t to Richard Key, being brought to this Court to be adjudged, is by the Court adjudged to be fourteene yeares of age and ordered to serve his said Master according to Law. *OB 1699–1713, Part 1, 1.*

1066. 19 Jan. 1698/99—Anne Pearle, serv^t to Capt William Houson, being brought to this Court to be adjudged, is by the Court adjudged to be fifteen years of age and ordered she serve her said Master according to Law. *OB 1699–1713, Part 1, 1.* [In the margin the name is spelled Howson.]

1067. 19 Jan. 1698/99—John Mason, serv^t to Thomas Hughlett, being brought to this Court to be adjudged is by the Court adjudged to be thirteen yeares of age & ordered he serve his said Master according to Law. *OB 1699–1713, Part 1, 1.*

1068. 19 Jan. 1698/99—Dowling Barry, serv^t to Mr John Bushrod, being brought to this Court to be adjudged, is by the Court adjudged to be fourteen yeares old and ordered he serve his said Master according to Law. *OB 1699–1713, Part 1, 1.*

1069. 19 Jan. 1698/99—John Poore, serv^t to Mr William Keene, being brought to this Court to be adjudged, is by the Court adjudged to be fourteen yeares of age and ordered he serve his said Master according to Law. *OB 1699–1713, Part 1, 1.*

1070. 19 Jan. 1698/99—Richard Duggle, serv^t to Mr John Bushrod, being brought to this Court to be adjudged, is by the Court adjudged to be fourteene yeares of age and ordered he serve his said Master according to Law. *OB 1699–1713, Part 1, 1.*

1071. 19 Jan. 1698/99—Michael Gill, serv^t to Thomas Shapleigh, being brought to this Court to be adjudged, is by the Court adjudged to be fifteene yeares of age and ordered he serve his said Master according to Law. *OB 1699–1713, Part 1, 1.*

1072. 19 Jan. 1698/99—James White, serv^t to Thomas Shapleigh, being brought to this Court to be adjudged, is by the Court adjudged to be fifteene yeares of age and ordered he serve his said Master according to Law. *OB 1699–1713, Part 1, 1.*

1073. 19 Jan. 1698/99—Symon White, serv^t to William Feilding, being brought to this Court to be adjudged, is by the Court adjudged to be fourteene yeares of age and ordered he serve his said Master according to Law. *OB 1699–1713, Part 1, 1.*

1074. 19 Jan. 1698/99—Matthew Carrell, serv^t to Mr William Keene, being brought to this Court to be adjudged, is by the Court adjudged to be seventeene yeares of age and ordered he serve his said Master according to Law. *OB 1699–1713, Part 1, 1.*

1075. 19 Jan. 1698/99—Michael Wood, serv^t to Capt William Jones, being brought to this Court to be adjudged, is by the Court adjudged to be fifteene yeares of age and a halfe and ordered he serve his said Master according to Law. *OB 1699–1713, Part 1, 2.*

1076. 19 Jan. 1698/99—Laurence Faugheigh, Servant to Edward Coles, being brought to this Court to be adjudged, is by the Court adjudged to be eighteene yeares of age and ordered he serve his said Master according to Law. *OB 1699–1713, Part 1, 2.*

1077. 19 Jan. 1698/99—Thomas Meighon, serv^t to Nicholas Merrica, being brought to this Court to be adjudged, is by the Court adjudged to be sixteene yeares of age and ordered he serve his said Master according to Law. *OB 1699–1713, Part 1, 2.*

1078. 19 Jan. 1698/99—John Allen, servant to Mr Cuthbert Spann, is being brought to this Court to be adjudged, is by the Court adjudged to be eighteene yeares of age and ordered he serve his said Master according to Law. *OB 1699–1713, Part 1, 2.*

1079. 19 Jan. 1698/99—Teige Kennady, serv^t to Hugh Stathem, being brought to this Court to be adjudged, is by the Court adjudged to be fifteene yeares of age and ordered he serve his said Master according to Law. *OB*

1699–1713, Part 1, 2.

1080. 19 Jan. 1698/99—Richard Brittain, serv^t to Henry Frankling, being brought to this Court to be adjudged, is by the Court adjudged to be thirteene yeares of age and ordered he serve his said Master according to Law. *OB 1699–1713, Part 1, 2.*

1081. 19 Jan. 1698/99—Robert Furney, being presented this Day to the Court by Capt Rodham Kenner to have his age adjudged for service, he haveing purchased the said Robert for Mr John Bertrand, the Court doe adjudge him to be twelve yeares old and ordered he serve his said Master ye sd Bertrand or his assignes according to Law. *OB 1699–1713, Part 1, 2.*

1082. 19 Jan. 1698/99—David Savage, servant to William Cornish, being brought to this Court to be adjudged, is by the Court adjudged to be fifteene yeares old and ordered he serve his said Master according to Law. *OB 1699–1713, Part 1, 2.*

1083. 19 April 1699—James Lane, servant to John Langsdon, being brought to this Court to be adjudged, is by the Court adjudged to be eleven yeares of age and ordered he serve his said Master according to Law. *OB 1699–1713, Part 1, 4.*

1084. 19 April 1699—Phillip Moglame [or Moglaime] & Cornelius Luitsey, serv^{ts} to Jno Webb, being brought to this Court to be adjudged, are by the Court adjudged to be both eighteene yeares of age and ordered they serve their said Master according to Law. *OB 1699–1713, Part 1, 4.*

1085. 19 April 1699—John Erwyn, serv^t to John Pope, being brought to this Court to be adjudged, is by the Court adjudged to be seventeene yeares of age and ordered he serve his said Master according to Law. *OB 1699–1713, Part 1, 4.*

1086. 19 April 1699—John Dowle, servant to Mr Christopher Neale, being brought to this Court to be adjudged, is by the Court adjudged to be eleven yeares of age and his master relinguishing him a year's service, It's ordered he serve his said Master the residue according to Law. *OB 1699–1713, Part 1, 4.*

1087. 19 April 1699—Henry Wilson, servant to Alexander Witherstone, being brought to this Court to be adjudged, is by the Court adjudged to be sixteene yeares of age and ordered he serve his said Master according to Law.

OB 1699–1713, Part 1, 4.

1088. 19 April 1699—William Hall, servant to George Barratt, being brought to this Court to be adjudged, is by the Court adjudged to be thirteene yeares of age and ordered he serve his said Master according to Law. *OB 1699–1713, Part 1, 4.*

1089. 19 April 1699—Loughly Flannerell, servant to Binsent Garner, being brought to this Court to be adjudged, is by the Court adjudged to be eighteene yeares of age and ordered he serve his said Master according to Law. *OB 1699–1713, Part 1, 5.*

1090. 19 April 1699—John Chisholme, serv^t to Mr William Harcum, being brought to this Court to be adjudged, is by the Court adjudged to be eighteene yeares of age and ordered he serve his said Master according to Law. *OB 1699–1713, Part 1, 5.*

1091. 19 April 1699—Archibald Stutson, serv^t to Robert Reeves, being brought to this Court to be adjudged to be nine yeares of age and ordered he serve his said Master according to Law. *OB 1699–1713, Part 1, 5.*

1092. 19 April 1699—Roderick Dingwell, serv^t to Charles Vollen, being brought to this Court to be adjudged, is by the Court adjudged to be fifteene yeares of age and ordered he serve his said Master according to Law. *OB 1699–1713, Part 1, 5.*

1093. 19 April 1699—Derby Connor & Jone Carty, serv^{ts} to Tho: Waters, being brought to this Court to be adjudged, are by the Court adjudged, the said Connor eighteen & the said Carty seventeene yeares old and ordered they both serve their said Master according to Law. *OB 1699–1713, Part 1, 5.*

1094. 19 April 1699—John Lockman, serv^t to Richard Oldham, being brought to this Court to be adjudged, is by the Court adjudged to be thirteene yeares of age and ordered he serve his said Master according to Law. *OB 1699–1713, Part 1, 5.*

1095. 19 April 1699—James Cushion, serv^t to Capt Francis Voyer, being brought to this Court to be adjudged, is by the Court adjudged to be nine yeares of age and ordered he serve his said Master according to Law. *OB 1699–1713, Part 1, 5.*

1096. 19 April 1699—Patrick Balden, serv^t to Capt Francis Voyer, being brought to this Court to be adjudged, is by the Court adjudged to be eight yeares of age and ordered he serve his said Master according to Law. *OB 1699–1713, Part 1, 5.*

1097. 19 April 1699—James Steward, serv^t to Richard Flynt Senr, being brought to this Court to be adjudged, is by the Court adjudged to be thirteene yeares of age and ordered he serve his said Master according to Law. *OB 1699–1713, Part 1, 5.*

1098. 19 April 1699—Andrew Peacock, serv^t to Capt Geo: Cooper, being brought to this Court to be adjudged, is by the Court adjudged to be sixteene yeares of age and ordered he serve his said Master according to Law. *OB 1699–1713, Part 1, 5.*

1099. 19 April 1699—Thomas Goggin, serv^t to Mr William Wildy, being brought to this Court to be adjudged, is by the Court adjudged to be seventeene yeares of age and ordered he serve his said Master according to Law. *OB 1699–1713, Part 1, 5.*

1100. 19 April 1699—James Mulroany, serv^t to Denis Conway, being brought to this Court to be adjudged, is by the Court adjudged to be sixteene yeares of age and ordered he serve his said Master according to Law. *OB 1699–1713, Part 1, 5.*

1101. 19 April 1699—Dennis Loyney, serv^t to Enoch Hill, being brought to this Court to be adjudged, is by the Court adjudged to be thirteene yeares of age and ordered he serve his said Master according to Law. *OB 1699–1713, Part 1, 6.*

1102. 19 April 1699—James Shaw, serv^t to John Jones being brought to this court to be adjudged, is by the Court adjudged to be seventeene yeares of age and ordered he serve his said Master according to Law. *OB 1699–1713, Part 1, 6.*

1103. 19 April 1699—Certificate is granted to Charles Dermott to the Assembly for takeing up a runaway serv^t belonging to Joseph Palmer by name Patrick Farrell, the said serv^t being taken up above fifteene miles from his house. *OB 1699–1713, Part 1, 6.*

1104. 26 April 1699—William Odohothy, petitioned this Court that under Certaine Considerations he was to serve James Nipper and his heires which considerations being not performed he therefore prayed order to be acquitted from his service and Jane Nipper not being present, she being Exec of the said James, It's ordered that she have notice to appeare next Court to answer the said Complaint. *OB 1699–1713, Part 1, 7.* [In the margin the name is spelled Odohoty.]

1105. 21 June 1699—Charles Savage, servant to Mr Hancock Lee, being brought to this Court to be adjudged, is by the Court adjudged to be fifteene yeares of age and ordered he serve his said Master or his assignes according to Law. *OB 1699–1713, Part 1, 16.*

1106. 21 June 1699—Robert Gorden, servant to Sam^{ll} Mahen, being brought to this Court to be adjudged, is by the Court adjudged to be fifteene yeares of age and ordered he serve his said Master or his assignes according to Law. *OB 1699–1713, Part 1, 16.*

1107. 21 June 1699—William Patten, servant to Mr John Howson, being brought to this Court to be adjudged, is by the Court adjudged to be thirteene yeares of age and ordered he serve his said Master or his assignes according to Law. *OB 1699–1713, Part 1, 17.*

1108. 21 June 1699—George Dunbarr, servant to Joseph Palmer, being brought to this Court to be adjudged, is by the Court adjudged to be fourteene yeares of age and ordered he serve his said Master or his assignes according to Law. *OB 1699–1713, Part 1, 17.*

1109. 21 June 1699—George Dunken, servant to Nicholas Lehugh, being brought to this Court to be adjudged, is by the Court adjudged to be sixteene yeares of age and ordered he serve his said Master or his assignes according to Law. *OB 1699–1713, Part 1, 17.*

1110. 21 June 1699—Allen Durrough, serv^t to Capt William Jones, being brought to this Court to be adjudged, is by this Court adjudged to be thirteene yeares of age & ordered he serve his said Master or his assignes according to Law. *OB 1699–1713, Part 1, 17.*

1111. 21 June 1699—Robert Gordon, serv^t to Thomas Huske, being brought to this Court to be adjudged, is by the Court adjudged to be fifteene yeares of age and ordered he serve his said Master or his assignes according to Law. *OB 1699–1713, Part 1, 17.*

1112. 21 June 1699—Dennis Mahoany, servant to Mr Samuell Smith being brought to this Court to be adjudged, is by the Court adjudged to be eighteene yeares of age and ordered he serve his said Master or his assignes according to Law. *OB 1699–1713, Part 1, 17.*

1113. 21 June 1699—Dunkan Thompson, servant to Henry Frankling, being brought to this Court to be adjudged, is by the Court adjudged to be ten yeares of age and ordered he serve his said Master or his assignes according to Law. *OB 1699–1713, Part 1, 17.*

1114. 21 June 1699—Morris Bowle, servant to Thomas Dameron, being brought to this Court to be adjudged, is by the Court adjudged to be nineteene yeares of age and ordered he serve his said Master or his assignes according to Law. *OB 1699–1713, Part 1, 17.*

1115. 21 June 1699—Darby Leonard, servant to John Ingram, being brought to this Court to be adjudged, is by the Court adjudged to be thirteene yeares of age and ordered he serve his said Master or his assignes according to Law. *OB 1699–1713, Part 1, 17.*

1116. 21 June 1699—William Kidd, servant to Mr John Nickless, being brought to this Court to be adjudged, is by the Court adjudged to be thirteene yeares of age and ordered he serve his said Master or his assignes according to Law. *OB 1699–1713, Part 1, 17.*

1117. 21 June 1699—Patrick Fairweather, serv^t to Barthol. Schrever, being brought to this Court to be adjudged, is by the Court adjudged to be fifteene yeares of age and ordered he serve his said Master or his assignes according to Law. *OB 1699–1713, Part 1, 17.*

1118. 21 June 1699—William Bowman, serv^t to Isaac Gaskins, being brought to this Court to be adjudged, is by the Court adjudged to be seventeene yeares of age and ordered he serve his said Master or his assignes according to Law. *OB 1699–1713, Part 1, 17.*

1119. 21 June 1699—Teigue Swillivant, serv^t to William Bletsoe, being brought to this Court to be adjudged, the Court are of opinion he is above nineteene yeares of age and ordered he serve the Custom of the Country. *OB 1699–1713, Part 1, 18.*

1120. 21 June 1699—James Kelly, servant to Loughly Conlin, being brought to this Court to be adjudged, is by the Court to be sixteene yeares of age and ordered he serve his said Master or his assignes according to Law. *OB 1699–1713, Part 1, 18.*

1121. 21 June 1699—William Browne, servant to Thomas Brewer, being brought to this Court to be adjudged, is by the Court adjudged to be fourteene yeares of age and ordered he serve his said Master or his assignes according to Law. *OB 1699–1713, Part 1, 18.*

1122. 21 June 1699—David Power, servant to Capt Rodham Kenner, being brought to this Court to be adjudged, is by the Court adjudged eleven yeares old and ordered he serve his said Master according to Law. *OB 1699–1713, Part 1, 18.*

1123. 21 June 1699—Daniell Hogan, serv^t to Capt Rodham Kenner, being brought to this Court to be adjudged, is by this Court adjudged to be ten yeares of age and ordered he serve his said Master or his assignes according to Law. *OB 1699–1713, Part 1, 18.*

1124. 21 June 1699—Humphrey Groome, servant to John Cockrell, being brought to this Court to be adjudged, is by the Court adjudged to be nine yeares of age and ordered he serve his said Master according to Law. *OB 1699–1713, Part 1, 18.*

1125. 21 June 1699—John Wilson, serv^t to William Smith, being brought to this Court to be adjudged, is by the Court adjudged to be fifteene yeares of age and ordered he serve his said Master or his assignes according to Law. *OB 1699–1713, Part 1, 18.*

1126. 21 June 1699—James Smith, servant to William Winder, being brought to this Court to be adjudged, is by the Court adjudged to be seventeene yeares of age & ordered he serve his said Master or his assignes according to Law. *OB 1699–1713, Part 1, 18.*

1127. 21 June 1699—John Conner, servant to Thomas Smith, being brought to this Court to be adjudged, is by the Court adjudged to be seventeene yeares of age and ordered he serve his said Master according to Law. *OB 1699–1713, Part 1, 18.*

1128. 21 June 1699—Mary Williams, servant to John Walters, being brought to this Court to be adjudged, is by the Court adjudged to be seventeene yeares of age and ordered she serve her said Master or his assignes according to Law. *OB 1699–1713, Part 1, 18.*

1129. 21 June 1699—Morris Bevin, servant to Richard Lattemore, being brought to this Court to be adjudged, is by the Court adjudged to be seventeene yeares of age and ordered he serve his said Master or his assignes according to Law. *OB 1699–1713, Part 1, 18.*

1130. 21 June 1699—David Smith, serv^t to John Bryan, being brought to this Court to be adjudged, is by the Court adjudged to be sixteene yeares of age and ordered he serve his said Master and his assignes according to Law. *OB 1699–1713, Part 1, 18.*

1131. 21 June 1699—John Marriner, serv^t to Isaac Ester, being brought to this Court to be adjudged, the Court are of opinion he is above nineteene yeares of age & ordered he serve the Custom of the Country. *OB 1699–1713, Part 1, 18.*

1132. 21 June 1699—Hugh Peterson, serv^t to John Lewis, being brought to this Court to be adjudged, is by the Court adjudged to be eighteene yeares of age and ordered he serve his said Master or his assignes according to Law. *OB 1699–1713, Part 1, 19.*

1133. 21 June 1699—James Conner, servant to Charles Ingram, being brought to this Court to be adjudged, is by the Court adjudged to be seventeene yeares of age and ordered he serve his said Master or his assignes according to Law. *OB 1699–1713, Part 1, 19.*

1134. 21 June 1699—William Moore, servant to Mr Thomas Wynter, being brought to this Court to be adjudged, is by the Court adjudged to be eighteene yeares of age and ordered he serve his said Master or his assignes according to Law. *OB 1699–1713, Part 1, 19.*

1135. 21 June 1699—John Low, servant to Richard Hudnall, being brought to this Court to be adjudged, is by the Court adjudged to be nineteene yeares of age and ordered he serve his said Master or his assignes according to Law. *OB 1699–1713, Part 1, 19.*

1136. 21 June 1699—William Wooll, servant to Lazarus Taylor, being brought to this Court to be adjudged, is by the Court adjudged to be fourteene yeares of age and ordered he serve his said Master or his assignes according to Law. *OB 1699–1713, Part 1, 19.*

1137. 21 June 1699—Mary Merry Hearty, servant to Thomas Taylor, being brought to this Court to be adjudged, is by the Court adjudged to be sixteene yeares of age and ordered he [she] serve his [her] said Master or his assignes according to Law. *OB 1699–1713, Part 1, 19.*

189

1138. 21 June 1699—Michael Rareday, servant to Thomas Everard, being brought to this Court to be adjudged, is by the Court adjudged to be eleven yeares of age and ordered he serve his said Master or his assignes according to Law. *OB 1699–1713, Part 1, 19.*

1139. 21 June 1699—Gillian Scannell, servant to John Trimlett, being brought to this Court to be adjudged, is by the Court adjudged to be nineteene yeares of age & ordered she serve her said Master or his assignes according to Law. *OB 1699–1713, Part 1, 19.*

1140. 21 June 1699—William Pedds, serv^t to William Coppage, being brought to this Court to be adjudged, is by the Court adjudged to be thirteene yeares of age and ordered he serve his said Master or his assignes according to Law. *OB 1699–1713, Part 1, 19.*

1141. 21 June 1699—James Spratt, servant to Anthony Haine [Haynie] being brought to this Court to be adjudged, is by the Court adjudged to be eighteene yeares of age and ordered he serve his said Master or his assignes according to Law. *OB 1699–1713, Part 1, 19.*

1142. 22 June 1699—Sam^{ll} Cammell, serv^t to Mr Christopher Garlington, being brought to this Court to be adjudged, is by the Court adjudged to be eighteene yeares of age and ordered he serve his said Master or his assignes according to Law. *OB 1699–1713, Part 1, 25.*

1143. 22 June 1699—Ambrose Hawkins, serv^t to Mr Christopher Garlington, being brought to this Court to be adjudged when he becomes a tythable, the Court are of opinion he is thirteene yeares of age. *OB 1699–1713, Part 1, 25.*

1144. 22 June 1699—William Odohothy, haveing petitioned this Court that he was bound under and for certaine considerations to serve James Nipper, his heires which considerations being not performed wherefore he prayed order to be acquitted from his said service, It's ordered that if Jane Nipper adm^r of the said James Nipper doe not appeare the next Court and prove the considerations performed the said William be free from his said service. *OB 1699–1713, Part 1, 25.* [At a court held July 1699 William Odohothy was set free, but Jane Nipper, the widow of James Nipper, appealed the case. *OB 1699–1713, Part 1, 37.*]

1145. 22 June 1699—Elizabeth Hunt, servant to Cloud Tullos, being brought to this Court to be adjudged, is by the Court adjudged to be seventeene yeares of age and ordered she serve her said Master or his assignes according to Law. *OB 1699–1713, Part 1, 25*.

1146. 22 June 1699—Joane Murfew, serv^t to Nicholas Edwards, being brought to this Court to be adjudged, is by the Court adjudged to be fifteene yeares of age and ordered she serve her said Master according to Law. *OB 1699–1713, Part 1, 30*.

1147. 22 June 1699—William Nellagon, servant to Nicholas Edwards, being brought to this Court to be adjudged, is by the Court adjudged to be seventeene yeares of age and ordered he serve his said Master according to Law. *OB 1699–1713, Part 1, 30*.

1148. 17 Aug. 1699—Ordered that John Simpkins serve his Mrs Eliz^a Downing or her assignes four months after his accustomed or Indenture time is expired, the said service being due for his running away & other expenses in takeing him up. *OB 1699–1713, Part 1, 58*.

1149. 20 Sept. 1699—Certificate is granted to Dan^ll Swillivant three hundred acres of Land for the transportation of six persons into this Colony (vizt) George Armstronge, John Chambers, John Fegan, Richard Vuxon, John Cannady and John Smith, the said Dan^ll Swillivant haveing made oath in Court that he never made use of any of the said Rights. *OB 1699–1713, Part 1, 65*.

1150. 20 Sept. 1699—Certificate is granted to Major Rodham Kenner for five hundred acres of Land for the transportation of ten persons into this Colony vizt Thomas Stott, Thomas Smith, Mathew Jackman, Phillip Sennett, Richard Burke, Daniell Howland, David Poore, Richard Cushion, Robert Ferne, and Elizabeth Wilcox, the said Major Kenner made oath in Court that he never made use of any of the said Rights or any part of them. *OB 1699–1713, Part 1, 65*.

1151. 20 Sept. 1699—Certificate is granted Rawl Travers three hundred acres of Land for the transportation of six persons into this Colony (vizt) Laurence Fox, Edward Peters, Robert McGregory, Gowen Steward, Elizabeth Dobson & James Letherborough, the said Mr Travers haveing made oath in Court that he never made use of any of the said Rights. *OB 1699–1713, Part 1, 65*.

1152. 21 Sept. 1699—Certificate is granted Capt John Cralle for one thousand and fifty acres of Land for the transportation of one & twenty persons into this Colony (vizt) John Cralle, Dan^ll Neale, Ignatius Oliver, John Mast, James Carne, Ralph Holmes, Sarah Hutchins, Elinor Browne, Wm Batting,

John Lindsey, Mary Williams, Tho: Fitzgerrard, Cornelius Allen, Patrick Codd, William Wool, Allice Evans & Dan[ll] Dane, Phill Welsh, Thomas Phillips, Robert Phillips, John Owen, the said Cralle haveing made oath in Court that he never made use of any of the said Rights. *OB 1699–1713, Part 1, 66.*

1153. 21 Sept. 1699—Certificate is granted M[r] Peter Coutanceau for five hundred & fifty acres of Land for the transportation of eleven persons into this Colony (viz) James Mortemore, John Aro, Denis Macarty, Edw[d] Folio, Marg[t] Chapman, John Bryan, Tho: Walters, Henry Hutson, William Parker, Mary Day & John Hayes, the said Coutanceau haveing made oath in Court that he never made use of any of y[e] sd rights. *OB 1699–1713, Part 1, 66.*

1154. 20 Dec. 1699—John Knight, serv[t] to M[r] Peter Coutanceau, being brought to this Court to be adjudged, is by the Court adjudged to be seventeene yeares of age and ordered he serve his said Master according to Law. *OB 1699–1713, Part 1, 89.*

1155. 20 Dec. 1699—George Wigginton, serv[t] to Richard Tullos, being brought to this Court to be adjudged, is by the Court adjudged to be fifteene yeares of age and ordered he serve his said Master according to Law. *OB 1699–1713, Part 1, 89.*

1156. 21 Feb. 1699/1700—Idmund [Edmund ?] Connale, serv[t] to John Lynton, being brought to this Court to be adjudged, is by the Court adjudged to be seventeen yeares of age and ordered he serve his said Master according to Law. *OB 1699–1713, Part 1, 91.*

1157. 21 Feb. 1699/1700—John Fogershie, serv[t] to Christ[r] Neale, being brought to this Court to be adjudged, is by the Court adjudged to be ten yeares old and ordered he serve his said Master according to Law. *OB 1699–1713, Part 1, 91.*

1158. 21 Feb. 1699/1700—Mary Robins, servant to Cap[t] William Howson, having had a Child in the time of her service, It's ordered she serve her said Master one whole yeare according to Law and ordered that she serve Cap[t] Peter Hack six months after her time expired in compensation of her fine of five hundred pounds tobacco which the said Hack hath in Court assumed to pay and it is further ordered that the said Cap[t] Peter Hack pay the same according to Law als Ex. *OB 1699–1713, Part 1, 91.*

1159. 21 Feb. 1699/1700—Martha Hunter, servant to James Nipper, haveing had a base child in the time of her service by Timothy Riley as she hath made oath & the said Nipper haveing in Court assumed to pay five hundred pounds of tobacco fine for further default, It's ordered she serve her said Master one yeare & a halfe according to Law and ordered the said James pay the said five hundred pounds of Tobo according to Law als Ex. *OB 1699–1713, Part 1, 91.*

1160. 21 Feb. 1699/1700—Richard Dollins, servant to John Dawson, being brought to this Court to be adjudged, is by the Court adjudged to be fifteene yeares of age and ordered he serve his said Master according to Law. *OB 1699–1713, Part 1, 91.*

1161. 21 Feb. 1699/1700—William Anderson, serv^t to Mr Tho: Rout, being brought to this Court to be adjudged, is by the Court adjudged to be thirteene yeares of age and ordered he serve his said Master according to Law. *OB 1699–1713, Part 1, 91.*

1162. 21 Feb. 1699/1700—Richard Williams, serv^t to Richard Lattemore, being brought to this Court to be adjudged, is by the Court adjudged to be fourteene yeares of age and ordered he serve his said Master according to Law. *OB 1699–1713, Part 1, 91.*

1163. 21 Feb. 1699/1700—William Dunawon, serv^t to Christ^r Neale, being brought to this Court to be adjudged, is by the Court adjudged to be eight yeares old and ordered he serve his said Master according to Law. *OB 1699–1713, Part 1, 91.*

1164. 21 Feb. 1699/1700—David Thomas, serv^t to Mr Richard Nutt, being brought to this Court to be adjudged, is by the Court adjudged to be fifteene yeares of age and ordered he serve his said Master according to Law. *OB 1699–1713, Part 1, 91.*

1165. 17 April 1700—John Williams, servant to Mrs Elizabeth Bankes, being brought to this Court to be adjudged, is by the Court adjudged to be fifteene yeares of age and ordered he serve his said Master or his assignes according to Law. *OB 1699–1713, Part 1, 93.*

1166. 17 April 1700—Elinor Williams, serv^t to Mr Wm Harcum, being brought to this Court to be adjudged, is by the Court adjudged to be eighteene yeares old and ordered she serve her sd Master or his assignes according to Law. *OB 1699–1713, Part 1, 93.*

1167. 17 April 1700—Tho: Wells, serv^t to Jno Ingram, being brought to this

193

Court to be adjudged, is by the Court adjudged to be thirteene yeares of age and ordered he serve his said Master or his assignes according to Law. *OB 1699–1713, Part 1, 93.*

1168. 17 April 1700—John Thomas, serv^t to Dan^{ll} Sivillivant, being brought to this Court to be adjudged, is by the Court adjudged to be twelve yeares of age and ordered he serve his said Master or his assignes according to Law. *OB 1699–1713, Part 1, 93.*

1169. 17 April 1700—Hugh Price, serv^t to Mr James Rogers, being brought to this Court to be adjudged, is by the Court adjudged to be twelve yeares of age and ordered he serve his said Master or his assignes according to Law. *OB 1699–1713, Part 1, 93.*

1170. 17 April 1700—Arthur Thomas, serv^t to Capt Peter Hack, being brought to this Court to be adjudged, is by the Court adjudged to be seventeen yeares of age but the said Arthur haveing affirmed to this Court that he had Indentures for five yeares but that he was cheated out of them by Capt William Thornton who brought him into this Country, It's ordered that if the said Arthur shall not produce his Indenture the next Court or take such Court as the Law prescribes in order to prove or make vallid his said Indenture that the said Arthur serve his said Master or his assignes untill he arrives to four and twenty yeares of age according to Law. *OB 1699–1713, Part 1, 93.*

1171. 17 April 1700—John Pasternell, serv^t to Richard Flynt Junr, being brought to this Court to be adjudged, is by the Court adjudged to be fourteene yeares of age But he haveing in Court asserted that he had Indentures but were deteyned by Mr Gunery, the Merchant of the shipp wherein he arrived, It's ordered that provided the said John shall produce such Indenture to the next Court then to serve his said Master such time as therein shall be specified otherwise to serve his said Master or his assignes four & twenty yeares according to Law. *OB 1699–1713, Part 1, 94.*

1172. 17 April 1700—John Mahughen, serv^t to Capt Thomas Winder, being brought to this Court to be adjudged, is by the Court adjudged to be thirteene yeares of age & ordered he serve his said Master or his assignes according to Law. *OB 1699–1713, Part 1, 94.*

1173. 17 April 1700—Katherine Sivillivant on her own and her brother Owen Sivillivant . . . haveing this day Complained to this Court that Capt William Thornton whose shipp they arrived herein did deteyne their Indentures from them and that she could procure proofe thereof ag^t the said M^r

Thornton and that the said Indentures were good and sufficient & could prove the same, It's ordered of the same as affirmed (shee giveing or causeing the said Mr Thornton to have notice of this order) before Mr John Harris upon his Report to the next Court & such proofe the said matter to be determined the next Court according to such evidence & proofe as above said. *OB 1699–1713, Part 1, 94.*

1174. 18 April 1700—Thomas Lock, serv^t to Charles Moorehead, being brought to this Court to be adjudged, is by the Court adjudged eleven yeares old and ordered he serve his said Master or his assignes according to Law. *OB 1699–1713, Part 1, 95.*

1175. 19 June 1700—Owen Sivillivant, servant to Charles Nelmes, being brought to this Court to be adjudged, is by the Court adjudged eleven yeares old and ordered he serve his said Master or his assignes according to Law. *OB 1699–1713, Part 1, 100.*

1176. 17 July 1700—Langhly Rytim, serv^t to Mr Edwd Sanders, haveing absented himselfe from his Master's service fower dayes in the beginning of this month & his Master expending fower hundred pounds of tobb^o in his persuit, It's ordered he serve halfe a yeare for the same and the said Langhly haveing since runaway & his Master moveing this Court that he might be punished, It's ordered he have twenty lashes well laid on his bare back. *OB 1699–1713, Part 1, 104.*

1177. 17 July 1700—Mary Ferrel, servant to Mrs Elizabeth Downing, haveing had a Bastard Child in her said Mistress her service, It's ordered shee serve her said M^{rs} one yeare for her Default according to Law and halfe a yeare for her fine, her said Mistress haveing assumed the payment of five hundred pounds of tobacco to the Parish. *OB 1699–1713, Part 1, 105.*

1178. 17 July 1700—Jonie Whitten, serv^t to Dennis Conaway, haveing had a bastard Child in the time of her service by Matthew Canniday, It's ordered that she serve her said Master one yeare for her default according to Law and ordered that the sherriffe take her into custody and bring her to the next Court to receive punishment. *OB 1699–1713, Part 1, 105.*

1179. 16 Aug. 1700—Grace Grey, serv^t to Sam^{ll} Mahen, haveing had a bastard Child in the time of her service by William Humphreys, serv^t to William Coppage as she hath made oath, It's ordered shee serve her said Master one yeare for her said default according to Law and halfe a yeare for her fine, her said Master haveing assumed the paym^t of five hundred pounds of Tobacco to the Parish for her fine. *OB 1699–1713, Part 1, 119.*

1180. 16 Aug. 1700—Dennis Conaway hath in Court assumed the paym^t of five hundred pounds of Tobb^o to the Parish for his servant Grace Grey fine she haveing had a Bastard. *OB 1699–1713, Part 1, 119.*

1181. 16 Aug. 1700—Grace Grey, haveing this day in Court sworne a Bastard Child to William Humphreys, serv^t to William Coppage, It's ordered that the said Humphreys after his Indented or accustomed time be expired be accountable for the maintaining of the said Child according to Law. *OB 1699–1713, Part 1, 119.*

1182. 16 Aug. 1700—Jane Duke, serv^t to Mr Joseph Hoult, Petitioning this Court for her freedom being adjudged before Lt Coll Sam^{ll} Smith & Mr Peter Presly to serve Peter Maxwell & Mary his wife untill one & twenty yeares of age, the Court are of opinion the Law will not obleidge her to serve longer then eighteene yeares of age and ordered shee be free. *OB 1699–1713, Part 1, 120.* [Although the word apprentice is not used here, Jane Duke was actually an apprentice. She was bound an apprentice to Peter Maxwell 1 April 1684, at the age of three. Girls bound as apprentices were not to serve beyond the age of 18. *OB 1678–98, Part 1, 227*, details the record of her being apprenticed.]

1183. 23 Aug. 1700—John Cockrell and his servant Henry Harding, haveing each attended this Court three dayes as evidence on the behalfe of John Scott ag^t James White as the said Cockrell hath made oath, It's therefore ordered the said Scott pay the said Cockrell for the same two hundred and forty pounds of tobacco als Ex. *OB 1699–1713, Part 1, 128.*

1184. 15 Jan. 1700/01—Joseph Phillips, serv^t to Hannah Frankling, being brought to this Court to be adjudged, is by the Court adjudged to be seventeene yeares of age and ordered he serve his said Master or her assignes according to Law. *OB 1699–1713, Part 1, 140.*

1185. 15 Jan. 1700/01—John Robinson, serv^t to Mr Charles Lee, being brought to this Court to be adjudged, is by the Court adjudged to be sixteene yeares of age and ordered he serve his said Master or his assignes according to Law. *OB 1699–1713, Part 1, 140.*

1186. 15 Jan. 1700/01—George Medford, serv^t to Mr Thomas Waddy, being brought to this Court to be adjudged, is by the Court adjudged to be fourteene yeares of age and ordered he serve his said Master or his assignes according to Law. *OB 1699–1713, Part 1, 140.*

1187. 15 Jan. 1700/01—Margaret Lay, serv^t to Patrick Pollick, haveing had a Bastard Child in the time of her service, It's ordered she serve her said Master one year for her said default according to Law & halfe a yeare for her fine, her sd Master haveing in Court assumed the paym^t thereof to the Parish. *OB 1699–1713, Part 1, 141.*

1188. 15 Jan. 1700/01—Mary Eyes, haveing moved this Court that her servant man named Patrick McConner lay'd violent hands on her contrary to an Act of Assembly in that case made and provided and moved the benefitt thereof and the said Patrick being absent, It's ordered the sherriffe bring him to the next Court to answer to his said Default. *OB 1699–1713, Part 1, 141.*

1189. 19 Feb. 1700/01—John Chipman, serv^t to Mr Sam^{ll} Mahen, being brought to this Court to be adjudged, is by the Court adjudged to be fifteene yeares of age and ordered he serve his said Master or his assignes according to Law. *OB 1699–1713, Part 1, 142.*

1190. 19 Feb. 1700/01—Nicholas Murfew, serv^t to Mr Daniell Sivillivant, being brought to this Court to be adjudged, is by the Court adjudged to be ten yeares old and ordered he serve his said Master or his assignes according to Law. *OB 1699–1713, Part 1, 142.*

1191. 19 Feb. 1700/01—Mary Laurence, serv^t to Capt Thomas Winder, haveing had a bastard Child in the time of her service by William Harding as she hath made oath in Court and the said Capt Winder haveing in Court assumed the paym^t of her fine, It's therefore ordered she serve her said Master one yeare & a halfe after her time by Indenture or Custome be expired according to Law and further ordered that the said William enter into bond with goods and sufficient security to save the parish harmless. *OB 1699–1713, Part 1, 143.*

1192. 19 Feb. 1700/01—Elizabeth Wilcox, serv^t to Robert Reeves, haveing had a Bastard Child in the time of her service by Robert Clifford as she hath made oath in Court, It's ordered shee serve her Master one yeare according to Law and that the sherr: give her twenty lashes on her bare back for her said offense and that the said Robert the Reputed father enter into bond with good & sufficient security to save the parish harmless. *OB 1699–1713, Part 1, 144.*

1193. 22 Feb. 1700/01—Ordered that the sheriffe take into his Custody Mary Robins, servant to Mrs Sarah Houson and Mary Farrell, servant to Mrs Downing, and bring them to the next Court to answer to such things as shall be alleadged against them by the Churchwardens of St Stephens Parish and that the sheriffe faile not att his Perrill to performe this order. *OB 1699–1713, Part 1, 153.*

1194. 19 March 1700/01—Patrik [Patrick] Conner, petitioning this Court that he hath served his full terme of time that he came in for part to Dennis Eyes and part to his wife since his decease, yett the said wife refuseth to pay him either Corne or Cloaths and prayed order for the same and Martha Eyes, wife of the said Dennis, by her attorney alleadging that shee was unprovided at present to answer the said Complaint and prayed time till next Court the matter is referred therefore till next Court. *OB 1699–1713, Part 1, 153.*

1195. 16 April 1701—Hugh Miller, servant to Sam^{ll} Mahen, being brought to this Court to be adjudged, is by the Court adjudged to be nine yeares old and ordered he serve his said Master or his assignes according to Law. *OB 1699–1713, Part 1, 159.*

1196. 16 April 1701—William Edwards, serv^t to Mr John Taylor, being brought to this Court to be adjudged, is by the Court adjudged to be nine yeares old But the boy produceing an Indenture for fourteen yeares the Court adjudge the Indenture to be good. *OB 1699–1713, Part 1, 159.*

1197. 16 April 1701—Mable Newgent, servant to Joseph Holt haveing had a bastard Child as she hath made oath by Daniell Murphew, alsoe servant to the said Holt, It's ordered shee serve her said Master for her said Default according to Law and halfe a yeare for her fine her Master haveing engaged to pay the same. *OB 1699–1713, Part 1, 159.*

1198. 21 May 1701—Charles Lockiere, serv^t to Mr John Cralle, being brought to this Court to be adjudged, is by the Court adjudged to be fifteene yeares old and ordered he serve his said Master or his assignes according to Law. *OB 1699–1713, Part 1, 162.*

1199. 21 May 1701—Mary Farrell, late servant of Mrs Downing, haveing had a Bastard Child for which formerly shee was ordered to serve for her said Default & alsoe her fine assumed by her said Mistress and the said Mary refuseing to declare the father of her said illegitamate Child, It's ordered that the sheriffe take her into Custody and secure her in prison untill shee shall upon her oath declare the father of her Child or tell the Court shall otherwise determine therein. *OB 1699–1713, Part 1, 162.* [At a court held 22 May 1701, Mary Farrell named John Lyon, servant to Mrs. Downing, as the father of the child. *OB 1699–1713, Part 1, 164.*]

1200. 22 May 1701—Mary Anderson, serv^t to Mr Richard Pemberton, haveing had a bastard Child as she hath made oath by her Master, It's ordered shee serve the Parish of St Stephens for her said default according to Law and ordered that the said Pemberton enter into bond with good sufficient security to save the said Parish harmless. *OB 1699–1713, Part 1, 163.*

1201. 22 May 1701—Ordered that the sheriffe take Mary Robins, serv^t to Mrs Sarah Howson, into his Custody and bring her to the next Court to answer for her default in concealing the father of a bastard Child for which she hath had service awarded in this Court against her formerly according to Law and ordered that the sheriffe faile not in duty executing this order as he will answer the Contrary at his perrill. *OB 1699–1713, Part 1, 165.*

1202. 18 June 1701—Susannah Payton, servant to Jane Yarratt, haveing had a Bastard Child by William Dugard, another servant of the said Jane, It's ordered shee serve her said Mistress for her said default according to Law and ordered that after his Indented or accustomed time [is] expired the sheriffe take the said William into Custody & keepe him untill he shall give sufficient caution to save the Parish harmeless thence forward and to reimburse the Parish for all charges till that time accrewing [accruing] and the said Susannah haveing made her estate from Court, It's ordered that the sheriffe take her into Custody and bring her to the next Court to suffer such Penalty as by Law in such Cases is Inflicted. *OB 1699–1713, Part 1, 166.*

1203. 18 June 1701—John Burge, serv^t to Mr Peter Coutanceau, being brought to this Court to be adjudged, is by the Court adjudged to [be] fourteene yeares old & Mr Coutanceau in fafour [favor] of the said John haveing owned that he bought the said John But for eight yeares, It's ordered therefore that he serve his said Master or his assignes the said terme of eight yeares & no longer. *OB 1699–1713, Part 1, 166.*

1204. 16 July 1701—Margaret Lawson, presumed to be a free woman, haveing had a bastard Child as she hath confessed upon her oath by a negro called Daniell Webb and the said Marg^t haveing informed this Court that shee is a covenanted servant to Mrs Sarah Howson, It's therefore ordered that Mrs Howson aforesaid have notice of this order and that if it shall not appeare that the said Margaret is servant to the said Mrs Howson the next Court that then the Churchwardens of St Stephens Parish forthwith take her into possession and dispose of her according to Law and if shee shall appeare to be such servant that after the expiration of such service the then Churchwardens shall dispose of the said Margaret as aforesaid. *OB 1699–1713, Part 1, 167.*

1205. 19 July 1701— . . . to view the body of Alice Evans, a woman serv^t of Capt John Cralle lying then dead at ye said Cralle's house in Cherry Poynt . . . to report how ye sd Alice came by her death importing these words . . . (vizt) that by what signes doe appeare upon the body of the said Alice Evans and by what our evidences doe declare we doe find Evans Roberts to be the cause of the said Alice her death. . . . *OB 1699–1713, Part 1, 168.*

1206. 19 July 1701—Anthony Jackson, servant to Edward Bennett, haveing absented himselfe from his Master's service sixteene dayes and the said Bennett haveing produced an Acc^t ag^t the said Jackson for expenses in retreiveing the said serv^t amounting to sixteene hundred and one pounds of tobacco, damages & Charges & six shillings . . . *OB 1699–1713, Part 1, 169.* [A jury heard the case, and Anthony was ordered to serve his master 20 months for all damages after the expiration of his indenture. *OB 1699–1713, Part 1, 169.*]

1207. 15 Oct. 1701—Mary Sivillivant, servant to Clement Aldridge, haveing had a bastard child in the time of her service, It's ordered she serve her said Master for her said default one yeare and a halfe according to Law, her said Master in Court haveing engaged to pay the fine. *OB 1699–1713, Part 1, 176.*

1208. 23 Jan. 1701/02—Cert:, according to Act of Assembly, is granted to Thomas Hobson for the Importation of ten persons into this Colony (vizt)

    John Topping   William Gay
    John Thompson   Susanna Read
    Dorothy Thompson Anne Fryer
    Richard Dobles   Henry Parry
    Margaret Lawson   Andrew Armsley

OB 1699–1713, Part 1, 195.

1209. 23 Jan. 1701/02—Phebe Whitters als Cooke, haveing in Court acknowledged herselfe to be ser^t to John Cockrell for ten yeares commencing from the fourteenth of this instant according to an Indenture for the said terme here in Court produced & that the said Indenture was not in any wise Clandestinely procured nor otherwise to enslave or entrap her into service, It's ordered shee serve the said terme according to such her Indenture with her own voluntary free will and consent. *OB 1699–1713, Part 1, 195.*

1210. 15 April 1702—James Hews, serv^t to Mr Joseph Hoult, being brought to this Court to be adjudged, is by the Court adjudged to be fourteene yeares of age and ordered he serve his said Master or his assignes according to Law. *OB 1699–1713, Part 1, 196.*

1211. 15 April 1702—John Hill, serv^t to Mr Thomas Waddy, being brought to this Court to be adjudged, is by the Court adjudged to be thirteen yeares of age and ordered he serve his said Master or his assignes according to Law. *OB 1699–1713, Part 1, 196.*

1212. 15 April 1702—Thomas Thackerell, serv^t to Mr Dennis Conaway, being brought to this Court to be adjudged, is by the Court adjudged to be fifteene yeares of age and ordered he serve his said Master or his assignes according to Law. *OB 1699–1713, Part 1, 196.*

1213. 15 April 1702—Catherine Luin [or Linn], serv^t to Mr Richard Rice, being brought to this Court to be adjudged, is by the Court adjudged to be fifteene yeares of age and ordered shee serve her said Master or his assignes according to Law. *OB 1699–1713, Part 1, 197.*

1214. 15 April 1702—Catherine Jones, serv^t to Bartholl: Schreever, haveing had a bastard Child in the time of her service, It's ordered she serve her said Master one yeare for her said default according to Law and halfe a yeare for her fine, her Master haveing in Court assumed the paym^t of the same. *OB 1699–1713, Part 1, 197.*

1215. 15 April 1702—Edith Gent, serv^t to Richard Price, haveing had a bastard Child in the time of her service, It's ordered shee serve her said Master one yeare for her said default according to Law and halfe a yeare for her fine, her Master haveing in Court assumed the payment of the same & the said Edith in Court haveing refused to make oath who was the father of the Child, It's ordered the sheriffe take the said Edith into safe Custody untill she shall make oath as aforesaid. *OB 1699–1713, Part 1, 197.* [At the next Court Edith Gent under oath declared that Richard Tullos was the father of the child. *OB 1699–1713, Part 1, 200.*]

1216. 15 April 1702—Capt Christ^r Neale, as being appointed Churchwarden of St Stephens Parish having presented Anne Williams, Rebecca Taylor, and Nicholas Liscombe, serv^t woman, each of them for haveing bastard Children & Bartholl: Leasure for keeping another man's wife, It's ordered ye sheriffe summon to make their appearance to answer to such things as shall there be objected against them. *OB 1699–1713, Part 1, 197.*

1217. 16 April 1702—Alexander Forjoy, servant to Mrs Elizabeth Kenner,

201

being brought to this Court to be adjudged, is by the Court adjudged to be thirteene yeares of age and ordered he serve his said M^{rs} or his assignes according to Law. *OB 1699–1713, Part 1, 199.*

1218. 17 June 1702—Thomas Dunabaugh, serv^t to Mrs Dorothy Span, being brought to this Court to be adjudged, is by the Court adjudged to be thirteene yeares old and ordered he serve his said M^{rs} or her assignes according to Law. *OB 1699–1713, Part 1, 206.*

1219. 17 June 1702—Mary Millbank, serv^t to Mr John Cockrell, being brought to this Court to be adjudged, is by the Court adjudged to be fourteene yeares of age and ordered she serve her said Master or his assignes according to Law. *OB 1699–1713, Part 1, 206.*

1220. 17 June 1702—Christopher Copperweight, serv^t to Major Rodham Kenner, being brought to this Court to be adjudged, is by the Court adjudged to be fourteene yeares old and ordered he serve his said Master or his assignes according to Law. *OB 1699–1713, Part 1, 207.*

1221. 17 June 1702—Turloah Bryan, serv^t to Mrs Elizabeth Bankes, being brought to this Court to be adjudged, is by the Court adjudged to be seventeene yeares of age and ordered he serve his said Master or his assignes according to Law. *OB 1699–1713, Part 1, 207.*

1222. 17 June 1702—Sarah Pannell, serv^t to John Cockrell, haveing had a Bastard Child in the time of her service, It's ordered shee serve her said Master for her said Default according to Law and halfe a yeare for her fine, her Master haveing in Court assumed the payment of the same. *OB 1699–1713, Part 1, 207.* [In the next entry, under oath Sarah Pannell said that John Robinson was the father of the child. Mr. Richard Haynie, attorney for Robinson, objected, stating that there was good reason to believe the child was a mulatto.]

1223. 17 June 1702—John Claughlin, otherwise called John Cofflin, serv^t to James Ginn, haveing petitioned this Court that he haveing served the Custome of the Country ought to have his freedome and it appearing that he hath served the terme of five yeares, hee the said John is therefore hereby declared to be and is hereby made free. *OB 1699–1713, Part 1, 207.*

1224. 17 June 1702—Mary Rogers, serv^t to Nicholas Liscomb, summoned to and appearing this Court and being demanded to render an acco^t upon her oath who was the father of a Bastard Child which shee lately had and the said Mary refuseing to make oath, It's ordered the sheriffe take her into Custody and putt her into goale and there to keepe her in safe Custody untill she shall give her oath as aforesaid. *OB 1699–1713, Part 1, 208.*

1225. 18 June 1702—Certificate is granted to Thomas Hobson for fifteene hundred Acres of Land for the Importation of thirty persons into this Colony vizt

John Mackdanell	James Allen
Mary Mackdanell	James James
Elizabeth Wilkes	James Macbeth
John Scott	Margaret ____
William Glage	Ellinor Coot
Andrew Peacock	Hugh Cannon
John Scott	Peter Platt
Daniell Linch	Mary Pledwele
Hugh Broughton	Joseph Hoult
Alice Argile	Francis Ward
Alexander Cammell	Thomas James
Phill Pitts	William Clay
Mary Evans	Mary Swetman
Joseph Bland	Henry Sanders
Thomas Shorthose	

They haveing all made oaths that they nor any other to the best of their knowledge ever made use of them. *OB 1699–1713, Part 1, 211.*

1226. 15 July 1702—Patrick Devin, serv^t to Sam^{ll} Mahane, being brought to this Court to be adjudged, is by the Court adjudged to be fourteene yeares of age and ordered he serve his said Master or his assignes according to Law. *OB 1699–1713, Part 1, 211.*

1227. 15 July 1702—Olliver Gardner, servant to Thomas Baker, being brought to this Court to be adjudged, is by the Court adjudged to be fourteene yeares of age and ordered he serve his said Master or his assignes according to Law. *OB 1699–1713, Part 1, 212.*

1228. 15 July 1702—John Maddison, serv^t to Mr John Harris, is by the Court adjudged to be twelve yeares old, he haveing Indenture for nine yeares only presented to the Court for Judgm^t when his levy becomes due. *OB 1699–1713, Part 1, 212.*

1229. 16 Sept. 1702—It appearing to this Court by sufficient Certificate and the Confession of the Party that John Chisnell, serv^t to Lt Coll. Sam^{ll} Griffin, hath absented himselfe, being run away from his said Master's service in the Choice time of his Crop eighty two dayes.... *OB 1699–1713, Part 1, 219.*

1230. 16 Sept. 1702—Certificate is granted to Major Rodham Kenner for seventeene hundred acres of land for the Importation of thirty four persons into this Colony (vizt)

Hugh Williams	Henry Gallion
Evan Hill	Evan Rann
Anne Price	Timothy Higgins
Joseph Parris	Robert Mitchell
John Macguart	Richard Dowgell
Margarett Laurence	Dowland Berry
Anthony Jackson	William Wilkins
Jane Murphew	John Skelle
Thomas Sadler	Thomas Knight
Jane Macksassion	Hannah Anderson
Owen Jones	Richard Calphen
Thomas Williams	Andrew Flannagon
John Poope	Thomas Lock
John ___	Richard Bently
William Dunnawan	George Screech
Willm Price	Ellinor ___
Sarah Richardson	Christopher ___

OB 1699–1713, Part 1, 220.

1231. 16 Sept. 1702—It appearing to this Court that Carroll Dunn, serv^t to Mr John Cralle, hath absented himselfe from his Master's service seventy five dayes by running away in the heith [height] of his Cropp.... *OB 1699–1713, Part 1, 220.*

1232. 16 Sept. 1702—It appearing to this Court that Joseph Elton, serv^t to Mr John Cralle, hath absented himselfe from his Master's service one hundred and two dayes by running away in the height of the Cropp.... *OB 1699–1713, Part 1, 220.*

1233. 17 Sept. 1702—Mary Rogers, serv^t to Nicholas Liscome, haveing had a Bastard Child as shee hath made oath before Mr John Coutanceau (one of her Majesty's Justices of the Peace for this County) begotten by her said Master and her said Master haveing in Court assumed the paym^t of five hundred pounds of tobacco for her fine, the said Mary is therefore acquitted from punishment & further service to her said Master and also ordered that the Churchwardens of St Stephens Parish where the said offence was committed after her indented or accustomed time shall be expired dispose of the said Mary to serve two yeares to the use of the said parish according to Law. *OB 1699–1713, Part 1, 223.*

1234. 25 Oct. 1702—Whereas Michell Kendy petitioned to this Court that he had served Mr John Taylor four yeares, being the full time that he came into this Country for & had Indenture to signifie ye same Signed by the Lord Mayor of the Citty of Dublin (which was by Mr William Thornton, Master of the shipp Anne of Dublin) in which the said Complainant came taken from him and destroyed and Dennis McFarly & haveing made oath that he did see such Indenture (being shipmate to the said Michaell and read them & that it was soe signed as aforesaid and other circumstances on the Comp^{lts} behalfe being made obvious to the Court. The Court doth therefore consider that the said Michaell be free and ordered the said Taylor pay him his Corne and Cloathes accustomed als Ex^o. *OB 1699–1713, Part 1, 225.*

1235. 25 Oct. 1702—Elizabeth Hunt, serv^t to Sarah Tullos, haveing had a bastard Child in the time of her service as she hath made oath by Wm Grady, It's ordered shee serve for her sd Default to her said M^{rs} according to Law and ordered that ye sheriffe take her into Custody & give her twenty lashes well laid on her bare back. *OB 1699–1713, Part 1, 226.*

1236. 18 Nov. 1702—Whereas Thomas Kehowe, his Master being present, petitioned this Court that being brought into this Country a serv^t sold to Richard Pemberton served his said Master according to ye tenure of his Indenture and prayed to be discharged from his said Master's service and an order for his Corne and Cloaths accustomed whereupon he produced his said Indenture Importeing that the said Thomas of his owne free will hath bound himselfe an apprentice to Henry Arther & his assignes for four yeares.... *OB 1699–1713, Part 1, 231.*

1237. 18 Nov. 1702—Anne Wiggins, servant to the estate of Capt Spencer Mottrom, haveing had a bastard Child in the time of her service and it being thought necessary to respite further proceedings in that matter till next Court, It's therefore ordered shee appeare the next Court alwaies [always] provided that shee shall not take any advantage, the cheife reasons of the said Respite being in favour of the said Anne. *OB 1699–1713, Part 1, 231.*

1238. 19 Nov. 1702—Whereas Derby Danheny, his master being present, petitioned this Court that being brought into this Country a serv^t & sold to Richard Pemberton, served his said Master according to the tenure of his Indenture & prayed to be discharged from his said Master's service & an order for his Corne and Cloaths accustomed whereupon he produced his Indenture importing that the said Darby of his owne free will hath bound himselfe an apprentice to Henry Arther & to his assignes for four yeares or according to the Custome of Virg^a sealed and signed by Henry Arther & attested Sam^{ll} Hearne not publick which Indenture is considered by the Court & adjudged good and it appearing that the said Term of four yeares are fully expired since the said Darbie's arrivall in this Country & whereupon it's ordered that the said Darby Danbeny bee & is hereby discharged from all service, one by virtue of his said Indenture and alsoe ordered that the said Richard Pemberton pay to the said Derby his Corne & Cloathes accustomed in such cases with Costs als Ex^o. *OB 1699–1713, Part 1, 233.* [Pemberton appealed to the governor and council.]

1239. 21 Oct. 1702—Patrick Quiff, serv^t to John Cockrell, haveing petitioned this Court to serve him four yeares who sent him into this Colony and was sold by Capt Voyer but for how long he knowes not but his Master refuses to discharge him notwithstanding his time aforesd is expired and it appeareing that the said Patrick's time will be expired the fourth of Christmas next, It's considered that the sd Patrick be then free & y^t his sd Master then pay him his Corne & Cloaths wth Costs als Execution. *OB 1699–1713, Part 1, 226.* [The name Quiff eventually became Keeve.]

1240. 20 Nov. 1702—Patrick Burne, his Master being present, petitioned this Court that Mr Francis Voyer brought him into this Country and sold him to Ignatius Olliver whome he served according to the tenure of his Indenture and prayed to be discharged from the service of his said Master and alsoe an order for his Corne and Clothes accustomed in such cases and produced his said Indenture signifieing that the said Patrick of his own free will hath bound himselfe an apprentice to Henry Arther and to his assignes for four yeares or according to the Custom of Virg^a sealed and signed Henry Arther . . . which said Indenture is by the Court considered who adjudges the same to be good. the terme of four yeares being fully compleated since the sd Patrick's arrivall here, therefore It's ordered that the said Patrick Burne bee and he is hereby discharged from all service due by the said Indenture and also that the said Ignatius Olliver pay him the said Patrick his said accustomed Corne and Cloaths with Costs. *OB 1699–1713, Part 1, 234.* [Burne could have been an apprentice rather than a servant; however, there is no mention of schooling or a trade.]

1241. 20 Nov. 1702—Anthony Kennedy, serv^t to John Addams, came into Court (together with his said Master this day and declared that Mr Francis Voyer brought him into this Country and sold him to the said John whom he served four yeares of his Indenture tho' the same was lost) he ought to doe but no longer and prayed that he might be discharged from his said Master's service and have order for his accustomed Corne and Cloathes. . . . *OB 1699–1713, Part 1, 234*. [Anthony Kennedy received his freedom.]

1242. 20 Nov. 1702—Daniell Hogan, servant to Major Rodham Kenner, petitioning this Court that he served his said Master the terme of four yeares according to the tenure of his Indenture as by good and sufficient evidence may appear but his said Master refuseing and denying to discharge him prayed he might be discharged & noe such Indenture or other cause appearing to make free and the said Daniell being formerly Judged in this Court, It's adjudged he serve according to the said Judgm^t. *OB 1699–1713, Part 1, 235.*

1243. 20 Nov. 1702—Anne Wiggins, serv^t to Capt Mottrom's estate, being presented for haveing a bastard Child and the said Anne by her attorney Dan^{ll} McCarty denied that she had any bastard Child and for tryall thereof putt herselfe upon the Country, It being late Capt Peter Presly hath engaged the said Anne shall appear tomorrow. *OB 1699–1713, Part 1, 235.*

1244. 17 Dec. 1702—Whereas Richard Kirkin petitioned this Court he had served his Master Wm Fletcher according to the tenure of his Indenture and prayed to be acquitted of all further service & his Corne and Cloathes paid him as is accustomed and the said Kirkin haveing produced his sd Indenture and the Court considering the same doe adjudged that he hath fully served his time unless some other Contract or otherwise shall appear to the Contrary he is therefore hereby made and declared free unless the said Fletcher shall appear the next Court and show reasons to the Contrary. *OB 1699–1713, Part 1, 235.* [At the next court Richard Kirkin received his freedom, and Fletcher was ordered to pay him his corn and clothes. *OB 1699–1713, Part 1, 238.*]

1245. 18 Dec. 1702—Mary Browne did this day in open Court upon her oath declare that Anne Wiggins now or late servant to Capt Spencer Mottrom's estate . . . was delivered of a man Child and that she (being in the house with the said Child and conversant therewith doth really believe that the said Child is a mulatto & hath heard the said Anne often owne that it was a mulatto begotten by a negro called Billy belonging to the said Mottrom's estate. *OB 1699–1713, Part 1, 237.* [At the next court Anne Wiggins was ordered to serve an additional year for her said default. *OB 1699–1713, Part 1, 238.*]

1246. 17 Feb. 1702/03—Martha Hunter, serv^t to James Nipper haveing had a bastard Child and refusing to declare the father, It's ordered the sheriffe take her into Custody & keepe her in Close Prison untill shee shall declare the father. *OB 1699–1713, Part 1, 238.* [At the court held 18 Feb. 1702/03, Martha Hunter, under oath, stated that Timothy Riley was the father of the child.]

1247. 18 Feb. 1702/03—William Olive, serv^t to John Reason, haveing runaway from his said Master's service nine dayes and the said Reason petitioning that besides his trouble he hath expended nine hundred pounds of tobacco & stands engaged to make satisfaction to John Pines in Lancaster County for goeing to James River & that way downe the Country in search of the said William. . . . *OB 1699–1713, Part 1, 238.*

1248. 19 Feb. 1702/03—James McDonnell, serv^t to John Laurence, haveing absented himselfe from his said Master's service twenty five dayes. . . . *OB 1699–1713, Part 1, 239.*

1249. 18 March 1702/03—William Macy, orphan son of Henry Macy deced, serv^t to John Laurence, haveing by George Escridge [Eskridge] his attorney, complained to this Court that he the said W^m hath attained to age to choose a guard^n & hath reason soe to doe but is presented by his sd Mast^r who wil not admit him to come to Court, It's ordered that if the said Laurence, haveing notice hereof by the sheriffe, shall not suffer the said William to come to the next Court, that the said Laurence then appear & the reasons to the Contrary. *OB 1699–1713, Part 1, 241.*

1250. 19 March 1702/03—James Ecles, servant to Joseph Humphryes, haveing contrary to Law struck his Master, It's ordered he serve his said Master for his said Default according to Law. *OB 1699–1713, Part 1, 246.*

1251. 19 May 1703—Anne Fryer, serv^t to Thomas Hobson, haveing had a bastard Child in the time of her service as she hath made oath by Andrew Armsby, serv^t alsoe to ye sd Hobson, It's ordered shee serve her sd Master one yeare for her sd default according to Law & halfe a yeare for her fine, her Master haveing assumed to pay the same. *OB 1699–1713, Part 1, 246.*

1252. 19 May 1703—Robert Clerke, serv^t to Sam^{ll} Mahens being brought to this Court to be adjudged, is by the Court adjudged to be fifteene yeares of age and ordered he serve his said Master or his assignes according to Law. *OB 1699–1713, Part 1, 246.*

1253. 19 May 1703—William Harcum, one of the Churchwardens of St Stephens Parish, haveing presented Anne Williams, Mary Ferrell, serv^t to Mrs Downing, Diane Collins, Mary Day, Ester, a woman at Gaar Edwards his house & Margaret Laurence, serv^t to Capt Tho: Winder for haveing had bastard Children, It's ordered that the sheriffe take the said women into custody untill they enter into bond wth good & sufficient security to appeare the next Court to answer for their Defaults. *OB 1699–1713, Part 1, 247.*

1254. 19 May 1703—Richd Baker, serv^t to Daniell Sivillivant, haveing absented himselfe from his Master's service four months and it appearing that the said Sivillivant hath beene at seven hundred pounds of tobacco expense in retreiving him by the oath of the said Sivillivant & his account in Court produced, inconsideration whereof together with his absented time, It's ordered he serve his said Master sixteene months after his Indented or accustomed time is expired. *OB 1699–1713, Part 1, 248.*

1255. 19 May 1703—William Macy, orphan sone of Henry Macy, serv^t of Jno Laurence, hath this day in Court made choice of Edward Wooldridge to be his guardian who is accordingly admitted. *OB 1699–1713, Part 1, 248.*

1256. 19 May 1703—Whereas in March Court last John Harrold under some conditions being bound to Capt Thomas Winder provided Mr John Cooke of Lancaster County should not show some reasons to the Contrary upon his appearance & debating the matter or the former order to be made null or confirmed & noe cause appearing to the Contrary the said former is confirmed & ordered the said Harrold serve the said Winder according to the directions of the former order. *OB 1699–1713, Part 1, 248.*

1257. 20 May 1703—William Ollive, serv^t to John Reason haveing made oath that he attended this Court as an evidence ten dayes on the behalfe of William Harcum agt David Williams & Rachell his wife, It's ordered the said Harcum pay the said Reason forty pounds of tobo per day according to Law for his servant's attendance als Execution. *OB 1699–1713, Part 1, 251.*

1258. 21 July 1703—Mary Dermott, orphan Daughter of Owen Dermott, serv^t to John Laurence, is by the Court adjudged to be free when shee attaines to the age of eighteene yeares which is the eight & twentieth day of this instant. *OB 1699–1713, Part 1, 255.*

1259. 18 Aug. 1703—Darby Danheny, complaining to this Court that the nineteenth day of November 1702 he obtained order against Richard Pemberton, his late servant, to be discharged from further service and for his Corne and Cloaths. *OB 1699–1713, Part 1, 258.* [Pemberton appealed to the General Court for a hearing, but he did not appear. Pemberton still refused to pay Darby his corn and clothes and was ordered to appear at the next court.]

1260. 18 Aug. 1703—Thomas Kehow, complaining to this Court that the nineteenth day of Novr 1702 he obtained order agt Richd Pemberton, his late Master, to be discharged from further service for his Corne & Cloathes accustomed.... *OB 1699–1713, Part 1, 258*. [Pemberton appealed to the General Court, but he never appeared to present his appeal. Still Pemberton refused to pay Thomas his corn and clothes.]

1261. 15 Sept. 1703—Certificate is granted to Mr John Carnegie for two thousand four hundred acres of land for the Importation of fifty eight persons into this Colony (vizt)

William Godnell	Francis Williard
Christopher King	William Nellagon
John Mason	Elizabeth Wilcox
William Ollive	Robert Reeves
William Seward	Matthew Benham
John Duke	Catherine Langsdon
John Mase	Stephen Clauckerett [?]
Robert Crouch	Humphry Veale
William Keene	Laurence Oneale
William Langsdon	Dan^{ll} Ologney
Anthony Hogherd	Evan Jones
Benjamine Coleman	Solomon Jones
Mary Nowell	David Murray
Mary Crouch	Henry Macbare
Hannah Staynie	Edward Rainsford
Elizabeth Hobson	Mary Gridly
Dennis Mohanny	Mary Savoy
Marg^t Cowland	Isaac Mardam
William Prichett	John Gill
Wm Mekinall	Patience Gridly
Joseph Taylor	Elizabeth Wollham
John Parsons	John Phipps
Daniell Clerke	Michaell Gill
Rebecca Clerke	James White

OB 1699–1713, Part 1, 260.

1262. 15 Sept. 1703—Ellinor Hewes, serv^t to John Jones (In consideration of the said Jones his purchasing her from a ... Master) of her own free will and unto Court & obleidges herselfe hereby to serve Jones one year after her Indenture or accustomed time expired & on the said Jones his motion the said Ellinore's petition relateing thereunto is admitted to Record. *OB 1699–1713 Part 1, 260.*

1263. 15 Sept. 1703—Charles Conner, late serv^t to Robert Jones deced, Petitioning this Court agt Maurice Jones Exec^r of the said Robt for his Corn & Cloaths due to him by Law the said Petition is continued to the next Court, the said Mr Maurice Jones not being present. *OB 1699–1713, Part 1, 260.*

1264. 15 Sept. 1703—William Wedderilse, late serv^t to Robert Jones deced, Petitioning the Court against Maurice Jones Exec. of the late said Robert for his Corne and Cloaths due to him by Law, the said Petition is continued the next Court, the said Mr Maurice Jones not being present. *OB 1699–1713, Part 1, 261.*

1265. 18 Sept. 1703—Upon Complaint made last Court by Derby Danheney, late serv^t to Richard Pemberton that the said nineteenth day of November 1702 he obtained order against his said Master for his freedom and Corne & Cloaths accustomed for which the said Pemberton appealed to the General Court but not presenting twas dismissed, It was ordered that unless the said Pemberton (having notice of that order) should show reason to the contary this Court the said Darby may have Judgm^t and whereas the said Pemberton hath now made his appearance and the said Darby moved by his attorney George Eskridge for a confirmation of the said order of the last Court. . . . *OB 1699–1713, Part 1, 266.* [Pemberton was ordered by the court to pay Darby his corn and clothes with cost of court, but Pemberton appealed to the governor and the council.]

1266. 18 Sept. 1703—Upon Complaint made last Court by Thomas Kehows, late servant to Richard Pemberton, that the nineteenth day of November 1702 he obtained order against his said Master for his freedom and corn and cloaths accustomed. . . . *OB 1699–1713, Part 1, 267.* [Pemberton appealed to the General Court, but he did not appear before the court the first time. He did appear at the next court and was ordered to pay Darby his corn and clothes with cost of court. Again Pemberton appealed to the governor and council.]

1267. 17 Nov. 1703—John Claughton, one of the grand jury, haveing presented Daniell Sivilivant for an unChristian like part in burying his serv^t maid or woman soe shallow that the Doggs or hoggs halled [hauled] her out of the ground, It's therefore ordered that the sheriffe take the said Sivillivant into Custody & bring him to the next Court & that the summon George Leasure, John & Thomas Hall, William Hoult & Sam^{ll} Churchill to give in their evidence the next Court on that behalfe. *OB 1699–1713, Part 1, 272.*

1268. 15 Dec. 1703—Judgm^t is granted William Wedderilse agt the estate of Robt Jones deced for his Corne and Cloaths according to Law and ordered that Capt Maurice Jones Exec^r of the said deced pay the same out of the said deced estate unto the said Wedderisle with costs of suit als Exec. *OB 1699–1713, Part 1, 275.*

1269. 15 Dec. 1703—Judgm^t is granted Charles Conner against the estate of Robert Jones for his Corne and Cloathes.... *OB 1699–1713, Part 1, 275.*

1270. 15 Dec. 1703—Judgm^t is granted Mary Nugent, late serv^t to Richd Hudnall, agt her sd Master for her Corne and Cloaths according to Law unless the said Hudnall shall appear the next Court and show reasons to the Contrary. *OB 1699–1713, Part 1, 275.*

1271. 15 Dec. 1703—Richard Baker, serv^t to Daniell Sivillivant, haveing made Complaint agt his said Master for his bad usage but not makeing out his said Compl^t, the Court are of opinion that he returne to his Master's service but the said Baker being very bare & naked, It's ordered that after his returne to his said Master's service his said Master forthwith see him well cloathed. *OB 1699–1713, Part 1, 275.*

1272. 15 March 1703/04—Thomas Malaughny, serv^t to Mr James Crean, haveing absented himself sixteene days from his Master's service & his Master haveing expended six hundred pounds of tobo in procuring him, It's ordered he serve his sd Master eight months after his time by Indenture as Custom is expired. *OB 1699–1713, Part 1, 280.*

1273. 17 May 1704—Whereas John Roberts, late servant to Josias Gaskins deced & since to Sam^{ll} Mahanes adm^r of the sd Gaskins, petitioned this Court that he had served his full time by Indenture, Custome or otherwise & prayed order for his Corne and Cloaths accustomed ag^t the said Gaskins his estate and it appearing to this Court that the said Roberts is free ordered the said Mahen ... pay the said Roberts his Corne and Cloaths accustomed out of the said Gaskins his estate with Costs als ex. *OB 1699–1713, Part 1, 287.*

1274. 17 May 1704—Anne Alberry, serv^t to Capt John Cralle, haveing had a bastard Child in the time of her service by Thomas Fitzgerrald as shee hath in Court made oath, It's ordered shee serve her said Master for her said Default according to Law and that the Churchwardens take a Legall Course with the reputed father and alsoe that she be remitted from punishment, Wm Medcalfe haveing in Court assumed the paym^t of her fine. *OB 1699–1713, Part 1, 287.*

1275. 17 May 1704—Whereas Elizabeth Ferldor petitions this Court agt Francis Hathaway for her freedome & produced an order of Wiccocomoco Vestry dated the eighth day of May 1688 in these words (vizt) It was then ordered by the above vestry that Elizabeth, the bastard Child of William Ferlder should be bound to Mr John Eustace to serve him according to Law and it appearing that shee hath attained to eighteene yeares of age, It is the Court's opinion that by the Seventh Act the 25th September 1672 the said Elizabeth is free and ordered shee be according free. *OB 1699–1713, Part 1, 288.*

1276. 17 May 1704—Judgm^t is granted Wm Jones late serv^t to Christ^r Dawson agt the sd Dawson for his Corne & Cloaths accaccustomed & one p^r of shooes als Execution unless the said Dawson shall appeare the next Court & show reasons to ye Contrary. *OB 1699–1713, Part 1, 288.*

1277. 17 May 1704—Elizabeth Hazelwood, serv^t to Christ^r Dawson, under complaint to the Court that shee is very much distempered & that her Master neglects her & will take noe care for a cure & otherwise misuses her very much and the said Dawson not being present to answer the said Complaint & this Court thinking it very expedient that some speedy course may be taken for ye preservation of the said Elizabeth, It's therefore ordered that the said Christ^r Dawson (haveing notice of this order) answer the said Elizabeth's complaint before Capt Tho: Winder & Capt Leonard Howson to be by them determined on Monday next at Capt Winder's house according as they shall import & adjudge of the premises. *OB 1699–1713, Part 1, 289.*

1278. 21 June 1704—Mary Bullery, serv^t to Mr Peter Coutanceau, haveing had a Bastard Child in the time of her service by John Driver, a taylor [tailor] as she hath made oath, It's ordered shee serve her said Master for her said default according to Law and halfe a yeare for her fine, her Master haveing in Court assumed the payment thereof to the Parish. *OB 1699–1713, Part 1, 290.*

1279. 21 June 1704—Timothy Shahanghuary, serv^t to Mr Peter Coutanceau, being brought to this Court to be adjudged, is by the Court adjudged to be fifteene yeares of age and ordered he serve his said Master or his assignes according to Law. *OB 1699–1713, Part 1, 290.*

1280. 21 June 1704—Phoebe Whitter, serv^t to John Cottrell, haveing had a Bastard Child in the time of her service as she hath made oath by Henry Harding, serv^t to the said Cottrell, ordered that the sheriffe take her into Custody and give her five and twenty lashes on her bare back [at] the next Court before the Court house Doore well laid on and ordered shee serve her said Master one yeare according to Law or pay one thousand pounds of Tobacco after her time by Indenture or Custome shall be expired. *OB 1699–1713, Part 1, 290.*

1281. 21 June 1704—John Emberson, serv^t to William Nelmes, haveing absented himself from his said Master's service forty nine dayes, It's ordered he serve his said Master in compensation according to Law ninety eight dayes and It appearing that the said Nelmes hath expended five hundred pounds of tobacco & sixteene shillings . . . in pursuit of the said John besides other troubles ordered he serve his said Master (including the ninety eight dayes) eleven months after his time by Indenture or Custome shall be expired. *OB 1699–1713, Part 1, 291.*

1282. 21 June 1704—Mary Follierd, serv^t to Mr Maurice Jones, haveing had a Bastard Child in the time of her service as she hath made oath by Dominick Newgent, It's ordered she serve her said Master for her said Default according to Law and that the sheriffe take her into Custody and give her five & twenty lashes well laid on but her said Master haveing in Court assumed the paym^t of her fine her punishm^t is Remitted, she haveing in Court promised to serve her said Master one whole year in Recompense thereof and furthered ordered the said Dominick enter into bond with good and sufficient security to save the Parish harmless. *OB 1699–1713, Part 1, 291.*

1283. 21 July 1704—Mary Williams, late serv^t of John Stott of Lancaster County, now servant to Dennis Vollen, for the consideration (as shee affirmes) of his redeeming her from a hard service, in Court assumes to serve the said Vollen one yeare after her Indenture or accustomed time be expired. *OB 1699–1713, Part 1, 306.*

1284. 29 Aug. 1704—Will of Daniel Suilevant . . . I give and bequeath to Vincent Cox my Servt boy Richard Baker. . . . *RB 1706–1720, 262.*

1285. 20 Sept. 1704—Katherine Jones, serv^t to Mr Batholl^w Schreever, haveing had a bastard child in the time of her service as shee hath made oath by Robert Mackey, It's ordered shee serve her said Master for her said Default according to Law & ordered that the sheriffe take her into Custody and give her five and twenty lashes on her bare back well laid on. *OB 1699–1713, Part 1, 310.*

1286. 20 Sept. 1704—Mary Chapman, serv^t to James Harrold, in Court haveing acknowledged that shee had a bastard Child in the time of her service, her fine for her said Default is remitted, her said Master in Court haveing assumed to pay the fine. *OB 1699–1713, Part 1, 311.*

1287. 21 Sept. 1704—Certificate is granted to Mr George Eskridge for one thousand acres of Land for the Importation of twenty persons into this Colony (Viz^t)

  Matthew Kelly   Wm Browne
  Nich^s Hutchinson   Wm Rennolds
  John Poor   Mary Caseley
  Alexander Salmon   Eliz^a Wooll
  Mary Bullery   Archibald Shusy
  Hon^r Frankling   John Houson
  Robert Teigue   Wm Henley
  Shahanna Shaw   Kath: Carty
  Alex^r Browne   Wm Henderson
  Tho: Burnett   Marg^t Murfy
OB 1699–1713, Part 1, 312.

1288. 21 Sept. 1704—Certificate is granted to Mr James Waddy for the Importation of tenn persons into this Colony for five hundred acres of Land (whose names are as followeth)
  George Violett   John Birke
  Anne Violett   John Cambell
  Charles Colgin   Francis Brookes
  Simon Holland   Gillian Scallin
  William Harsell   Mary Parsons
OB 1699–1713, Part 1, 312.

1289. 21 Sept. 1704—Certificate is granted to Capt Richard Haynie for two hundred & fifty acres of Land for the Importation of five persons into this Colony vizt
  Jno Butler   Patrik Fisher
  James Fleming   Eliz^a Sheppard
  Robt Hughs
OB 1699–1713, Part 1, 312.

1290. 21 Sept. 1704—Certificate is granted to John Laurence for one hundred acres of Land for the Importation of two persons into this Colony vizt John Williams and Jaine MacDannell. *OB 1699–1713, Part 1, 312.*

1291. 22 Sept. 1704—Certificate is granted to Hugh Callan for two hundred acres of Land for the importation of four persons into this Colony (vizt) Hugh Callan, Marg^t Callan, Eliz^a Cousedy, & Kath Chalan [Callan ?], the said Hugh haveing made oath he never made use of these Rights. *OB 1699–1713, Part 1, 314.*

1292. 18 Oct. 1704—Katherine Line, serv^t to Richard Rice, haveing absented herselfe from her Master's service five and twenty dayes & her said Master haveing beene at severall expenses to about the value of six hundred pounds of tobacco besides his own person six dayes to which he hath made oath, It's ordered she serve her sd Master seven months according to Law after her Indented or accustomed time shall be expired. *OB 1699–1713, Part 1, 317.*

1293. 18 Oct. 1704—Anne Fryer, serv^t to Thomas Hobson, haveing had a Bastard Child in the time of her service by Andrew Armsly as she hath made oath, It's ordered shee serve her said Master for her said Default according to Law and halfe a yeare for her fine, her Master haveing in Court assumed the paym^t of the same. *OB 1699–1713, Part 1, 317.*

1294. 22 Feb. 1704/05—Certificate is granted to Capt George Eskridge for two thousand nine hundred & fifty acres of Land for the Importation of [fifty] nine persons into this Colony

Thomas Millar	Abraham Proctor
John Ashton	John Dowly
Jonathan Palfry	Christopher Petty
Edmond Bowes	John Conner
Mary Westerby	Phillip Autrobus
Mary Frankling	Marg^t Fitzmorris
Mary Conalan	Henry Puckney [or Pinckney]
Mary Prise	John Thomas
James Jones	Francis Thomas
Elizabeth Jones	Susanna Unthank
Thomas Oxx	Wm Lambert
John Joyne	Wm Jones
Thomas Seddon	Wm Provis
Joane Seddon	Joseph Atkins
Evan Morgan	Thomas Simms
Richard Prise	George Dodson
John Davis	Anne Dodson
David Savige	James Neale
Wm Janeway	Thomas Lane
John Skimage	Wm Stephenson
George Groves	James Genn
Mary Barnes	Mary Genn
Thomas Moore	John Coflin [or Cofflin]
Henry Commons	Arthur Bell
Henry Brabin	John Laland

John Crostit	Wm Thompson
Patrick Quiff	David Thomas
David Straughan	John Arsbell
Robert Smith	Thomas Genn
Sarah Anderson	

OB 1699–1713, Part 1, 322.

1295. 22 Feb. 1704/05—Edward Laurence, late serv^t of Henry Dawson deced, petitioning this Court agt Katherine Dawson, Henry Dawson & John Conaway adm^rs of the said deced, for his Corne and Cloaths, haveing served his time according to Custome, It's therefore ordered that the adm^rs of the sd Dawson pay him his Corne & Cloaths together with Costs als Exec unless they appeare the next Court and show reasons to the Contrary. *OB 1699–1713, Part 1, 322.*

1296. 25 March 1704/05—William Seward, Petitioning this Court agt his late Master John Reason for his Corne and Cloaths he served his full time according to the Custome of this Country, It's ordered that unless the said Reason appeare the next Court and show reason to the Contrary the sd Seward may have Judgm^t. *OB 1699–1713, Part 1, 332.*

1297. 16 May 1705—Timothy Higgins, late serv^t to John Hany Petitioning this Court for his Corne and Cloaths haveing served his full time according to Custome, It's ordered the said Haynie pay him his Corne and Cloaths accustomed with Costs als execution unless the said Haynie shall appeare the next Court & show reason to the Contrary. *OB 1699–1713, Part 1, 333.*

1298. 16 May 1705—John Woolse, late serv^t to Christ^r Dawson, Petitioning this Court for his Corne & Cloaths haveing served his full time according to Custome, It's ordered the said Dawson pay him his Corne and Cloaths accustomed with Costs als Ex^on unless the said Dawson shall appeare at the next Court and show reasons to the Contrary. *OB 1699–1713, Part 1, 333.*

1299. 17 May 1705—Judgm^t is granted William Seward agt John Reason, his late Master, for his Corne and Cloaths according to Law and ordered he pay the same unto the said Seward with Costs als Ex^on. *OB 1699–1713, Part 1, 336.* [In the court order dated 22 July 1714, John and Mary Seward, son and daughter of William, were ordered to serve Thomas Hobson according to terms of an indenture signed by Hobson and Seward. *OB 1713–19, 60.*]

1300. 17 May 1705—Edward Laurence, late serv^t of Henry Dawson deced, petitioning this Court for his Corne and Cloaths according to Law agt

Katherine Dawson, Henry Dawson & John Conaway adm[rs] of the said deced, It's ordered that if the said adm[rs] doe not appear the next Court & show reasons to the Contrary that then the said Edw[d] have judgm[t], he proveing that he have served his time lawfully. *OB 1699–1713, Part 1, 336.*

1301. 18 May 1705—Katharine Fletcher affirmeing to this Court that shee is a free woman and that John Webb deteynes her as a serv[t] under pretence of an assignement from Hugh Callan, It's ordered that the said Webb be cited to the next Court to show cause if any he can for his soe deteyning the sd Katharine. *OB 1699–1713, Part 1, 337.*

1302. 18 May 1705—Cap[t] Maurice Jones, haveing moved this Court that his serv[t] Simon Haverson hath some objections to make about his personal service being assigned by John Ryan to him, the said John for the terme of four yeares from the nine and twentieth day of March 1705 and nothing appeareing to the Court but that the said assignment is good. It's ordered the said Haverson serve the said Jones the sd terme. *OB 1699–1713, Part 1, 337.*

1303. 18 July 1705—Elizabeth Macey, serv[t] to Thomas Gill, being brought to this Court to be adjudged, is by the Court adjudged to be sixteene yeares of age and ordered shee serve her said Master or his assignes according to Law. *OB 1699–1713, Part 1, 340.*

1304. 18 July 1705—George Dunbarr, complayneing to this Court that his Master Richard Hudnall did abuse him in a barbarous manner & his stripes appearing unreasonable to this Court, It's ordered that the said Richard Hudnall be cited to the next Court to answer the said Compl[t] and that the said George Dunbarr be and remaine with Charles Nelmes untill the said Court. *OB 1699–1713, Part 1, 340.*

1305. 18 July 1705—Upon the petition of Bridgett Taylor, covenant serv[t] to William Mason who petitioned for liberty to seeke remedy for her cure of lingering distemper, her said Master refuseing her the same in her distress, It's ordered that shee have liberty to seeke remedy for cure of her sd distemper and that her said Master hinder her not. *OB 1699–1713, Part 1, 341.*

1306. 18 July 1705—David Browne & Manly Browne, sons of David Browne, petitioning this Court ag[t] George Hill who intermarryed Mary Flynt Exer[ix] of Tho: Flynt deced for deteyning them as servants contrary to Law and upon what conditions they knew not, It's ordered that the sheriffe cite the sd Hill and his wife to the next Court to show reasons if any they can for their soe deteyning the sd David & Manly Browne. *OB 1699–1713, Part 1, 341.* [At a court held Aug. 15, 1705, David and Manly were ordered to return to Hill and his wife and serve them until they arrived at the age stated in the indenture. *OB 1699–1713, Part 1, 345.*]

1307. 19 July 1705—Katharine Fletcher, moveing this Court for her freedome from her service to Mr John Webb & an assignm^t being produced in Court from Marie V [?] Fletcher to Hugh Callan of the said Katherine by the name of Katherine Collaghan & proved by the oaths of John Hughlett & an assignm^t endorsed from Hugh Callan to the sd Webb, the Court adjudged the sd assignm^t good and ordered the said Katherine serve the said Webb untill the expiration of two yeares from the date of the said Fletcher's asignment. *OB 1699–1713, Part 1, 343.*

1308. 17 Aug. 1705—Tho: Norton, serv^t to David Spence, haveing made oath that he attended this Court thirty two dayes as an evidence on the behalfe of Jno Haynie p^{lt} ag^t John Stott Def^t and the sd Spence declareing in Court he would be satisfied with eight hundred pounds of tobacco & Cask for his sd serv$^{t's}$ attendance, It's ordered the said Haynie pay the same unto the sd Spence with Costs. *OB 1699–1713, Part 1, 353.*

1309. 17 Aug. 1705—James Rogers was attached to answer John Pope in a Plea of the Case for that (that is to say) whereas the Def^t pretending to be a Doctor and takeing upon himselfe the Cure of diverse distempers & diseases and being at the house of the p^{lt} on or about the first day of June 1700 and the p^{lt} haveing a serv^t Jno Ervyn troubled with a distemper commonly called the yaws.... *OB 1699–1713, Part 1, 353.*

1310. 21 March 1705/06—Certificate is granted Capt George Eskridge for four hundred and fifty acres of Land for the Importation of nine persons into this Colony vizt

Jane Harrison	Thomas Cavernott
William Thomson	Rachell Newton
Matthew Chettwood	Uriah Bryant
William Dyelsoild	Kath: Talbott
John Williams	

OB 1699–1713, Part 1, 373.

1311. 21 March 1705/06—Certificate is granted Capt George Eskridge for one thousand & fifty acres of Land for the Importation of twenty one persons into this Colony vizt

John Laughee	Katherine Fling
George Jackson	Margarett Bryan

Arthur Kauselaugh	Isabell Davis
John Roach	Ellinor Hunt
Thomas Rock	Mary Olliver
Dennis Rooarke	Edward Kelley
Patrick Earne	Allice White
James Theary	Katherine Keaton
Anthony Delany	Mary Lane
John Connell	Mary Wheeler
John Poore	

OB 1699–1713, Part 1, 375.

1312. 21 March 1705/06—George Jackson brought into this Country without Indenture by Capt Sam^{ll} Ellis and sold to Sarah Tullos for seven yeares and the sd George in Court acknowledging that he is willing and ready to serve his said Mistress the sd terme of seven yeares, It's therefore ordered that he serve her or her assignes that time and noe longer. *OB 1699–1713, Part 1, 375.*

1313. 21 March 1705/06—Certificate is granted to Capt George Eskridge for the Importation of twenty one persons into this Colony for one thousand & fifty acres of Land vizt

Robert Reeves	Thomas Ryder
Charles Moorehead	Sam^{ll} Ball
Thomas Flatman	John Walker
Thomas Prise	Turlur Conner
Anthony Bateman	Solomon Mason
Mary Lilley	Thomas Jackson
Jane Shirly	Robt Harrison
Richard Booth	James Stanly
John Poore	John Floyd
John Wilkins	Francis Wheeler
James Russell	

OB 1699–1713, Part 1, 376.

1314. 21 March 1705/06—Certificate is granted to Capt George Eskridge for three hundred acres of Land for the Importation of six persons into this Colony (vizt)

Patrick Quiffe	Andrew Fisher
John Medly	Margery Merritt
Margaret Medly	John Cleron

OB 1699–1713, Part 1, 376.

1315. 21 March 1705/06—Cert: is granted Mr George Eskridge for two

hundred acres of Land for the Importation of four persons into this Colony vizt
    John Lyon   Humphry Dunaby
    John Hayes   Mary Milbanks
OB 1699–1713, Part 1, 376.

1316. 21 March 1705/06—Certificate is granted to Capt George Eskridge for two hundred and fifty acres of Land for the Importation of five persons into this Colony (vizt)
    Henry Harding   Pheebe Whitter
    Laurence Gamwell   Edmond Plea
    Thomas Dickenson
OB 1699–1713, Part 1, 377.

1317. 21 March 1705/06—Certificate is granted Capt George Eskridge for one hundred and fifty acres of Land for the Importation of three persons into this Colony vizt
    John Davis   David Savige
    Morris Braseele
OB 1699–1713, Part 1, 377.

1318. 21 March 1705/06—Certificate is granted George Eskridge for one hundred acres of Land for the Importation of two persons into this Colony vizt
    John Jameson   Hugh Price
OB 1699–1713, Part 1, 377.

1319. 17 Aprill 1706—John Connell, serv^t to Mr Joseph Hoult, being brought to this Court to be adjudged, is by the Court adjudged to be twelve yeares of age & ordered he serve his said Master or his assignes according to Law. *OB 1699–1713, Part 1, 377.*

1320. 17 April 1706—Jonathan Hemoney, being brought to this Court to be adjudged when he becomes a tythable, is by the Court adjudged to be tenn yeares of age. *OB 1699–1713, Part 1, 377.*

1321. 17 Aprill 1706—John Poore, serv^t to Bartholl: Leasure, being brought to this Court to be adjudged, is by the Court adjudged to be tenn yeares of age and ordered he serve his said Master or his assignes according to Law. *OB 1699–1713, Part 1, 377.*

1322. 17 April 1706—Patrick Bready, serv^t to Dennis Conway Junr, being brought to this Court to be adjudged, is by the Court adjudged to be tenn yeares of age & ordered he serve his said Master or his assignes according to Law. *OB 1699–1713, Part 1, 377.*

1323. 17 April 1706—Certificate is granted Capt George Eskridge for two thousand three hundred & fifty Acres of Land for the Importation of forty seven persons into this Colony (vizt)

David Kenner	Thomas Lolly
Hugh McDarmil	Edward Butler
Will Kalleron	Ellinor Helbert
Thomas Keale	John McLanna
James Loope	William Siddon
Owen Doyle	Ellinor Phillips
Thomas Redish	Ellinor Morris
Laurence Trea	Roger Dey
Laurence Forne [or Ferne]	Thomas Corne
George Baskervill	Patrick Aminner [or Aminuer]
Nora Higgins	Edmund Kennall
Tagor King	Sarah Carty
Margaret Hand	Susana Palonert [?]
Honno^r Wells	Sam^{ll} Mitchell
Toby Kelly	Elizabeth Patten
Michaell Kelly	Sam^{ll} Short
Margaret Morris	John James
Henry Hambrooke	William James
Patrick Sarchfeild	Jeremiah Grantham
Thomas Burke	George Newton
Teaugne Kelly	Anne Meuach [?]
Patrick Naster	Tomson Gayer
Alice Mealy	Ellinor Cannon
Margarett Mulley	

OB 1699–1713, Part 1, 378.

1324. 17 Aprill 1706—William Beane, servant to William Arledge, complayneing to this Court that his sd Master doth not Cloath him as he ought to doe, It's ordered the sd Beane returne home to his Master's service, the sd Arledge haveing in Court promised to Cloath him fitting for such servant. *OB 1699–1713, Part 1, 378.*

1325. 15 May 1706—Onesiphorus Harvey, petitioning this Court agt his serv^t woman Anne Grin Dorothy for absenting herselfe from his service and the sd Anne appearing & pray it might lye cont'd [continued] to the next Court

& that Mr Schreever might be summoned, It's ordered the sheriffe summon ye sd Schrever to ye next Court to give his evidence therein. *OB 1699–1713, Part 1, 380.*

1326. 15 May 1706—Rosamond Wills, petitioning this Court ag^t Isaac Hester for her freedom, upon the sd Hester's motion the cause is continued to the next Court. *OB 1699–1713, Part 1, 380.*

1327. 17 July 1706—Plato, an Indian Boy belonging to Mr Hancock Lee, being brought to this Court to be adjudged, is by the Court adjudged to be five yeares old. *OB 1699–1713, Part 1, 385.*

1328. 18 July 1706—Mary Dennis, serv^t to Thomas Gill, being much distemper'd & comeing into Court & declareing herselfe to be willing to serve her sd Master two yeares after her time by Indenture or Custome is expired provided he will endeavour for her cure which he in Court engageing to doe, It's ordered shee serve her sd Master the said terme after Indented or accustomed time shall be expired. *OB 1699–1713, Part 1, 386.*

1329. 18 July 1706—Rosamond Wells, petitioning this Court for her freedom being bound by two paire of Indentures bearing the same date unto Isaac Hester which said Indentures being produced and perused by the Court—The Court are of opinion and doe adjudge the said Indentures not good and doe therefore order the said Wells be free. *OB 1699–1713, Part 1, 387.*

1330. 21 Aug. 1706—William Onellican, late serv^t to Robert Reeves, petitioning this Court for his Corne & Cloathes haveing served his said Master according to Law and the said Reeves not appearing, It's therefore ordered the sheriffe summon the said Reeves to the next Court to answer the said Complaint. *OB 1699–1713, Part 1, 393.*

1331. 21 Aug. 1706—Ann Gadd, serv^t to Thomas Miller, haveing had a bastard Child in the time of her service by Carroll Dun as she hath made oath, serv^t to Richd Hews, It's ordered shee serve her sd Master for her sd default according to Law and ordered the sherriffe take her into Custody & bring her to ye next Court to render punishment as ye Law Directs. *OB 1699–1713, Part 1, 393.*

1332. 21 Aug. 1706—Ellinor Maddin, serv^t to Mr Joseph Hoult, haveing had a bastard Child in the time of her service by her fellow serv^t James Hughs as she hath made oath, It's ordered shee serve her sd Master for her sd default according to Law and halfe a year for her fine, her Master haveing in Court assumed the payment thereof. *OB 1699–1713, Part 1, 393.*

1333. 19 Nov. 1706—Whereas it hath beene Certified to this Court by Capt John Cralle that Phillip S__ett [not legible], servant to Col. Rodham Kenner deced, hath absented himselfe from his said Master's service forty eight dayes as by his owne confession and before evidence, It's therefore ordered he serve the sd Deced's estate ninety six dayes for his said Default according to Law. *OB 1699–1713, Part 1, 402.*

1334. 19 Nov. 1706—Phebe Whitter, serv^t to John Cottrell, being brought to this Court for haveing a Bastard Child, It's ordered the sheriffe take her into Custody & give her five & twenty lashes upon her bare back well laid on for her sd default according to Law. *OB 1699–1713, Part 1, 402.*

1335. 19 Nov. 1706—Peter Barly, serv^t to Thomas Rout, being brought to this Court to be adjudged when he becomes tythable being brought into this Country by Indenture for nine yeares is by the Court adjudged to be tenn yeares of age. *OB 1699–1713, Part 1, 402.*

1336. 18 Dec. 1706—It's ordered the sheriffe of this County take into his Custody Elizabeth Lynne, serv^t woman of Enoch Hills, Mary Williams, serv^t to Richd Russell & Lovis Bee, being presented to this Court by the grand jury for haveing Bastard children & them in safe Custody to keepe untill they enter into bond with good security for their appearance at the next Court to answer their Defaults. *OB 1699–1713, Part 2, 423.*

1337. 19 March 1706/07—Arthur Kensloe, serv^t to the estate of Coll Rodham Kenner deced, aged thirteen yeares, being brought to this Court by Capt Francis Kenner & Capt Christ^r Neale Exec^{rs} of the sd deced to be adjudged how long he should serve, he by his Indenture being bound for Maryland and it appearing to this Court that serv^{ts} in Maryland serve but till they are two & twenty yeares of age, It's therefore ordered the sd Kensloe be free att that age. *OB 1699–1713, Part 2, 432.*

1338. 19 March 1706/07—Mary Williams, serv^t to Richard Russell, being presented to this Court by the grand jury for haveing a Bastard Child and her sd Master in Court assumeing the paym^t of her fine to the parish, It's ordered shee serve her sd Master for the same according to Law. *OB 1699–1713, Part 2, 432.*

1339. 19 March 1706/07—Bridgett Fitzgerrald, serv^t to Mr Thomas Hughlett, being presented to this Court for haveing a bastard Child by John

Conner as she hath made oath and her said Master in Court assumeing the paym^t of her fine to the parish, It's therefore ordered shee serve her sd Master therefore as alsoe for her default according to Law. *OB 1699–1713, Part 2, 432.*

1340. 19 March 1706/07—Certificate being made to this Court by Capt John Cralle that John Williams, serv^t to Mrs Elizabeth Bankes, absented himselfe from his sd Mistress's service twenty eight daies, It's therefore ordered he serve his said Mistress fifty six dayes for his sd Default according to Law & fourteene dayes for her Charges in Recovering the sd serv^t againe. *OB 1699–1713, Part 2, 432.*

1341. 23 May 1707—An agreem^t made by Joseph Phillips, serv^t to Richard Russell with his said Master before Coll. George Cooper, one of her Majesty's Justices of the Court, this day being presented to the Court and the said Phillips in Court haveing acknowledged the agreem^t the same is on the sd Mr Russell's motion admitted to Record. *OB 1699–1713, Part 2, 453.*

1342. 16 July 1707—Hugh Fullerton, serv^t to Richard Oldham, being brought to this Court to be adjudged when he becomes tythable is by the Court adjudged eleven years old. *OB 1699–1713, Part 2, 460.*

1343. 16 July 1707—Solomon Bowles, petitioning this Court that he hath served Doctor William Harcum his full time according to Law and that the sd Harcum notwithstanding refuses to pay his Corne & Cloathes as ye Law directs, It's therefore ordered the sheriffe summon the sd Harcum to the next Court to answer the said Complaint. *OB 1699–1713, Part 2, 462.*

1344. 20 Aug. 1707—William Williams, serv^t to Mr Richard Russell, being brought to this Court to be adjudged when he becomes tythable, is by the Court adjudged thirteene yeares old. *OB 1699–1713, Part 2, 476.*

1345. 20 Aug. 1707—Solomon Bowles, petitioning this Court ag^t Doct^r Wm Harcum for his freedom & Corne & Cloathes accustomed by Law, and it appeareing to this Court that the sd Bowles hath served his full terme to the sd Harcum, It's therefore ordered that he be free and Judgm^t granted the sd Bowles ag^t ye sd Harcum for his Corne & Cloathes by Law accustomed & ordered the sd Harcum pay the same unto the sd Bowles with costs als Ex^{on}. *OB 1699–1713, Part 2, 479.*

1346. 17 Sept. 1707—Katherine Jones, Petitioning this Court that shee hath served her Master, Bartholl: Schreever, her full accustomed time according to

Law and that he refuses to deliver her her Corne & Cloathes accustomed, It's therefore ordered the sheriffe summon the sd Schreever to the next Court to answer the sd Compl^t. *OB 1699–1713, Part 2, 487.*

1347. 18 Nov. 1707—Judgm^t is granted George Dunkin ag^t Nicholas Lehugh for his Corne and Cloaths according to the old Law, he haveing served the said Lehugh his full Indented time and ordered the sd Lehugh pay the same to the sd Dunkin only deducting two bushells & a halfe of Corne pd by ye sd Lehugh for ye sd Dunkin by order of Capt John Howson with Costs of suite als Ex. *OB 1699–1713, Part 2, 491.*

1348. 19 Nov. 1707—Martha Boyd, serv^t to John Shaw of Wiccocomoco Parish in this County, being presented to this Court for haveing a bastard Child by Dan^{ll} McCarty as she hath made oath and the sd Martha in Court assumeing to serve her sd Master one yeare for the paym^t of her fine & he assumeing to pay the same to the sd parish, It's therefore ordered shee serve her sd Master one yeare for ye same as alsoe for her sd default according to Law. *OB 1699–1713, Part 2, 491.*

1349. 19 Nov. 1707—Dan^{ll} McCarty in Court assumeing to pay unto John Shaw one thousand pounds of tobacco or to serve him the full terme of one whole yeare provided the sd Shaw should keepe a base child sworne to the sd McCarty in Court by Martha Boyd and the sd Shaw assumeing soe to doe, It's therefore ordered the sd McCarty pay the sd Shaw one thousand pounds of tobacco or serve him the sd terme. *OB 1699–1713, Part 2, 491.*

1350. 19 Nov. 1707—Ellinor Reader, servant to Mrs Elizabeth Downing, being presented to this Court for haveing a bastard Child by Joseph Gadis, serv^t to Mr John Cole, as shee hath made oath, It's therefore ordered shee serve her sd Mistress for her sd default according to Law and that the sheriffe give her twenty lashes on her bare back well laid on for her said offence as alsoe that the sheriffe summon the sd Gadis to the next Court to answer his sd offense. *OB 1699–1713, Part 2, 492.*

1351. 21 Jan. 1707/08—Upon the Petition of James White therein setting forth that he haveing served Mr John Haynie Junr his full accustomed & demanding his Corne & Cloathes of his sd Master due according to Law who refuses to pay him the same, It's therefore ordered unless the sd Haynie appeare at the next Court & answer the sd Compl^t, Judgm^t shall pass against him by Default. *OB 1699–1713, Part 2, 501.*

1352. 19 Feb. 1707/08—Judgm^t is granted James White ag^t his late Master

John Haynie Junr for his Corne & Cloaths according to Law, he haveing served his full accustomed time as the Law directs and ordered the sd Haynie pay him the same forthwith together with Costs als Ex. *OB 1699–1713, Part 2, 505.*

1353. 17 March 1707/08—Thomas Wallise, serv^t to Mr John Cralle, being brought to this Court to be adjudged, is by the Court adjudged to be twelve yeares old and ordered he serve his said Master or his assignes according to Law. *OB 1699–1713, Part 2, 507.*

1354. 17 March 1707/08—Mary Daly, presented by ye grandjury for haveing a Bastard Child & appeareing in Court sweareing ye same to be begotten by John Shaw, It's therefore ordered that the sheriffe take the sd Shaw into his Custody & him safely to keep untill he enter into bond with good & sufficient security for his appearance at ye next Court or into bond to save ye Parish of Wiccocomoco harmless and alsoe that he take ye sd Default according to Law. *OB 1699–1713, Part 2, 509.*

1355. 17 March 1707/08—Mary Rutt, serv^t to Richard Price, presented by ye grandjury for haveing a Bastard Child & not appeareing & her Master in Court assumeing for her appearance ye next Co^{rt}, ye same is continued. *OB 1699–1713, Part 2, 509.*

1356. 17 March 1707/08—Phebe Whitter, serv^t to Mr John Cotrell, being presented to this Court by ye grandjury for haveing a bastard Child, It's ordered the sheriffe take her into his Custody and give her twenty lashes on her bare back well laid on for her sd Default according to Law. *OB 1699–1713, Part 2, 509.*

1357. 19 May 1708—Katherine Line, serv^t to John Nelmes, being presented to this Court for haveing a Bastard Child as she hath made oath by Thomas Ryder, It's ordered that shee serve her sd Master for her said Default according to Law as alsoe for her fine, her Master haveing in Court assumed the paym^t of the same to ye Parish of St Stevens [Stephens]. *OB 1699–1713, Part 2, 515.*

1358. 19 May 1708—William Carpenter, bringing a boy to this Court to be adjudged when he becomes a tythable, he being brought into this Colony by Indenture for six yeares, is by the Court adjudged to be fourteene yeares of age. *OB 1699–1713, Part 2, 515.*

1359. 20 May 1708—Katherine Thawe [or Thane], serv^t to Mr Richard

Neale, being brought to this Court to be adjudged, is by ye Court adjudged to be fifteene yeares old & ordered shee serve her sd Master or his assignes according to Law. *OB 1699–1713, Part 2, 518.*

1360. 16 June 1708—Mr John Taylor, presenting his serv^t Wm Edwards to this Court & praying he might be Levyey [levy] free untill he is capable of workeing, he being much distemper'd and the sd Edwards appeareing to be distempered and uncapable of service, the Court doe therefore consider that the sd Taylor be free from paying any Levy for the sd Edwards this two yeares. *OB 1699–1713, Part 2, 528.*

1361. 16 June 1708—Daniell Davis, servant to Parish Garner, haveing absented himselfe from his sd Master's service fifty three daies as his said Master hath made oath in Court, It's therefore ordered that he serve his sd Master for his sd Default according to Law, and it appeareing alsoe that his said Master has expended eight hundred pounds of tobacco for takeing up and bringing home the sd servant as per Certificate thereof & other good proofe to the Court, It's therefore further ordered that he serve his said Master for the same according to Law. *OB 1699–1713, Part 2, 529.*

1362. 21 July 1708—Judgm^t is granted Mary Dennis, late serv^t of George Kesterson for her Corne and Cloathes according to Law to ye Custome of this Country and ordered the said George Kesterson pay her the same together with Costs als Ex^{on}. *OB 1699–1713, Part 2, 530.*

1363. 17 Nov. 1708—Upon the Petition of Mary Rich, a mulatto therein setting forth shee is deteyned a serv^t Contrary to Law & Prayed an attorney might be assigned her for the Recovery of her freedome, Capt George Eskridge is by ye Court assigned her attorney for y^t purpose. *OB 1699–1713, Part 2, 550.*

1364. 17 Nov. 1708—It appearing to this Court by a Certificate that James Fullerton, late serv^t of James Oldham but now serv^t to Capt Richd Hews, did absent himselfe from his late Master's service two months as alsoe that his sd late Master expended two hundred pounds of tobacco in takeing him up, It's therefore now ordered that he serve his sd present Master for the same according to Law after his Indented or accustomed time shall be expired. *OB 1699–1713, Part 2, 551.*

1365. 20 Jan. 1708/09—Mary Phillips, petitioning this Court ag^t her late Master, Richard Russell, for deteyning her Corne & Cloaths accustomed, shee haveing served him her full indented time, It's ordered the sheriffe summon the said Russell to the next Court to answer ye premises. *OB 1699–1713, Part 2, 563.*

1366. 20 April 1709—Ellinor Maddin, serv^t to Mr Joseph Holt, being presented to this Court for haveing a bastard Child by her fellow serv^t, James Hews, as she hath under oath and confessing alsoe to the Court that shee hath agreed to serve her sd Master two yeares from the first day of March next ensuing for his payment of this & alsoe a former fine to the Parish, It's therefore ordered that shee serve the sd terme soe agreed upon. *OB 1699–1713, Part 2, 571.*

1367. 20 April 1709—Thomas Barnes in behalfe of Mr Joseph Hoult assumes ye paym^t of five hundred pounds of tobacco to ye Church Wardens of St Steven's [Stephens] parish, it being Ellinor Maddin's fine for a bastard Child. *OB 1699–1713, Part 2, 571.*

1368. 20 April 1709—Thomas Barry, serv^t to John Hartly & sold to the sd John by Capt Edward Collins, haveing lost his Indenture but comeing into Court & owning himselfe willing to serve his sd Master five yeares, It's ordered that he serve him the sd terme and then to be discharged. *OB 1699–1713, Part 2, 572.*

1369. 20 April 1709—Thomas Barry, serv^t to John Hartly, being brought to this Court to be adjudged when to pay Levy, is by ye Court adjudged thirteene yeares of age. *OB 1699–1713, Part 2, 572.*

1370. 20 April 1709—Upon the motion of John Burge (late serv^t to Peter Coutanceau gen^t deced) who is lately free, It's ordered that Mrs Katherine Palmer, surviving adm^x of the sd deced, pay him his Corne & Cloaths according to Custome out of the sd dower's estate wth Costs als Ex^{on}. *OB 1699–1713, Part 2, 573.*

1371. 20 April 1709—John Luttrell, servant to Sarah Tullos, moveing this Court for Liberty to Choose his guardian to take care of his Land dureing his minority & nominating John Tullos, the sd Tullos is accordingly by the Court admitted his guardian for that purpose and ordered the sd Luttrell serve his full time of service to his sd M^{rs} without ye molestation of the sd John Tullos Jr. *OB 1699–1713, Part 2, 573.*

1372. 15 June 1709—John Baker, serv^t to William Nelmes, being brought to this Court to be adjudged when he becomes tythable, is by the Court adjudged to be fourteene yeares old. *OB 1699–1713, Part 2, 579.*

1373. 20 July 1709—Phillip Shaw, serv^t to Henry Boggass, imported into this Country by Indenture, in Court agreeing with his sd Master to serve him tenn yeares from the fourteenth day of Aprill last, his said Master in Court assumeing in Consideration thereof to teach the sd Shaw or cause him to be taught to Read, write & Cypher and at the end or expiration of the sd terme to give him a suite of aparrell more than is by the Law in such cases accustomed. *OB 1699–1713, Part 2, 583.* [It appears that Shaw may have been first a servant and later agreed to serve his master as an apprentice. In turn Boggass was to teach him to read, write, and some math.]

1374. 20 July 1709—Thomas Wood, servant to Robert Boyd, being brought to this Court to be adjudged when he becomes tythable, is by the Court adjudged to be thirteene yeares of age. *OB 1699–1713, Part 2, 583.*

1375. 20 July 1709—Edmond Mady, being brought to this Court to be adjudged when he becomes a Tythable, is by the Court adjudged to be fourteene yeares old. *OB 1699–1713, Part 2, 584.*

1376. 20 July 1709—William Calvin, serv^t to John Hill, haveing absented himselfe from his said Master's service thirty dayes and alsoe it appeareing to the Court that the said Hill hath expended two thousand one hundred & eighty pounds of Tobacco in pursueing & apprehending the said serv^t, It's therefore ordered the said Calvin serve his said Master for his sd Default & ye aforesd expence the terme of two yeares and four months after his Indented time shall be expired. *OB 1699–1713, Part 2, 585.*

1377. 21 July 1709—Thomas Walker, servant to John Linsey, being brought to this Court to be adjudged when he becomes a tythable, is by the Court adjudged to be fourteene yeares of age. *OB 1699–1713, Part 2, 587.*

1378. 22 Sept. 1709—Rachell, a mulatto girle belonging to the estate of John Webb deced, being presented to this Court for haveing a bastard Child by Arthur Thomas as shee hath made oath in Court, It's therefore ordered she serve her said Master's estate according to Law after her time by Custome or Law shall be expired. *OB 1699–1713, Part 2, 619.*

1379. 23 Sept. 1709—David Savage, Petitioning this Co^{rt} ag^t his late Master W. [not legible] Cornish for his Corne & Cloaths, It's ordered the sherife summon ye sd Cornish to the next Court to answer ye same. *OB 1699–1713, Part 2, 630.*

1380. 21 Dec. 1709—Capt Richard Hews, informeing this Court that Sarah Hutchins, now serv^t to Elizabeth Banks, hath a Child by a mulatto slave, It's ordered the sheriffe summon the said Sarah to ye next Court to answer ye premises. *OB 1699–1713, Part 2, 632.*

1381. 21 Dec. 1709—Thomas Wells, serv^t to Mr Jno Ingram, haveing absented himselfe from his sd Master's service some time and his said Master haveing expended two hundred pounds of tobbo for bringing him home, It's ordered he serve his sd Master for ye same & alsoe for his sd Default according to Law. *OB 1699–1713, Part 2, 635.*

1382. 17 Feb. 1709/10—Ellinor Hawkins, Petitioning this Court ag^t Sam^{ll} Blackwell & Margery his wife, relict of Joseph Hudnall deced, for deteyning her s serv^t & alsoe her Corne & Cloaths due by Law, It's therefore ordered the sheriffe summon the sd Blackwell and his wife to the next Court to answer the said Complaint. *OB 1699–1713, Part 2, 639.* [At a court held on 16 March 1709/10, a trial by jury was held and Ellinor was ordered to be discharged and Samuel Blackwell ordered to pay her corn and clothes together with costs of court. *OB 1699–1713, Part 2, 646, 647.*]

1383. 16 March 1709/10—Daniell Davis, haveing absented himselfe from the service of his Mrs Mary Price, widow, her service for the space of twenty daies & his sd M^{rs} haveing expended seven hundred pounds of Tobacco to bring him home, It's ordered he serve his said M^{rs} for the same as alsoe for his said Default according to Law. *OB 1699–1713, Part 2, 646.*

1384. 16 March 1709/10—William, a mulatto begotten by a Negro on a white woman & seven years old this instant March, is by the Court bound to serve Mary Price, widd^o, & her assignes according to Law. *OB 1699–1713, Part 2, 646.*

1385. 17 March 1709/10—John Williams, covenant servant to Phillip Rogers, haveing absented himselfe from his Master's service eight & twenty daies and alsoe the said Rogers haveing expended twenty shillings sterl: for bringing him home as he hath in Court made oath which the Court vallues at three hundred pounds of Tobacco, It's therefore ordered the said Williams serve the sd Rogers for the same as alsoe for his sd Default according to Law *OB 1699–1713, Part 2, 651.*

1386. 17 May 1710—Thomas Allen, servant to Mr Thomas Downing haveing absented himselfe from his said Master's service one hundred sixty

231

four daies & his master haveing expended three hundred forty four pounds of Tobacco to Recover him againe as appears by accounts, It's therefore ordered the sd Allen serve his sd Master for ye same as alsoe his default according to Law. *OB 1699–1713, Part 2, 658.*

1387. 21 June 1710—Thomas Wood, serv^t to Robt Boyd, haveing runaway and absented himselfe from his sd Master's service eight daies & his master haveing in Court made oath that he expended two hundred & thirty pounds of Tobacco in recovering him againe, It's therefore ordered that he serve his said Master three months & tenn daies in Lieu of the sd Tobacco expended and according to Law for his sd default after his Indented or accustomed time shall be expired. *OB 1699–1713, Part 2, 663.*

1388. 22 June 1710—Hugh Bristow, serv^t to John Hill, haveing runaway and absented himselfe from his said Master's service thirty eight daies and his Master haveing expended seven hundred pounds of Tobacco in Recovering him againe, It's therefore ordered that he serve his said Master tenn months & a halfe in lieu of the said tobacco expended and according to Law for his said Default after his Indented or accustomed time shall be expired. *OB 1699–1713, Part 2, 669.*

1389. 19 July 1710—Wiliam Phillips, a mulatto belonging to Mrs Elizabeth Banks, being one and twenty years old ye ninth day of March next is by the Court bound to serve the said Elizabeth or her assignes untill he arrives to the age of twenty four yeares, the said Elizabeth during the sd Terme finding & allowing the sd serv^t competent cloathing, meat, drink, washing and lodging. *OB 1699–1713, Part 2, 676.*

1390. 20 July 1710—Mary Jackson, petitioning this Court that shee hath since her arrivall into this Colony served Coll. Rodham Kenner deced in his life time & Capt Christopher Neale & Capt Francis Kenner, his Exec^{rs}, since his death the space of five yeares and upwards, yett the said Neale and Kenner Exec^{rs} as aforesd refuses to discharge her & pay her Corne & Cloaths which shee conceives to be due, It's therefore ordered that the sheriffe summon the said Capt Neale & Capt Kenner to the next Court to answer the said Petition. *OB 1699–1713, Part 2, 679.*

1391. 16 Aug. 1710—Ebenezer Ram, serv^t to John Haynie, petitioning this Court that his sd Master Cloaths him not as he ought to doe, It's therefore ordered that his master take him home and Cloath him as is Convenient for such a serv^t or upon the next just Complaint he be removed from his said service as the Law directs. *OB 1699–1713, Part 2, 686.*

1392. 16 Aug. 1710—Ebenezer Ram doth in Court bind himselfe together with the Consent of his former Master, John Haynie, to serve Tho: Thorne from this present time till next Christmas come twelve months. *OB 1699–1713, Part 2, 687.*

1393. 24 Jan. 1710/11—This Indenture made this 24 day of January in ye year of Our Lord 1710 Between Alexander Sollomon of the parrish of Cople in ye County of Westmoreland laborer of the one part & Patrick Burn of the Parrish & County aforesd planter of the other p^t Wittnesseth y^t ye sd Alexander doth covenant & agree with the sd Patrick to serve him ye said Patrick, his Exec^{rs} or assignes from the day of ye date hereof for & dureing ye full terme & time of four years from thence next ensueing in all such lawfull employm^t as ye sd Patrick his Exec^{rs} etc shall think fitt to imploy him in Consideration he ye said Patrick Burn for himselfe, his Exec^{rs} & assignes doth covenant & agree to & with ye said Alexander Sollomon to find him sufficient meatt, Drink, washing, Lodging & apparrell dureing ye said Terme & to pay to Wm Rust for ye said Alexander ye sume of six hundred pounds of Tobacco & to pay to ye widdow Smyth in ye Provence of Maryland for ye said Alexander the sume of five hundred pounds of Tobacco & at the expiration of ye aforesaid Terme of four years to pay & deliver to him ye said Alexander one young mare of four years old, one new saddle & Bridle and one new suit of Clothes fitt for him ye said Alexander of Kersey or Serge & then to discharge him from this Indenture in Testimonie whereof Both parties hath interchangeably thereunto sett there hands & affixed there seales the day and year above written.

             Alexand^r W Sollomon

RB 1710–13, 100.

1394. 21 March 1710/11—Mr John Ingram, makeing it appear to this Court that his serv^t Thomas Wells haveing absented himselfe from his said Master's service for the apprehending of whom his Master haveing expended four hundred pounds of tobacco, It's therefore ordered that he serve his said Master for the same after his Indented or accustomed time shall be expired according to Law. *OB 1699–1713, Part 2, 709.*

1395. 21 March 1710/11—Marea, a mulatto serv^t belonging to Mr Joseph Holt, being brought to this Court to be adjudged for haveing a bastard Child shee is by the Court adjudged to serve her said Master for her Default and Trouble according as the Law directs. *OB 1699–1713, Part 2, 710.*

1396. 22 March 1710/11—Katherine Line, serv^t to Eliz^a Walters, widdow being presented to this Court for haveing a Bastard Child and covenanting in Court to serve her sd M^rs for three yeares for her Default, paying her fine & saveing the Parrish of Wiccocomoco harmless from ye sd Child, It's therefore [ordered] that shee serve her sd M^rs or her assignes the sd Terme of three yeares. *OB 1699–1713, Part 2, 711.*

1397. 22 March 1710/11—Christopher Maise doth hereby in Court obleidge himselfe, his heires, Exec^rs to pay unto the Churchwardens of Wiccocomoco parish ... for the time being five hundred pounds of Tobacco on demand, it being for Katharine Line's fine for haveing a Bastard Child & ordered he pay the same wth Costs als Ex^n. *OB 1699–1713, Part 2, 711.*

1398. 22 March 1710/11—Mary Jackson, petitioning this Court that shee is a free woman and that Christ^r Neale & Francis Kenner Gent Exec^rs of Rodham Kenner Gent, deced doe keepe and constraine her to Labor contrarie to all Justice & Equity, It's therefore ordered the sheriff summon the said Christ^r Neale & Francis Kenner Exec^rs as aforesd to make their appearance att the next Court to answer the premises. *OB 1699–1713, Part 2, 712.*

1399. 22 March 1710/11—Thomas Lock this day came into Court & assumeing to serve Mr Richard Nutt three yeares from Christmas next (to be employed in teaching the sd Nutt's children to read) & not to worke in the ground under an overseer, In consideration whereof the sd Nutt assumes to teach the sd Lock to write & Cypher as farr as he can, It's therefore ordered that the sd Lock serve ye sd Nutt the terme aforesd and that he teach the sd Lock to write & Cypher as aforesd. *OB 1699–1713, Part 2, 713.*

1400. 22 March 1710/11—Richd Williams, petitioning this Court that he hath served his full time of service with Mr Richard Lattimore yett, the sd Lattimore refuses to let him goe free or pay him what by Law is accustomed, It's therefore ordered that ye sheriffe summon the said Lattimore to the next Court to answer ye premises. *OB 1699–1713, Part 2, 713.*

1401. 16 May 1711, Inventory of the estate of Mary Hughlett—1 servant named Thomas Allen, 2000 lbs. *RB 1710–13, 32.*

1402. 16 May 1711, Inventory of the estate of Richard Russell—1 woman serv^t named Alice Shadock, 2000; 1 servant lad named Wm Williams at 2200. *RB 1710–13, 36.*

1403. 16 May 1711, Inventory of the estate of Vincent Garner—2 negro men, 16000^lbs. *RB 1710–13, 47.*

1404. 16 May 1711—Francis Opalbow, serv^t to Peter Revir, comeing into Court and affirmeing to the Court that he had agreed with and was willing to serve his said Master the space of three yeares after his Indented time should be expired in Consideration that his sd Master had bought him from a hard Master, It's therefore ordered he serve his said Master the said Terme as aforesd. *OB 1699–1713, Part 2, 716.*

1405. 17 May 1711—Richard Williams, Petitioning this Court that Richard Lattimore, his late Master, detained him in his service Contrary to Law as alsoe his Corne & Cloaths to him due and belonging and the said Lattimore appearing and in Court affireming he had paid the sd Williams his Corne & Cloaths and alsoe had discharged him from him, the sd Lattimore's service & that he would likewise give him a Coate for some small matter done & the said Williams makeing noe objection ag^t the same, the Suits Dismis^t. *OB 1699–1713, Part 2, 724.*

1406. 20 June 1711—Patrick Grady, servant to Christopher Conaway, brought to this Court for absenting himselfe from his Master's service & it appeareing to the Court that he absented himselfe from his said Master's service twenty six daies & that his Master expended two hundred pounds of Tobacco for apprehending him as Mr John Claughton affirmed to ye Court, It's therefore ordered that the sd Grady serve his sd Master for his sd Default and alsoe for his sd two hundred pounds of Tobacco expended in takeing him according to Law. *OB 1699–1713, Part 2, 732.*

1407. 10 July 1711—Katharine Carty, serv^t to Mr Clem^t Spellman, presented by the grandjury for haveing a bastard Child & haveing sworne to the father before a Justice & Mrs Hannah Spellman, haveing in Court assumed the Paym^t of her fine to the Parrish of St Stevens [Stephens], It's therefore ordered that the sd Katharine serve her said Master for the paym^t of her fine to the Parrish and alsoe for her said Default according to Law. *OB 1699–1713, Part 2, 736.*

1408. 18 July 1711, Inventory of the estate of Robert Boyd—a servant boy having between 4 & 5 yeares to serve, 1800. *RB 1710–13, 70.*

1409. 15 Aug. 1711, Inventory of the estate of Doctor James Rogers—1 serv^t man named Hugh 2 y^{rs} to serve, 1200. *RB 1710–13, 102.*

1410. 19 Sept. 1711—Alexander Solomon, late serv^t of Patrick Burne from whom Wm Metcalfe hath purchased him, having assumed in Court to serve the sd Metcalfe six years from this day according to an Indenture ... *OB 1699–1713, Part 2, 749.*

1411. 20 Sept. 1711—Ann Enderby, late Servt of Jno Keine, for the Consideration of discharging her from the sd Keine, her sd master's service, doth hereby in Court assume to serve Robt Davis or his assignes the terme of four years from this time forward, the sd Davis therefore in Court having assumed to pay the sume of twelve hundred pounds of tobacco unto the sd Keine and ordered that the sd Ann serve the sd Davis or assig^s as aforesd the sd term of four years according to her sd assumption. *OB 1699–1713, Part 2, 756.*

1412. 19 Dec. 1711—Wm Medcalfe for the Consideration of the Cure of a maladay to be perfected in a sore legg of Robert Jackson's wch in Court he hath assumed to perform by & with the Consent of the said Jackson here in Court the said Cure performed but not otherwise is to have of the said Robert Jackson six monthes service & ordered in case the said Medcalfe shall perform ye said Cure that the said Jackson shall performe his said service. *OB 1699–1713, Part 2, 758.*

1413. 20 Feb. 1711/12—Tho: Wood, serv^t to Ann Boyd, having petitioned this Court ag^t his sd Mistress for hard usage, It's ordered that the sherr: cite the sd Anne to the next Court to answer the Complaint of her sd serv^t. *OB 1699–1713, Part 2, 768.*

1414. 21 Feb. 1711/12—Arthur Kenslow, serv^t to the estate of Rodham Kenner gent^l deced, having petitioned this Court concerning his freedome wch the Court having Consulted are of opinion and accordingly doe order that he serve three years from ye nineteenth day of March next at the expiration of wch term his due performance of his lawfull service ye Court adjudge that he shall be then free. *OB 1699–1713, Part 2, 770.*

1415. 19 March 1711/12—Tho: Wood, serv^t to Ann Boyd, having runaway from his sd Mistress's imploym^t, absented himselfe seven dayes, It's ordered he serve for his sd Default according to Act. *OB 1699–1713, Part 2, 772.*

1416. 18 June 1712—Alice Chadock, serv^t to Tho: Smyth, having had two Bastard Children at a Birth by Wm Williams, serv^t also of the sd Smyth, It's ordered that she serve her sd Master for her sd default according to Law and upon the motion of ye sd Alice & her ... It's ordered that she serve her sd master after her accustomed or indented time expired one yeare in Consideration of her sd Master's paying the fine wch he hath in Court assumed to pay to the use of the parrish of St Stephens als Exec. *OB 1699–1713, Part 2, 783.*

1417. 19 June 1712—Hono^r Conner, serv^t to Jno Burne, petitioned this Court that she hath served her accustomed or indented time & prayed shee might be free and that her master pay to her her Corn & Clothes wch the sd Burn (appearing in Court) opposed alledging that her sd time was not expired and whereupon the sd Burn & Conner mutually consented & agreed (to witt) that the sd Hon^r Coner should be free & have her Corn & Clothes provided shee would bind her son to serve ye sd Burn untill he attained twenty one years of age, and on the sd Burn's motion wth the Consent as aforesd of ye sd Hon^r her sd son Jno Conner is bound an apprentice to serve ye sd Burn untill he attain ye age of one & twenty years, ye sd Burn during the sd term finding ye sd Conner wth Sufficient apparell, dyett, washing & lodging & teaching him to read ye Byble and ordered that the sd Hon^r be free & y^t sd Burn pay her her Corn and Clothes accustomed wth Costs als Exec. *OB 1699–1713, Part 2, 785.*

1418. 16 July 1712, Inventory of the estate of Joseph Hoult—one molato man named Jno haveing eleven years to serve at 500 per year, 5500; things belonging to the estate of the s^d dec^d not appraised, Paid James Hughs for freedom Clothes and all my wearing clothes . . . Ann Hoult. *RB 1710–13, 205.*

1419. 16 July 1712—Oliver Garner, having petitioned this Court ag^t Henry Hopkins for his freedom Corn & Clothes accustomed for that he had served ye sd Hopkins his master his Indented or accustomed time and the sd Hopkins having made oath y^t ye sd Oliver during the time of his service hath absented himselfe there from forty dayes, It's ordered he serve his sd Master ye sd term of forty dayes for his sd Default. *OB 1699–1713, Part 2, 788.*

1420. 16 July 1712—Eliz^a McColly, serv^t to Tho: Gill, having had a bastard Child in the time of her service by Antho: Baker as she hath made oath in Court & her sd Master wth the approbation & desire of ye sd Eliz^a having assumed to pay her fine & keep her sd Child from the charge of ye parrish, her punishment is therefore Remitted, shee having agreed in Consideration thereof to serve her sd Master as alsoe four years and ordered shee performe the sd service after her Indented or accustomed time shall be expired. *OB 1699–1713, Part 2, 789.*

1421. 20 Aug. 1712, Will of Thomas Matthew—Item whereas my loving Brother in Law Capt Jno Cralle & my old & faithfull serv^{ts} Mr. James Genn and Mary his wife have manifested every great faithfullness & Industry in ye managem^t of my affaires both whilst I dwelt in Virginia & will that my said brother Cralle & the sd James Genn & his said wife may quietly remaine &

reside in & upon & in ye peaceable Possession of the houses & lands now in their Respective Tenures during their respective lives.... *RB 1710–13, 215.*

1422. 17 Dec. 1712—An Appraisement of the Estate of Capt Jno Graham ... 2 years service of a white hand named Daniel James, 1600 lbs. tobacco; a serv^t boy named Matthew Simonds about five years to serve, 3000 lbs. tobacco. *RB 1706–20, 194.*

1423. 17 Dec. 1712—Rachell Day, a mulatto serv^t to the orphants of Jno Webb deced, having had a bastard Child by Negro Will (Capt Kenner's slave) as she hath made oath in Court, It's ordered she serve for her sd default according to law. *OB 1699–1713, Part 2, 803.*

1424. 17 Dec. 1712—Tho: Welsh and James Stepfort, serv^ts to Maurice Jones gent^l, being brought to this Court to be adjudged how old they are, are adjudged ye sd Thomas to be twelve and the sd James to be eleven years old. *OB 1699–1713, Part 2, 803.*

1425. 18 Feb. 1712/13—This Indenture made the eighteenth of Feb. Anno Dom 1712.13 Between Richd Hues & Edward Coles Churchwardens of Saint Stephens parrish in Northumberland County of the one and Edward Sanders one of the Exec^rs of Jno Webb dec^d for & in behalfe of Sarah Webb, the daughter of the said Jno Webb dec^d of the other part, Wittnesseth that whereas by Act of Assembly It is Provided that if any woman serv^t shall have a bastard Child by a negro & the Churchwardens of the parrish where such Child shall be borne shall bind the said Child to be a Servant untill it shall be thirty one years of age and Rachell Webb als Day, servant to the said Sarah Webb having had a bastard Child by a negro Pursuant to the said law, It is therefore hereby Covenanted & agreed by the said Churchwardens that the said Child named Winifred born in June last for the consideration of the said Sanders his allowing the said Winifred dureing the said Terme sufficient apparrell, dyett, washing & lodging saving the said parrish harmless shall serve & she is hereby bound to serve the said Sarah Webb her heirs & assigns from the day of the date hereof untill shee the sd Winifred shall attaine to the age of thirty one years according to law in Wittness of the premises the said parties have sett their hands & signed, sealed & delivered in the presence of ye Justice & acknowledged in Northumberland County Court by Capt Richard Hues & Mr Edwd Coles, Churchwardens of St Stephens parrish the 19th Feb^r 1712/13 & is recorded. *RB 1710–13, 270.*

1426. 18 Feb. 1712/13—By ye information of Capt Geo: Eskridge ... to this Court y^t he has a suspicion that one Danl Conoly, a serv^t man belonging to Capt

Jn⁰ Cralle of this County & one Jack, a negro man belonging to Madam Eliz^a Bankes of this County, were guilty of burning of a ship in ye river Cone on the 8th day of this instant, It is therefore ordered y^t the sherr: or his Deputy doe forthw^th take a sufficient number of men wth him & take into Custody ye sd Danl & Jack & bring them before this Court where they may be examined concerning the premises. *OB 1699–1713, Part 2, 808.*

1427. 18 Feb. 1712/13—Thomas Wood, serv^t to Wm Fallen, came into Court & offered on his own free will and voluntary consent to serve his sd Master three years after his indented or accustomed time shall be expired for the Consideration of his sd Master's teaching him ye sd Wood or causing him to be taught to read, write and Cypher for the due performance of wch the sd Wm Fallen and Jn⁰ Pope doth hereby oblige themselves their heirs Exec^rs admin^rs joyntly & severally in the penal sum of six thousand pounds of tobacco to be pd to the sd Tho: Wood, his heirs, or assigns upon making out his sd Master's faylure in Complyance with such performance and whereupon it is ordered that the sd Tho: Wood serve the sd Wm Fallen (after his sd indented or accustomed time [is] expired) the sd term of three years as aforesd. *OB 1699–1713, Part 2, 809.*

1428. 19 Feb. 1712/13—Winnifred Day (als Webb) her Indenture for service to Sarah Webb on ye motion of Edwd Sanders is admitted to record. *OB 1699–1713, Part 2, 809.*

1429. 19 Feb. 1712/13—Daniel Conoly, serv^t to Capt Jn⁰ Cralle, having been taken into ye sherriff's Custody upon suspicion of being a Principall actor in burning the ship Nightingale or Biddeford Capt Jn⁰ Drew commander in Cone river in this County and the sd Daniel Conoly having been charged wth the said fact by Geo Eskridge gent^l . . . & strictly examined in Court & the circumstances wheron the sd suspicion was groundless duely considered and the Court not finding any lawfull cause to confine him, he is therefore released from the Sherr^s Custody. *OB 1699–1713, Part 2, 809.*

1430. 18 March 1712/13—Phillip Magrah, servant to Henry Hopkins, being brought to this Court to be adjudged how old he is, is adjudged to be eighteene years old. *OB 1699–1713, Part 2, 812.*

1431. 20 May 1713—Danl Connell, serv^t to Capt Jn⁰ Cralle, having been committed unto ye sherr^s Custody upon suspicion of felony and brought to this Court upon the motion of George Eskridge gentl attorney gen^ll & It is ordered that the sherr: putt him, ye sd Danl in Irons & Confine him Close prison & produce him here tomorrow for his tryall and also ordered that the sherr:

239

summon Henry Boggess & Mary Butler to make their appearance at his tryall & give in their evidence on behalfe of our soveriegn Lady ye Qu ag^t the sd Danl and also ordered y^t David Savage and William Way give their attendance on ye behalfe aforesd. *OB 1699–1713, Part 2, 815.*

1432. 20 May 1713—Terence Murphew, serv^t to Wm Heath, is by ye Court adjudged to be fifteen years old & ordered that he serve his sd Master according to Law. *OB 1699–1713, Part 2, 816.*

1433. 21 May 1713—Tho: Lock, serv^t to Richard Nutt, having petitioned this Court ag^t his sd Master, It's ordered that the sherr: cite the sd Nutt to make his appearance the next Court & answer the Complaint of the sd Lock. *OB 1699–1713, Part 2, 818.*

1434. 21 May 1713—Daniel Davis, serv^t to Wm Price, having petitioned this Court for his freedom & Corn & Clothes accustomed, It's ordered that the sherr: cite the sd Price to make his appearance at ye next Court to answer the sd Davis his Complaint. *OB 1699–1713, Part 2, 818.*

1435. 21 May 1713—Danl Connell, serv^t to Capt Jno Cralle, having been brought before this Court on suspicion of felony & divers evidences examined & sworn on behalfe of our sovereign Lady the Queen ag^t the sd Danl & nothing proved materiall touching the discovery of the felony whereof he stands accused, But it being made evident to the Court by the testimony of his sd Master & other proofe & circumstances that ye sd Danl is a stubborn, pilferring, unruly serv^t, a night walker, companion of negroes & greatly suspected to be as well an actor with as a concealor of their thefts and evill practices being also of a very lewd life & bad behaviour, It is therefore ordered that the sherr: cause him forthwith to be tyed in the Court house yard or feild and twenty lashes to be given him on his bare back well layd on & afterwards that the sherr: confine him untill the evening and cause him then againe to be tyed as aforesd have nineteen lashes more well layd on upon his bare back & y^t he be then released from confinem & sent home to his master. *OB 1699–1713, Part 2, 818.*

1436. 17 June 1713—Matthew Miller, serv^t to Tho: Gill, being brought to this Court to be adjudged what age he is, the Court adjudge him to be thirteen years old. *OB 1699–1713, Part 2, 820.*

1437. 18 June 1713—Danl Davis, serv^t to Wm Price, having petitioned this Court for his freedom and it appearing to this Court that he hath two years to serve from the fifteenth day of July next, It is therefore ordered that he return home to his sd Master's service & serve him or his assigns untill his sd time shall be expired. *OB 1699–1713, Part 2, 824.*

1438. 30 Oct. 1713—Wm Wayland, serv^t to Thomas Gill, is by the Court adjudged to be ten years old and on the sd Gill's motion, it is ordered he serve his sd Master according to Law. *OB 1713–19, 3.*

1439. 30 Oct. 1713—Edwd Ryan, serv^t to Tho: Gill, upon the motion of his sd Master, is adjudged to be eight years old & ordered he serve his sd master according to law. *OB 1713–19, 3.*

1440. 18 March 1713/14—Catherine Hughs, late serv^t to Teleife Alverson, petitioned this Court ag^t the sd Teleife for his noncomplyance with the performance of what he stands ingaged to Comply with to the sd Catherine by vertue of an order of this County Court, a conditional order is granted the sd Catherine ag^t the sd Telife for a thousand pounds of tobacco unless the said Teleife shall appear next Court & show reasons to the Contrary. *OB 1713–19, 27.*

1441. 16 June 1714—Inventory of Peter Coutanceau . . . one servant man one year to serve, 1100 lbs. of tobacco, [no name given]; one servant woman named Sarah, [no surname and no price given]. *RB 1706–20, 216.*

1442. 16 June 1714—Laurance Conner, a serv^t boy belonging to Jno Lewis on ye sd Lewis his motion is adjudged to be fifteen years old. *OB 1713–19, 42.*

1443. 16 June 1714—Solomon Northen, serv^t to Mr Jno Ingram, having runaway from his sd Master with two negroes, one of the sd Ingram's & the other belonging to Lazarus Dameron and the sd Ingram & Dameron produced their acc^{ts} upon their oathes for their trouble, charge and expences in recovering & regaining the sd Solomon & Negroes (who had transported themselves in a boat or vessel across the Bay to some Island) amounting to three thousand three hundred & sixty pounds of tob^a which was consulted & allowed by the Court and the sd Ingram having assumed the payment of twelve hundred & fourteen pounds of tob^a part of their sd expences unto the sd Lazarus Dameron, it being his whole claim out of the sd Joynt expence, It is therefore ordered upon the motion of the sd Ingram (being therwith contented) that ye sd Solomon Northen for his sd Default & in consideration of his absented time & the expences aforesd serve the sd Ingram or his assigns after his the sd Solomon's indented or accustomed time shall be expired the full term of four yeares & no longer. *OB 1713–19, 43.* [Solomon Northen was actually an apprentice. He was bound to John Ingram 17 Oct. 1711. *RB 1710–13, 113*. In the document above, one would think he was a servant.]

1444. 22 July 1714—Wm Hart, serv^t to Coll. Peter Hack, having runaway from his master's service and been six dayes absent and it appearing y^t his sd master hath pd two hundred pounds of tob^a for the taking up of the sd serv^t above ten miles from home, It is therfore ordered that the sd W^m serve his sd Master three monthes for his sd expense & twelve dayes for the time absented according to law. *OB 1713–19, 58.*

1445. 23 July 1714—Walter Sterling, serv^t to Tho: Ashburne, is by the Court adjudged to be thirteen years old. *OB 1713–19, 65.*

1446. 16 Feb. 1714/15—Michael Lowry, serv^t to Wm Metcalfe, having runaway from his sd Master's service and been absent forty six dayes and the sd Metcalfe having produced his acco^t ag^t the sd Lowry for his trouble & Charges (allowed by the Court) amounting to six hundred & eighty pounds of tob^a, It is ordered that the sd Lowry in consideration of his sd time absented and by his sd Master's Charge, trouble & expence as aforesd serve his sd Master or his assignes one year one month and eight dayes after his Indented or accustomed time shall be expired. *OB 1713–19, 93.*

1447. 17 March 1714/15—Jno Baskafeild, a poor distempered man having complained to this Court that he hath been unlawfully detained (by Phillip Bustle, Edward Lewis & others) as a serv^t under some pretensions of curing his malady and nothing appearing to this Court from any of ye sd pretenders who here made their appearance, the sd Baskafeild is therefore hereby discharged to apply himselfe to the Churchwardens of St Stephens parish for releife rendering satisfaction if cured. *OB 1713–19, 107.*

1448. 20 July 1715—Catherine Lyon, serv^t to Lilia Waters, having had a bastard Child (as she hath made oath by Wilt), an Indian (belonging to the Wiccocomoco town) in the time of her service, it is ordered she serve her said mistress for her sd default according to law and half a year for her fine (her sd Mistress paying the fine) after her indented time expires. *OB 1713–19, 125.*

1449. 20 July 1715—Lelia Waters doth hereby confess Judgm^t unto ye Churchwardens of Wicco^{co} parish for ye sum of five hundred pounds of tob^o for ye consideration of halfe a years service due to her paying the same for Catherine Lyons fine for a Bastard Child and ordered the said Lelia Waters pay ye said five hundred pds of tobacco for ye use of ye sd parish als Exec^n. *OB 1713–19, 125.*

1450. 20 July 1715—Saml Webb als Day, a mulatto serv^t to Mrs Jane Yarrett, having petitioned this Court ag^t his sd Mistress for his freedom on her motion the same is continued till the next Court. *OB 1713–19, 126.*

1451. 21 Sept. 1715—Robert Watts and John Taylor, serv^{ts} to Mr Jno Copedge, having unlawfully absented themselves from their said Master's service eighty dayes and the sd Jno Copedge having produced his acc^t to this Court ag^t his sd serv^{ts} wherein he charges the sum of seven thousand eight hundred & forty four pounds of tobacco expences for sending after, pursuing and taking them up wth other charges by the Court considered & allowed and by the sd serv^{ts} here present not gainsayed nor objected against, It is therefore ordered that ye sd serv^{ts} in consideration of their sd absented time and their sd Master's said expences serve their sd Master or his assigns after their Indented or accustomed time of service shall be expired each of them five years four months & ten dayes according to law. *OB 1713–19, 130.*

1452. 21 Sept. 1715—Tho Taylor als Wm Harmwood, serv^t to Mark Harding having absented his sd master's service eighty dayes unlawfully and his sd Master having put his acco^t into this Court ag^t the sd serv^t (who was here present which upon a regulation thereof and noe materiall objection by the sd serv^t made ag^t the same) amounts to the sum of three thousand nine hundred & thirty nine pounds & a halfe of tobacco, It is therefore ordered in Consideration of the sd absented time & ye acc^t aforesd (being for expences in pursueing, takeing up & other charges) that he the aforesd Taylor als Harmwood serve his said Master or assigns after his accustomed or indented time that be expired five years three months & thirteen dayes according to law in that case made and provided. *OB 1713–19, 131.*

1453. 22 Sept. 1715—Mr Wm Barnes of Sommersett County in the Province of Maryland having apprehended and taken up without the governm^t one Robt Watts & Jno Taylor, serv^{ts} to Mr Jno Copedge & Tho: Taylor als Wm Harmwood, serv^t to Mark Harden (which were runaway from their said master's service & brought home, the said serv^{ts} to their sd masters) exhibited an acc^t unto this Court ag^t the sd Runaways for eleven pounds, six Shill: & nine pence & prayed sattisfaction. And the said serv^{ts} being here present and heard the sd acc^t read containing divers articles for sundry goods & commodities wch they had of him ye sd Barnes together with their imprisonm^t & other Charges and making noe objection to any part of ye sd acco^t the same is by the Court allowed and ordered that each of the said runaways (to witt) Robt Watts, Jno Taylor & Tho: Taylor als Wm Harmwood in Compensation of ye said acc^t (being valued in Tob^o by the Court at five shill: p cent wch amounts to four thousand five hundred & thirty five pounds of tob^o besides the Costs) serve the said Barnes or his assigns for the said charges & acc^t two yeares (agreeable to act of assembly in that law provided preportioned to each serv^t at eight hundred pounds of tobacco p annum) after their time of service ended which they are to serve their present masters aforesd and on ye sd Barnes his motion the Court confides & hereby enter their opinion that if any of the sd serv^{ts} shall be disposed of by their present masters before their time of service shall be expired ye master or masters of such disposed serv^t or serv^{ts} shall take sufficient security of ye Purchaser of such serv^t or serv^{ts} provided they shall Comply with their service duely to such purchaser & shall be living at ye expiration thereof that they shall be then forthcoming to the sd Mr Wm Barnes or his assigns for their due Complyance wth this order on his behalfe any thing herein contained to the Contrary notwithstanding. *OB 1713–19, 135, 136.* [In the Index the name is Harding.]

1454. 18 May 1716—Alexand^r Salmon, serv^t to Wm Metcalfe having runaway & absented himself from his said Master's service three years eleven months and two and twenty dayes and his sd master having produced an acco^t in Court (approved & allowed) for his necessary trouble & experience in procuring his sd serv^t amounting to eleven hundred & twenty pounds of tobacco, Judgm^t is therefore granted ye sd Wm Metcalfe ag^t the said Alex^r Salmon and ordered that the sd Alex^r (after his indented or accustomed time shall be expired) serve ye said Metcalfe or his assignes in Consideration of his said unlawfull absenting himselfe from his sd master's service as aforesd and his sd Master's expenses as aforesd the term of nine years four months and eight dayes according to law in the like case made and provided. *OB 1713–19, 170.*

1455. 18 May 1716—Roger Moor, a negro transported serv^t (but no slave) to Richd Hudnall having been committed into the sheriff's Custody by precept from Mr John Ingram, one of his Majesty's Justices of the peace.... *OB 1713–19, 171, 172.* [A long court order in which Roger Moor was accused of breaking into the house of Thomas Eves and stealing certain items of clothing. Roger was found guilty and was ordered to receive 39 lashes on his bare back well laid on at the common whipping post. Richard Hudnall paid his fine, and he was released from jail. Roger was to enter into sufficient security in the penalty of forty pounds sterling for his good behavior.]

1456. 21 Nov. 1716—Phillip McGraugh, servant to Andrew Donelson, having absented himself from his master's service 43 Dayes & his master having produced his acc^t against him, amounting unto 250 pd of Tob^o he paid for taking him up, it is ordered he should serve for his fault & his master's sd expense of one yeare & eleven months after his Indented or accustomed time shall be expired. *OB 1713–19, 185.*

1457. 16 Jan. 1716/17—Elizabeth Murphew, serv^t to William Medcalf, came into Court and agreed to serve her said Master the term of one whole year after her Indented or accustomed time is expired and ordered that she perform the same accordingly. *OB 1713–19, 188.*

1458. 16 Jan. 1716/17—Tho: Wryon, servant to Tho: Hughlett, is judged to be fourteen years of age. *OB 1713–19, 190.*

1459. 17 Jan. 1716/17—James Wooden, servant to Hannah Harcum, is judged by the Court to be ten years of age. *OB 1713–19, 190.*

1460. 20 March 1716/17—James Cunningham, servant to Mrs Ann Hoult, is judged by the Court to be fifteen years of age. *OB 1713–19, 199.*

1461. 20 March 1716/17—Eliz^a Welsh, servant to Tho: Cunningham, made a complaint to this Court that her Indentures were altered & the word four years is struck out & five years inserted, the Court having examined Tho: Smith upon oath in relation to the premises who declared that he heard the sd Elizabeth say before she was sold to the said Cunningham that she had five years to serve (and ordered that she serve the said term of five yeares accordingly) which said Indenture is admitted to record. *OB 1713–19, 200.*

1462. 20 March 1716/17—Tho: Walker, serv^t to Tho: Pittman, came into Court & acknowledged his Indenture then given into Court by the sd Walker which he acknowledged to be his Indenture & by which he is willing to serve & the said Indenture is admitted to record. *OB 1713–19, 200.*

1463. 20 March 1716/17—Matthew Mitchell, servant to Wm Nelms, is judged by the Court to be fifteen years of age. *OB 1713–19, 201.*

1464. 20 March 1716/17—Tho: Welsh, servant to Christopher Garlington, is adjudged to be fifteen years of age. *OB 1713–19, 201.*

1465. 21 March 1716/17—Robert Homes, servant to Nicholas Lancaster, came into Court & acknowledged his Indenture for six years and ordered that he serve his said master according to the tennor of the same. *OB 1713–19, 201.*

1466. 17 April 1717—Jno Marson, servant to Mr Edward Coles, is by the Court adjudged to be eleven yeares of age which said Marson was sold to the said Coles by one Nathaniel Wattson, the said Marson having agreed to serve ye said Coles eight yeares to commence from the date hereof. It's therefore ordered that he serve his said Master the said term of eight years accordingly. *OB 1713–19, 204.*

1467. 16 May 1717—Sylvester Carty, a servant Boy belonging to Mr Charles Lee, is by the Court adjudged to be twelve yeares old and the said Lee having produced an Indenture in Court for seven years belonging to the said Carty and the said Carty having agreed to serve his said Master the Term of seven years according to the Tennor of the Indenture aforesaid and ordered that he perform the same accordingly and on the said Lee's motion, the said Indenture is admitted to Record. *OB 1713–19, 213.*

1468. 16 Oct. 1717—Richard Kenneday, a serv^t boy belonging to Elizabeth Million, being brought to this Court to be adjudged, is adjudged to be twelve years of age. *OB 1713–19, 251.*

1469. 18 Dec. 1717—Sarah Hudson, serv^t to Mr Barth^o Schrever, having runaway and absented her self from her said Master's service one hundred & forty nine dayes and her said Master having produced an Acco^t in Court for his necessary trouble, expenses in procureing his said serv^t amounting to the sum of two hundred pounds of Tobacco to which he hath made oath in Court, Judgment is therefore granted the said Schrever against the said Sarah Hudson and ordered that the said Sarah (after her Indented or accustomed time is expired) serve the said Schrever or his assignes in Consideration of her said unlawfull absenting her self from her said Master's service as aforesaid and her Master's expenses as aforesaid the Term of one whole year and Twenty three dayes according to Law. *OB 1713–19, 251.*

1470. 18 Dec. 1717—Amy Hatch, a serv^t woman belonging to Capt John Cralle which he purchased of Capt Edwad Collins for the Term of four yeares, came into Court and doe voluntarily consent and agree to serve the said Cralle or his assigns five years to commence from the date hereof provided she might not be compelled to worke in the ground and ordered that she serve the said Cralle or his assigns as aforesd the said Term of five yeares in all such Lawfully services and employment as he or they should employ her about except working in the ground aforesaid for and dureing ye term of five yeares as aforesaid anything herein contained to the contrary notwithstanding. *OB 1713–19, 252.*

1471. 19 Feb. 1717/18—Elizabeth McColley, a servant woman which

Robert Wilson bought of Thos Gill, came into Court and agreed to serve the said Wilson or his assigns the Term of six yeares to commence from the day of the date hereof to be released from the said Gill and ordered that she serve the said Wilson or his assigns as aforesaid the Term of six yeares accordingly. *OB 1713–19, 257.*

1472. 20 Feb. 1717/18—Thos Gardner, a servant boy belonging to Thos Smith, is by the Court adjudged to be eleven yeares old. *OB 1713–19, 260.*

1473. 20 Aug. 1718—Herman Hinderson, serv^t to Mr Robert Jones, is by the Court adjudged to be three yeares old last Chistmas and ordered that he serve his said Master according to Law. *OB 1713–19, 275.*

1474. 20 Aug. 1718—Andrew Cullealley, servant to Capt Maurice Jones, is by the Court adjudged to be fourteen years of age. *OB 1713–19, 275.*

1475. 21 Aug. 1718—John Taylor, servant to John Jordon, having runaway and absented himselfe from his said Master's service fourteen dayes and his said Master having produced an Account in Court for the trouble and necessary expences in procuring his said serv^t amounting to the sum of five hundred and Twelve pounds of Tobacco to which he hath made oath in Court, Judgment is therefore granted the said Jordon against the said Taylor and ordered that the said John Taylor (after his Indented or accustomed time shall be expired) serve the said Jordon or his assigns in Consideration of his said unlawfull absenting himself from his said Master's service as aforesaid and his Master's expences as aforesd the sum of ___ [no amount entered]. *OB 1713–19, 277.*

1476. 18 March 1718/19—Jerremy Dare, serv^t of James Gardner, judged to be twelve years old. *OB 1713–19, 309.*

1477. 20 May 1719—John Murdock, serv^t to Geo: Murdock, judged to be six years old. Wm Tully, serv^t to Jos: Humphry, judg'd to be eleven years old.

Charles Russell, serv^t to Graves Eves, having run away from his Master's service & been thirty four days absent, it appearing that his said Master hath paid three hundred & fifty pounds of Tobo. for taking up the said serv^t, it is therefore ordered that the said Cha: serve his said master five Callender Months & one week for his said expenses & sixty eight days for the time absented according to law. *OB 1713–19, 316, 317.*

1478. 20 May 1719—Attkins Dynon, serv^t of Wm James, having run away from his said Master's service & been absent fifteen days, it's therefore order'd that he serve his said Master thirty days for ye time absented according to law. *OB 1713–19, 317.*

1479. 20 May 1719—Ralph Smithhurst, serv^t to Mrs Mary Hughs, having runaway from his said Mistress and it appearing that his s^d Mistress has paid ye sum of 1424 Pounds Tobb^o for charges in taking up her said servant, it is ordered ye said servant serve his Mistress 21 months & a week and he having been run away from his service 18 days, it is ordered that he serve ninety six Days according to Law. *OB 1713–19, 323.*

1480. 18 June 1719—John Day, a servant to William Grinstead, having caus'd his said Master to be at ye Charges of 400^lbs Tobb^o for taking him up when running away, it is ordered he serve his said Master six months and he being absent from his said Master's service thirteen weeks & three days, it is further order'd that he serve his master six months and three weeks according to Law. *OB 1713–19, 323.*

1481. 20 Aug. 1719—Marguritt Pine was Judg'd by this Court to serve her Master, Mr Samuell Heath, Three months and three weeks for his charge of 250^lbs Tobb^o paid to Doctor Thornton occasion'd by the said servant's laying violent hands on her self, ordered that the said Marguritt Pine serve the said time to her said Master according to Law. *OB 1713–19, 334.*

1482. 20 Aug. 1719—Upon the motion of Jane Myars to this Court setting forth that she had brought up Christian Penny, a base born Child from an Infant, ordered that the said Christian serve the said Jane Myars till she arrive to the age of eighteen years. *OB 1713–19, 334.*

1483. 18 Nov. 1719—John Glan, serv^t of Sam^ll Winstead, Judged to be 10 years old. *OB 1713–19, 345.*

1484. 18 Nov. 1719—Thaddeus Dorgan and Joan his wife, servants of Timothy Greenham (agreed with their said Master to serve him one whole year above their Indented time in consideration that he would keep them together) and on the said Greenham's motion it's admitted to Record. *OB 1713–19, 345.*

1485. 18 Nov. 1719—Judith Bowling, serv^t of Ann Hould, came into Court and swore that John Figrow (a mulatto) was the father of a bastard child that she was lately brought to bed with, it is therefore ordered that after her Indented time is expired and a year for her Mistress's trouble she be sold by the

Church Wardens according to Law. *OB 1713–19, 347.*

1486. 20 Jan. 1719/20—Ellin Flynt, serv^t of Henry Bangess, came into Court and swore a bastard Child to Edward Hogan, the s^d Ellen voluntarily consented to serve her said master two years and a half for the paying her fine and the trouble of the house. *OB 1713–19, 351.*

1487. 20 Jan. 1719/20—Bridgett Kelly, serv^t of Mrs Jane Yarrat, came into Court and swore a bastard Child to Thos Allen, order'd that she serve her mistress according to Law. *OB 1713–19, 351.*

1488. 20 Jan. 1719/20—Ellenore Ring, serv^t of Wm Bowman, came into Court and voluntarily agreed to serve her said Master six years from her coming into the Country. *OB 1713–19, 353.*

1489. 18 May 1720—John Mockridge, serv^t of Stephen Hall, Judg'd to be 18 years old. *OB 1719–29, 10.*

1490. 18 May 1720—John Cambell, son of John Cambell, servant to Andrew Flannegan, Judg'd to be six years old. *OB 1719–29, 10.*

1491. 18 May 1720—Elizabeth Phillips, serv^t to Robert Davis, came into Court and agreed in presence of this Court with her said Master to serve him six months for his payment of five hundred pounds of tobacco to the Church Wardens of St Stephens Parrish for her having a bastard Child. *OB 1719–29, 10.*

1492. 18 May 1720—Alex^r Nelson, a serv^t to Mr Jno Opie, judged to be 16 years old. *OB 1719–29, 10.*

1493. 15 June 1720—Gilbert Murray, serv^t to John Crump, haveing absented himself from his said Master's service sixteen Days, the said Crump haveing made oath thereto upon the sd Crump's motion ordered that he serve his said master according to law. *OB 1719–29, 15.*

1494. 16 June 1720—Mary Mahon, serv^t to Elizabeth Rout, haveing had a bastard Child agrees with her said Mistress before the Court to serve her a year and seven months for her sd M^{rs} trouble & her . . . and paying her fine (after her Indented time is expired) and ordered by this Court that she serve the said time according to law. *OB 1719–29, 18.*

1495. 16 June 1720—John Crump came into Court and swore that Gilbert

Murray, his servant, absented himself from his service 26 Days and that he has paid one thousand pounds Tobb° for taking him up, Ordered that the said Murray serve his said Master above his Indented time one wole year and three months and fifty two Days according to law. *OB 1719–29, 23*.

1496. 20 July 1720—Upon the Petition of Marguritt Burn order'd that Mrs Mary Hughs pay her her freedom Corn according to Law. *OB 1719–29, 25*.

1497. 20 July 1720—George Green, serv^t of Thomas Ashburn, haveing runn away from his said Master one Day, Ordered that he serve his said Mast: two Days and three months for his payment of 200$^{\#}$ Tobb° for taking him up according to law. *OB 1719–29, 25*.

1498. 20 July 1720—Will of Elizabeth Banks . . . Item. It is my will that my mulatto man named John Spence be free and discharged from Servitude from me and my heirs immediately after my Decease. . . . *RB 1718–26, 128*.

1499. 21 July 1720—William Higgens, servant of Wm Grinstead, came into Court and agreed with his said master to serve him one whole year after his Indented time in Consideration his master will keep him to the trade of a Taylor and cause him to be learnt to cut out Cloaths. *OB 1719–29, 29*.

1500. 16 Oct. 1720—Will of Dennis Conway . . . Item. I give unto my Loving Wife Anne Conway a Negroe called Cupid to her and her heirs with a Servant named Patrick Mackmouris [or Mackmourn]. *RB 1718–26, 261*.

1501. 15 Feb. 1720/21—Upon the Pet [petition] of John Kennedy ord [ordered] serv^t to Thomas Smith. *OB 1719–29, 31*.

1502. 15 Feb. 1720/21—Patrick Murfey, serv^t to Wm Hobson, is judg'd to be 12 years old. *OB 1719–29, 32*.

1503. 16 Feb. 1720/21—Mr Wm Keen's Discharge of a mulatto man named Jn° Spence, formerly belonging to Mrs Elizabeth Banks, was this Day presented to this Court by Richard Lee and on his motion it's admitted to record. *OB 1719–29, 34*.

1504. 16 Feb. 1720/21—Elizabeth McColley came this Day into Court and voluntarily agreed to serve her said master David Smith two years above her Indented time in consideration of his giving her two suits of stutt [?] cloaths, a pair of Boddice [bodice], shooes and stocking, head Cloaths and gloves, a hood and shifts, one suit of the said Cloaths the said Elizabeth is to have upon

Demand with necessarys and the other att her freedom, the said Smith haveing bought her of a former master partly enjoyns the said McColley to make this agreement. *OB 1719–29, 35.*

1505. 16 Feb. 1720/21—Jane Sallaway, servant to Thomas Genn, came into Court & voluntarily agreed to serve her said Master one year above the Indented time on condition the said Genn uses his true endeavour to cure the said Jane of an ailment she's now troubled with by sallivation [salivation ?] or otherwise (it's thought proper and on the said Genn's motion it's admitted to record). *OB 1719–29, 37.*

1506. 15 March 1720/21—Inventory of the servants and slaves belonging to Mrs. Elizabeth Banks . . . Elizabeth Williams, about six months to serve; Charles Boulton, a mulatto about 11 years old born of an English woman; John Spence, sett free. . . . *RB 1718–26, 170.*

1507. 16 March 1720/21—Henry Kenney, servant to Thomas Smith, haveing made it appear to ye Court that he had an Indenture for four years being proved by the oaths of Jasper Steward and Thomas Webb, the said Kenney haveing served the said Smith that term, it is the Court's oppinions that the said Kenney is free from any further service due to his master. *OB 1719–29, 39.*

1508. 19 July 1721—John Lockier, servant of Capt Maurice Jones, having runn away from his said Master's service the space or time of Twenty one days and the said Jones having exhibited an acco^t to the Court of seven hundred Twenty Five pounds of Tobbaco, the said Jones has been all the charge of is taking up the said runnaway ordered that the said Lockier serve his said master after his Indenture time is expired forty two Days and ten Kallender months and a half and eleven Days according to law. *OB 1719–29, 41.* [After his indented time John Lockier was to serve John Stepto three months and 26 days because Lockier, when he ran away, had taken with him a Negro boy belonging to Stepto. This is in the very next entry.]

1509. 19 July 1721—Ralph Smithhurst, serv^t of Mrs Mary Hues dec^d, having run away from his service, ordered that he have twenty lashes on his bare back and that Capt George Eskriege Exec^{rs} of the said Dec^d have liberty to put on the said servant Irons. *OB 1719–29, 41.*

1510. 19 July 1721—Mary Mackmenis, a servant woman to Charles Nelms, came into Court and before the Court agreed with her said Master to serve him six months above her Indented time in consideration of his being at the charge in haveing her sallivated and useing his true endeavour of haveing her made a cure of an ailment, the said servant is now afflicted with. *OB 1719-29, 42.* [In the Index her name is McMennis.]

1511. 19 July 1721—Robert Porin, servant of John Foushee, haveing absented himself three Days from his said master's service and the said Foushee being att the charge of seventy pounds of Tobb^o in taking the said servant up, ordered that he serve his said master according to law. *OB 1719-29, 43.*

1512. 20 July 1721—John Maguire, serv^t of William Nelms, having assaulted a certain John Lacy upon the King's road and the evidences proving the facts ag^t him ordered that he have thirty nine lashes well laid on upon his bare back which was performed accordingly. *OB 1719-29, 45.*

1513. 20 July 1721—Inventory of the estate of William Price . . . a servant man named Robert, £5; a servant man named James, £10. . . . *RB 1718-26, 209.*

1514. 6 Sept. 1721—Inventory of the estate of Bartholomew Leazure . . . a man servant, £2. *RB 1718-26, 213.*

1515. 20 Sept. 1721—John and Agnis Cambell, serv^{ts} to Mrs Anne Hoult, came this day into Court and voluntarily agreed to serve their said mistress a year each of them after their Indented time was expired and on the said Anne Hoult's motion it's admitted to Record. *OB 1719-29, 49.*

1516. 20 Sept. 1721—Chatty Fergus, serv^t of Robt Reeves, haveing absented herself thirty Days from her s^d Master's service and he being att the charge of four hundred pounds of Tobb^o in takeing her up, ordered that the said servant serve her said Master eight Kallender months after her Indented time is expired. *OB 1719-29, 49.*

1517. 20 Sept. 1721—Fearnot Crowder, serv^t to Mr Jno Ingram, came into Court and agreed to serve her said Master two years above the Indented time and on the said Ingram's motion it's admitted to record. *OB 1719-29, 49.*

1518. 20 Sept. 1721—Mary Swords, servant of Mary Price, came into Court and agreed to serve her said Mistress Ten months above her Indented time in consideration of her said Mistress paying on her acco^t six hundred pounds Tobbacco. *OB 1719-29, 51.*

1519. 20 Dec. 1721—Mary Mahony, servant of Eliz: Rout, is ordered by this Court to serve her said Mistress three months above her Indented time on acco^t of her said Mistress paying two hundred pounds Tobb° for being taken up when runn away. *OB 1719–29, 58.*

1520. 17 Jan. 1721/22—Upon the Petition of Ann Fry ordered that Mr Robt Jones pay her her freedom Rites [rights] according to law, that is to say three barrels of Indian Corn and forty shillings or the value thereof in goods with Costs als execution. *OB 1719–29, 58.*

1521. 17 Jan. 1721/22—Thomas Caterton came into Court and agreed to serve his Master William Trussell four years from this day in Consideration of his giveing him a pair shooes and stockins and his Freedom Cloaths as the law allows. *OB 1719–29, 60.* [In the Index the name is Cotterton.]

1522. 17 Jan. 1721/22—Eliz: McDermot agrees to serve her Master, Jn° Lunceford, Junior, eighteen months above her Indented time in Consideration his giveing her a gown and peticoat above what the law allows. *OB 1719–29, 60.* [In the Index the names are Dermot and Lunsford.]

1523. 17 Jan. 1721/22—Mary Rawlins, serv^t of Thomas Cunningham, came into Court and swore that James Blackwood, serv^t of the said Cunningham, was father of a bastard Child that she lately had and in Consideration of the said Cunningham's paying her fine to the parrish and keeping the said bastard 4 years from the parrish, she obliges herself to serve her said master 4 years from the date hereof. *OB 1719–29, 60.*

1524. 17 Jan. 1721/22—Mary Fitzgarold, servant of Richd Clayton, came into Court and voluntarily agreed to serve Wm Trussel six years and a half above her Indented time in Consideration of his clearing her of her former matter. *OB 1719–29, 60.*

1525. 21 Feb. 1721/22—Upon the Petition of Mary Anley, formerly serv^t to Josias Dameron, ordered that the said Dameron pay her her Freedom Dues wch is Fiveteen bushells of Indian Corn and Forty Shillings Current money or the value thereof in goods als execution. *OB 1719–29, 63.*

1526. 21 Feb. 1721/22—Katherine Ferguson, serv^t of Robt Reeves, came into Court, she haveing had a bastard Child, ordered that she serve her said Master according to law and in consideration of her said Master paying her fine, she agrees to serve him nine months above her Indented time. *OB 1719–29, 64.*

1527. 21 March 1721/22—Upon the Petition of Judith Laycock ordered that she be free from her master, John Claughton, and that she be paid by her said master her freedom Dues according to Law. *OB 1719–29, 68.*

1528. 22 March 1721/22—Margaret Christian, serv^t of Mr John Keen, haveing been presented by ye grand Jury for haveing a bastard Child, ordered that ye sheriff take her into Custody and bring her to the next Court. *OB 1719–29, 70.*

1529. 16 May 1722—Inventory of the estate of Thomas Webb . . . 2 white servants, £6. *RB 1718–26, 284.*

1530. 16 May 1722—Jane Stevens, formerly servant to Wm Self, came into Court & voluntarily agreed to serve Wm Knott three years above her Indented time in consideration of the said Knott, his buying her of her former Master. *OB 1719–29, 73.*

1531. 20 June 1722—Elizabeth Philips, haveing been presented by the grand jury for haveing a bastard Child, came into Court and swore it to her Master, Robert Davis. John Hanie [Haynie] Junr came into Court and entered into a recognizance with the said Davis to keep the said child from being a charge to the Parrish and ordered that the said Elizabeth be sold as the law directs after her Indented time is expired. *OB 1719–29, 75.*

1532. 17 July 1722—Inventory of the estate of Mr Jno Ingram . . . 2 white servants. . . . *RB 1718–26, 287.*

1533. 18 July 1722—Caron Clinton, servant of Robert Davis, haveing beaten & abused his said Master, ordered by this Court that after his Indented time is expired, he serve his Master for the said abuse one whole year according to Law. *OB 1719–29, 77.*

1534. 18 July 1722—Mary Peak, servant to James Lewis, agrees to serve her said Master five years and eleven months from this Day in consideration of his paying the Doctor for her cure. *OB 1719–29, 78.*

1535. 18 July 1722—Margaret Christian, serv^t of Mr John Keen, is ordered to serve her said Master one whole year after her Indented time is expired for haveing a mulatto bastard Child, ordered that when her time to her master be expired she be delivered up to the Church Wardens of Saint Stephens parrish for the time being for the payment of fiveteen pounds Curr^t money or to be sold for five years. *OB 1719–29, 78.*

1536. 15 Aug. 1722—Indenture between William Gill and Catherine Poor . . . Witnesseth that the said Catherine Poor for and in Consideration of one suit of apparrel to her in hand paid att and before the ensealing and delivery of these presents by the said William Gill the receipt whereof the said Catherine doth here by acknowledge as well as for the consideration & covenants in and by these presents expressed and by the said Wm Gill to be performed, observed and fullfill'd the said Catherine Poor . . . of her own free and voluntary will doth covenant, promise and agree to and with ye said Wm Gill to serve . . . ye full and just term and term of four years and five months . . . in all such lawfull Services and Employment as he the said Wm Gill, his heirs, etc. shall employ her . . . during which term the said Catherine the lawfull commands of her said master . . . shall gladly do and obey . . . in Consideration of which said Service the said Wm Gill doth by these presents for himself, his heirs, Exec^{rs} and assigns Covenant, promise and agree to and with the said Catherine Poor to provide for and allow the said Catherine Poor and her Child which she hath now and with her named Richd Poor Sufficient Diet, washing and Lodging during the said term Sufficient for such in their Circumstances . . . and also att the expiration of the aforesaid term to pay and allow unto the said Catherine one good new gown and petticoat, one pair of shooes, two Shifts, one pair of Stockins, one apron, two new capps, one handkerchief and also to let the said Catherine att the expiration of the said term with her said son Richard depart clearly accquitted of any Charge for the maintenance of the said Child during ye said term. . . . *RB 1718–26, 288, 289.*

1537. 15 Aug. 1722—Catherine Poor came into Court and acknowledged an Indenture for service to Wm Gill and on his motion, it's admitted to record. *OB 1719–29, 83.*

1538. 15 Aug. 1722—Jane Flint came into Court and voluntarily agreed to serve James Furnett (in Consideration of his buying her of her former Master) from this Day of December come two years. *OB 1719–29, 84.*

1539. 20 Feb. 1722/23—Upon the Petition of William Whayland and Edward Rion, serv^{ts} of Mr Th^o Gill, ordered that James McCallaugh and Wm Jones be summoned by the sheriff to the next Court to answer the said Petition. *OB 1719–29, 97.*

1540. 20 Feb. 1722/23—Ginneter Conner came into Court and agreed to serve Richard Denny one year more than her Indented time in Consideration of his buying her of her former master and useing his endeavour by means within himself of cureing her of an ailment that she now has. *OB 1719–29, 99.*

1541. 25 April 1723—Thomas Heath Preferred his Claim for taking up a white servant man named Jno Fitzgarrald belonging to one Thomas Stone of Westmorland County, he being above Ten miles from the place of his residence and the said Heath making oath before the Court that he hath rec^d no satisfaction on that Acc^t, Certificate is granted him for allowance to the General Assembly. *OB 1719–29, 102.*

1542. 25 April 1723—Judith Bowlin, servant to Mrs Ann Holt, came this Day into Court and swore a bastard Child to Patrick Martin, servant to Thomas Gill, the said Judith likewise agreeing with her said Mistress to serve her a year above her Indented time in Consideration of her paying her fine. *OB 1719–29, 104.*

1543. 25 April 1723—Upon the Petition of Wm Whayland and Edward Rion agst their Master, Thomas Gill, for their freedom several evidences appearing and being examined by the Court upon their taking it into Consideration, it is their oppinion that they return to their service and serve their s^d Master untill the time of their being adjudged by a former order of Court is expired. *OB 1719–29, 105.*

1544. 25 April 1723—Patrick Conoley, haveing brought his servant Th^o Morgan to this Court for running away and produceing an acco^t ag^t ye said Morgan for his absenting himself and other Charges, it is the oppinion of the Court that he serve his s^d Master five months and Twenty days (the said Conoley paying two hundred pounds of Tobb^o for takeing him up) and eighty Days for his absence above his Indented time. *OB 1719–29, 106.*

1545. 17 July 1723—Inventory of the estate of Capt John Opie . . . 1 white serv^t named Alex^{dr} Nelson. . . . *RB 1718–26, 408.*

1546. 21 Aug. 1723—Upon the Complaint of Sam^{ll} Webb als Day, serv^t of Mrs Jane Yarratt, setting forth that he is entitled to Freedom and evidences appearing and proveing to the Contrary, ordered that the said servant serve his said Mistress untill ye seventh Day of August one thousand and seven hundred Twenty five. *OB 1719–29, 113.*

1547. 21 Aug. 1723—Ordered that Thomas Matthews, servant to Allen Harvey, serve his said Master eight months and twenty Days (for his . . . five hundred and ninety pounds of Tobb⁰ and two Days absence) when his Indented time is expired, his said Master haveing made oath thereto. *OB 1719–29, 113.*

1548. 22 Aug. 1723—Maurice Gibbons, haveing brought his serv^t James Burk before this Court (and makeing oath that he has paid and is to pay six hundred pounds of Tobb⁰ to several persons for takeing his said serv^t up) when he absented himself which was Fifty Days, Ordered that the said serv^t serve his said Master after his Indented time is expired twelve months and a week according to Law. *OB 1719–29, 114.*

1549. 18 Sept. 1723—Thomas Simpson, Servant of Henry Aublin, is ordered to serve his said Master eight months and Twenty Six days after his Indented time is expired, he haveing absented himself from his said Master's service which occassioned him to be att the Charge of paying five hundred and ninety pounds of Tobb⁰ to which the said Aublin hath made oath and the said Servant was absent two Days. *OB 1719–29, 122.*

1550. 20 Nov. 1723—Matthew Cox, serv^t to Mr John Champion, is by the Court adjudged to be twelve years old. *OB 1719–29, 123.*

1551. 20 Nov. 1723—Mack Mack Million, Servant of Wm Metcalf, having runn away from his said Master's Service three months and Four Days and his said Master haveing been of the expence of one hundred and Twenty pounds of Tobb⁰ in getting him to which he hath made oath, ordered that he serve his said Master until his Indented time is expired according to law. *OB 1719–29, 124.* [In the Index the last name is McMillion.]

1552. 20 Nov. 1723—Winnefred Halfpenny, haveing runn away from her Master Ch^a Hammond seven Days and he haveing been att the expence of two hundred pounds of Tobb⁰ in getting her again to which he hath made oath, ordered that after her Indented time is expired she serve her said Master six months and Fourteen Days according to Law. *OB 1719–29, 125.*

1553. 20 Nov. 1723—Thomas Matthews, Servt of Allen Harvey, having Runn away from his Master one and Twenty Days and gott into the Province of Maryland which occasioned his said Master to be at the expence of Four hundred and seventy two pounds of Tobb⁰ for prison fees and getting him again to which he the said Harvey hath made oath, ordered that after his Indented time is expired he serve his Master according to Law. *OB 1719–29, 125.*

1554. 20 Nov. 1723—James Burk, servant of Mary Price, haveing Runn away from his Mistress one and Twenty Days and got into ye Province of Maryland which occasion'd his said Mistress to be att the expence of Four hundred and Seventy two pounds of Tobb^o for Prison fees and getting him again to wch the said Mary hath made oath, order'd that after the expiration of his Indented time he serve his said Mistress according to Law. *OB 1719–29, 125.*

1555. 20 Nov. 1723—Winnefred Fern, serv^t to Ephraim Hughlett, haveing run away from her said Master and he haveing been at the expence of three hundred and Fifty Six pounds of Tobb^o, ordered that after her Indented time is expired she serve her said Master according to Law which is three months and six Days. *OB 1719–29, 126.*

1556. 20 Nov. 1723— . . . William Grinstead's serv^t woman for a base Child. . . . *OB 1719–29, 127.*

1557. 15 Jan. 1723/24—Jane Arrenthrew, a servant woman of Ch^a Craven, came into Court and swore that a certain Duncan McCoy was the father of her base born Child and ordered that she serve the said Craven for the trouble of his house in lying. . . . *OB 1719–29, 129.*

1558. 15 Jan. 1723/24—Thomas Morgan, serv^t of Patrick Connaly, came into Court and voluntarily agreed to serve Joseph Nutt four years from Christmas last in Consideration of his clearing him of his former master. *OB 1719–29, 132.*

1559. 15 Jan. 1723/24—Upon the motion of Charles Craven, Jane Arrenthrew is by the Court ordered to serve him according to Law for his being att the Charge of haveing her taken care of dureing her being with Child and lying in. *OB 1719–29, 132.*

1560. 18 March 1723/24—Elizabeth Phillips, servant of Robt Davis, haveing been Presented by the grand Jury for haveing a bastard Child and haveing this day rec^d twenty lashes on her bare back, ordered that she serve her said master one year above her Indented time for the trouble of his house according to law. *OB 1719–29, 137.*

1561. 18 March 1723/24—Feamot Crowder, servant to Mrs Ann Ingram, haveing (by the information of Capt Philip Smith, one of the Church Wardens of Wiccocomoco Parrish) had a bastard Child ordered that she serve her said

Mistress one year above her Indented time for the trouble of her house according to Law. *OB 1719–29, 137*. [A Fearnot Crowder, daughter of Thomas Crowder, was bound an apprentice to Charles Ingram 18 Aug. 1709. *OB 1699–1713, Part 2, 604*. It is possible this could be the same person.]

1562. 18 March 1723/24—Upon the pe^t [petition] of Catherine Fowler, formerly serv^t of William Grinsted, ordered that her said master pay her her freedom dues which is Fifteen bushels of Indian Corn and Fourty shillings in money or the value thereof in goods according to Law with Costs. *OB 1719–29, 138*.

1563. 18 March 1723/24—John Iron, servant to Abraham Ingram, haveing absented himself from his Master's service Forty two days and the said Ingram paying two hundred pounds of Tobb^o for takeing his said serv^t up when he runn away and for his own Trouble going after him ten days att fiveteen pounds of Tobb^o a day by the Judgment of this Court, ordered that the said servant serve his said Master above his Indented time according to Law. *OB 1719–29, 139*.

1564. 20 May 1724—Additional Inventory of the Estate of Mrs Eliz^a Burn ... 1 serv^t Boy Jno Conner about seven years to serve, £6. ... *RB 1726–29, 112*.

1565. 20 May 1724—Upon the Petition of Marg^t Pines who was formerly a serv^t to Mr Sam^{ll} Heath ordered that he pay her Tenn Bushells of Indian Corn and Seventeen Shillings and nine pence in money or the value thereof in goods according to Law. *OB 1719–29, 146*.

1566. 17 June 1724—Upon the motion of Hanah Malony, formerly a serv^t to Cary Keble, setting forth that there is still due from the s^d Keble her Freedom dues, the Court hearing the severall allegations on both sides and the said Keble produceing a Discharge from under the said Melony's hands in Consideration of her being sett free severall months before her Indented time was expired, it was the Court's oppinion that there was nothing due to her. *OB 1719–29, 153*.

1567. 17 June 1724—Edward Welch, servant of Robert Carter Esqr, haveing absented himself eight Days from his said Master's service, is ordered that he serve his said Master according to Law. *OB 1719–29, 154*.

1568. 15 July 1724—George French, servant to William Reeves, being brought before this Court by his said master, and he makeing oath that he absented himself Sixty one Days and that he was in pursuit of his said servan four Days on horseback, it is the oppinion of this Court that he serve his said Master six months and ten Days after his Indented time is expired. *OB 1719–29, 158.*

1569. 15 July 1724—Judith Bowlin, servant to Mrs Ann Holt, came into Court and made oath that the true Father of her bastard Child was John Jackson, a foreigner. *OB 1719–29, 158.*

1570. 15 July 1724—Ordered that Judith Bowlin, serv^t to Ann Holt, serve her said Mistress after her Indented time, on order of Court, is expired one year according to Law for having a bastard Child. *OB 1719–29, 158.*

1571. 15 July 1724—It appearing to this Court that Judith Bowlin, serv^t to Ann Holt, has served her Indented time, ordered that the said Ann Holt pay her her freedom dues which is fiveteen Bushells of Indian Corn and Forty Shillings in money or the value thereof in goods with Costs als Execution. *OB 1719–29, 158.* [All three of the above entries of Judith Bowlin are on the same page.]

1572. 15 July 1724—Catherine Jones, serv^t to Mr Thomas Cralle, came into Court and voluntarily agreed to serve Grant Inesberry two years above her Indented time in Consideration of his buying her of her former Master. *OB 1719–29, 159.*

1573. 16 Sept. 1724—Mary Cavener, servant to Richd Oldham, haveing absented herself from her said Master's service thirty one Days and the said Oldham haveing been att the Charge of a Man and horse going in pursuit of her three Days, he haveing made oath thereto ordered that the said Cavener serve her said Master after her Indented time is expired two Kallender months, 3 weekes, four days according to Law. *OB 1719–29, 160.*

1574. 20 Jan. 1724/25—Catherine Jones, serv^t to Thomas Hobson, came into Court and for some Consideration to them best known voluntarily agreed to serve her said Master three years above her Indented time. *OB 1719–29, 166.*

1575. 20 Jan. 1724/25—Susannah Betts came into Court and voluntarily agreed to serve the Exec^{rs} of Thomas Webb dec^d in behalf of the said Webb's orphans one year above her Indented time. *OB 1719–29, 166.*

1576. 20 Jan. 1724/25—Edward Neale, formerly Servant to Richard Rout, came into Court and agreed to serve John Smith to Christmas next. *OB 1719–*

29, 166.

1577. 20 Jan. 1724/25—Upon the Pet [Petition] of John Oxendine als Figro vs Ann Hoult, the Def^t came into Court and objected against his petition because it was preferr'd nine months before, the said Oxendine als Figro was entitled to Freedom and it appearing to this Court by the oaths of Wm Willday and Elizabeth his wife that ye sd Oxendine als Figro was free in June last past, it is the oppinion of this Court that he is free from any services that the said Ann Holt can or may claim from him and it being the further oppinion of this Court that they not agreeing that the said Oxedine als Figro should have any Claim from his said Mistress for his serving her above his Indented time, it is ordered that the said Ann Holt pay all Costs that has accrued on occasion of this suit since Sept^{br} last. *OB 1719–29, 167.*

1578. 17 Feb. 1724/25—John Markin, serv^t to Wm Christopher, haveing absented himself from his said Master's service nineteen Days & his master being att the expence of Four hundred & Tenn pounds of Tobb^o in getting him again to his service, ordered by this Court that he serve his said Master one year & one month and Ten days after his Indented time is expired. *OB 1719–29, 170.*

1579. 17 Feb. 1724/25—Abraham Ingram came into Court and made oath that his servant John Iron has absented himself from his master's service eighty Days, it is therefore ordered by this Court that the said John Iron serve his said Master Five Kallender months and Tenn Days after his Indented time & other orders of Court for his servitude be expired. *OB 1719–29, 171.*

1580. 17 March 1724/25—Ann Conner als Prichard came into Court and voluntarily agreed to serve Cary Keble his heirs four years from this Day in Consideration of his now giveing her a suit of good apparell and finding her sufficient Cloaths, Diett and Lodging to have her learn'd to sew, knitt and spin and att ye expiration of the time or Term aforesaid, the s^d Keble or his heirs is to give her a Suit of new Cloathes (to Witt) a gown and pettycoat, two shifts, two aprons, two Capps, two handkerchiefs, a pair of new shooes and stockins and a Heiffer and a Sow with Pigg. *OB 1719–29, 172.* [Because she was to be taught a trade, Ann Conner very well could have been an apprentice.]

1581. 17 March 1724/25—William Trussell came into Court and made oath that his serv^t Mary Fitzgarrald absented herself from his service Seven days and that he was four days on acc^t of getting her for which he is allowed sixty pounds of Tobb^o, ordered that the said Ann Fitzgerrald serve her said

Master after her former order of Court or Indenture time is expired. *OB 1719–29, 173.*

1582. 19 May 1725—Hanah Melony came into Court and made oath that Joshua Harrison, serv^t to Robert Carter Esqr, was the Father of her base born Child. *OB 1719–29, 179.* [In the Index the name is spelled Mellony.]

1583. 19 May 1725—John Marquiss, serv^t of William Christopher, haveing absented himself from his said Master's service four Days and his said Master haveing made oath that he was att the expence of Two hundred pounds of Tobb^o in recovering his said servant and Fifteen pounds of Tobb^o for horse and man, order'd that the said serv^t serve his said Master three Kalender months and sixteen days after his Indented time or order of Court is expired. *OB 1719–29, 182.*

1584. 19 May 1725—Edward Neal, servant of Michael Tobin, haveing absented himself from his said Master's service four days, order'd that he serve his said Master eight days according to Law. *OB 1719–29, 182.*

1585. 16 June 1725—Wm Gardner, serv^t of Mr Richard Blackburn, came into Court and acknowledged an Indenture for eight months service to ye said Blackburn in Consideration of his being absent four months from his said master's service, the said Blackburn accquitting the said Gardner of all other charges that accrues on that acco^t. *OB 1719–29, 184.*

1586. 18 Aug. 1725—Whereas Hanah Melony, Marg^t Megeneys and Ann Lynch was bound over to this Court by Ge^o Ball gen^t, one of the Majesty's Justices of the peace for this County and being convicted by evidence together with their own Confession, ordered y^t the sheriff give the said Hanah Melony, Marg^t Megeneys and Ann Lynch twenty five lashes each well laid on their bare backs att the Common Whipping post and that they be discharged paying Costs. *OB 1719–29, 185.*

1587. 18 Aug. 1725—George Woodbridge, serv^t to Thomas Grinsted, haveing moved to this Court to be discharged from his said Master and the said Grinsteed coming before the Court and agreeing thereto, ordered by this Court that the said Woodbridge be discharged from his said Service. *OB 1719–29, 185.*

1588. 18 Aug. 1725—Upon the pe^t [petition] of Sarah Nichols, formerly serv^t to Thos Gill, Judgm^t is granted her ag^t the said Gill for the sum of one hundred and sixty six pounds Tobb⁰, it being for five months Service which is ordered to be paid with Costs als execution. *OB 1719-29, 186.*

1589. 18 Aug. 1725—Upon the Petition of Robert Cole order'd that Robt Harrison be summoned by the sheriff to the next Court to answer the said petition. *OB 1719-29, 187.*

1590. 5 Sept. 1725—John Markell, haveing absented himself from his master, Wm Christopher's service, four Days and his Master being att the Charge of one hundred pounds of Tobb⁰ in takeing him up, order'd that the said Markel serve his said Master seven weeks and one Day according to Law. *OB 1719-29, 193.*

1591. 15 Sept. 1725—Edward Welsh, serv^t of Robert Carter Esqr, haveing absented himself fourteen days from his said Master's service and his said Master haveing been att the Charge of Two hundred pounds of Tobb⁰ in takeing him up, order'd that the said Welch serve his s^d Master Four months after his Indented time or former order of Court is expired and moreover that he pay James Webb his now overseer thirty pounds of Tobb⁰ for goeing after him a day or as much time as the Tobb⁰ comes to according to Law. *OB 1719-29, 193.*

1592. 15 Sept. 1725—Thomas Hope, serv^t of Mrs Elinor Haynie, haveing absented himself Twenty Days from his said M^{rs} service, order'd that he serve his said Mrs Forty Days according to Law. *OB 1719-29, 193.*

1593. 16 Dec. 1725—John Hudnall vs John Oxender Def^t pleads owes nothing. *OB 1719-29, 198.*

1594. 20 April 1726—John Johnson, servant to Col. Peter Presly, haveing runn away from his said Master and he being att the Charge of one hundred forty five pounds of Tobbacco for takeing him up, order'd that the said Johnson serve his said Master sixty six days according to Law. *OB 1719-29 210.*

1595. 20 April 1726—Mary Peak came into Court and voluntarily agreed to serve John King two years above her Indented time in consideration of his haveing cured her of the Keykicksey. *OB 1719-29, 211.*

1596. 20 April 1726—Edward Neale came into Court and agrees to serve Timothy Stamps untill Christmas next and from that time to the end and term of three years more in Consideration that the said Stamps pay his debts and give him a suit of Cloaths att the expiration of ye said term or time. *OB 1719–29, 211.*

1597. 20 April 1726—Thomas Cole, serv^t of Hannah Rice, is by the Court adjudged to be fourteen years old. *OB 1719–29, 211.*

1598. 20 July 1726—Terrence Smith, Servant to John Rose, haveing struck his said Master and broke the windows of his Master's house and committed several other enormities, being brought to the barr confess'd the same, It is therefore ordered that the said servant serve his said Master one whole year above his Indented time or former order of Court being expired according to the Act of Assembly in that Case made and provided. *OB 1719–29, 216.*

1599. 20 July 1726—John Markell, Servt of Wm Christopher, haveing absented himself from his master's service two Days and the said Christopher haveing been at the expence of Two hundred and forty pounds of Tobb^o upon oath in getting his said serv^t, ordered that the s^d Markel serve his said Master three Kallendar months three weeks and three days after his Indented time and former order of Court is expired. *OB 1719–29, 218.*

1600. 19 Oct. 1726—Richard Rapson, servant of Thomas Cunningham, came into Court with the said Cunningham and agreed to discharge his said Master of his Freedom dues provided he be this day discharged from his said Master's Service which was agreed on by the said Cunningham and Rapson. *OB 1719–29, 231.*

1601. 17 Nov. 1726—Robert Ross, servant of one Frances Porter of Talbert County in Maryland, having run away from his said Master & taken up by Cary Keble of the Dividing Creek & lyeing in this County['s] goal seventy six days. Ordered that he be sold at outcry by the sheriff to pay the charges due by Law of this Country for his being taken up & lyeing in goal for eight years & fifteen days. Order'd that he serve above the Indented time of eight years & fifty days, one year seven months and six days the prison fees & other charges amounting to Twelve hundred & eighty pounds of Tobacco. *OB 1719–29, 234.*

1602. 15 Feb. 1726/27—Will of William Fallin ... Item. I give to my Negro Jamme Jamme that I had of Thomas Webb his freedom after the Term of four years Expired. ... *RB 1726–29, 33.* [In the inventory of William Fallin the name is James.]

1603. 8 Feb. 1726/27—Will of Robert Bradly ... I give to my son John Flynt and to his wife one orphan boy called Richard Booth. ... *RB 1726–*

29, 49.

1604. 15 March 1726/27—Inventory of William Fallin . . . 1 Negro man named James, four years to Serve, £10. *RB 1726–1729, 64b.*

1605. 15 March 1726/27—Inventory of the estate of John Cottrell . . . 1 Servant woman Named Ann Barrom, £6; 1 Servant man Named John M^{c}eldemar, £6. *RB 1726–29, 69.*

1606. 15 March 1726/27—Eliz^a Fouls, serv^t of Lewis ap Lewis, swears a bastard child of Robt Hues, serv^t of James Farned. Lewis ap Lewis agrees to pay to the Church Wardens of St Stephens for the use of the said parish the sum of Five hundred pounds of Tobacco at the Laying of the next Levy for the said Fouls fine. And the said Eliz^a Fouls agrees to serve her said Master one whole year above her indented time for his paying the said Tob: and order'd that she serve her said Master according to Law for her having the said Child. *OB 1719–29, 256.*

1607. 15 March 1726/27—Jno Ordery, serv^t of Jno West, having run away from his said Master six days & his said M^r being after him 5 days on horseback wch he is allow'd 30 p day upon oath & his said Master being obliged to pay Two hundred pounds of Tobacco for taking up the said servant. Ordered that he serve his said Master twelve days for his six days absence & Twenty two weeks & five days for his allowance of Three hundred & fifty pounds of Tobacco above his Indented time with costs. *OB 1719–29, 256.*

1608. 19 April 1727—Hannah Clark, servant of Anne Christopher, came into Court & agreed to serve her said Mistress one whole year above her indented time besides one whole year allow'd by law for the trouble of the said Mistress house allowed by law, In Consideration of her said Mistress paying Five hundred pounds of Tobacco to the Church Wardens of St Stephens Parish as a fine by Law laid on the said Hannah for having a bastard Child wch is now dead. *OB 1719–29, 258.*

1609. 27 April 1727—Will of George Howell . . . Item if Elizabeth Webster remain in the Service of my Wife or Child till she arrives to the age of Eighteen years, I do give her one Cow and Calf and a Suit of Cloaths. . . . *RB 1726–29, 116.*

1610. 20 Sept. 1727—Edward Welsh, serv^t of the Honble Robt Carter, Esqr, having run away from his said master one year three months & eighteen days & his Master being at the charge of Two hundred & eighty pounds of Tobacco to retake him, order'd that the said Welsh serve his said Master Two years seven months & six days for his one year three months & eighteen days absence & also four months & ten days for his charges after him above his Indented time with Costs. *OB 1719–29, 278.*

1611. 25 Jan. 1727/28—George Eves, having preferr'd his claim for taking up a serv^t man named James Griffin belonging to John Jordon of Northumberland County above Ten Miles from the place of his Residence & the said Eves making Oath that he hath receiv'd no satisfaction, Certificate is granted him for allowance to the General Assembly. *OB 1719–29, 285.*

1612. 17 April 1728—Mary Martin, formerly a servant of James Webb, came into Court and volluntarily agrees to serve John Basie one year above her Indented time in Consideration of his buying her of her former Master and his giveing her a suit of good stuff Cloathes above what is allow'd for her freedom dues. *OB 1719–29, 288.*

1613. 18 April 1728—Judgment is granted to Wm Moon against Robert Harrison for one suit of cloaths (Viz^t) a Coat Jacket & breeches of Kersey or other good substantial Cloath, one hatt, two Shirts and one p^r of Shoes (it being for his freedom Dues by Indenture) wth Costs als Exec. *OB 1719–29, 291.*

1614. 18 April 1728—John Ranson, servant of Richard Oldham Junr, haveing run away ninety Days and his Master being eighty eight Days after him at five shillings p^r [per] day and expending six pound eighteen shillings & six pence one hundred pounds of Tob^o in retaking him, order'd that he serve his said Master according to Law. *OB 1719–29, 296.*

1615. 17 July 1728—Thomas Walker, servant of Frances Knight, came into Court and produced an Indenture by which it appear'd that he was free from his said Mistress upon the petition of the said Walker ordered that the said Frances Knight pay him his Freedom Dues according to Law with Costs als Execution but in Consideration of the great scarcity of Corn order'd that no Execution Issue for Corn until the last of November. *OB 1719–29, 303.*

1616. 21 Aug. 1728—James Scrivner, servant of Alexander Edwards, judged to be fourteen years old. *OB 1719–29, 304.*

1617. 22 May 1729—Upon the motion of Co^{ll} Peter Presly, he brings an Indented servant named Andrew Cralle before the Court who pretended to be a Gardner and was at the wages of eight pounds sterling p year, the Court being Inform'd by several gent^m who had been the said Cralle's work that he knew nothing of the Gardner's Trade are of oppinion that he be cut of his wages & be Deem'd as a Common Indented Servant. *OB 1719–29, 340.*

1618. 10 June 1729—Thomas Parr came into Court and voluntarily agreed to serve Thomas Gill six years from this Day in Consideration that the said Gill Release him from all other contracts or obligations for Service. *OB 1719–29, 343.*

1619. 16 July 1729—William Crain, serv^t of Wm Robinson, with the Lease of the s^d Robinson in writing, came into Court and acknowledged an Indenture for four years service to Richard Harrison. *OB 1719–29, 345.*

1620. [page worn]—Thomas Hicks, servant of Thomas Gill, came into Court and agreed to serve his said master six years [page worn] Indented time and not to claim his freedom dues until the six years were expired in Consideration [page worn] let Katherine Hues his servant free at Christmas next and at the same time [page worn] said Katherine. *OB 1729–37, 1.*

1621. 10 March 1729/30—Thomas Hicks, formerly a servant to Thomas Gill, came into Court and agreed to serve John Allgood [page worn] years above his time of service acknowledged to the said Gill at September Court last, in consideration the said Allgood give to Katherine, wife of the said Thomas Hicks, her board four years and a half from this time and likewise find him the said Thomas Hicks one suit of good Duroys upon demand besides what be due to him by Law when his time of Service is expired. *OB 1729–37, 9.*

1622. 17 June 1730—Abraham Low came into Court and agreed to serve Mr Matthew Zuill three years & eleven months from this Day in Consideration of his buying him of Thomas Brown, his former master. *OB 1729–37, 13.*

1623. 19 Aug. 1730—Robert Leitch, servant to Sam^{ll} Heath Decd, came into Court and agreed to quit his Claim to all that is or shall be due to him for Service to the said Heath and to make all the negroes Cloaths for this ensuing year in Consideration that the Exec^{rs} of the said Decd Discharge him from any further service when the said Cloathes are finished. *OB 1729–37, 16.*

1624. 19 Aug. 1730—Thomas Hicks, servant of Andrew Cottrell, came into Court and Volentarily agreed to serve his said Master Twelve years from the first Day of this month in consideration that he give him at the expiration of the said time a Suit of good New Drugget Cloaths, a hat, a pair of shoes and stockens and a fine new shirt above what the Law allows Servants for their freedom Dues. *OB 1729–37, 18.*

1625. 19 Aug. 1730—Saml Simms, Servant of John Smith, haveing been convicted for Dealing with a Negro Man slave belonging to Mrs Hannah Shapleigh for goods of the vallue of one hundred & Twenty pounds of Tobb^o order'd that he pay to Mrs Hannah Shapleigh four hundred and eighty pounds of tob^o or receive on his bare back eighteen Lashes upon which Thomas Simms came into Court and entered himself Security for the said Fine which he is order'd to pay to the said Hannah Shapleigh with Costs als Execution. *OB 1729–37, 18.*

1626. 18 Nov. 1730—Ann Scrivener came into Court and acknowledged six years service to Wm Smout above her Indented time in Consideration of his Buying her of Hugh Kelly, her former master. *OB 1729–37, 24.*

1627. 18 Nov. 1730—Thomas Wallis came into Court and acknowledged to serve Alexander Edwards until Christmas next and from thence four years in Consideration of his Buying him of his former Master. *OB 1729–37, 24.*

1628. 17 Feb. 1730/31—Richard Braden, Servant of James Farned, haveing Run away from his said Master five months & 8 Days and his master being at the expence of man and horse Six Days in Retakeing him at 30 pounds of Tob^o p Day, ordered that the said Braden Repay his said Master by Service according to Law after his Indented time is expired with Costs. *OB 1729–37, 29.*

1629. 21 April 1731—Honour Clark came into Court and agreed to Serve Eliz^a Brown one year and three quarters above her Indented time for paying her fine to Wiccocomoco parish for her haveing a Bastard child. *OB 1729–37, 31.*

1630. 15 March 1731/32—John Ranson, Servant of Richard Oldham, having absented himself from his said Master's service thirteen days and his master being at forty five pounds of Tobacco Charge in retakeing him, order'd that he Serve his s^d Master, his heirs or assignes for his said Default according to Law after his other time of Service is expired. *OB 1729–37, 33.* [In the Index the name is Ransom.]

1631. 19 April 1732—James Hayes, Servant of John Lewis Jun., having absented himself from his said Master's service fifty Days and his Master haveing been at three hundred twenty-three pounds in Retakeing him, ordered that he serve his said Master for the same after his other time of service is expired according to Law. *OB 1729–37, 55.*

1632. 19 April 1732—Mary Jinkins, Servant of Thomas Webster, came into Court and agreed to serve her said Master Two years above her Indented time in Consideration that he Learn her to Read, Write, Knit & Spin, and household Work. *OB 1729–37, 55.* [Apparently in the beginning Mary was a servant; now she is willing to serve him longer provided he teach her the things cited.]

1633. 20 April 1732—John Walters, Servant of Robert Clark, is by the Court adjudged to be Tenn years old. *OB 1729–37, 57.*

1634. 20 April 1732—Thomas Jones, Servant of Robert Clark, is by the Court adjudged to be thirteen years old. *OB 1729–37, 57.*

1635. 8 May 1732—William Hill Jun came into Court and produced a Certificate under the hand of Matthew Kenner gent for his takeing up Thomas Hicks, a servant belonging to Andrew Cottrell of this County above Tenn miles from home. . . . *OB 1729–37, 61.*

1636. 16 Aug. 1732—Upon the Complaint of Roger Kaine and Henry Voy, Servants of David Beathan, that their said Master did not keep them with sufficient Cloathing and Diet, upon a full hearing the Court are of Opinion and do order that the said Beathan give them Two good Shirts, a pair of Summer Drawers and warm Winter Cloathing such as Servants usually wear each year and sufficient Diet and Lodging. *OB 1729–37, 63.*

1637. 21 Sept. 1732—Mary Moor, Servant of Ambros Fielding, haveing been Delivered of a Bastard Child that is Dead that she serve her said Master for her said Default after her other time of service is expired according to Law, and the said Mary Moor agrees to serve her said Master Twelve months more in Consideration of his paying her fine to the Churchwardens of Wiccocomoco parish. *OB 1729–37, 72.*

1638. 17 Jan. 1732/33—Andrew Burn, formerly Servant to Richard Dudly, came into Court and agreed to serve Richard Smith three years from the first Day of May next in Consideration that the said Smith hath payd fifteen hundred pounds of Tobacco for Discharging the said Burn's Debts and agrees to find him the said Burn at the expiration of his Service a good Suit of Druggit [drugget] Cloaths, a hat, Shoes and Stockens and three good Shirts. *OB 1729–37, 72.*

1639. 17 Jan. 1732/33—Timothy Harris, Servant of George Conway, came into Court and agreed to quit his freedom Dues in Consideration of his Master's quitting him Two months of his service. *OB 1729–37, 74.*

1640. 19 April 1733—John Hudson, Servant of John Lewis gent, haveing absented himself from his said Master's service and his Master being at the Charge of three hundred and Sixty Six pounds of Tobacco in Retakeing him, order'd that he serve his Master for his said Default after his other time of Service is expired according to Law. *OB 1729–37, 89.*

1641. 17 May 1733—Andrew Cottrell Complained to the Court that he had a Servant named Mary Saunders then at the Court who pretended that she came there to petition for her freedom, the said Mary was called to the Barr and her allegations heard but the said Andrew asserting that she was his Servant by Indenture, she is remanded to her service but on the motion of Mr William Arbuckle in favour of the said Mary, it is considered that she have Liberty to appear at the next Court to make good her allegations. *OB 1729–37, 100.*

1642. 10 July 1733—Thomas Hicks, servant of Andrew Cottrell, haveing absented himself from his Master's Service nine Days, order'd that he serve for his offence after his other time of service is expired according to Law, and he receive on his bare back Twenty one Lashes. *OB 1729–37, 101.*

1643. 15 Aug. 1733—James Willson, servant of Thomas Gill, haveing run away and absented himself from his Master's Service Twenty three Days and his master being at the Charge of Six hundred and fifteen pounds of Tobacco and one pound fourteen Shillings and nine pence Current money in Retakeing him, order'd that he serve his said Master for his said offence after his other time of Service is expired according to Law and order'd that the money that is Charged against the said Servant be Discharged in Tobacco at 12/6 pc^t. *OB 1729–37, 105.*

1644. 15 Aug. 1733—Thomas Griffin, Servant of Joseph Hudnal, having runaway and absented himself from his master's service thirty six Days and his master being at the Charge of Six hundred & fifteen pounds of Tobacco and one pound fourteen Shillings and Nine pence in retakeing him, order'd that he serve his said Master for his said offence after his other time of Service is expired according to Law and that the mony that is Charged against the said Servant be Discharged in Tobacco at 12/p C^t. *OB 1729–37, 106.*

1645. 16 Aug. 1733—Honour Clark, Servant of Elizabeth Brown, haveing runaway and absented her self from her Mistress's Service Six Days and her Mistress being at the Charge of four hundred pounds of Tobacco in Retakeing her, order'd that she serve her said Mistress (after her other time of Service is expired) for her said offence and for the Costs.... *OB 1729–37, 108.*

1646. 19 Sept. 1733—In this action of Trespass for assault and Battery Depending in this Court between Jane Arranthrough Pltf and Richard Hudnal Deft for the Sum of fifty pounds Current money Damage as in the Declaration is set forth at a Court held for this County on this 19th Day of April last, the Deft by his attorney Defended the force and Injury and for plea said that the said Jane was his hired Servant and was very lazie and Insolent in her behaviour towards him and that he only gave her moderate Correction which was the assault in the Pltf's Declaration set forth and at a Court held for this County on the 15th Day of August last the Pltf Replyd that by any thing in the above pleading alledged she ought not to be Barred from haveing her action for that the Deft of his own proper wrong and without any such Cause as he in pleading alledged on her an assault did make as she in her Declaration had set forth and this she prayed might be enquired of by the Country and the Deft in like manner the tryal of which Jane was then referred until this Day when a Jury were called to the barr and sworn to by the Issue Joyn'd who Viz^t Ormsby Haynie, Saml Blackwell, Winder Kenner, Richard Booth, Thomas Dameron, Thomas Harcom, Howson Kenner, Andrew Cottrell, John Downing, Christopher Dameron, went from the Barr and after awhile brought in their Verdict in these words Viz^t We the Jury do find for the Pltf Damage forty shillings Current mony Winder Kenner foreman, Judgment is therefore granted to the said Jane against the said Richard for the said sum of fifty shillings Current money Together with one attorney's fee and Costs als execution. *OB 1729–37, 115.*

1647. 22 Nov. 1733—Upon the petition of Catherine Jones seting forth that she is unjustly Detained a servant by Elias Martin, the said Elias appear'd and failing to make good his claim to her service, it is considered by the Court that she be Discharged from any further Service to the said Elias. *OB 1729–37, 125.*

1648. 20 March 1733/34—Upon the petition of James Conner, formerly Servant of Charles Nelms, decd., order'd that the Executors of the Last Will and Testament of the said Decd pay to the said James his freedom Dues according to Law with Costs als Execution. *OB 1729–37, 133.*

1649. 27 April 1734—John Strickland and Darby Tool, Servants of John Lewis gent and Linsez Opie, being charged with fellonsiously Takeing a

Silver Spoon belonging [to] the said John Lewis, were brought to the Barr and the evidence of Alexander Broadie, being taken in behalf of our Sovereign Lord the King and what the said John and Darby could say in their own Defence against the said accusation fully heard, it is considered by the Court that the said John & Darby Receive at the public whiping post for their offence in this matter thirty nine lashes each on their bare Backs well layd on and that they serve their said masters after their time by Indenture is expired according to Law for the Charges hereby occasioned together with nine Days for their loss of time Dureing their Imprisonment that their said masters be accountable to the County after their service is expired for the Costs hereby occasioned. *OB 1729–37, 143.*

1650. 20 April 1734—Thomas Hicks, a servant belonging to Andrew Cottrell of St. Stephens parish in this County, Charged with felloniously Burning a Tobacco house belonging to his said Master, one other Tobacco house belonging to Abner Neale and one other Tobacco house belonging to George Curtis, all of the aforesaid parish, Confesed he did some time since Christmas last burn the Tobacco house aforesaid belonging to his said master with a quantity of Tobacco at that time lodged in same and that on the Wednesday night after Easter last he did also Burn the Tobacco house aforesaid belonging to the said Abner Neale with what things were then Lodged in that house but Denied the Burning the other tobacco houses laid to his Charge, whereupon it is the opinion of the Court that the said Thomas Hicks ought to be Tryed for the aforesaid facts at the General Court and the said Thomas was committed to the goal of this County from whence it is ordered that he be forthwith removed to the publick goal at W^{ms}burg as the Law Directs and it is further ordered that Notice be given to his majesties attorney general that the aforesaid Andrew Cottrell and Abner Neale tho they were not examined on this occasion would be material evidences against the said Thomas Hicks at his tryal in the General Court. *OB 1729–37, 143.*

1651. 15 May 1734—Judgment is granted to Ann Scrivner against William Smoot for her freedom Dues according to Law and a Callico gound [gown] and apron, a pinner fine shift, handkerchief and pair of shoes Due to the said Ann from the said William by agreement order'd that the said William pay the same to the said Ann with Costs als Execution. *OB 1729–37, 148.* [In the Index the name is spelled Schrivner.]

1652. 16 May 1734—In the difference Depending in the Court between Chas Lawrence, Servant of Winder Kenner Pltf and his said master Deft, the Court, having heard the evidence in behalf of the Pltf and Deft, are of opinion that the said Charles is not free and that he is in June next but Twenty nine years old, order'd that he return to his Master's Service. *OB 1729–37, 150.*

1653. 19 June 1734—Upon the petition of Mary Palmer, late servant of William Rankin Decd, order'd that Wm Hudnall and Ellis Gill Exec^{rs} of the said Decd Render and unto the said Mary Twelve yards of Sarge, seven yards of good Dowlace, a pair good shoes & Stockens, 1 yard and half fine Linnen for Caps and a hankerchief, it appearing to be the said Mary's Right for her freedom Dues als execution. *OB 1729–37, 155.*

1654. 16 Oct. 1734—Honour Clark, Servant of Eliz^a Brown of Wiccocomoco parish, haveing had a Bastard Child which she has sworn to Timothy Harris and failing to pay her fine, order'd that the sheriff give her Twenty five lashes according to Law and also that the said Honour serve her said Mistress after her other time of Service is expired as the Law Directs in that Case. *OB 1729–37, 167.*

1655. 21 Nov. 1734—Hester Wattson, Servant of Capt Philip Smith, haveing absented her self from her Master's service Two hundred and Twenty Days order'd that she serve for her said Default after her other time of Service is expired four hundred and forty Days and for the Costs hereby occasioned according to Law. *OB 1729–37, 171.* [In the Index the name is spelled Watson.]

1656. 19 Feb. 1734/35—James Tool, servant of Mr John Lewis, having run away sixty days from his said Master & his being at the expence of Five thousand Seven hundred & eighty five pounds of Tobacco for taking him up, order'd that he serve his said Master after his Indented time is expired seven years six months and twenty days for his s^d expenses according to Law. *OB 1729–37, 178.*

1657. 19 Feb. 1734/35—Thomas Borgan, servant of Alexander Brodie, & Silvester Kennedy, servant of John Gill, is committed for felloniously stealing several goods belonging to Christian Jones being both brought to the Barr, the evidence against them (Viz^t) Christian Jones, Eliz^a Bush & Mary Coleman were examined & the prisoners heard in their defence. It is the opinion of the Court that the said prisoners for the aforesaid offence receive on their bare backs Thirty nine lashes well laid on at the publick whipping post, Twenty of them forthwith & the remainder tomorrow about 12 o clock and ordered that their aforesaid Masters either give security for each of their servants good behaviour or for their wearing a large Iron collar (each of them) about their necks with points twelve inches long at least during the whole time of their service. *OB 1729–37, 178.*

1658. 19 Feb. 1734/35—John Strickland, servant of Mr John Lewis, having run away Twenty five days from his said Master & his being at the expense of Thirteen hundred & fifteen pounds of Tobacco for taking him up. Order'd that he serve his said Master after his indented time is expired one year nine months & ten days for his said expence according to Law. *OB 1729–37, 178.*

1659. 15 Oct. 1735—Mary Coleman, servant of James Seebry, came into Court & voluntarily acknowledged to serve ye s^d Seebry six years from this Day in consideration whereof the s^d Seebry oblidgeth himself to pay her on demand three & half yards of good Dowlas, a good large silk hankerchief, a pare of English shoos besides her freedom Dues when her s^d time will be expired. *OB 1729–37, 199.*

1660. 15 Oct. 1735—Thomas Floyd, servant to Richd Lansdale, haveing absented himself four days from his Master's service & his Master haveing been att ye Charge of two hundred & twenty four pounds of tob^o for takeing him up, ordered that he serve for his s^d offence after his other time of service is expired. *OB 1729–37, 200.*

1661. 19 Nov. 1735—Thomas Evans, servant to Joseph Robinson, being Brought before this Court for running away & absenting himself from his master's service thirty nine days & his master being att ye expence of four hundred & ninety pounds of tob^o in Retakeing him ordered that ye s^d Thomas Evans Repay his s^d master by service according to Law after his Indented time is expired with Costs. *OB 1729–37, 203.*

1662. 21 Jan. 1735/36—On ye Petition of Abigal Seebry for her service wages amounting to three hundred & ninety seven pounds of tob^o against ye estate of Richd Tullos Dec^d in ye hands of Wm Hughlett adm^r of ye s^d Dec^d ordered the s^d Hughlett pay ye same before any of her Debts with Costs als Ex out of ye estate of ye s^d Tullos within one year from ye date hearof [hereof] assets in his hands. *OB 1729–37, 208.*

1663. 22 Jan. 1735/36—John Ransom, serv^t to Mary Oldham, being brought before this Court for absenting himself from his s^d Mistress's service ordered he serve the s^d Mary Oldham three months after his Indented time shall be expired with Costs als ex. *OB 1729–37, 209.*

1664. 16 June 1736—On ye Petition of Sam^{ll} Bear, servant of John Chilton, ordered that he return unto his s^d Master's Service untill next Court at which time he is to have his farther Tryall & ordered that Margaret Caddell be summoned to ye next Court to give her evidence between ye s^d Bear & his s^d

master. *OB 1729-37, 227.*

1665. 21 July 1736—Thomas Floyd otherwise John came into Court & voluntarily of his own free will agreed to serve Winfield Wright for the term of six years from the date hearof [hereof] on Consideration whereof the s^d Wright obliges himself to find the s^d Floyd sufficient meat, drink, Lodging & apparell dureing ye s^d term according to ye Custom of ye County. *OB 1729-37, 233.*

1666. 26 July 1736—Sam^{ll} Snow of this County came into Court & produced a certificate under the hand of Matthew Zuill gen^t for his takeing up a Runaway man servant named William Finlay belonging to Capt Isaac Allerton of Westmoreland County (above ten miles from his master's home) & upon his making oath that he never Received any sattisfaction for ye same, Certificate is granted him for allowance by ye General assembly. *OB 1729-37, 237.*

1667. 26 July 1736—Lamberth Dodson of Richmond County came into Court & produced a certificate from under the hand of John Waughop gen^t for his takeing up a runaway Servant man named Charles Murrow belonging to William Walker of Richmond County (ten miles from his master's home) & upon his making oath that he never Received any sattisfaction for ye same. Certificate is granted him for allowance by ye General assembly. *OB 1729-37, 237.*

1668. 26 July 1736—John Cary of Richmond County came into Court & produced a Certificate from under the hand of John Lewis gen^t for his takeing up a runaway serv^t named William Sloughman, servant to David Ringeade of Spotsilvania County (ten miles from his master's home). . . . *OB 1729-37, 237.*

1669. 18 Aug. 1736—On ye Pet^n of Sam^{ll} Peer, servant of John Chilton, seting forth that he was free & had served his full time which he aledged was five years, ye s^d Sam^{ll} Peer & his master leaving it to ye judgm^t of ye Court whether ye s^d Peer was free or not & John King, Mary Watkins & Margaret Caddel evidences between ye s^d Partys being sworn & their evidence considered by ye Court after haveing heard ye arguments on both sides it is ye opinion of ye Court that the s^d Sam^{ll} Peer return to his master's service & serve him untill he hath Compleated seven years from his arrival in Virginia & serve his s^d Master seven Callendar months after ye afores^d seven years are expired for sattisfaction of ye Costs of this suit & sattisfying ye evidences for their attendance. *OB 1729-37, 239.*

1670. 18 Aug. 1736—John King, serv^t to Joshuah James, made oath that he attended three days as an evidence of John Chilton against his servant Sam^{ll} Peer, ordered that ye s^d John Chilton pay ye s^d Joshuah James for his s^d servant's attendance according to Law with Costs als Ex. *OB 1729–37, 239.*

1671. 18 Aug. 1736—Mary Watkins, serv^t of John Coppedge, made oath that she attended three days as an evidence for John Chilton. . . . *OB 1729–37, 239.*

1672. 13 Dec. 1736—John McGuier, a servant boy belonging to ye Revd Francis Peart, was judged to be eleven years old. *OB 1729–37, 247.*

1673. 13 Dec. 1736—James Tool, servant to John Lewis, came into Court & promised to serve his s^d master truly & faithfully for ye term of five years ensuing ye Date hereof & on failure he is to serve his whole time which is considerably longer which was ordered to be Recorded. *OB 1729–37, 250.*

1674. 13 June 1737—On ye motion of Mr Sam^{ll} Blackwell against his servant Catherine Cassedy ordered that she serve him according to Law for absenting her self seven days from her s^d master's service & likewise for ye sum of two hundred & forty pounds of tob^o expended by her s^d master in Retakeing of her after her Indented time is expired. *OB 1729–37, 259.*

1675. 11 June 1737—Elizabeth Thomas, servant of Thomas Walker, made oath that she attended four days as an evidence for Wm Wildy against Thomas Parry, ordered she be p^d [paid] for her s^d attendance according to Law. *OB 1729–37, 263.*

1676. 11 June 1737—John Hurst, servant of Thos Hurst, seting forth by Pet^n [petition] that he was of age & ought to be free & Thomas Hurst appearing to answer to ye s^d Pet^n did before ye Court Consent & agree that ye s^d John Hurst should be free from his s^d service & it is ordered by ye Court that ye s^d Thomas Hurst pay the Costs of this suit als ex. *OB 1729–37, 263.* [This entry has been marked through; however, on page 266 the same names appear in another court order.]

1677. 8 Aug. 1737—On ye Petition of John Hurst against Thomas Hurst for a whole suit of apparell, ordered the s^d Thomas Hurst Deliver him the Cloaths he took from him & over & above that he give him a good new hat & a new pare of shoos & Stockens with ye Costs of this suit als Ex. *OB 1729–37, 266.*

1678. 8 Aug. 1737—George McGibonny, servant to Mr John Cralle, haveing run away into Maryland & absented himself from his s^d Master's service one whole month & his master being at ye Charge of one thousand eight hundred & twenty five pounds of tob^o in Retakeing him, ordered that he serve his said Master (after his other time of service is expired) for his s^d offence & for the Costs hereby occasioned according to Law. *OB 1729–37, 266*. [In the Index the name is spelled McGibbony.]

1679. 8 Aug. 1737—Mary Bond, servant of Mr John Cralle, haveing run away into Maryland & absented her self from her s^d Master's service one whole month & her Master being at ye Charge of one thousand eight hundred & twenty five p^d [pounds] of tob^o in Retakeing her & she haveing stole one gound [gown] from her mistress valued at one hundred pounds of tob^o, ordered that she serve her s^d Master for her s^d offence (after her other time of service is expired) for her s^d offence & for the Costs hereby occasioned & ye gound according to Law in that Case made & provided & it appearing to ye Court that ye s^d Mary Bond made use of a forged Certificate, it is ordered that the sheriff put her in ye Pillory & that she stand there two hours. *OB 1729–37, 266.*

1680. 8 Aug. 1737—William Smith, servant of Joshuah James, haveing run away & absented himself from his master [page worn] fifteen days & his master being at ye Charge of two hundred ninety six pounds & one [page worn] of tob^o [page worn] him ordered that he serve his s^d Master (after his other time of Service is expired) for his s^d offence [page worn] the Costs hereby occasioned according to Law in that Case made & provided. *OB 1729–37, 267.*

1681. 8 Aug. 1737—John Whealand, servant to Joshuah James, haveing run away & absented himself from his s^d master's service fifteen days & his master being at ye Charge of two hundred pounds & one quarter of tob^o in Retakeing him ordered that he serve his s^d Master (after his other time of service is expired) for his s^d offence & for ye Costs hereby occasioned according to Law in that Case made & provided. *OB 1729–37, 267.*

1682. 12 Sept. 1737—Robert Shiels, Servant to Peter Presly, being Brought before the Court & Convicted of Resisting & Strikeing his s^d Master, it is ordered that he serve his s^d master one year after his time of Service expired for his s^d offence with Costs. *OB 1737–43, 1.*

1683. 10 Oct. 1737—On ye Petition of Ann Jones, serv^t of Thos Rout, for her Freedom Dues ordered that the s^d Rout be summoned to appear at ye next Court to answer ye s^d Pet^n. *OB 1737–43, 5.*

1684. 10 Oct. 1737—Hester Flood, serv^t of Wm Barret, came into Court & of her free will & Consent agreed to serve Thomas Harding one year after her Indented time expired in Consideration of the s^d Harding's buying her from ye s^d Wm Barret which is ordered to be Recorded. *OB 1737–43, 6.*

1685. 13 Feb. 1737/38—In ye Petition of James Brenane, serv^t of Nathaniell Rigin, ordered that ye s^d Rigin pay him his freedom Dews [dues] according to Law in that case made & provided with Costs al^s Ex^{to}. *OB 1737–43, 20.*

1686. 13 Feb. 1737/38—On ye motion of Moses Oldum against Sarah Sampson, his servant, for one year's service for haveing a bastard Child which his servant ordered she pay him ye s^d year's service after her Indented time expired according to Law with Costs al^s Ex^{to}. *OB 1737–43, 21.*

1687. 28 Feb. 1738/39—Will of Thomas Hall . . . Item. I give unto my Loveing Wife Hannah Hall one servant wench named Ann Jones. . . . *RB 1738–43, 169a.*

1688. 19 March 1737/38—Jannet Hunter, serv^t of James Fontaine, came into Court & by her s^d master's consent & she relinguishing her freedom Dews [dues] at her Request was sett free by ye Court from any service to him her s^d Master on acc^t of her Indenture. *OB 1737–43, 33.*

1689. 11 April 1738—James Brenam, haveing absented an attachm^t under the hand of Coll. Peter Presly, one of the Majistrates of this County, against the estate of Nathaniell Riggin for two Barels [barrels] of Corn, thirty shillings & gun of ninety shillings price & the sheriff of this County haveing thereupon returned March ye 18th 1737/8 then attached ye estate Nathaniel Riggin's for use James Brenam executed by me as followeth to 1 black horse & som [some] tob^o Joseph Hudnall sub sh: & the debt appearing to be justly Due from ye s^d Nathaniell Riggin ye s^d Brenam haveing made oath thereto ordered the s^d attached goods be sold for ye s^d Debt & Costs. *OB 1737–43, 37.*

1690. 8 May 1738—Elizabeth Jones, servant of Mr John Foushee, being delivered of a bastard Child at his house in ye Parish of St Stephens, it is ordered that ye s^d Elizabeth Jones serve her s^d Master one year (for ye trouble he has been at) after her other service expired according to Law with Costs als ex^{to}. *OB 1737–43, 40.*

1691. 8 May 1738—Mr Travis Colston, one of ye Churchwardens of St Stephens Parish, informing ye Court that Hannah Hopkins, servant of Ann

Sebree, was Delivered of a bastard Child, ye s^d Hannah Hopkins (not being able to pay her fine to ye Parish) ordered ye sheriff give her twenty five lashes on her bare back well layd on & that she serve her s^d Mistress one year after her Indented time expired according to Law with Costs als Ex^{to}. *OB 1737–43, 40.*

1692. 12 June 1738—Robert Phealand, servant to Wm James, came into Court & agreed to serve his s^d Master six months after his Indented time expired & Relinguish his freed Dues on Consideration of his s^d consideration of his s^d master buying him when he was to be sold to other persons to whom he was unwilling to be sold. *OB 1737–43, 43.*

1693. 13 June 1738—Elizabeth Guin, servant of William Hughlet, came into Court & agreed to serve her s^d master one year after her Indented time expired on Condition that her s^d Master shall not put her to work at the how [hoe] dureing her servitude but employ her in other work in ye house which is ordered to be Recorded. *OB 1737–43, 56.*

1694. 13 June 1738—Silvester Nono, shoomaker servant of Wm Taite gent, came into Court & agreed to serve his s^d Master one year after his Indented time expired on Condition that his s^d Master shall not dureing s^d Term put or oblige him to do any planter's work but keep him chiefly to his trade. *OB 1737–43, 56.*

1695. 14 Aug. 1738—Ealse Collins, servant of John Hartgrove, haveing run away into Maryland & absented her self from her s^d Master's service sixty days & her s^d master being at ye Charge of one thousand four hundred & fifty pounds of tob^o in retakeing her ordered that she serve her s^d Master (after her other time of service is expired) for her s^d offence & for ye Costs hereby occasioned according to Law in that Case made & provided & pay ye Costs of this prosecution. *OB 1737–43, 60.*

1696. 9 Oct. 1738—Ann Daley, servant of John Gaskins, being brought before ye Court & convicted of being delivered of a mulatto bastard Child at ye house of her s^d Master, ordered that she serve her s^d Master in recompence of ye loss & trouble occasioned thereby one whole year after her time by Indenture expired according to Law in that Case made & provided. *OB 1737–43, 66.*

1697. 9 Oct. 1738—Ann Daley of St Stephens Parish, servant of John Gaskins, on her oath Confessed that Charles, a mulatto belonging to Stephen Haynie, was the father of a mulatto bastard Child she was lately Delivered of in ye parish aforesd, it is therefore ordered that upon ye expiration of her time to her present Master she pay down to ye Churchwardens of ye Parish afores^d for ye use of ye s^d Parish fifteen pounds of Current money or be sold for five years to ye use afores^d being ye fine inflicted by Law for ye afores^d offence. *OB 1737–43, 66.*

1698. 25 Oct. 1738— ... To James Lewis of this County for takeing up Catherine Cassedy, servant of Sam^ll Blackwell of this County, 200 lbs tob^o. ... *OB 1737–43, 72.*

1699. 25 Oct. 1738— ... to Sam^ll Nelms of this County for takeing up William Duggin, servant of William Durn of Essex County, 200 lbs tob^o. ... *OB 1737–43, 72.*

1700. 25 Oct. 1738— ... to James Daughity & Charles Betts Junr of this County for takeing up John Berry, servant of Henry Williams of Richmond County, 200 lbs tob^o. ... *OB 1737–43, 72.*

1701. 25 Oct. 1738— ... to Simon Bowley of this County for takeing up Arthur Murphy, serv^t of James Murphy of Westmoreland County, 200 lbs tob^o. ... *OB 1737–43, 72.*

1702. 8 Jan. 1738/39—Mary Doland, servant of Thomas Genn, being brought before ye Court & Convicted of being Delivered of a bastard Child at ye house of her s^d Master, ordered that she serve her s^d master in recompense of ye loss & trouble occasioned thereby one whole year after her other time of service expired according to Law in that Case made & provided with Costs.

The s^d Mary Doland refuseing to pay her fine ordered ye sheriff give her twenty lashes at ye common whiping post. *OB 1737–43, 77.*

1703. 8 Jan. 1738/39—Robert Shiels & William Simmons, servants of Peter Presly Esqr, haveing run away into Maryland & absented themselves from their Master's service seventy days each & their s^d master being at ye Charge of four thousand three hundred & forty nine pounds of tob^o in Retakeing them ordered that they serve their s^d Master after their other time of service is expired for ye s^d offence & for the Costs thereby occasioned according to Law. ... *OB 1737–43, 77.*

1704. 9 April 1739—John Hader, servant of John Coleman, came into Court & voluntarily agreed to serve his s^d Master two years besides his Indented time on Condition that his s^d Master will not sell him to any other person dureing ye time of his servitude which was ordered to be Recorded. *OB*

1737–43, 83.

1705. 9 April 1739—John Williams, servant of John Irons, haveing run away into Maryland & absented himself from his s^d master's service five months & twenty five days & his master being at ye Charge of one thousand eight hundred & sixty pounds of tob^o & five pounds ten shillings Current money, ye money (to be paid at ye rate of 100 lbs of tob^o for ten shillings) in retakeing him, ordered that he serve his sd master (after his other time of service is expired) for his s^d offence & for the Costs hereby occasioned according to Law in that Case made & provided. *OB 1737–43, 83.*

1706. 9 April 1739—On the Petition of Elizabeth Voucher, servant of James Harris, against the s^d Harris Dismist. *OB 1737–43, 83.*

1707. 9 April 1739—Else Collins, servant of John Hartgrove, haveing runaway & absented her self from her s^d Master's service twenty one days & her master being at ye Charge of five hundred & fifty five pounds of tob^o in retakeing her, ordered that she serve her s^d master (after her other time of service is expired) for her s^d offence for the Costs hereby occasioned according to Law in that Case made & provided. *OB 1737–43, 84.*

1708. 14 May 1739—John Bradfield, servant of Richd Hudnall, haveing run away & absented himself from his s^d master's service fifteen Days & his master being at ye Charge of five hundred & thirty nine pounds of tob^o in retakeing him, ordered that he serve his s^d Master (after his other time of service is expired) for his s^d offence & for the Costs thereby occasioned.... *OB 1737–43, 91.*

1709. 14 May 1739—James Lattes, servant of David Fluker, haveing run away & absented himself from his s^d master's service fifteen days & his master being at ye Charge of four hundred & eighty six pounds of tob^o in retakeing him, ordered that he serve his s^d Master (after his other time of service is expired) for his s^d offence & for the Costs thereby occasioned.... *OB 1737–43, 91.*

1710. 11 June 1739—Mary Morgan, servant of Richard Tomson, being brought before ye Court & Convicted of being Delivered of a mulatto Bastard Child at ye house of her s^d Master, ordered that she serve her s^d Master in Recompense of the loss & trouble occasioned thereby one whole year after the time of her other service expired.... *OB 1737–43, 95.* [In the next entry Mary Morgan was ordered to pay to the churchwardens £15 of current money or be sold for five years.]

1711. 9 July 1739—On ye Complaint of James Fontaine against Joseph Walker, servant to ye s^d Fontaine for resisting & strikeing his s^d Master, ordered that the sheriff of this County take ye s^d Joseph Walker & cause him to appear before ye next Court to be held for this County to answer the s^d Complaint. *OB 1737–43, 100.*

1712. 10 Sept. 1739—Mary Neale, formerly serv^t to Ann Sebree & now servant to Charles Downing came into Court & voluntarily acknowledged & agreed to serve her s^d Charles Downing fourteen months after her Indented time expired in consideration of ye s^d Downing's buying her from ye s^d Ann Seebre which on ye motion of ye s^d Downing was ordered to be Recorded. *OB 1737–43, 106.*

1713. 8 Oct. 1739—Inventory of the Estate of Mr William Hobson . . . 1 Servant boy Ric^h Thomas, £1 10s. . . . *RB 1738–43, 52.*

1714. 10 Dec. 1739—On ye Petition of Spencer Lawrence, a mullatto, against Richard Kenner for his freedom continued. *OB 1737–43, 119.*

1715. 11 Feb. 1739/40—On ye petition of Sarah Samson, servant of Moses Oldham, for her freedom dues, ordered that the s^d Moses Oldham pay her her freedom Dews [dues] according to Law in that Case made & provided with Costs als Ex^o. *OB 1737–43, 122.*

1716. 10 March 1739/40—On ye Petition of Mary Kelly, servant of Jonathan Hammondtree, against her s^d Master, ordered the s^d Hammondtree be summoned by ye sherif to answer the s^d Petition next Court. *OB 1737–43, 126.*

1717. 10 March 1739/40—Spencer Laurence vs Richard Kenner for his freedom severall evidences for ye s^d Lawrence being sworn & examined by ye Court, it is the opinion of the Court & they order that the s^d Lawrence be free next Court except Mrs Footman makes it appear by her evidence which is to be taken by Capt Hack that he is not yet thirty one years of age & pay him for his month's service if he detaines him. *OB 1737–43, 127.*

1718. 10 March 1739/40—On ye motion of Edward Rogers against Mary Bolin, a mulatto born the thirty first day of March 1723 & was the 19th day of March one thousand seven Hundred & twenty five by John Shapleigh & Thomas Cralle gent., Churchwardens of St Stephens Parish, bound unto Mrs Anne Holt, her heirs & assignes from the day of the date of s^d Indenture until the ye s^d Mary Bolin attaine to ye age of eighteen years, ye s^d Mary Bolin's Mother Judy Bolin haveing sworn that ye s^d Mary was got by a white man notwithstanding which oath it is now ye oppinion of ye Court that the s^d Mary Bolin was got by a white man; it is therefore ordered that the s^d Mary Bolin Return to her service & serve the heirs or assignes of ye s^d Ann Holt untill she attaine ye age of thirty one years from the afores^d day of her birth being the first day of March one thousand seven hundred & twenty three. *OB 1737–43, 129.*

1719. 14 April 1740—Spencer Lawrence, a mulatto, vs. Richard Kenner for his freedom, it appearing to ye Court by the Deposition of Mrs Elizabeth Footman taken in Westmoreland County by Henry Lee gen^t that the s^d Spencer Lawrence hath yet two years to serve from ye second day of this instant month of April before he attaines ye age of thirty one years, ordered that he ye s^d Lawrence return to his s^d Master's Richard Kenner's service (except he can by other evidence make it appear that he is thirty one years of age) & serve him, his heirs or assigns until the 2^d day of April one thousand seven hundred & forty two & pay ye Cost of this prosecution. *OB 1737–43, 130.*

1720. 14 April 1740—On the Petition of John Adams, servant of Matthew Zuill gen^t, seting forth that he was free, the Court haveing considered the same order that the s^d John Adam return to his master's service & serve him till ye nineteenth day of April next & pay Costs. *OB 1737–43, 131.*

1721. 12 May 1740—Ann Daly, servant of Richard Smith, came into Court & agreed to serve her s^d master one year after her Indented time is expired in Consideration of ye s^d Smith's buying her time from George Pickering, her former master who she was not willing to serve. *OB 1737–43, 132.*

1722. 13 May 1740—Catherine Jordan vs. John Rout, the Court adjudge & order that the s^d John Rout sett the s^d Catherine Jordan free & give her a Certificate of her freedom & pay ye Costs of this prosecution. *OB 1737–43, 139.*

1723. 16 May 1740—... William Tounsend of this County for takeing up Thomas Poolton, servant to Thomas Murphy of Lancaster County, 200 lbs. tob^o. *OB 1737–43, 141.*

1724. 9 June 1740, Inventory of the estate of Swanson Prichard—... one negro woman named Hannah for 5 years, £10. ... *RB 1738–43, 81.*

1725. 9 June 1740—Pursuant to an order of last Court, Mary Kelly, a mulatto, was brought before ye Court that she is a mulatto born of a white woman & lyable by Law to be bound by ye Church wardens of Wico^o Parish until she attaine ye age of thirty one years, it is therefore ordered that y^e

Churchwardens of ye afores^d Parish take her in their Custody & sell her for ye use of ye s^d parish untill she attaine the age of thirty one years to ye Highest bidder for next years pay & that out of the produce of ye sale the s^d Churchwardens pay all her just Debts with Costs. *OB 1737–43, 144.*

1726. 11 Aug. 1740—Mary Range, servant of Winder Kenner, being presented by the grand jury for haveing a mullato Bastard of which she was lately delivered in ye Parish afores^d, ordered that upon ye expiration of her time to her present master she pay Down to ye Churchwardens of ye Parish afores^d for the use of the afores^d Parish fifteen pounds Current money or be sold for five years to ye use afores^d being ye fine inflicted by Law for ye afores^d offence. *OB 1737–43, 152.*

1727. 19 Aug. 1740—On ye motion of of Winder Kenner, judgment is granted him against Mary Range for one year's service to the trouble at his house, she being Delivered there of a mulatto bastard according to Law in that Case made & provided. *OB 1737–43, 156.*

1728. 8 Sept. 1740, Division of the estate of Richard Lee. Mrs. Judith Lee allotted the third part of her Dec^d Husband's Estate—... 1 Negro boy bound till 21 years of age named Stephen, £10. ... *RB 1738–43, 94.*

1729. 13 Oct. 1740—John Greenstreet made oath to a discharge from service given by Wm Teage to Peter Greenstreet which is ordered to be Recorded & a Certificate given by ye Clerk according to Law to ye s^d Peter Greenstreet. *OB 1737–43, 161.*

1730. 14 Oct. 1740—churchwardens of St Stephens Parish vs Elizabeth Turner, it appearing to the Court that ye s^d Elizabeth Turner was lately Delivered of a mulatto bastard in ye parish afores^d & she not being able to pay her fine or give sufficient Caution for ye same, ordered that the Churchwardens of s^d parish sell the s^d Elizabeth for to serve the term of five years to the use of ye afores^d Parish according to Law in that Case made & provided. *OB 1737–43, 169.*

1731. 14 Oct. 1740—Ann Thomas of St Stephens Parish, being brought before the Court confest [confessed] on oath that she was lately delivered of a mulatto bastard Child at the house of Mrs Clark Hobson sen, her present mistress, it is therefore ordered that on ye expiration of her service due to her s^d mistress that the Churchwardens of ye afores^d Parish sell her for five years to the use of the afores^d Parish according to Law. ... *OB 1737–43, 169.* [In the next entry Ann was ordered to serve her mistress one year after her indented time is expired.]

1732. 10 Nov. 1740—Elizabeth Turner, being brought before the Court & Convicted of being lately delivered of a mullatto bastard Child at the house of Lewis Lamkin, ordered that she serve the s^d Lamkin in recompence of the loss & trouble occasioned thereby one whole year according to Law in that Case made & provided. *OB 1737–43, 170.*

1733. 10 March 1740/41—Moses Oldham, complaining to ye Court that Sarah Sampson, a servant woman of his was delivered of a bastard Child at his house before the time of her service due to him was expired, it is therefore ordered that the s^d Sarah Sampson serve the s^d Moses Oldham one year for the trouble of his house according to Law in that Case made & provided. *OB 1737–43, 179.*

1734. 10 March 1740/41—Thomas Floyd, servant of Nicholas Cary, came into Court & agreed to serve his s^d Master two years besides his former time in Consideration whereof his s^d master obliges himself to keep him dureing s^d time employed & working at ye trade of a blacksmith & teach him ye same to ye best of his skill. *OB 1737–43, 180.*

1735. 13 April 1741—On the motion of Thomas Webster, Patrick Marshal, servant of ye s^d Webster, came into Court & agreed to serve his s^d master three months after his Indented time expired & to quit his freedom dues in Consideration whereof his s^d Master oblidges himself to give him at ye expiration of s^d term a Coat & breeches of peudesoy. *OB 1737–43, 182.*

1736. 13 April 1741—Peter Faushew, servant of George Ball gen^t, came into Court & agreed to serve his s^d master one year after his Indented time expired on Consideration of ye s^d Ball's buying him of his former master & that the s^d Ball employ him as a miller to keep & tend his mill dureing s^d time which was ordered to be Recorded. *OB 1737–43, 182.*

1737. 11 May 1741—Ann Daley, servant of Richard Kenner, came into Court & Confessed that she ran away & was absent seven weeks & Richard Tomson made oath that he was at ye Charge of fifty six pounds of tob^o in retakeing her ordered she serve her s^d master for ye same according to Law. *OB 1737–43, 194.*

1738. 8 June 1741, Inventory of the estate of Charles Craven—... 1 Servant man John Pursley, £7. ... *RB 1738–43, 125.*

1739. 10 Aug. 1741—Ann Owens, servant of Lindsey Opie, came into Court & voluntarily agreed to serve his s^d Master one year after her Indented time expired in Consideration of his buying her of her former master, Wm Eskridge. *OB 1737–43, 213.*

1740. 10 Nov. 1741—Thomas Pulham, serv^t of Saml Snow, haveing run away & absented himself from his s^d Master's service two days & his master being at the Charge of two hundred & eighty nine pounds of tob^o in retakeing him, ordered he serve his s^d master (after his other time of service is expired) for his s^d offence & for his Costs hereby occasioned according to Law in that Case made & provided. *OB 1737–43, 236.*

1741. 14 Dec. 1741—Churchwardens [of] St Stephens Parish vs Mary Range for haveing a mullatto Bastard Child, the s^d Mary Refuseing to pay her fine ordered that the Churchwardens of s^d Parish sell her for five years according to Law in that Case made & provided. *OB 1737–43, 242.*

1742. 11 Jan. 1741/42—On the petition of Thomas Webster against his servant man, Patrick Martial, seting forth that the s^d servant abused him by words & Blows Contrary to Law, Judgment is granted that the s^d Webster against the s^d Martial, his servant, for one year's service for his s^d offence after his other time of service expired & ye Costs of this prosecution pursuant to the act of assembly in such Cases made & provided. *OB 1737–43, 244.* [In the Index the name is spelled Marshall.]

1743. 11 Jan. 1741/42—On the Prayer of Mr Richard Kenner on acc^t of Spencer Lawrence, a mullatto serv^t, which came into Court & agreed that provided the s^d Kenner would now set him from his service he would Relinguish his freedom Dewes [dues] to the s^d Kenner in consideration thereof which was ordered to be Recorded. *OB 1737–43, 246.*

1744. 12 April 1742—On the petition of Mary Taylor vs Moses Oldham for freedom Dues, ordered the s^d Oldham be summoned to appear at the next Court to answer the s^d Petition. *OB 1737–43, 255.*

1745. 10 May 1742—On the Petition of Thos Webster vs Patrick Marshall, his serv^t, for running away from him continued. *OB 1737–43, 268.*

1746. 11 May 1742—On the Petition of Mary Taylor, servant of Moses Oldham, for freedom Dewes [dues], ordered her s^d Master pay her fifteen bushels of Indian Corn & forty shillings in money or the value thereof in goods according to Law & the Charge of this prosecution als Ex. *OB 1737–43, 274.*

1747. 10 June 1742—Patrick Marshall, servant of Thomas Webster, haveing run away & absented himself from his s^d master's service & his master being at the Charge of five hundred & forty pounds of tob^o in retakeing him, ordered he serve his s^d Master (after his other time of service is expired) for his s^d offence & the Costs hereby ocasioned according to Law in that Case made & provided. *OB 1737–43, 280.*

1748. 10 June 1742—Our Sovereign Lord, the King, vs. Sam^{ll} Beachum, John King, Lewis Hudson, & James Barwell, Runaway Sailors from Capt William Finch, master of the ship Alexander Rideingal Pattuxin in Maryland from whom they had taken a boat etc. when they run away etc. & the s^d Capt haveing recovered the s^d boat etc., they are acquitted as to that point & the s^d Capt Finch being willing to release Sam^{ll} Beachum & Lewis Hudson, it is ordered that John King & James Barwell be forthwith sent with a propper gard [guard] to the s^d Capt Finch, he paying the prison fees & Charges of takeing them up & that the s^d Sam^{ll} Beachum & Lewis Hudson be forthwith Conveyed from Constable to Constable to one of his Majesty's ships of warr in the Colony as the Law directs. *OB 1737–43, 275.* [In the above document it is not possible to ascertain whether the men named are apprentices or servants; however, it is obvious they were not at liberty to leave the ship.]

1749. 12 July 1742—John Sherredon came into Court & voluntarily of his own accord agreed to serve Mr Cavan Dulany six months in Consideration of s^d Dulany's buying him from his former Master after his Indented time & other service of ord^r of Court be expired. *OB 1737–43, 283.*

1750. 13 July 1742—Robert White came into Court & voluntaryly bound & obliged himself to serve John Boggess for the term of eighteen months from this day in Consideration of the s^d Boggess paying all the Costs & Charges, prison fees, etc. ocasioned by a Certain prosecution in behalf of our sovereign Lord the King against the s^d Robert White & a certain Mary Quarum on suspicion of fellony. *OB 1737–43, 290.*

1751. 14 Dec. 1742—Barbary Jones, servant of Ormsbe Haynie, came into Court & relinquished her freedom dues due by her s^d master on condition that she be now set free, haveing yet about ten months to serve which was ordered to be Recorded & the s^d serv^t set free, her s^d master agreeing thereto. *OB 1737–43, 317.*

1752. 10 Jan. 1742/43—Mary Punnby [or Punisby], servant of James

Stuart, by Consent of her s^d Master came into Court & agreed to serve James McGoo & his assignes for the time of five years from the twenty fifth day of December last past though she had not so long time to serve her s^d Master Stuart in Consideration the s^d McGoo should buy her time from her s^d Master which was ordered to be Recorded & Certified. *OB 1737–43, 319.*

1753. 27 Jan. 1742/43, Inventory of the estate of John Donaway— . . . a Servt man three years to Serve so Distempered with Sore legs that we think him to be worth nothing. . . . *RB 1738–43, 226.*

1754. 14 Feb. 1742/43—On the motion of Joseph Wildy Plt. against his servant woman, Mary Morgan Def^t, who was lately delivered of a bastard Child in his house, ordered that the s^d Def^t serve her s^d Master for the trouble of his house after the time of her service expired one year according to Law. *OB 1737–43, 323.*

1755. 14 Feb. 1742/43—Mary Morgan, formerly serv^t of Joseph Wildy but now serv^t of Joseph Robinson, came into Court & voluntarily agreed to serve the s^d Robinson one year & four months after her other time of service is expired in Consideration of his paying her fine to the Parish for haveing a bastard Child & the Costs hereby ocasioned. *OB 1737–43, 324.*

1756. 13 June 1743—Presentm^t grand jury vs Ann Thomas of St Stephens Parish for being lately Delivered of a mulatto bastard Child, the s^d Ann Thomas came into Court & confessed the fact & she not being able to pay fifteen pounds Current money, the fine inflicted by Law for her s^d offence, ordered the sheriff sell her to the highest bidder to serve five years from the date hereof, the money or tob^o, the . . . set for to go to the use of the afores^d Parish according to Law. *OB 1737–43, 345.*

1757. 11 July 1743—John Smith & John White, servants of Richd Hudnall, haveing runaway twice & absented themselves from their s^d Master's service fifty days each & their master being at the Charge of thirteen hundred pounds of tob^o in retakeing them, ordered that they serve their s^d Master (after their other time of service is expired) for their s^d offence & for the Costs hereby ocasioned according to Law in that Case made & provided. *OB 1737–43, 353.*

1758. 8 Aug. 1743—Mary Bond, servant to James Lewis, agreed before the Court to serve her s^d Master one year after her Indented time of service is expired. *OB 1737–43, 362.*

1759. 14 Nov. 1743, Inventory of the estate of Mrs. Clark Hobson— . . . 1

mulatto girl 23 years to serve, £5. . . . *RB 1743–49, 6.*

1760. 14 Nov. 1743—Mary Palmer of St Stephens Parish, servant of John Tally, for haveing a Mullatto bastard. *OB 1737–43, 367.*

1761. 14 Nov. 1743—Jeremia Wells, servant of Robt Jones gen^t, haveing run away & absented himself from his s^d master's service two months & thirteen days & his master being at the Charge of nine pounds eighteen shillings Current money in Retakeing him & the Court allowing that he shall be allowed one hundred pounds of tob^o for every eight shillings & four pence of the s^d charges, ordered that the s^d Wells serve his s^d Master (after his other time of service is expired) for his s^d offence & for the Costs hereby ocasioned according to Law in that Case made & provided. *OB 1737–43, 368.*

1762. 13 Feb. 1743/44, Inventory of the estate of Dr. David Alexander— . . . 1 servant man named Peter, 1s 6d. . . . *RB 1743–49, 12a.*

1763. 9 April 1744—William Simmons alias Roberts, servant of Coll. Peter Presly, haveing run away into Maryland & absented himself from his s^d Master's Service four months & his s^d master being at the Charge of eleven pounds five shillings & ten pence Current money & one thousand one hundred & forty pounds of tob^o (the money to be Computed in tob^o at one penny p^r pound) in retakeing him, ordered the s^d Simmons serve his s^d Master (after his other time of service is expired) for his s^d offence & for the Costs hereby ocasioned according to Law in that Case made & provided. *OB 1743–49, 16.*

1764. 9 April 1744—James Harriot, Blacksmith servant of Coll. Peter Presly, haveing run away into Maryland & absented himself from his s^d Master's Service four months & his s^d Master, being at the Charge of eleven pounds five shillings & ten pence Current money & three hundred pounds of tob^o (the money to be Computed in tob^o at one penny p^r pound) in retakeing him, ordered the s^d Harriot serve his s^d Master (after his other time of service is expired) for his s^d offence & for the Costs hereby ocasioned according to Law in that Case made & provided. *OB 1743–49, 16.*

1765. 11 June 1744—On the Complaint of George Kerr, servant of Francis Brown, ordered that the s^d servant forthwith return to his Master's service & that the s^d Francis Brown with Henry Miller his security do enter into Recognizance to our Sovereign Land & the king in the sum of forty pounds Current money to be Levyed of their Lands & Tennements, goods & Chattels on Condition that the s^d Francis Brown shall be of good behavior for the term of one year from the date hereof towards the s^d George Kerr then this

Recognizance to be voyd otherwise to remaine in full power & vertue. *OB 1743–49, 23.*

1766. 11 June 1744, Inventory of the estate of James McGoo— ... 1 serv^t woman named Mary Ponseby, £4. ... *RB 1743–49, 38a.*

1767. 9 July 1744—Mary Williams, servant of John Ashburn, haveing runaway & absented herself from her s^d master's service six days & he being at the Charge for two hundred pounds of tob^o in retakeing her, ordered she serve her s^d Master (after her other time of service is expired) for her s^d offence for the Costs hereby ocasioned according to Law in that Case made & provided. *OB 1743–49, 30.*

1768. 30 Aug. 1744— ... to William Hames J^r of Richmond County for takeing up Mary Wallis, servant of John Ashburn of this County, 180 lbs. tob^o; to William Airs of this County for takeing up a Runaway servant named John Spence belonging to Thomas Golothon of Westmoreland County. *OB 1743–49, 33.*

1769. 11 Sept. 1744—William Simmons, servant of Coll. Peter Presly, haveing runaway & absented himself from his s^d Master's service twenty four days & his s^d Master being at the Charge of one pound three shillings & three pence in retakeing him (for which money the Court allows one pound of tob^o for each penny, which amounts to two hundred & twenty nine pounds of tob) ordered that he serve his s^d Master (after his other time of service is expired) for his s^d offence & for the Costs hereby ocasioned according to Law in that Case made & provided. *OB 1743–49, 36.*

1770. 17 Sept. 1744—James Harriot, servant of Coll. Peter Presly, haveing run away & absented himself from his s^d Master's service twenty four Days & his s^d master being at the Charge of one pound three shillings & three pence in retakeing him (for which money the Court allows one pound of tob^o for each penny which amounts to two hundred & twenty nine pounds of tob^o) ordered that he serve his s^d Master (after his other time of service is expired) for his s^d offence & for the Costs hereby ocasioned according to Law in that Case made & provided. *OB 1743–49, 36.*

1771. 9 Oct. 1744—On the Complaint of Mary Wallis, a servant, against her master John Ashburn ordered the s^d Complaint ly [lie] till her appearance. *OB 1743–49, 41.*

1772. 13 Nov. 1744—Mary Wallace, servant of John Ashburn, haveing run away & absented her self from her s^d master's service twenty five days & her s^d Master being at the Charge of one hundred & fifty pounds of tob^o in retakeing her, ordered that she serve her s^d Master (after her other time of service is expired) for her s^d offence & for the Costs hereby ocasioned according to Law in that Case made & provided. *OB 1743–49, 46.*

1773. 10 Dec. 1744—On the Information of Spencer Ball & Ellis Gill, Churchwardens of St Stephens Parish, against Margaret Burn, late servant of Gilbert Harrold, ordered the sheriff take the s^d Margaret Burn in Custody (for being lately delivered of a bastard Child) & Cause her to appear at the next Court to answer the s^d information. *OB 1743–49, 48.*

1774. 10 Dec. 1744—John White, servant of Francis Brown, came into Court & agreed to serve his s^d Master three years after his other time of service expired in Consideration of his s^d Master's buying him from Richd Hudnall, his former master, which agrem^t was ordered to be Recorded. *OB 1743–49, 49.*

1775. 10 April 1745—On the presentm^t of the grand jury versus Margaret Burn for haveing a bastard Child in St Stephens Parish in this County, the s^d Margaret being called & not appearing, on the motion of _____ [name of person not stated], gent^t, one of the Churchwardens of the afores^d Parish, judgment is granted him against the s^d Margaret & Gilbert Harrold, her security, for five hundred pounds of tob^o, being the fine inflicted by Law for the afores^d offence which the s^d Margaret & Gilbert are ordered to pay at the laying of the next levy for s^d Parish to use of the poor thereof with Costs. . . . *OB 1743–49, 57.*

1776. 13 May 1745—On the petition of John Sherridon, formerly serv^t of Nicholas Cary, for his freedom Dues, ordered the s^d Nicholas Cary be summoned to appear at the next Court to answer the s^d Petition. *OB 1743–49, 61.*

1777. 8 July 1745—Mary Wallace, servant of James Alexander, came into Court & agreed to serve her s^d master one year after her indented time expired in Consideration of his buying her of her former master. *OB 1743–49, 71.*

1778. 9 July 1745—On the Petition of John Sherridon Pl^f & Nicholas Cary Def^t for his freedom Dues, the s^d Def^t being called & not appearing judgm^t is granted the s^d Pl^f against the s^d Def^t for ten bushels of Indian Corn, thirty shillings in money or the value in goods & one fuzee or Musket of the value of twenty shillings at least, ordered the said Def^t pay the same unto the s^d Pl^f with Costs & fifteen shillings for one attorney's fee else execution. *OB 1743–*

49, 75.

1779. 13 Aug. 1745—James Gibson alias Johnson, formerly servant of Arthur Collen, haveing runaway & absented himself from his s^d master's service six months & nineteen days & his s^d master being at the Charge of one pound thirteen shillings & nine pence in retakeing him, ordered that he serve Shapleigh Neale his present master (after his other time of service is expired) for his s^d offence & for the Costs hereby ocasioned according to Law in that Case made & provided. *OB 1743–49, 82.*

1780. 13 Jan. 1745/46, Inventory of the estate of Joshua James— . . . a Servant named Joseph Richards one year to serve, £1 15s; 1 Servant named John McMillion 2 years to Serve, £5. . . . *RB 1743–49, 119.*

1781. 10 Feb. 1745/46—Patrick Carrol, servant to William Seebre, came into Court & acknowledged to serve his s^d master two years after his indented time expired in consideration whereof his s^d master obliges himself to teach him the trade of a tight cooper. *OB 1743–49, 97.* [Carrol was actually an apprentice.]

1782. 14 April 1746—Elizabeth Stanfield, servant of John James, haveing run away & absented her self from her s^d master's service twenty Days & her s^d master being at ye Charge of three hundred & ninety three pounds of tob^o in retaking her, ordered that she serve her s^d Master (after her other time of service is expired) for her s^d offence & for the Costs hereby occasioned according to Law in that Case made & provided. *OB 1743–49, 101.*

1783. 9 June 1746—On the pet^n of Elizabeth Wilkey, late serv^t of Saml Nelms J^r, for her freedom dues, ord^d the s^d Nelms be summoned to appear at the next Court to answer the s^d Petition. *OB 1743–49, 111.*

1784. 9 June 1746, Inventory of the estate of Edward Mason—. . . 1 Servant man named George Simmenet, £8. . . . *RB 1743–49, 147a.*

1785. 13 Oct. 1746—Elizabeth Standfield, servant to John James, came into Court and agreed to serve John Christopher one year and an half after her indented time is up on Consideration of his Buying her from her said master which is ordered by the Court accordingly. *OB 1743–49, 118.*

1786. 15 Oct. 1746—On the Petition of Elizabeth Wilkie against Samuel Nelms Junr for her freedom dues, It is order'd that the said Nelms pay her forty shillings worth of goods in some store in this County and that he pay the Costs of this suit. *OB 1743–49, 127.*

1787. 9 Feb. 1746/47, Inventory of the estate of Morris Gibbons— . . . 1 Negro girl named Hannah Nicken 5 years to serve, £6. . . . *RB 1743–49, 170.*

1788. 10 Feb. 1746/47—The Court doth adjudge Robert Greenwater, a servant Boy belonging to the Reverend Mr David Morthland, to be fourteen years of age. *OB 1743–49, 152.*

1789. 13 April 1747, Inventory of the estate of Peter Bearcroft— . . . 1 Servant named George Willson having 4 years & 5 months to serve. . . . *RB 1743–49, 198a.*

1790. 11 May 1747, Inventory of the estate of the Rev. Moses Robertson— . . . a servant woman named Sarah Gaskall having two years to serve, £2 10s. . . . *RB 1743–49, 208.*

1791. 13 July 1747—Ordered that Dorothy Lord, servant to David Lattimore, serve his said master one year extraordinary as the law directs for having a Bastard Child.

On the information of the Church Wardens of Wiccomoco Parish ag^t Dorothy Lord for having a Bastard Child, It is ordered that the said Dorothy be whip'd at the Public whipping post according to Law. *OB 1743–49, 218.*

1792. 13 July 1747—James Guttree, servant to John Oldham, came into Court and confessed that he run away and was absent from his master's service forty six Daies and his master making oath that he was at the expence of six hundred and seventy Pounds of Tobacco in getting him, It is ordered that he serve his said Master for the said offence according to Law. *OB 1743–49, 220.* [In the Index the name is spelled Guttry.]

1793. 14 Sept. 1747—Ann Turner, servant to Thomas Webster, agrees to serve Doctor Alexander Maver the remainder of the time she has to serve the said Webster and also to acquit him, the said Maver, her freedom dues on Consideration of his curing her of a veneral [venereal] decease [disease]. *OB 1743–49, 239.*

1794. 14 Sept. 1747—Peter Runey, servant to Collin Campbell, agrees to acquit his said master his freedom dues on Consideration of his setting him free. *OB 1743–49, 240.*

1795. 15 Sept. 1747—James Burke, servant to Manley Brown, came into

Court and agrees to forgive his said master his freedom dues on Consideration of his said Master's setting him free. *OB 1743–49, 253.*

1796. 9 Nov. 1747—James Guttree, servant to John Oldham, confessed he was absent from his said master's service forty seven daies, the said Oldham making oath that he was at the expence of two hundred Pounds of Tob⁰ in getting him, order'd he serve his said master for the same according to Law and it is ordered that the said Oldham have leave to put an Iron Coller [collar] on his said servant's neck. *OB 1743–49, 260.*

1797. 17 Jan. 1747/48—James Guttrie, servant to John Oldham, who run away and was absent from the service of his said master forty six daies and his master being at the expence of nineteen hundred and five Pounds of Tobacco in getting him again, order'd that he serve his said master after his other time of service is expired for the said offence and charges according to Law. *OB 1743–49, 266.*

1798. 13 March 1747/48, Inventory of the estate of George Conway— . . . 1 Servant boy named Samuel Hope, 1s. . . . *RB 1747–49, 260.*

1799. 11 April 1748, Will of Daniel Suillevant— . . . Item I give & Bequeath to Vincent Cox my Servant Boy Richard Backer and the said Vincent to pay to my Cozen George Hutton a Servant Boy when he shall attain to the age of twenty one years at which time my will is that he shall Possess the Land above Bequeathed. . . . *RB 1743–49, 266a.*

1800. 9 May 1748—William Smith came into Court and give up his right of the service of Elizabeth Boggess Beswick who was some time agoe bound to him to William Taite gent. *OB 1743–49, 309.* [She is actually an apprentice. She was bound first to William Smith with William Taite as security. *OB 1743–49, 101.*]

1801. 11 July 1748—William Whitby and Mary Willis, servants to William Taite gent, acknowledged they had absented their said Master's Service for two daies each of them and the said Taite making oath that he was at the expence of one pound eighteen shillings in getting them. It is ordered they serve their said Master for the same according to Law, and it is the Court's opinion that the above expences be discharged in Tobacco at one penny per pound. *OB 1743–49, 340.*

1802. 11 July 1748—John Stephen's Servant to John Elmor agrees to forgive his said Master his freedom dues on Consideration of his said Master's setting him free. *OB 1743–49, 340.*

1803. 14 Nov. 1748—Termance [or Tennance] Teagins, a servant man belonging to John Mayes, agrees to forgive his said Master his freedom dues on Consideration of his setting him free. *OB 1743–49, 401.*

1804. 14 Feb. 1748/49—Martha Bryant, confessing she had lately been delivered of a Bastard Child, which is a mulatto, It is ordered she pay the Churchwardens of Saint Stephens Parish fifteen pounds immediately or be sold according to Law and that the child be bound out by the Churchwardens according to Law. *OB 1743–49, 421.*

1805. 14 Feb. 1748/49—Martha Bryant came into Court and agreed to serve Charles Betts Junr one year after her other time of service is expired on Consideration of the said Betts Buoying [buying] her. *OB 1743–49, 428.*

1806. 13 June 1749—On the Petition of Anne Thomas against Israel Fogg & Leah his [wife] for her freedom dues, It is ordered that they pay her the hundred pounds of Tobacco & her Costs by her in this behalf expended. It appearing to the Court that they have already paid her some part. *OB 1743–49, 490.*

1807. 13 June 1749—Emanuel Decoly, a servant man belonging to Richard Hudnall, having Runaway & absented himself from his said Master's Service thirty four Days and his said Master making oath that he was at the expence of Fifteen Shillings & Ten pence & Two hundred & thirty Pounds of Tobacco in getting him again, ordered that the said Servant serve his said Master after his other time is expired for the said offence according to Law & that the Tobacco be rated at 10 pc^t. *OB 1743–49, 492.* [The name Decoly determined by looking at the Index.]

1808. 13 June 1749—On the motion of Robert Christopher, leave is given him to put an Iron Collar about his servant Daniel Rian's neck. *OB 1743–49, 493.*

1809. 14 Aug. 1749—Jeremiah Wells, servant to John Jones, acknowledging that he had absented himself from his Master's service Fourteen Months & eighteen Days and his said Master making oath that he was at the expense of Twelve pounds fifteen Shillings & Ten pence in getting him again, It is ordered that the said Servant serve his said Master (after his other time of Service is expired) for the same according to Law and that the said Money be rated in Tobacco at Ten Shillings per Hundred pounds. *OB 1743–49, 507.*

1810. 14 Aug. 1749—John Elom, Servant to Manly Brown jun^r, agrees to serve his said master after his other time of Service is expired eighteen months in consideration of the said Brown's bying [buying] him from Nicholas McGennis. *OB 1743–49, 507.*

1811. 14 Aug. 1749—Eleanor McDaniel agrees to serve Spencer Ball gent. Two years from this Day on consideration of the said Ball's becoming her Security for keeping her Bastard Child off the Parish & for the Clerk's Fees on the information of the Churchwardens against her. *OB 1743–49, 507.*

1812. 23 Aug. 1749—Margaret Wainwright came into Court and agreed to serve William Harding Fourteen Months from the first of this instant on consideration of his being Security for her appearance at the next General Court to give evidence on behalf of our Sovereign Lord the King against Richard Warwick committed for Felony. *OB 1743–49, 514.*

1813. 1 Dec. 1749, Will of Sarah Haynie—... I give & Bequeath unto my Son George Haynie my Servant Boy named Peter Myers.... *RB 1747–49, 273.*

1814. 10 April 1750—Ann Field, a Servant Woman belonging to Peter Presly gen^t, being brought before the Court for having a Bastard Child, It is ordered that she receive twenty five lashes on the bear [bare] back at the common whiping Post and that she serve her s^d Master one year besides her time. *OB 1749–53, 20.*

1815. 10 May 1750—At a Court held ... for the examination of George Afflax, Wm Simmons, John Ridehouse, James Gregory, Nicholas Meeds, & Anne Fields on Suspicion of their being guilty of Feloniously murdering Peter Presly gen^t, their late Master. *OB 1749–53, 22.* [Those named above were committed to jail and later led to the bar. John Ridehouse, James Gregory, and Anne Fields were allowed as witnesses against Afflax, Simmons, and Meeds. After hearing the evidence, the court decided there was sufficient evidence for the case to be heard in Williamsburg.]

1816. 10 May 1750—... before the Justices of the County Court of North^d of our Lord the King at the Courthouse came Bushrod Fauntleroy, William Harding, John Foushee for Magdaline Pingo, his servant.... *OB 1749–53, 23.* [Those named above appeared at the courthouse in the city of Williamsburg to give evidence in the trial of George Afflax, William Simmons, and Nicholas Meeds.]

1817. 10 May 1750—Ordered that John Ridehouse be kept in goal to give testimony agst the aforesaid Prisoners in June Court and not to be Discharged till then. *OB 1749–53, 23.*

1818. 8 July 1750, Inventory of the estate of James Booth— ... 1 Servant man named John Smith. ... *RB 1, 343.*

1819. 9 July 1750, Inventory of the estate of Robert Jones— ... a Servant man called Jerimiah Will. ... *RB 1, 345.*

1820. 15 Aug. 1750—At a Court held ... for the examination of Geo Wilson, a servant man belonging to Jno Maith, charged with Felony in Breaking & entering the storehouse of Wm Smith & stealing thereout two quart Bottles & two quarts of Rum. *OB 1749–53, 76.* [George Wilson was tried and found guilty. He was to receive 39 lashes on his bare back at the whipping post.]

1821. 10 Sept. 1750—Isabell Mills, a Servant Woman belonging to Rodham Neale, is by her said Master discharged from his Service upon her agreeing never to demand her freedom dues. *OB 1749–53, 82.*

1822. 8 Oct. 1750—On the Petition of Mathew Bowlin for his freedom dues from Phillip Fisher. It is ordered that the said Bowlin be discharged from the service of the said Fisher & he is to be excluded from his freedom dues. *OB 1749–53, 89.*

1823. 18 Dec. 1750— ... at the Courthouse came Robert Middleton, Andrew Morgan, William Garland for his Servant Edward Davis & William Clarke of the said County. ... *OB 1749–53, 113.*

1824. 11 March 1750/51—Elnor McDaniel, being brought before this Court for having a Bastard Child on the Complaint of Spencer Ball gent, her Master. It is ordered that she serve her said [master] one year besides her said time and that she Receive on her bare back at the Common Whiping Post 25 Lashes well laid on—and it is ordered that the sheriff cause imediate execution thereof to be done. *OB 1749–53, 121.*

1825. 8 April 1751—On the Petition of Anne Smith, late Servant of Robert Jones deced. It is ordered that Samuel Blackwell gent Pay her her freedom dues and Costs out of the estate of the said Jones. *OB 1749–53, 141.*

1826. 9 April 1751—On the Petition of Mary Sennit against Anne Fauntleroy for her Freedom dues, It is the opinion of the Court that she recover the same together with her Costs by her in this behalf expended. *OB 1749–53, 155.*

1827. 9 April 1751—On the Petition of Andrew Forbus against George Jones & Eliz[a] his wife for his Freedom dues. It is the opinion of the Court that he recover the same together with his Costs by him in this behalf expended. *OB 1749–53, 155.*

1828. 13 May 1751—On the Complaint of Samuel Carter against Peter Bateman, a Servant Man belonging to Richard Lee Esq[r], the said Samuel having declared he was in danger of his life. It is the opinion of the Court that the said Baiteman receive twenty nine lashes well laid on and that he be then delivered to the Constable who is to deliver him to the said Carter. *OB 1749–53, 161.*

1829. 13 May 1751—On the Petition of Richard Thomas against Judith Hobson for his freedom dues. It is ordered that she be summoned to appear at the next Court to answer the said Petition. *OB 1749–53, 162.*

1830. 10 July 1751—John Fitzpatrick, a Servant man belonging to W[m] Taite gent, having absented himself from his said Master's Service twenty seven Daies and his s[d] Master making oath that he was at the expense of thirteen hundred pounds of Tob[o] in retaking the said Runaway. It is ordered he serve his said Master according to Law & that he receive twenty Lashes well laid on at the Publick whiping Post. *OB 1749–53, 202.*

1831. 10 July 1751—Cornelious Daughity, a Servant man belonging to Rodham Neale, having absented himself from his said Master's Service thirty one Daies and his said master making oath he was at the expence of eleven hundred pounds of Tobacco in retaking the said Runaway. It is ordered that he serve his said Master according to Law and that he receive twenty Lashes well Laid on at the Publick whiping Post. *OB 1749–53, 202.*

1832. 11 July 1751— . . . the examination of Peter Baterman, a convict servant man belonging to Richard Lee Esq[r], charged with Felony & Burglariously breaking and entering the store house of Charles Campbell, merchant, and stealing thereout divers goods to the value of £20 as also breaking and entering the house of Richard Booth and stealing thereout sundrie goods to the value of twenty shillings. *OB 1749–53, 209.* [In the next entry the name is spelled Bateman; in the Index it is spelled Batemain. Bateman was brought before the court. After hearing evidence from several witnesses, it was decided he should be tried at the next General Court in Williamsburg.]

1833. 11 July 1751—John Smith, a Servant Man belonging to Samuel Eskridge, came into Court and agreed to serve his said Master till Christmas come twelve month and to acquit his said Master his Freedom dues on Consideration of his giving him a new Suit of Kersey, a Hatt, two Shirts, one pair of shoes and stockins at the expiration of the aforesaid time. *OB 1749–53, 211.*

1834. 14 Nov. 1751—To James Crain of this County for taking up Edward Davis, a Servant Man belonging to William Garland of Richard County, 90 lbs. tobacco. *OB 1749–53, 249.*

1835. 14 Nov. 1751— . . . To Robert Bryant of this County for taking up Tho[s] Barnes, a Servant man belonging to Rodham Neale of the same County, 90 lbs. tobacco. . . . *OB 1749–53, 249.*

1836. 14 Nov. 1751— . . . To William Townsend of this County for taking up Daniel Rion, a Servant man belonging to James Clarke of Westmoreland County, 180 lbs. tobacco. . . . *OB 1749–53, 249.*

1837. 10 Feb. 1751/52—Upon the Complaint of Daniel Rion [or Rian], a Servant Boy belonging to Robert Christopher, It is ordered by the Court that the said Christopher immediately find the said Rion wastecoat & shirt such as are sufficient & Customary for Servants to wear. *OB 1749–53, 252.*

1838. 13 April 1752, Inventory of the estate of Edward Boollock— . . . 1 Servant man named John Poynting, £15. . . . *RB 2, 108a.*

1839. 13 April 1752—Magdalan Pingo, a servant woman belonging to John Foushie gent, this Day came into Court and relinquished her Freedom dues upon her said Master's discharging her from his Service which he having agreed to, she is discharged accordingly. *OB 1749–53, 270.* [In the Index the name is spelled Magdalin.]

1840. 12 July 1752, Inventory of the estate of Travers Colston— . . . Robert Smee & Ned Lee Serv[ts] for 6 years, £28. . . . *RB 2, 128a.*

1841. 14 July 1752—On the Petition of George Lax ag[st] W[m] Greenwood for his Freedom dues, It is ordered that the said Greenwood pay the same & Costs according to Law. *OB 1749–53, 314.*

1842. 9 Oct. 1752—Upon the Complaint of Philip Fisher against Eleanor Bennit, a Servant woman belonging to the said Fisher for having a Bastard Child, the said Eleanor was this Day brought before the Court who made oath that William Booth was Father of the said Child. It is therefore ordered that the said Eleanor serve her said Master one whole year and over and above the time mentioned in her Indenture and she not being able to pay the fine in such Cases presented by Law. It is further ordered that she receive Twenty five Lashes on her Bare Back well laid on and that the sheriff cause execution thereof to be done and that she be thence discharged. *OB 1749–53, 355.*

1843. 9 Oct. 1752—The Petition of Philip Landy against Sarah Moon is dismissed. *OB 1749–53, 357.*

1844. 12 Feb. 1752/53—Anne Waters, a Servant woman belonging to Willoughly Lewis, came into Court and discharged her said Master from paying her her freedom dues. *OB 1749–53, 373.*

1845. 12 Feb. 1752/53—William Owen & Mary Harrison, Servants belonging to John Hanks, came into Court and agreed to serve their s^d Master one year upon their having Liberty to marry & if they should have any Children during their Service aforesaid they are each of them to serve one year more. *OB 1749–53, 373.*

1846. 7 April 1753—Thomas Ball produced an account against his runaway Servant man Andrew Clarke for four Days absence & one Pound Ten Shillings expended in retaking the said Runaway which being allowed by the Court was Sworn to by the said Ball and It is ordered that the said Andrew serve his Master for the same according to Law. *OB 1749–53, 391.*

1847. 9 July 1753—Sarah Wilson, a Servant Woman belonging to William Greenwood, being convicted of Bastardy & not Procuring any person to pay her fine, It is ordered that she be whipt according to Law & that she serve her Master one whole year according to Law. *OB 1753–56, 7.*

1848. 10 July 1753—Nathaniel Wilson & James Berry, Two Servant Men belonging to David Galloway gent, were this Day brought before the Court and their Master Produced an Account against them for absenting themselves from his Service Three Days each & for his expences in retaking them which being allow'd by the Court was Sworn to b[y] the said Galloway & Ordered to be

Recorded and it's ordered that the said Servants Serve their said Master Six Months each to Satisfy his expences aforesaid & that they serve according to Law for the time they were absent. *OB 1753–56, 18.*

1849. 10 Sept. 1753—Daniel Rian, a Servant Boy belonging to Richard Thomas, came into Court and agreed to discharge his Master from paying him his Freedom dues in Consideration of his said Master's discharging him from his Service. *OB 1753–56, 48.* [In the Index the name is spelled Ryan.]

1850. 29 Oct. 1753—Fielding Hudson Produced a Certificate granted him for taking up Robert Baylie, a Servant Man belonging to Stephan Peacok of the County of Richmond and made oath that he had received no satisfaction for the same, ordered that it be Certified to the next General Assembly. *OB 1753–56, 56.*

1851. 10 Dec. 1753—Ordered that the Executors of John Oldham jun^r deced pay unto Thomas Betts his freedom dues according to Law. *OB 1753–56, 64.*

1852. 12 March 1754, Will of Mary Quarom— ... I give to my Servant Boy William Watson one Colt when he arrives of age. I likewise leave the said Servant boy Wm Watson Ten Shillings to buy him a Saddle when he comes of age.... *RB 3, 69.*

1853. 11 March 1754, Inventory of the estate of John Sutton— ... paid Dorothy Lord her Freedom Deeds [Dues ?], £2 10s.... *RB 3, 75.*

1854. 13 May 1754—Richard Hull gen^t produced an account against his Runaway Servant Man James Brown for Sixty Six Days absence & eight hundred & Twenty five pounds of Tobacco expended in retaking the said Runaway which being allowed by the Court was sworn to by the said Hull and It is Ordered that the said James Serve his Master for the same & his Costs in this behalf expended amounting to Twenty five Pounds of Tobacco according to Law. *OB 1753–56, 138.*

1855. 8 July 1754—James Guttry, a Servant Man belonging to John Routt, came into Court and agreed to give up his freedom dues in consideration of his said Master's discharging him from his Service & paying him one hundred & fifty pounds of Transfer Tobacco. *OB 1753–56, 158.*

1856. 12 Aug. 1754—Spencer Ball and Richard Hull gentl: produced accounts against their servant men, William Walson & Francis Rowes, which was examin'd by the Court & order'd that they serve their said Masters according to Law, and if the Maryland Law for taking up Runaway servants from Virginia is more than two hundred pds of tob⁰, It is the opinion of the Court that the s^d Ball & Hull receive the same. *OB 1753–56, 184.*

1857. 15 Aug. 1754—To Thomas Williams of this County for taking up John Western, a servant man belonging to John Sorrell of Westmorland County, 180 lbs. Tob⁰. *OB 1753–56, 213.*

1858. 25 Aug. 1754—To Ezekil Hayden of Lancaster County for taking up John Pinn, a servant man belonging to Richard Hudnall of this County, 90 lbs. tob⁰. *OB 1753–56, 213.*

1859. 25 Aug. 1754—To William Garner of this County for taking up Rawleigh Pinn, a servant boy belonging to Richard Seldon of Lancaster County, 90 lbs. tob⁰. *OB 1753–56, 213.*

1860. 25 Aug. 1754—To Abraham Beacham of this County for taking up Alex^a Frazier, a servant boy belonging to Spencer Airiss of Westmorland County, 180 lbs. tob⁰. *OB 1753–56, 213.*

1861. 25 Aug. 1754—To Thomas Williams for taking up Joseph Pyle, a servant man belonging to Richard Lee of Westmorland County, 90 lbs. *OB 1753–56, 213.*

1862. 11 Nov. 1754—Ordered that John Hardey, a servant man belonging to Spencer Ball gen^t, serve his said Master after his former time of Service expired for eighty four days absence & for three thousand one hundred & seventeen pounds of tob⁰ for charges in taking up according to Law. *OB 1753–56, 232.*

1863. 10 Feb. 1755—William Booth, a servant man belonging to Phillip Fisher, came into Court, and with the consent of the s^d Fisher he agrees to serve his s^d master after his former time of service is expired eight months & also discharges his said Master of his freedom dues, upon condition that his s^d Master keeps his Child which Child is to be deliver'd to the said Booth at the expiration of the afores^d time. *OB 1753–56, 262.*

1864. 14 April 1755—James Aubrey, a servant man belonging to John Foushee gen^t, came into Court and agreed to discharge the s^d Foushee from paying him his freedom dues in consideration of the said Foushee's buying him from his late master James Bayley of Westmorland County. *OB 1753–56, 292.*

1865. 14 April 1755—Upon the Complaint of Mrs Anne Taite against Nanny Taylor, a servant woman belonging to William Taite gen^t for resisting her said Mistress, It is order'd that she serve a year after her former time of service is expired for so doing according to Law, and that she receive on her bare back Thirty nine lashes well laid on for threating [threatening] to burn her master's house & threating to strike her said mistress. *OB 1753–56, 293.*

1866. 14 July 1755—Eleanor Bennett, a servant woman belonging to Phillip Fisher, came into Court and agreed to serve her s^d master one year after her Indented time of service is expired & to Discharge him from her freedom dues, In consideration that the s^d Fisher will take care & provide for a Child which she the s^d Bennett has living with him, which he the s^d Fisher agrees to do. *OB 1753–56, 346.*

1867. 14 July 1755—Mary Owen, a servant woman belonging to John Ross in the Province of Maryland, having been taken up as a runaway, was this day brought before the Court, and it appearing to them by the affidavit of William Angell that the s^d Owen had the leave of her said master to be absent from his service, she is according discharged. *OB 1753–56, 346.*

1868. 15 July 1755—Anne Taylor, a convict servant woman belonging to Thomas Ball of this County who stands charged with great Larcany in Stealing a silverspoon, the property of William Taite gen^t of the value of four Shillings Curr^t money and being arraigned of the premises, upon her arraignment she pleaded not guilty, and thereupon divers witnesses to wit Mary Willis, James Brown & Elizabeth Ball were sworn & examined, whereupon it seems to the Court by the evidence afores^d that the s^d Anne is guilty of the Larcany afores^d & thereupon it is ordered that she receive thirty nine lashes on her bare back well laid on, and it is said to the sherriff that he cause imediately execution thereof to be done, and that she be thence discharged. *OB 1753–56, 355.*

1869. 8 Sept. 1755—Order'd that John Young, a servant boy belonging to David Boyd, serve his said Master after his former time of Service is expired till he make satisfaction for Three hundred pounds of tob^o for charges in taking up when runaway & for twelve days absence according to Law. *OB 1753–56, 364.*

1870. 22 March 1756—Laurence Feagins of this County for taking up John

John Sryer, a servant man belonging to Robert Franks of the Bourough of Norfolk, 180 lbs. tobacco. *OB 1753–56, 487.*

1871. 12 April 1756, Inventory of the estate of James Booth—... 1 Servant man sold to James Crain, £5 0s 6d. .... *RB 3, 290.*

1872. 12 April 1756—John Longerwood, a servant man belonging to Ralph Wormly Esq:, being committed to the goal of this County as a Runaway, and being suspected of burning the s^d goal. After the examination of sundry witnesses touching the same, It is ordered that he receive thirty nine lashes on his bare back well laid on & then sent to his said Master. *OB 1753–56, 494.*

1873. 13 Dec. 1756—Order'd that John Young, a servant man belonging to David Boyd, serve his said Master after his former time of Service is expired till he makes satisfaction for Fifteen Shillings Curr^t money, charges in taking him up when runaway and for Sixty three days absence according to Law & that he also receive twenty five Lashes on his bare back well laid on. *OB 1756–58, 91.*

1874. 11 April 1757—To Jacob Haynie of this County for taking up Margaret Ross, a servant woman belonging to Tobias Purcell of Richmond County, 180 lbs. tob^o. *OB 1756–58, 139.*

1875. 11 April 1757—To William Blackerby of this County for taking up William Evere, a servant man belonging to Susannah Grey of Richmond County, 180 lbs tob^o. *OB 1756–58, 139.*

1876. 12 Sept. 1757—On the Petition of George Nicholson & Anne his wife against William Johnstone for freedom dues, Order'd the sherriff summon the Johnstone to appear at the next Court to answer the same. *OB 1756–58, 208.*

1877. 12 Sept. 1757—Mary Osburn, a servant woman belonging to John Webb, personally appeared in Court and agreed to discharge her said Master from paying her freedom dues, In Consideration of his Purchasing her from Philip Fisher, her late master. *OB 1756–58, 208.*

1878. 11 Oct. 1757—The Petition of George Nichelson and Anne his wife against William Johnstone is continued till next Court. *OB 1756–58, 232.*

1879. 11 Oct. 1757—Rachiel Ligthgow, a servant woman belonging to James Craine, came into Court & agreed to serve her said master eighteen months after her present time of service is expired, In consideration of his having her cured of her Disorder. *OB 1756–58, 236.*

1880. 11 April 1758—The Petition of Edward Barrat against George Haynie for freedom is Dismissed. *OB 1756–58, 291.* [Barrat, or Barrett, was actually an apprentice. He was bound to George Haynie 9 Feb. 1756.]

1881. 12 June 1758—It is order'd that John Crawford, a servant man belonging to Samuel Steel, serve his said master after his time of service is expired till he make satisfaction for one pound three shillings & three pence for Charge in taking up when runaway and for two days absence according to law. *OB 1756–58, 304.*

1882. 14 Aug. 1758—Grace Payne, a servant woman belonging to John Wilkins, personally came into Court and gave up her freedom dues on Consideration of her s^d Master's Discharging her from his Service. *OB 1756–58, 323.*

1883. 11 Sept. 1759—Patrick Gibney, a servant man belonging to Richard Hudnal, was brought before the Court for absenting himself from his s^d master's service who made oath he was at the expence of 180$^\#$ of Tob^o in Taking up the said runaway. It is therefore ordered he serve his said master after his time of service is expired according to Law for the s^d 180$^\#$ of Tobacco and Costs amounting to fourteen pounds of Tobacco. *OB 1758–62, 107.*

1884. 10 Oct. 1758, Will of Thomas Self—... Item I give unto my son Wm Self my Servant named William Dickson, the said William Dickson to serve him my said son till he is twenty one years old and one set of wedges & some Cooper and Carpenter too.... *RB 4, 314.*

1885. 14 April 1760—Mary Wilson, a servant woman belonging to Ezekiel Hudnal, this day came into Court and agreed to serve her said master over & above her time of service two years upon Consideration of her said Master's curing her of the fowl [foul] disease, and if she is not cured then this agreement to be void. *OB 1758–62, 172.*

1886. 12 May 1760—Anne Osborn, a servant belonging to John Knight, Came into Court and agreed to serve her said master over & above her usual time of service two years in Consideration of her said Master's Curing her of the foul disease and paying the Costs and if the said John Knight agrees that if she is not Cured the above agreement to be void. *OB 1758–62, 179.*

1887. 9 June 1760—Samuel Hoomes, a Servant man belonging to William Taite gen^t, came into Court and agreed to serve his said master over & above his time of service nine months upon Consideration of his said Master's having him cured of the foul disease and discharging him of Twenty Shillings paid by the s^d Taite for the taking up of the said Hoomes and the said Taite agreed that if the said Hoomes was not Cured the above agreement should be void. *OB 1758–62, 199.*

1888. 10 June 1760—Upon the Complaint of William Taite ag^t James Fitzmorris, his servant, for his misbehaviour to him. It is order'd that he receive thirty nine lashes on his bare back well laid on at the Publick Whipping poast [post], and it is further order'd the sherriff cause imediate execution thereof to be done & that he be thence discharged. *OB 1758–62, 204.*

1889. 8 Dec. 1760—Robert Sibbalds brought before the Court his Servant man Wm Wirre for absenting himself from his said Master's Service Ten days, and it is order'd he serve his said master after his time of Service for the same according to Law and also for his expences amount[in]g to fifteen Shillings and it is order'd he recieve thirty one lashes on his bare Back. *OB 1758–62, 238.* [Later the name is spelled Wier.]

1890. 9 Feb. 1761—Upon the Complaint of William Greenwood against his servent man Patrick Gibney for absenting himself from his service eighteen days and for five hundred and ninety pounds of tobacco his expence in taking the said Gibney, It is order'd that the said Patrick Gibney serve his said master over & above his time of service for the same according to Law. *OB 1758–62, 239.*

1891. 13 April 1761—Upon the Complaint of William Taite gen^t against James Fitzmorris his servant for misbehaving to his said Master, It is order'd he receive Ten Lashes at the Common Whiping post & then be discharged. *OB 1758–62, 268.*

1892. 22 May 1761—To Constantine Rock of this County for Taking up Patrick Gibney, a servant man belonging to Wm Greenwood of this County, 90$^\#$ tob^o. *OB 1758–62, 269.*

1893. 14 Sept. 1761—Elizabeth Purchet, a Servant Woman belonging to William Greenwood, was brought before the Court for absenting herself from her said Master's Service Fifteen Days and her Master making oath he was at the expence in retaking her of 180$^\#$ Tob^o and 20s. It is ordered she serve for the same after her time of Service is expired according to Law and that the account be Recorded and that she pay Costs. *OB 1758–62, 322.*

1894. 8 March 1762—Robert Sibbards brought before the Court his Servant Man Named William Wier for absenting Three months and Five Days from his Service and made oath he was at the expence of seventeen Shillings and Six Pence at different times in taking him for which it is ordered he serve after the expiration of his Service according to Law and the Account is ordered to be Recorded. *OB 1758–62, 362.*

1895. 12 April 1762—John Abby, Servant to Richard Hull gent., came into Court and agreed to pay his Master Five Pound Curr^t Money or Serve him Four Months after his Time of Service is expired upon Condition the said Hull pays for the said Abby Five Pound to any Person that shall cure the said Abby of the Foul Disease and pay Costs of entering this order etc. *OB 1758–62, 368.*

1896. 15 June 1762—Upon the complaint of Robert Sibbards against his Servant Man for Thirty seven Days absence and one Pound Ten Shillings which the Sibbards made oath he was at the expence of in retaking the said Servant, this being the Second complaint. It is ordered the Sheriff Sell the Servant to the highest Bidder and apply the money according to Law. *OB 1758–62, 398.* [The servant is Wier.]

1897. 8 Nov. 1762—Upon the complaint of Spencer Ball gen^t against George Anderson his servant for offering violence to his s^d master, It is order'd that for the s^d offence he serve his s^d master after his former time of service is expired according to Law & also receive on his bare back 39 lashes well laid on at the Public whiping post & be then remanded to goal. *OB 1762–66, Part 1, 3.*

1898. 13 Dec. 1762—Upon the Petition of Joseph Beatley, a servant, against John Yapp, his Master, It appearing to the Court that the s^d Yapp hath removed out of the Colony, order'd the s^d Beatley be discharged from any further service of his s^d Master. *OB 1762–66, Part 1, 19.*

1899. 9 May 1763—On the Petition of John Nicholas Smith by William Roane, his attorney, for his servant to be allowed for attending this Court in the suit between Joseph Samson Pl^t and Jesse Clutton Def^t, It is ordered that the said Jesse Clutton pay unto James Davis Fourteen hundred and eighty two pounds of tob^o for Twenty eight days attend^a at this Court & for Coming & Returning Sixteen Miles Six times and Fifteen Miles eleven times as a Witness for the said Clutton at the suit of the s^d Joseph Samson. *OB 1762–66, Part 1, 94.*

1900. 11 July 1763, Bill of sale from William Trussell to Thomas and George Simpson—... Gave granted, bargained & Sold and by these presents Do grant, bargain and Sell unto the said Thomas & George Simpson their Heirs, Exors, Adm^rs, or assigns, to wit, one negro girl named Hannah also my right of servitude of a Mulatto boy named Willoughby.... *RB 6, Part 1, 244.*

1901. 12 July 1763—Upon the motion of Sinah Scallion, a mollato Servant belonging to William Greenwood for her freedom. It appearing to the Court on examination of sundry witnesses that she is of the age of Thirty one years, ordered that she be therefore Discharged. But in Case the said Greenwood at the next Court Can make appear from the Register or any other undoubted Proof that she is not of that age, Then she then return to her aforesaid service & it is further ordered that she be allowed freedom dues. *OB 1762–66, Part 1, 180.*

1902. 12 Sept. 1763—It is ordered that John Payne, a servant man belonging to Richard Bowes, serve his said Master after his former time of service is expired untill he make satisfaction for the sum of seventeen pounds thirteen shillings and six pence Curr^t money of Virg^a which the s^d Bowes made oath that he had expended in Taking him up when Run away etc. as also for Ninety one days absence according to Law, and that the s^d John Payne receive Twenty Lashes on his bare back well laid on. *OB 1762–66, Part 1, 203.*

1903. 10 Oct. 1763—On the motion of William Greenwood by his attorney against his late serv^t Sinah Scallion, It is ordered that George Ball and Joseph McAdam gen^t take the Deposition of Jane Mott. And in Case it appears that the s^d Sinah is not of lawfull age that she then serve the s^d Greenwood according to Law. *OB 1762–66, Part 1, 227.*

1904. 12 Dec. 1763—Sarah Maughan, a servant woman belonging to the estate of Sarah Harding deced, Came into Court and agreed to Relinguish her freedom dues on Consideration of her freedom. *OB 1762–66, Part 1, 251.*

1905. 9 Jan. 1764—For the examination of Jonathen Crooke, a servant man belonging to Robert Sibbalds, charged with Felony in Stealing money from the s^d Sibbalds. The above named Jonathen Crooke being committed to the goal of this County charged with the Felony aforesaid was led to the Barr, and therefore Divers witnesses were Produced, Sworn and examined upon the

Premises and the Prisoner heard in his own Defence and upon Consideration of the evidence of the s^d witnesses & the Circumstance of the Case, It was the opinion of the Court that the Prisoner ought not to be tryed for the said supposed Fact by the General Court, but ought to be discharged from his Imprisonment afores^d And he was according Discharged. *OB 1762–66, Part 1, 261, 262.*

1906. 9 Jan. 1764—The Depositions taken between William Greenwood and his servant Sinah Scallion is continued till next Court for argument. *OB 1762–66, Part 1, 262.*

1907. 12 March 1764—It appearing to the Court that Sinah Scallion, a servant woman belonging to William Greenwood, is not yet free (as before have been Represented). It is order'd that she forthwith return to her s^d Master & serve according to Law. *OB 1762–66, Part 1, 275.*

1908. 11 June 1764—On the motion of Mary Enjer against Phillip Fisher for freedom dues, It is order'd that the sheriff summon the s^d Fisher to appear at next Court. *OB 1762–66, Part 2, 349.*

1909. 11 June 1764—Mary Enjer being summon'd to appear at this Court upon the Information of the Churchw^{ns} of St Stephens Parish against her for having a Bastard Child, & she not appearing, It is Considered by the Court that for this s^d offence she forfeit and pay Fifty Shillings on 500$^{\#}$ Tob^o to the said Churchwardens for the use of the poor of the s^d Parish & that she also pay the Costs of this Prosecution with an attornies fee, and Newton Keene gen^t agrees to pay the same. *OB 1762–66, Part 2, 348.*

1910. 9 July 1764—Judgment upon Petition is granted to Mary Enjer against Phillip Fisher for three pounds ten shillings due for freedom dues which is order'd to be paid with Costs. *OB 1762–66, Part 2, 375.*

1911. 11 Sept. 1764—On the motion of James Nicken by his attorney against George Ingram for his freedom, It is order'd that the sheriff summon the s^d Ingram to appear at next Court untill which time the s^d Nicken is to abide with Joseph Ball. *OB 1762–66, Part 2, 411.*

1912. 9 Oct. 1764—On the motion of Samuel Byrn against his former Master John Thomas for freedom dues, It is order'd the sherriff summon the s^d Thomas to appear at the next Court. *OB 1762–66, Part 2, 420.*

1913. 9 Oct. 1764—Upon a former motion of James Nicken against George

Ingram for freedom, the s^d Nicken now being called & not appearing, It is order'd the sherriff cause him to appear at the next Court. *OB 1762–66, Part 2, 423.*

1914. 13 Nov. 1764—Upon the Petition of James Nicken alias Bateman against George Ingram, on hearing the allegations of each party, It is order'd that the s^d Bateman serve the s^d Ingram & his assigns Four years from the date hereof During which time the s^d Ingram is to find him sufficient Diet & Cloathing. *OB 1762–66, Part 2, 435.*

1915. 13 Nov. 1764—Judgment upon Petition is granted Samuel Burn against his late Master John Thomas for three pounds ten Shillings on account of his freedom dues which is order'd to be paid with Costs. *OB 1762–66, Part 2, 436.*

1916. 13 Nov. 1764—Order'd that Samuel Burn pay unto John Moore Fifty pounds of tob° for two days attendance at this Court as a Witness for the s^d Burn against John Thomas. *OB 1762–66, Part 2, 436.* [Sarah Moore and Martha Bussell were also to be paid 50 pounds of tobacco each for two days attendance at court as witnesses for Burn.]

1917. 9 April 1765—William Taite agrees to give his Servant man named Dennis McCarty two years of his Service, For which the s^d McCarty promises and agrees to learn the s^d Taite's Negro man Jacob the Blacksmith's Trade, also the trade of a Cooper, Smith Braizer [Brazier] & Tin Smith and behave honestly, soberly & faithfully the remaining part of the time. William Taite agrees to give his Servant man named Mathew Lenord one year, on Consideration he behaves honestly, soberly & faithfully as a servant should do for the other part of his Servitude. *RB 6, Part 2, 545.*

1918. 9 April 1765—Articles of agreement between William Taite gen^t and his Servants, Dennis McCarty and Mathew Leonard, was this day agreed too by the Parties & admitted to Record. *OB 1762–66, Part 2, 475.*

1919. 8 July 1765—It is order'd that Patrick Malloy, a servant man belonging to Robert Sibbalds, serve his said Master his former time of service is expired untill he make satisfaction for Six Months absence and eleven hundred & six pounds of tob° p[er] year & that he also receive Ten lashes on his bare back well laid on. *OB 1762–66, Part 2, 552.*

1920. 20 July 1765—John Sydnor produced a Certificate for taking up William Webb, a servant man, who made oath that he hath rec^{ed} no satisfaction for the same, 180 lbs. tobacco. *OB 1762–66, Part 2, 548.*

1921. 20 July 1765—George Shepherd produced a Certificate for taking up Patrick Malloy, a servant man belonging to Robt Sibbalds of this County, who made oath that he hath reced no satisfaction for the same, order'd it be Certified to the next General Assembly, 180 lbs. tob^o. *OB 1762–66, Part 2, 548.* [At the same court William Barrot also produced a certificate for 180 pounds of tobacco for taking up Malloy.]

1922. 12 Aug. 1765, Inventory of the estate of William Harding— ... 1 white woman Servant named Sarah M Eranire [or McEranire].... *RB 6, Part 2, 590.*

1923. 12 Aug. 1765—It is order'd that Mathew Leonard, a servant man belonging to William Taite gen^t, serve his said master after his former time of service is expired according to law untill he make satisfaction for Twenty pounds one shilling and nine pence Charges in pursuing and taking him up when runaway and also for sixty seven days absence. *OB 1762–66, Part 2, 552.*

1924. 12 Aug. 1765—It is order'd that Samuel Holms, a servant man belonging to William Taite gen^t, serve his said Master after his former time of service is expir'd according to law untill he make satisfaction for Twenty two pounds twelve shillings and four pence half penny, Charges in taking him up when runaway and also for sixty seven days. *OB 1762–66, Part 2, 552.*

1925. 14 Oct. 1765, Will of Hannah Higgins— ... my desire is that John Ashburn shall have Stephen Day. ... *RB 6, Part 2, 638.* [This could be a servant or a slave.]

1926. 8 Sept. 1766—Order'd that Sarah Masker, a servant woman belonging to John Smith, serve her s^d Master one year after her former time of service is expired for having a Bastard Child. *OB 1762–66, Part 2, 665.*

1927. 9 Feb. 1767, Inventory of the estate of George Kerr— ... 1 Servan woman sold for £12 1s 0d. ... *RB 7, 27.*

1928. 11 May 1767—Upon the Complaint of Mary Fitzgerrele, a servan woman belonging to Robert Sibbalds, for ill usuage, on hearing the parties, I is order'd that she return to her service & that the s^d Robert use her better fo the usuage. *OB 1767–70, 69.*

1929. _ July 1767, Sales of the estate of William Taite— . . . 1 servant woman Mary Hynton sold to Mrs Anne Taite for 5s. . . . *RB 8, 465.*

1930. _ July 1767, Sales of the estate of William Taite— . . . a Servant man Thomas Dunn sold to James Crain for £5; to Spencer Thomas a servant man, Wm Walkins, £13 12s 6d. . . . *RB 8, 468.* [The name could be Watkins, but this clerk usually crossed his t's.]

1931. 13 Oct. 1767—Upon the Petition of George Christie against his Master William Ball for ill usuage, It is order'd that the sherriff summon the s^d Ball to appear at the next Court to answer the same. *OB 1767–70, 132.* [At the next court the suit was discontinued.]

1932. 11 Jan. 1768—The complaint of Edwin Lunsford against his Master Peter Beane for his Freedom is dismissed & the s^d Edwin order'd to return to his s^d Master's service. *OB 1767–70, 139.*

1933. 14 March 1768—Upon the motion of William Greenwood by his attorney against his servant, Sinah Scallion, for further service. It is considered that the s^d Scallion hath served her full time & that she be accordingly discharged. *OB 1767–70, 171.*

1934. 14 Nov. 1768—Upon the Petition of Winefred Range, a free molatto, against Betty Toulson for her freedom, on hearing the Parties, It is the opinion of the Court the s^d Winefred hath attain'd to the age of Thirty one years whereupon the same is order'd to be Certified. *OB 1767–70, 314.*

1935. 9 Oct. 1769, Inventory of the estate of Col. John Bell— . . . 1 Servant woman Christian Robertson about four years to serve, £10. . . . *RB 7, 407.*

1936. 12 March 1770—Upon the Petition of Nicholas Range against Winder Kenner for his freedom, It is Considered by this Court, from the evidence produced, that the said Range will be free at the expiration of two months from this time. *OB 1767–70, 451.*

1937. 9 April 1770—Upon the motion of Alice Turner against Allen S. Shiverell for her freedom, It is order'd that the sheriff summon the s^d Shiverell to appear at the next Court. *OB 1767–70, 462.*

1938. 14 May 1770—Upon the Petition of Alice Turner against Allen S. Shiverell for her freedom, on examination of her Indentures, it appearing to the

Court that they are Insufficient, she is therefore discharged from further service & the said Alice Turner here in Court relinguishes her right to freedom dues on having her youngest Child given up. *OB 1767–70, 484.*

1939. 15 May 1770—John Carnaby, a servant man belonging to David Boyd, this day in Court agreed to serve his said Master one year after his former time of service is expired for his the s^d Carnaby's being absent from his s^d Master sometime. *OB 1767–70, 488.*

1940. 18 May 1770, Inventory of the estate of the Hon. Presly Thornton— ... Betty Wilson near two years to serve, £6. ... *RB 8, 19.*

1941. 18 May 1770, Inventory of the estate of the Hon. Presly Thornton— ... Thomas [no last name given], a Taylor, 5 1/2 years to Serve, £30. ... *RB 8, 19.*

1942. 9 April 1771—Upon the motion of Spencer Thomas, a molatto, against his Master Henry Boggess for his freedom, It is order'd the said Boggess be summoned to appear at next Court. *OB 1770–73, 93.*

1943. 10 June 1771—Order'd that Jane Mills, a Servant woman belonging to Nathaniel Wilson, serve her s^d Master after her former time of service is expired untill she make satisfaction for seventeen days absence and three pounds five shillings Charges in taking her up when runaway according to law. *OB 1770–73, 145.*

1944. 10 June 1771—Order'd that Spencer Thomas pay unto Judith Coleman Twenty five pounds of tob^o for one days attendance at this Court as a Witness for him ag^t Henry Boggess. *OB 1770–73, 145.* [Spencer Thomas also was ordered to pay Hannah Dunaway, Juna Blewford, and William Lewis as witnesses.]

1945. 11 June 1771—On the motion of Grace Thomas against her Master Thomas Airs for freedom, It is order'd the sherriff summon him to appear at the next Court. *OB 1770–73, 146.*

1946. 11 June 1771—Spencer Thomas, a Servant belonging to Henry Boggess, came into Court & agreed to serve William Lewis three years from Christmas next on his said Lewis's purchasing him of his present master, the s^d Henry Boggess. *OB 1770–73, 146.*

1947. 11 June 1771—Order'd that Mathew Wilson, a servant man belonging to Rodham Kenner gen^t, serve his s^d Master after his former time of service is expired untill he make satisfaction for six months absence and twenty two shillings & six pence, charges in taking up when run away according to law. *OB 1770–73, 149.*

1948. 8 July 1771—Grace Thomas, a molatto   Pl^t   Petition for
                       v   her freedom
          Thomas Airs   Def^t
This day came the parties by their attornies & after hearing the Witnesses produced on both sides, It is considered by the Court that the Pl^t is a free person & she is order'd to be discharged accordingly. *OB 1770–73, 160.*

1949. 10 July 1771—On the motion of Elin^o Bussell for her freedom, It is order'd that Francis Kenner & Hannah his wife be summoned to appear at the next Court. *OB 1770–73, 178.*

1950. 9 March 1772—John Sebree's motion ag^st George Astin, his master, for his freedom, on hearing the witnesses Tis the opinion of the Court that he is of full age on which he is discharged. *OB 1770–73, 262.*

1951. 9 March 1772—On the motion of Jane Mills for ill usuage from Nath^a Wilson, it is order'd by the Court be that the shff summon the s^d Nath^a Wilson to appear at the next Court. *OB 1770–73, 264.*

1952. 13 April 1772, Inventory of the estate of Maj. William Taite— . . . William Watkins, a Servant, £20. . . . *RB 8, 455.*

1953. 13 April 1772, Inventory of the estate of Maj. William Taite— . . . Billy, £12 (free at 31). . . . *RB 8, 456.*

1954. 13 April 1772, Sales of the estate of William Taite— . . . a servant man, Matthew Lonard, sold to William Flood for £5 10s. . . . *RB 8, 464.* [The name could be Lenard.]

1955. 14 April 1772—Jane Mills having Complained to this Court against Nathl Wilson, her master, for ill usuage, on hearing the Parties, It is that she serve her s^d Master two months after her former time of Service is expired and that the sheriff Carry her home to her s^d Master. *OB 1770–73, 293.*

1956. 14 April 1772—Ordered that Jane Mills pay unto Spencer Haynie 25 lbs. tob^o for one day's attendance at this Court as a Witness for her against Nathl Wilson. *OB 1770–73, 293.*

1957. 9 Nov. 1772—The motion of Jane Mills, a Servant woman belonging to Nathl Wilson, for ill usuage is Dismist. *OB 1770–73, 464.*

1958. 9 Aug. 1773—Upon Complaint of James Walker against his Master Benjamin Clarke for freedom on hearing the Witnesses, it is the opinion of the Court that the s^d Walker is of full age whereupon he is discharged from further service. *OB 1773–83, 56.*

1959. 14 Feb. 1774—Upon the Complaint of Jane Mills against her Master Nathaniel Wilson for ill usuage (by consent of the s^d Wilson), it is ordered that she be sold by the sherriff of this County for the Term of Three Years & six Months, & that the produce of such sale be paid to the s^d Nathl Wilson. *OB 1773–83, 122.*

1960. 14 Nov. 1774, Inventory of the estate of James Toulson— . . . Augustine to be free at 31 years of age £25; John to serve till D^o, £25; Joe to serve till D^o, £20; Lettice to serve till D^o, £10; Rachell to serve till D^o, £15; Massco to serve till d^o and her Child Charlotte about one month old to serve till 18 years of age, £20. . . . *RB 9, Part 2, 498.*

1961. 14 Nov. 1774—Elizabeth Dawson, having been commited of having a Mulatto Bastard Child, it is ordered that she be sold for the term of Five years & the produce of such sale be applied to the use of St Stephens Parish. *OB 1773–83, 226.*

1962. 10 July 1775—Upon the Complaint of John Parrot against William Foalks for ill usuage, it is ordered that the Sherriff take the s^d William into his Custody & him safely keep untill he enters into Bond wth Sufficient Security to keep the peace & be of good behaviour towards all his Majesties Kings people for the space of one year. *OB 1773–83, 237.*

1963. 9 Dec. 1776—Upon Complaint of Mellicent Harcum against Winifred Airs for ill usuage, the said Mellicent having taken the usual oath, it is order'd that the Sherriff take into his Custody the body of the s^d Winifred Airs & her safely keep until he enters into Bond with two sufficient Securities, the Principal in £20 & the Securities in £10 each, that the s^d Winifred keep the peace & be of good behaviour towards all the people of this Commonwealth & more especially towards the said Mellicent, for the space of one whole year. *OB 1773–83, 275.*

1964. 10 March 1777—The motion of Alic, a mulatto woman, by Leroy Peachey gent., her attorney, against her Master John S. Woodcock for her freedom. On a full hearing of the Witnesses, it is order'd that she return to her Service, the Proof being quite insufficient. *OB 1773–83, 287.*

1965. 12 May 1777, Inventory of the estate of John Knight—... 1 white servant man, £12.... *RB 10, 169.*

1966. 10 Aug. 1778, Inventory of the estate of Rev. John Leland—... 1 Negro girl Nan free at 31 years, £60; Negro boy John free at 31 years, £75; 1 Negro boy Elijah free at 21 years, £30; Negro boy Spencer free at 21 years, £35.... *RB 10, 344.*

1967. 11 Aug. 1777—On the motion of Joseph Hudnal against Jane Mills, his Servant woman, who absented herself from her said Master's Service during her servitude five weeks, It is ordered that she pay to her said Master for such absence eighty three pounds of Tob° & six shillings and that she return to service till Thursday next after which Time she is to be free from her said Master. *OB 1773–83, 301.*

1968. 13 Oct. 1777—On the motion of Joseph Ball against William Blackerby for harbouring a servant boy of the name of J^{no} Oliver, it is ordered that the said servant return to his master's service. *OB 1773–83, 305.*

1969. 14 April 1778—On the motion of Joseph Ball against Milly Thomas, a mulatto (a Servant till she arrives to the age of 31 years), to serve him the said Ball three years for having three bastard children after her Time of servitude was expired. It is the opinion of the Court that the said motion illegal and contrary to Justice; therefore it is ordered to be dismissed. *OB 1773–83, 319.*

1970. 13 July 1778—On the motion of Nelly Dyches against James Ball, John Craine, Joseph Williams & Kenner Cralle gent., ordered that the sheriff Summon them to appear at the next Court to show cause why they retain as Servants Henry, Robert, Billy, Thomas Dyches her children & also that Kenner Cralle & James Ball as churchwardens do then appear. *OB 1773–83, 329.* [Robert, Billy (William), and Thomas Dykes were bound out by the churchwardens of St. Stephens parish 14 Nov. 1774. *(OB 1773–83, 226.)* More than likely they were apprentices and not servants. Evidently, in the court order here, Nelly Dyches is attempting to have her children returned to her.]

1971. 13 Oct. 1778—On the Complaint of Susanna Walker in behalf of Winifred Walker against Bennett Boush for Ill Treatment. Ordered that the sherif summon the said Bennett Boush to appear here at the next Court to said

County on the Second Monday in November next Then & there to answer the premises. *OB 1773–83, 342.*

1972. 8 Oct. 1781, Inventory of the estate of Joseph Ball— ... John Oliver, mulatto boy, that has to serve till 5th Day of Decr 1786, £30. ... *RB 11, 114.*

1973. 10 Oct. 1785—Upon the petition of John Popler who was a Servant to William Rice deced. and with the Consent of Richard Rice and Thomas Walker Admors. of the said deced. Ordered that he be Discharged from any further Service of the said Admors, the said Popler first arguing to Exonerate them from any Covenants expressed in a certain Indenture made between the Churchwardens of St. Stephens Parish and the said William Rice deced. *OB 1783–85, 395.*

1974. 10 Jan. 1791, Inventory of the estate of Nathan Pullin— ... 1 negroe boy Isaac, a servant to the age of 21 years, £10; 1 negroe girl Jude to serve to the age of 18 years, £8. ... *RB 14, 397.*

1975. 12 Oct. 1795—Ordered that it be certified to whom it may concern that it appears to the satisfaction of the Court that John Evans, a mulatto residing within this County, is free. *OB 1790–95, 579.*

1976. 12 Oct. 1795—Ordered that it is certified to whom it may concern it appears to the satisfaction of the Court that Francis Bee, a mulatto residing within this County, is free. *OB 1790–95, 579.*

ADDITIONAL DOCUMENTS

1977. 18 Nov. 1655, Will of George Nott—I give & bequeath unto Thomas Hall, (hee to be bound by Indenture by Order of County Court) one Cow Calfe to be delivered for his use three yeares before the expiration of his freedom. ... *RB 1652–58, 72.*

1978. 18 Feb. 1718—Jno Chauhady, serv^t to Jno Forrester, judged to be eight years old. *OB 1713–19, 299.*

1979. 10 April 1769—Upon the motion of Joseph Dameron by his attorney against Spencer Kelly who he alledges is his servant, and now going at large, under pretence of his being free, It is considered by the Court on the testimony of Bartholomew Dameron who is the only witness that the s^d is not yet free; it is therefore order'd that he return to his service accordingly. *OB 1767–70, 352.*

INDEX

All names of persons have been indexed according to document number. Names of places, rivers, and ships have not been indexed. Look for all possible spellings of a name.

Abby
   John 1895
Abraham
   Greene 106
   Thomas 1028
Acton
   Francis 135
Adam
   Thomas 888
Adams
   Deborah 763
   John 837, 1241, 1720
   Summar 375
   Summer 181
Adannough
   Teage 717
Aday
   Stephen 313
Addison
   Hugh 100
Adington
   Benjamin 705
Adire
   Alexander 976
Afflax
   George 1815, 1816
Ager
   John 590

Agura
   Joane 136
Ailey
   Joane 434
Ailiff
   Anne 419
Aires/Airs
   John 155, 218
   Thomas 1945, 1948
   William 1768
   Winifred 1963
Airiss
   Spencer 1860
Alberry
   Anne 1274
Alderidge/Aldridge
   Clement 1207
   George 20
   William 294
Aldwell
   Thomas 980
Alexander
   David 1762
   James 734, 1777
Alford
   Richard 13
   Thomas 404

Allcocke
    William 250
Allen/Allon
    Cornelius 1152
    James 93, 132, 200, 274, 439,
        480, 503, 1225
    John 647, 1078
    Ralph 1050
    Thomas 1386, 1401, 1487
    William 152
Allenson
    Thomas 245
    William 147
Allerton
    Isaac 334, 361, 381, 1666
    Mr. 349
Allgood
    John 1621
Allgrove
    Nicholas 429
Althorp
    John 800
Alverson
    Teleife 1440
Alverton
    Sileife 697
Amee
    Joseph 833
Amery
    Kath: 503
    William 503
Amie
    John 441
Aminner
    Patrick 1323
Amorite
    Isaac 306
Anderson
    George 1897
    Hannah 1230
    James 911, 917
    Mary 1200

Anderson (cont.)
    Robert 41
    Sarah 758, 1294
    William 284, 1161
Angell
    William 116, 1867
Anketell
    Francis 33
Anley
    Mary 1525
Apleton
    Capt. 684
Arbuckle
    William 1641
Archer
    Richard 1047
    William 282, 347, 493, 494
Argile
    Alice 722, 1225
Arledge
    William 1324
Armsby
    Andrew 1251
Armsley/Armsly
    Andrew 1208, 1293
Armstronge
    George 1149
    Henry 941, 983
    Thomas 840
Arney
    Roger 371
Arnold
    Alic 435
    Alice 475, 514
Aro
    John 821, 1153
Arpin
    Thomas 136
Arranthrough/Arrenthrew
    Jane 1557, 1559, 1642, 1646
Arsbell
    John 1294

Arshridge
　Thomas 313
Arther
　Henry 1236, 1238, 1240
Ash
　John 306
　Robert 775
Ashburn
　John 1767, 1768, 1771, 1772, 1925
　Thomas 1445, 1497
Ashton
　Charles 441
　Col. 461
　Isabell 248
　James 8
　John 1294
　Peter 142, 205, 230, 294, 296, 386, 441
Ashwin
　John 132
Askew
　Mary 314
Askwith
　John 313
Astin
　George 1950
Aston
　Jeffery 150
Atkins
　John 404, 519
　Joseph 460, 1294
　Robert 294
Atwell
　Thomas 13
Aublin
　Henry 1549
Aubourne
　Mary 821
Aubrey
　James 1864

Auger
　Jone 179
Austeene
　Col. 684
Austen/Austin
　James 304, 353, 354, 368, 476, 632, 921
　Joseph 921
　Thomas 993
Autrobus
　Phillip 1294
Ayres
　Katherine 294
Ayrie/Ayry
　Richard 845, 868

Backer
　Richard 1799
Backster
　Thomas 57
Bacon
　William 118
Bailes
　John 146, 157
Baily/Baley/Bayley/Baylie/Bayly
　James 1864
　Jane 481
　John 842, 998, 1004
　Joseph 404
　Mary 77
　Robert 1850
Baineham
　Alexander 22
　Ann 22
Baker
　Allice 788
　Anthony 1420
　Edward 684
　Hugh 519, 532
　John 1372
　Richard 1254, 1271, 1284
　Robert 832

Baker (cont.)
    Theodore 69, 1050
    Thomas 863, 935, 976, 1039, 1227
Balden
    Patrick 1096
Baldridge
    Thomas 1
    William 1
Balerod
    James 2
Ball
    Ann 71
    Elizabeth 1868
    George 1586, 1736, 1903
    James 1970
    Joseph 1911, 1968, 1969, 1972
    Samuel 502, 1313
    Spencer 1773, 1811, 1824, 1856, 1862, 1897
    Thomas 1846, 1868
    William 1931
Ballingall
    William 101, 407
Balterman
    Margaret 404
Bamfold
    John 734
Banbury
    Stephen 115
Bancroft
    William 193
Bandenall
    Thomas 532
Bangess
    Henry 1486
Banister
    Richard 737
Bankes/Banks
    Elizabeth 1005, 1165, 1221, 1340, 1380, 1389, 1426, 1498, 1503, 1506

Bankes/Banks (cont.)
    Thomas 718, 897, 989
Bankley
    Samuel 734
Banning
    Emlin 306
Barbar/Barber
    John 406, 595
    Robert 519, 591, 748
    Thomas 758
Bardon
    John 100
Bareman
    Peter 1828
Barker
    William 294
Barklett
    Robert 740
Barly
    Peter 1335
Barn
    James 373
Barnes
    James 212
    John 313
    Mary 1294
    Thomas 785, 1367, 1835
    William 1453
Barrat/Barratt/Barrett/Barrot
    Edward 1880
    George 853, 1088
    Mr. 396
    Thomas 392, 393, 394, 395
    William 1684, 1921
Barrom
    Ann 1605
Barrow
    Margaret 55
    Robert 357
Barry
    Dowling 1068
    Thomas 1368, 1369

Barwell
 James 1748
Bashaw
 Margaret 147
Basie
 John 1612
Baskafeild
 John 1447
Baskervill
 George 1323
Bassell
 Morris 1065
Bateman/Batman
 Anthony 1313
 James 1914
 Jane 232, 241
 John 135, 244
 Mary 135
 Peter 1828, 1832
Bater
 John 272
Bateson
 Samuel 833
Battin
 William 313
Batting
 William 1152
Batts
 William 509
Batty
 William 252
Baule
 Richard 722
Beacham/Beachamp/Beachum/
Becham
 Abraham 1860
 Ann 688
 Daniel 169, 333
 Samuel 1748
Beane
 Peter 1932
 William 1324

Bear
 Samuel 1664
Bearcroft
 Peter 1789
 Thomas 901
Beard
 John 981
 Lewis 313
Bearmore
 John 505, 547
Beasley/Beesly
 William 66, 68, 115
Beathan
 David 1636
Beatley
 Joseph 1898
Beavan
 Joseph 193
Beavin
 Anne 183
Beazles
 John 941
Bedle
 Elizabeth 8
Bee
 Francis 1976
 Lovis 1336
Beeton
 Joseph 734
Bell
 Arthur 1294
 John 313, 1935
 William 313
Benbow
 ___ 382
Benes
 William 419
Benham
 Mathew 822, 1261
Bennett/Bennit
 Christopher 245
 Edward 550, 833, 1206

Bennett/Bennit (cont.)
    Eleanor 1842, 1866
    Elizabeth 16, 833
    John 16, 49, 115
    Onesephorus 571, 572
    Richard 88
    William 242, 243, 415, 488, 829
Benson
    John 129
Bently
    Hannah 527
    Matthew 313
    Richard 1230
Beorane
    James 1054
Berry
    ___ 104
    Dowland 1230
    Francis 56
    Israell 800
    James 1848
    John 1700
    Robert 666, 673, 674, 775
    Thomas 884, 1054
Bertrand
    John 1081
Besouth
    William 812
Beswick
    Elizabeth Boggess 1800
Bethell
    William 28
Betts
    Charles 758, 1700, 1805
    Elizabeth 174, 330
    Susannah 1575
    Thomas 1851
    William 23, 293, 514, 722, 758
Beverly
    Robert 729

Bevin
    Morris 1129
    William 478
Biggs
    Phillip 180
Birch
    John 381
Bird
    Timothy 1044
Birk/Birke
    John 1033, 1288
Bishop
    Ralph 261
Bittle
    Hannah 27
Blach [or Biach]
    Thomas 997
Black
    Jack 579
Blackburn
    Richard 1585
Blackerby
    William 1875, 1968
Blackley
    Peter 714
Blackwell
    Charles 650, 715
    Josias 222, 361
    Margery 1382
    Samuel 1382, 1646, 1674, 1698, 1825
Blackwood
    James 1523
Blagg
    Thomas 50
Blake
    William 427
Blanck
    Susanna 174
Bland
    Joseph 860, 981, 1225

Bledsoe/Bletsoe
    George 624, 631
    William 1119
Bleufeild
    ____ 723
Blewford
    Juna 1944
Blitto
    John 26
Blome
    Bartho: 35
Blumstone
    Sarah 176
Boaz
    John 855
Boggess
    Henry 1373, 1431, 1942, 1944, 1946
    John 1750
Boharry
    William 228
Boles
    William 193
Bolin
    Judy 1718
    Mary 1718
Bolt
    Jane 289
Bonam/Bonum
    Grace 1
    John 519
    Sarah 1
Bond
    Mary 1679, 1758
Boolock
    Edward 1838
Booth
    James 1818, 1871
    Richard 770, 1313, 1603, 1646, 1832
    William 1842, 1863
Borgan
    Thomas 1657
Boswell
    William 128
Boulton
    Charles 1506
    Philip 432
Bound
    John 210
Bourne
    James 1041
    Terrence 1035
Boush
    Bennett 1971
Bowen
    John 325, 667, 801, 818
Bowes
    Edmond 1294
    Richard 1902
Bowle
    Morris 1114
Bowles
    John 288
    Solomon 1343, 1345
Bowley
    Simon 1701
Bowlin/Bowling
    Judith 1485, 1542, 1569, 1570, 1571
    Mathew 1822
Bowman
    William 1118, 1488
Bowyer
    Andrew 327
    Thomas 515
Boxberry
    Samuel 195
Boy
    John 510, 511
Boyd
    Ann 1413, 1415
    David 941, 1869, 1873, 1939

Boyd (cont.)
    Martha 1348, 1349
    Robert 1374, 1387, 1408
Boyer
    Richard 298
Brabin
    Henry 1294
Bradberry
    Elizabeth 274
Braden
    Richard 1628
Bradfield
    John 1708
Bradford
    Sarah 136, 153
Bradley/Bradly
    Henry 382
    John 294
    Mary 382
    Richard 696, 716
    Robert 286, 1603
    William 128
Brady
    ____ 915
    Owen 833
Bragg
    Henry 894
    Peter 272
Brale
    Nathaniel 324
Branch
    John 79, 684
    Mary 79
Brasor
    Margaret 177
    Richard 177
Brasseele/Brassell/Brassill
    Morris 982, 1065, 1317
Bready
    Patrick 1322
Brenam/Brenane
    James 1685, 1689

Brent
    Gyle 33, 684
    Hugh 684
    Margaret 33
    Mary 33
Brereton
    George 578
    Henry 1049
    Major 650
    Thomas 196, 404, 501, 511, 558, 592, 594, 613, 725, 786
    William 404, 450, 512, 519, 557
Brett
    George 549
Brewer/Brewers
    Sarah 133
    Thomas 133, 206, 234, 277, 366, 684, 818, 1008, 1121
Briars
    Thomas 288
Brickfeild
    Mary 152
Bride
    Abigall 165
Bridge
    Abigall 99
Bridgeman
    Nathaniel 684
    Thomas 267
Bridges
    Elizabeth 4
    Francis 37
    Hercules 37
Bridley
    Robert 151
Brierie
    Robert 236
Bright
    Thomas 654

Brighton
    George 255
Brigma
    John 240
Brigsby
    John 294
Brisco
    Phillip 259
Brissin
    William 709
Bristow
    Hugh 1388
Brittain/Brittaine/Britton
    Edward 386
    Fran: 433
    Franc: 408
    Francis 684
    Richard 1080
Britten
    Lyonell 85
Broadie
    Alexander 1649
Brocke
    William 313
Brockett
    June 81
Brodhurst
    Anne 15
    Elizabeth 15
    Susan 15
    Walter 15, 46
Brodie
    Alexander 781, 1657
Brookes/Brooks
    Ann 714
    Elizabeth 626
    Francis 1288
    John 409, 480, 650
    Nicholas 368
Broughton
    Hugh 722, 1225
    Mary 236

Broughton (cont.)
    Mathew 236
    Thomas 140, 174, 188, 236
Brown/Browne
    Alexander 1008, 1287
    Anne 265
    Benjamin 637
    David 1306
    Elinor 1152
    Elizabeth 1629, 1645, 1654
    Francis 1765, 1774
    George 531, 650
    James 1854, 1868
    Manly 1306, 1795, 1810
    Martin 306
    Mary 1245
    Peter 256
    Phillip 203
    Richard 433
    Thomas 313, 1622
    William 265, 690, 1121, 1287
Brunaugh
    Patrick 562
Brunton
    Thomas 42
Bryan
    Ann 389
    John 389, 586, 1058, 1130, 1153
    Margaret 1311
    Richard 625, 633
    Samuel 1912
    Turloah 1221
Bryant
    Daniel 1026
    John 684, 1003
    Kath: 800
    Martha 1804, 1805
    Richard 611
    Robert 1835
    Uriah 1310

Bryery/Bryerley/Byerley
   Christopher 732, 734
   Robert 637, 746, 787
Buckler
   William 313
Buckley
   Thomas 539
   William 287
Budd
   Eleanor 91
   Richard 89, 159
Bulbrooke
   Nicholas 155
Bullery
   Mary 1278, 1287
Bullock/Bullocke
   Samuel 245
   William 66
Bunbury
   Thomas 239
Bundy
   Elizabeth 294
   Robert 734
Burchard
   John 222
Burdman
   John 709
Burge
   John 1203, 1370
Burgess
   Henry 1486
   Richard 712, 981
Burinstone
   Frances 245
Burk/Burke
   Elizabeth 1042
   Henry 734
   James 1548, 1554, 1795
   John 992
   Richard 1024, 1150
   Thomas 1323
   William 1043

Burn/Burne/Byrn
   Andrew 1638
   Elizabeth 1564
   John 1417
   Margaret 1773, 1775
   Marguritt 1496
   Patrick 1240, 1393, 1410
   Samuel 1912, 1915, 1916
Burnell
   Thomas 553
Burnett
   Thomas 1287
Burrage
   John 869
Burrell
   Robert 207
Burrett
   Richard 117
Burton
   Ann 97
Bush
   Elizabeth 1657
   John 1016
Bushell
   Benjamin 307
   Richard 548
   Roseland 403
Bushrod
   John 1068, 1070
   Thomas 986
Bussell
   Elin^o 1949
   Martha 1916
Bustle
   Phillip 1447
Butcher
   John 313
   Margaret 313
Butler/Buttler
   Edward 1323
   Joane 117
   John 245, 271, 722, 731, 1289

Butler/Buttler (cont.)
    Mary 1431
    Thomas 409, 684
Buxton
    John 313
Buzzell
    Richard 602
Byram
    Abraham 295

Cadamy
    Kathein 703
Caddel
    Margaret 1664, 1669
Cale
    Susan 12
Calfew
    Richard 1018
    William 1018
Callan/Callon
    Hugh 786, 1291, 1301, 1307
    Margaret 1291
Calphen/Calphew
    Richard 1000, 1230
Calvert
    William 654
Calvin
    Charles 941
    William 1376
Cambell
    Agnis 1515
    John 1288, 1490, 1515
Cammell
    Alexander 650, 722, 1225
    John 40, 112, 976, 986
    Samuel 650, 980, 1142
Camnwell
    James 915
Campbell
    Charles 1832
    Collin 1794

Camplaime
    Thomas 775
Canady/Cannady/Canniday
    Jerimiah 392, 396
    John 1149
    Matthew 1178
Cane
    Charles 297
Cannon
    Ellinor 1323
    Hugh 722, 1225
Carey
    John 465
Carmickell
    George 74
Carnaby
    John 1939
Carne
    James 1152
Carnegie
    John 1261
Carpenter
    Francis 148
    Hannah 106
    Phillip 164
    Simon 135
    William 713, 1358
Carre
    Martha 545
Carrell/Carrol
    Matthew 1074
    Patrick 1781
Carter
    David 212
    Honora 576, 577, 585
    John 69, 964
    Robert 1567, 1582, 1591, 1610
    Samuel 1828
Cartwright
    Peter 519
Carty
    Dennis 717

Carty (cont.)
   Jone 1093
   Katherine 1287, 1407
   Sarah 1323
   Sylvester 1467
Cary
   John 509, 1668
   Nicholas 1734, 1776, 1778
Caseley
   Mary 1287
Casey
   Richard 1040
Casleton
   Robert 23
Cassedy
   Catherine 1674, 1698
Casterson
   Thomas 253
Castide
   Cormeck 650
Caterton
   Thomas 1521
Caulker
   Thomas 296
Cavenah/Cavernaugh/Covenah
   David 1039
   Mary 734
   Thomas 989
   William 993
Cavener
   Mary 1573
Cavernott
   Thomas 1310
Cawsey
   John 294
Cess
   John 28
Chaberline
   Rebecca 364
Chadborne
   William 403

Chadock
   Alice 1416
Chafee
   John 642
Chalan
   Katherine 1291
Chalkley
   Henry 660
Challienge
   Margery 21
   Samuel 21
Chambers
   John 1149
   Mary 793
Champion
   John 578, 658, 768, 783, 1550
Chandler/Chanler
   Thomas 782
   William 781
Chapman
   Jeffrey 241
   Margaret 970, 1000, 1018, 1153
   Mary 1286
   Richard 313
   William 103
   Winter 58, 59, 60
Charigon
   John 795
Charles
   Henry 759, 795
Chauhady
   John 1978
Chaukerett
   Stephen 822, 1261
Cheksheir
   Clement 519
Chettwood/Chetwood
   Matthew 1310
   Matthias 1005
Chewes
   Robert 784

Chewes (cont.)
    Thomas 784
Chilcock
    Robert 775
Childermas/Childermasse
    Thomas 774, 847
Chilton
    Edward 702
    John 1664, 1669, 1670, 1671
Chin
    John 581
    Michael 824
Chipman
    John 1189
Chisholme
    John 1090
Chisnell
    John 1229
Chivanne
    Peter 559
Christian
    Margaret 1528, 1535
Christie
    George 1931
Christmas
    Franc: 335, 345
Christopher
    Anne 1608
    John 1785
    Robert 1808, 1837
    William 1578, 1583, 1590, 1599
Church
    John 737, 739
Churchell
    Hannah 314
Churchill
    Samuel 1267
Churrell
    Samuell 303
Clark/Clarke
    Andrew 1846

Clark/Clarke (cont.)
    Benjamin 1958
    Christopher 734
    Dennis 201, 338, 339, 344, 349, 350, 383
    Edward 836, 940
    Frances 922, 938
    George 434, 484
    Hannah 1608
    Henry 228
    Honour 1629, 1645, 1654
    James 1836
    John 188, 201, 216
    Robert 117, 1633, 1634
    William 33, 1823
Clauckerett—see Chaukerett
Claughlin
    John 1223
Claughton
    James 303, 437, 538, 697, 743, 791
    John 1267, 1406, 1527
    Nicholas 220
Claveron
    Elizabeth 951
Clay
    Francis 28, 227, 426
    William 722, 1225
Clayton
    Nicholas 347
    Richard 1524
Cleaves
    Ann 734
Clement
    Elizabeth 263
    William 263, 268
Clenes
    John 40
Clerke
    Daniel 1261
    Rebecca 1261
    Robert 1252

Cleron
    John 1314
Clever
    Marge: 52
Clew
    John 79
Clifford/Cliford
    Henry 272
    Robert 985, 1192
Clinton
    Caron 1533
Clissen
    Phillip 1060
Cloberry
    John 11
Cloud
    Mary 406
Clurshene [?]
    Mary 69
Clutton
    Jesse 1899
Cocke
    Faith 271
    Thomas J. 724
    William 43
Cockerill/Cockrell/Cockrill
    Andrew 101
    John 346, 473, 579, 960, 961,
        985, 1007, 1048, 1124,
        1183, 1209, 1219, 1222,
        1239
    Thomas 12
Cockron
    Andrew 167
Codd
    Col. 623, 644, 704
    Patrick 1152
    St. Leger 645, 653, 704
    St. Roger 644

Coffee
    Robert 596
Cofflin/Coflin
    John 1223, 1294
Colclough
    Elizabeth 233
    George 8, 32, 42, 92, 108, 145,
        156, 171, 172, 180, 222,
        233, 334
    Ursula 108
Cole/Coles
    Anna 137
    Constance 222
    Edward 229, 431, 519, 566,
        567, 591, 650, 748, 1076,
        1425, 1466
    Fran: 378
    Grace 517
    John 814, 888, 986, 1350
    Richard 65, 68, 72, 136, 137,
        203, 215, 221, 230, 256,
        264, 291, 320, 329, 332,
        337, 343
    Robert 1589
    Thomas 1597
Coleman
    Benjamin 1261
    John 884, 1704
    Judith 1944
    Mary 1657, 1659
    Richard 117
Colgin
    Charles 1288
Collaghan
    Katherine 1307
Colledge
    Hezekiah 160
Collen
    Arthur 1779
Collins
    Diane 1253
    Ealse/Else 1695, 1707

Collins (cont.)
    Edward 1368, 1470
    Piles 311
Colloughcor
    Anne 664
Colsorom
    James 43
Colston
    Travis 1691, 1840
Colton
    Thomas 222, 233
Colvin
    Peter 313
Colyar
    William 427
Coman
    Elizabeth 136
    Richard 136
Comey
    Deborah 110
Commons
    Henry 1294
Compton
    Henry 684
Conalan
    Mary 1294
Conalley/Connale/Connaly/Connell/
Conoley/Conoly
    Daniel 1426, 1429, 1431, 1435
    Idmund 1156
    John 1311, 1319
    Margaret 117
    Patrick 1544, 1558
Conaway/Conoway/Conway
    Anne 1500
    Christopher 1406
    Dennis 650, 1100, 1178, 1180,
        1212, 1322, 1500
    George 1639, 1798
    Henry 549
    John 728, 1295, 1300
Cone
    John 3
Conepesarke
    Thomas 33
Conger
    William 77
Coningto
    John 180
Conlin
    Loughly 1120
Conner/Connor
    Ann 1580
    Charles 1263, 1269
    Derby 1093
    Ginneter 1540
    Hono^r 1417
    James 1133, 1648
    John 1127, 1294, 1339, 1564
    Laurance 1442
    Patrick 1194
    Turtlur 1313
Cook/Cooke
    Anne 961
    Isaac 404
    John 1256
    Phoebe 960, 961, 985, 1209
    Richard 775
Cooper
    George 892, 1098, 1341
    Gilbert 97
    John 355
    Mary 734
    Sampson 152
    Samuel 152
    Thomas 340
Coot/Coote
    Elinor 1225
    George 229
Cope
    John 559, 734
Copedge/Coppage/Coppedge
    John 1451, 1453, 1671

Copedge/Coppage/Coppedge (cont.)
   Thomas 736
   William 380, 412, 958, 1140, 1181
Cople
   Henry 958
Copperweight
   Christopher 1220
Corbell
   Angell 55
   Anne 55
   Clement 55
   Gabriel 55
   John 55, 650, 696, 807
Corbett
   Thomas 294
Corbin/Corbyn
   Henry 194
   John 838
Corend
   Edward 4
Corey
   Cornelius Omney 117
Corker
   William 309, 351
Corne
   Thomas 1323
Cornish
   William 285, 449, 589, 664, 684, 1082, 1379
Corvell
   Mathew 303
Cossens
   John 340, 597
Cotesford
   Richard 33
Cotoone
   Anthony 801
Cotroy
   Stephen 520
Cottell
   Martha 13

Cottrell/Cotrell
   Andrew 1624, 1635, 1641, 1642, 1646, 1650
   John 1280, 1334, 1356, 1605
Countall
   Geo: 441
Coupter
   William 134
Court
   Mary 889
Courtnall/Courtnell
   George 429, 441, 749
Courtney
   James 880
Cousedy
   Elizabeth 1291
Coutanceau/Coutanshaw/ Coutansheau/Cotanchew/ Cuttanceau
   John 273, 288, 290, 468, 507, 560, 561, 583, 623, 659, 802, 824, 889, 891, 1233
   Kath: 856
   Mr. 790, 803
   Oliver 441, 480
   Peter 821, 1000, 1018, 1022, 1057, 1058, 1153, 1154, 1203, 1278, 1279, 1370, 1441
   Thomas 524
   William 650
Cowland
   Margaret 1261
Cowt
   John 703
Cox
   Faith 270, 589
   James 801
   Joanne 557
   Mathew 595, 1550
   Richard 678, 704, 724, 728, 749, 785

Cox (cont.)
    Vincent 65, 66, 68, 72, 258, 1284, 1799
Coxen
    Samuel 155
Coynia
    Zachariah 852
Crabb/Crabe
    William 306, 629
Crabtree
    Daniel 385
Crage
    John 650
Crain—see Crane/Crean
Cralle/Crawley
    Andrew 1617
    John 821, 1064, 1152, 1198, 1205, 1231, 1232, 1274, 1333, 1340, 1353, 1421, 1426, 1429, 1431, 1435, 1470, 1678, 1679
    Kenner 1970
    Miles 734
    Thomas 1572, 1718
Crane/Crean
    James 1272, 1834, 1871, 1879, 1930
    Jane 882
    John 1970
    Margaret 771, 809, 849
    William 1619
Craven
    Charles 1557, 1559, 1738
    John 631
Cravener
    William 13
Crawford
    John 1881
Creedwell
    George 313
Criss
    Patrick 97

Cristom
    David 48
Croass
    James 784
Croft
    William 427
Crooke
    Jonathen 1905
Crosse
    James 760
    Thomas 482, 784
Crosthead
    William 559
Crostit
    John 1294
Crouch
    Mary 1261
    Robert 1261
    Symon 810
Crow
    Polonia 355
Crowde
    Siscily 151
Crowder
    Fearnot 1517, 1561
    Thomas 1561
Crowell
    Edward 4
    Jane 27
Crue
    Wiliam 513
Crump
    John 1493, 1495
Crumption
    John 828
Cubb
    Jane 294
Cullealley
    Andrew 1474
Cundiffe
    Richard 859

Cunningham
  James 1460
  Thomas 1461, 1523, 1600
Cunny
  George 108
  John 764
Cursom/Cursome
  Francis 684, 690
Curtis
  George 1650
  John 1043, 1044
  Pitts 1011
  Thomas 734
Cushion
  James 1095
  Richard 1150
Cussion
  Richard 1062
Cutler
  Thomas 624

Dabbs
  John 675, 775
Daley/Daly
  Ann 1696, 1697, 1721, 1737
  Mary 1354
Dalton
  John 988
Dameron
  Bartholomew 185, 702, 922, 1979
  Christopher 1646
  Dorothy 414
  George 667
  Joseph 1979
  Josias 1525
  Laurence 149, 185
  Lazarus 1443
  Thomas 1114, 1646
Damisson
  Peter 754

Dance
  Noah 111
Dane
  Daniel 1152
Danes
  William 86
Danheny
  Darby 1259
  Derby 1238, 1265
Daniell
  Thomas 363
Dankington
  Thomas 71
Dansy
  Dav: 371
Danvers
  Kate 427
Dare
  Jerremy 1476
Darrows
  Ann 25
  Thomas 25
Das
  Thomas 313
Dashield
  James 166
Daughity
  Cornelious 1831
  James 1700
Daulson
  John 734
Davenport
  Mr. 684
Davey
  Walter 703
David
  William 200
Davies
  Evan 240
  John 684, 776, 777, 779
  Thomas 688

Davis
- Daniel 1361, 1383, 1434, 1437
- David 288, 833
- Edward 1823, 1834
- Evan 323
- Henry 427, 1052
- Hester 823
- Isabell 1311
- James 650, 1899
- John 222, 334, 590, 632, 772, 823, 1294, 1317
- Kath: 442, 443, 444
- Mathew 823
- Robert 1411, 1491, 1531, 1533, 1560
- Thomas 752, 929
- William 593, 659

Dawes
- Thomas 198

Dawson
- Christopher 1276, 1277, 1298
- Elizabeth 1961
- Henry 1295, 1300
- John 322, 1160
- Katherine 1295, 1300
- Thomas 314
- William 939

Day
- Elinor 380
- George 58, 146
- John 928, 1480
- Mary 888, 928, 1153, 1253
- Prissilla 738
- Rachel 928, 1423, 1425
- Samuel 1450, 1546
- Stephen 1925
- Winifred 1425, 1428

Deadman
- William 351

Deawy
- William 1051

Decoly
- Emanuel 1807

deContee
- Michael 589

deJerzey
- Peter 734

Delany
- Anthony 1311

Dell
- Richard 378

deMarratt/Demerratt
- Luke 712, 981

Dennis
- Henry 284
- John 698
- Mary 1328, 1362

Denny
- Richard 1540

Dermott
- Charles 1103
- Mary 1258
- Owen 1258

Deuvenant
- Thomas 650

Devill [?]
- Richard 30

Devin
- Patrick 1226

Dew
- John 269, 453
- Thomas 734

Dey
- Roger 1323

Diamond
- Peter 762

Dickenson
- Thomas 1316

Dicks
- Mary 56

Dickson
- Joseph 305
- William 1884

Dingwell
  Roderick 1092
Dinney
  Edward 653
Discoll
  Fran: 714
Dixon
  Priscilla 908, 926
  Thomas 245
Doak
  James 986
Dobles
  Richard 1208
Dobson
  Elizabeth 1151
Dodd
  John 723
Dodson
  Anne 1294
  George 1294
  Lamberth 1667
Doggett
  Elizabeth 722
Doland
  Mary 1702
Dolien
  Dermot 117
Dolin/Dollin
  Jane 401, 402, 433
Dollins
  Richard 1160
Dollor
  Daniel 13
Domundy
  Michael 734
Donaway/Donoway
  John 423, 1753
Donelson
  Andrew 1456
Donne
  Walter 42

Dooly
  Dan: A 800
Dorgan
  Joan 1484
  Thaddeus 1484
Dorll
  Morgan 378
Dorothy
  Anne Grin 1325
Dorrell
  Thomas 143
Doughty
  Mary 153
Dowgell
  Richard 1230
Dowlane
  William 398
Dowle
  John 1086
Dowly
  John 1294
Downes
  Mary 734
Downing/Downinge
  Charles 1712
  Elizabeth 1148, 1177, 1350
  John 715, 795, 817, 831, 895,
    906, 986, 997, 1646
  Mr. 650
  Mrs. 1193, 1199, 1253
  Thomas 1052, 1386
  William 197, 419, 568, 590,
    641, 650, 652, 710, 726
Dowry
  Mary 136, 137
Doyle
  Denis 951
  Owen 1323
Drake
  Phillip 545, 630
Draper
  John 68, 115

Draper (cont.)
    Joseph 399
    Josias 399
    Thomas 399
Drew
    John 1429
Drinkwater
    William 433
Driscoll
    Florence 565
Driver
    John 1278
Dryer
    Alice 477
Ducket
    John 232
Dudley
    Richard 1638
Dugard
    William 1202
Duggin
    John 210
    William 1699
Duggle
    Richard 1070
Duglas
    Alexander 654
    John 62
Duke
    Jane 1182
    John 1261
    Thomas 703
Dulany
    Cavan 1745
Dun—see Dunn, Dunne
Dunabaugh
    Thomas 1218
Dunaby
    Humphrey 1315
Dunaway
    Hannah 1944
Dunawon
    William 1163
Dunbarr
    George 1108, 1304
Duncombe
    Anne 462
Dunelay
    James 758
Dunken/Dunkin
    George 1109, 1347
Dunkington
    Thomas 36
Dunn/Dunne
    Carroll 1231, 1331
    Francis 915
    Robert 734
    Samuel 52
    Thomas 1930
    Walter 167, 281, 650, 670, 845, 988
Dunnawan
    William 1230
Dunnidge
    John 98
Durant
    George 182
Durn
    William 1699
Durrough
    Allen 1110
Dyches/Dykes
    Billy 1970
    Henry 1970
    Nelly 1970
    Robert 1970
    Thomas 1970
Dyelsoild
    William 1310
Dyer
    Edward 142
    Hannah 175
    John 826

Dyer (cont.)
　Thomas 318
Dymsey
　Philip 639
Dynon
　Attkins 1478

Earle
　John 71, 263
　Mary 147, 215, 221, 230, 245, 263, 264
Earne
　Patrick 1311
East
　John 964
　William 703
Ecles
　James 1250
Ecock
　Thomas 800
Edee
　Andrew 901
Edenborough
　Andrew 39
Edmonds
　George 189
Ednee/Edney
　James 775, 836, 920, 964
Edwards
　Alexander 1616, 1627
　Gaar 1253
　Mary 28, 136
　Nicholas 1146, 1147
　Prudence 302
　William 1196, 1360
Efford
　Thomas 153
Ellery
　Nicholas 240
Ellet/Elliot
　George 610, 621
　Mathew 314

Ellet/Elliot (cont.)
　Robert 13
Ellis
　Edward 737
　Samuel 1312
Elliston/Ellistone
　George 390, 392
　Gerv: 834
　Jervas 502
Elmor
　John 1802
Elom
　John 1810
Elson
　John 948
Elton
　Joseph 1232
Elvis
　Joseph 440
Emberson
　John 1281
Emerson
　John 1046
Emery
　Kath: 439
Enderby
　Ann 1411
England
　An: 368
English
　Alice 332, 337
　George 150, 184, 186
　Walter 188
Enjer
　Mary 1908, 1909, 1910
Ensworth
　John 27
Eranire
　Sarah M 1922
Ereale
　Humphrey 650

Ervyn
  John 1309
Erwyn
  John 1085
Eskridge
  George 1249, 1287, 1294, 1310, 1311, 1313, 1314, 1315, 1316, 1317, 1318, 1323, 1363, 1426, 1429, 1431, 1509
  Samuel 1833
  William 1739
Essex
  Elizabeth 9, 92, 108
  Isaac 1131
  John 9, 225
Ester
  Isaac 1131
Esto
  Joshua 96
Eustace
  John 765, 840, 850, 910, 949, 1275
Evans
  Alice 1152, 1205
  Elizabeth 464, 478
  Henry 28
  John 404, 911, 917, 1975
  Mary 181, 668, 722, 1225
  Morditay 368
  Morgan 498
  Phillip 307, 738
  Thomas 1661
  William 380
Everard
  Thomas 1138
Evere
  William 1875
Everson
  Cornelius 634
Every
  George 684

Eves
  George 1611
  Graves 1477
  Thomas 1455
Ewes
  John 684
Eyes/Eyse
  Dennis 650, 870, 902, 912, 980, 1194
  Martha 1194
  Mary 1188

Fagan
  John 858
Fairweather
  Patrick 1117
Fallen
  William 1427, 1602, 1604
Fammer
  Elizabeth 588
Fanning
  Edward 437
Farlowe
  William 171, 180
Farmer
  Anne 821, 828, 879, 881
  William 881
Farned
  James 1606, 1628
Farnefold
  John 579, 611, 625, 650, 752, 929, 976
Farrel/Farrell
  Mary 997, 1193, 1199
  Patrick 1103
Fasshoe
  Richard 403
Faugheigh
  Laurence 1076
Fauntleroy
  Anne 1826
  Bushrod 1816

Faushew
  Peter 1736
Feagins
  Laurence 1870
Fegan
  John 1149
Feild—see Field
Feilding—see Fielding
Fell
  Owen 209
Fenner
  Richard 149
Fergus
  Chatty 1516
Ferguson
  Katherine 1526
Ferdldor/Ferlder
  Elizabeth 1275
  William 1275
Fern/Ferne
  Robert 1150
  Thomas 854
  Winnefred 1555
Ferrel/Ferrell
  Mary 1177, 1253
Fetherstone
  Thomas 215
Field/Fields/Feild
  Abraham 136
  Ann 52, 1814, 1815
  Edward 758
Fielding
  Ambrose 433, 549, 578, 580, 614, 656, 676, 1637
  Edward 976
  Joseph 528, 557, 576, 577, 585
  Richard 401, 408
  William 1073
Figro/Figrow
  John 1485, 1577
Finch
  William 1748

Finlay
  William 1666
Fipps—see also Phipps
  John 886, 896, 971
Fish
  John 313
Fisher
  Andrew 1314
  Henry 839
  Joseph 314, 356
  Mary 314
  Patrick 1289
  Phillip 1822, 1842, 1863, 1866, 1877, 1908, 1910
Fitzgarold/Fitzgarrald/Fitzgerrald/Fitzgerrele
  Bridgett 1339
  John 1541
  Mary 1524, 1581, 1928
  Thomas 1152, 1274
  William 936
Fitzherbert
  William 313
Fitzmorris
  James 1888, 1891
  Margaret 1294
Fitzpatrick
  John 1830
Flamagon
  Dam: 738
Flannagon/Flannegan
  Andrew 1230, 1490
Flannerell
  Loughy 1089
Flatman/Flattman
  Thomas 696, 1313
Fleet
  John 33
Fleming
  Alexander 313
  James 1289

Fletcher
    Katherine 1301, 1307
    Marie 1307
    William 1244
Fling
    Katherine 1311
Flint—see Flynt
Flood
    Hester 1684
    William 1954
Florence
    William 142
Flowers
    John 910
    Mary 408
    William 308, 684
Floyd
    John 1313
    Mary 210
    Thomas 1660, 1665, 1734
Fluker
    David 1709
Flynt
    Ellin 1486
    Jane 1538
    John 1603
    Mary 1306
    Mr. 398
    Peter 923, 939, 944
    Richard 102, 120, 144, 158,
        212, 373, 436, 756, 772,
        776, 777, 779, 1097, 1171
    Thomas 821, 925, 1306
Foalks
    William 1962
Fogershie
    John 1157
Fogg
    Israel 1806
Folio
    Edward 1153

Follierd
    Mary 1282
Fontaine
    James 1688, 1711
Footman
    Elizabeth 1719
    Mrs. 1717
Forbus
    Andrew 1827
    William 615
Ford
    Abraham 707
    John 720
Forjoy
    Alexander 1217
Forne
    Laurence 1323
Forrester
    Edward 1010
    John 1978
Forroughbush/Fourobush
    William 366
Forsett
    Hugh 111
Forsithe
    Thomas 313
Fortice
    Richard 313
Foster
    John 815
    Seth 31, 134
    Thomas 33
Fouch
    Hugh 168, 481
    Robert 506
Foulks
    Thomas 903
Fouls
    Elizabeth 1606
Foushee
    John 1511, 1690, 1816, 1839,
        1864

Fowke
   Elizabeth 313
Fowle
   William 399
Fowler
   Catherine 1562
Fowne
   Thomas 698
Fox
   David 684
   Laurence 933, 1151
Foxcroft
   Isaac 163
Francefois
   Elizabeth 152
Frances/Francis
   Evan 840
   Joan 714
   Jone 784
   Sarah 303
Franklin/Frankling
   Hannah 1184
   Henry 986, 1080, 1113
   Hon^r 1287
   John 376
   Mary 1294
Franks
   Robert 1870
Frazier
   Alexander 1860
Freake
   William 3
Freebone
   Rachel 969
Freeman/Freman
   John 351, 811
   Timothy 313
French
   George 1568
Friend
   Thomas 824

Frier
   Edward 3
Frigham
   Anne 404
Frissell
   John 64
Frost
   John 801
Fry
   Ann 1520
Fryer
   Anne 1208, 1251, 1293
Fulbrook
   Lau: 734
Fulfort
   Humphrey 104
Fuller
   Jane 228
Fullerton
   Hugh 1342
   James 1364
Furbush
   William 133
Furnett
   James 1538
Furney
   Robert 1081
Furshaw
   Michael 591
Fuse
   Thomas 556
Fynney
   Isabell 495

Gadd
   Ann 1331
Gadis
   Joseph 1350
Gage
   John 294
Gallaway—see Galloway

Gallee
 Peter 519
Gallion
 Henry 1012, 1230
Galloway
 Andrew 1011
 David 1848
Gamber
 Domanew 151
Gambles
 John 627
Gammonds
 Phil: 800
Gamwell
 Laurence 1316
Gardee
 Ad: 519
 Pet: 519
Gardener/Gardner
 James 1476
 John 300, 355
 Nathaniel 232
 Olliver 1227
 Thomas 1472
 William 1585
Garland
 William 1823, 1834
Garlington
 Christopher 219, 242, 243, 276, 335, 341, 352, 377, 415, 488, 508, 573, 621, 657, 663, 684, 702, 719, 780, 865, 883, 957, 1142, 1143, 1464
 Joane 686
 Mr. 331, 610
Garner
 Binsent 1089
 Nathaniel 421
 Oliver 1419
 Parish 1361
 Vincent 1403

Garner (cont.)
 William 1859
Garnesey
 James 235
Garnet/Garnett
 Sarah 276, 377
 William 542
Garrard
 Margrett 944, 956
Gaskall
 Sarah 1790
Gaskins/Gaskoyne
 Henry 774, 847
 Isaac 1118
 John 1696, 1697
 Joseph 986
 Josias 562, 826, 1028, 1273
 Thomas 224, 417, 519, 646, 941, 1038
Gately
 Joseph 986
Gatinge
 Edward 306
Gay
 William 1208
Gayer
 Tomson 1323
Gayland
 James 121
Gaylard
 James 234
Gaylord
 Mr. 546
Gayner
 Hugh 355
Gearding
 James 737
Geate
 Anne 583
Gemball
 Alexander 436

Genn
    James 1294, 1421
    Mary 1294, 1421
    Thomas 1294, 1505, 1702
Gent
    Edith 1215
George
    Sarah 265
Gerrard
    Elizabeth 855, 888
    Margret 939
    Thomas 73
Gibbins/Gibbons
    John 81
    Maurice 1548
    Morris 1787
Gible
    Richard 83
Gibney
    Patrick 1883, 1890, 1892
Gibson
    James 1779
    John 207, 270
Gilbert
    Elizabeth 313
    Francis 220, 256
    Henry 265
    James 723
Gilbird
    Rose 84
Gill
    Anne 784
    Ellis 1653, 1773
    John 1261, 1657
    Michael 1071, 1261
    Thomas 682, 1059, 1303, 1328, 1420, 1436, 1438, 1439, 1471, 1539, 1542, 1543, 1588, 1618, 1620, 1621, 1643
    William 1536, 1537
Gillen
    Julian 519
Gilpin
    Jane 33
Gilsen
    Elizabeth 81
Ginn
    James 1223
Giouer
    Edward 85
    Thomas 85
Givyer
    Anne 269
Glage
    William 1225
Glan
    John 1483
Glover
    Daniel 74
Glyn
    Samuel 302
Goare
    Jane 551
Goche/Gouche
    Jefferey 123, 139
    Samuel 139, 615, 618
Godding
    Mary 775
Godfrey
    John 69
Godnell
    William 1261
Goff
    William 453
Goffes
    Robert 596
Goggin
    Thomas 1099
Gold
    Richard 328
Golo
    Richard 289

Golothon
  Thomas 1768
Gomayar
  Sarah 100
Gonogar
  Edmund 117
Goodale
  Thomas 35
Goodwyn
  Edward 158
Goozy
  John 417
Gorden/Gordon
  Robert 1106, 1111
Gore
  Jane 411
Goreham
  John 655
  Miles 655
Goreing
  Devorax 13
Gosling
  Samuel 115
Gosse
  James 698
Grace
  Sarah 271
Grady
  Patrick 1406
  William 1235
Graham
  Jane 640
  John 403, 1422
Grandee
  Rachell 519
  William 249
Grant
  Alexander 709
Grantham
  Jeremiah 1323
Graves
  Anne 584
Gray
  Francis 2
  James 301
  Miles 135
Green
  Elizabeth 695, 775
  George 1497
  James 378
  Robert 232
  Thomas 13
  Tymothy 684
Greene
  Robert 313
Greenham
  Timothy 1484
Greening
  Anthony 684
Greensteed
  William 154
Greenstone
  Anne 805
  John 805
Greenstreet
  John 1729
  Peter 1729
Greenwater
  Robert 1788
Greenwood
  William 1841, 1847, 1890, 1892, 1893, 1901, 1903, 1906, 1907, 1933
Gregg
  Andrew 872
Gregory
  Anne 180
  James 1815
  Mary 140
Gregson
  Thomas 313
Gresall
  James 10

Grey
    Andrew 1030
    Grace 1179, 1180, 1181
    Susannah 1875
Gridly
    Mary 887, 1261
    Patience 1261
Griffin
    Alexander 388
    David 79
    James 1611
    Mary 761
    Michaell 637
    Samuel 1020, 1229
    Thomas 1644
    William 388, 462
Griffith
    David 652
    John 313, 665
    Thomas 26
Griggs
    Mary 44
Grigson
    Richard 79
Grimes/Grymes
    Edward 13, 941
    Ellenor 245
Grimstead/Grinstead/Grinsted
    John 806
    Thomas 806, 1587
    William 806, 1480, 1499, 1556, 1562
Grin
    Anne 1325
Groome
    Humphrey 1124
Groves
    George 1294
    Jane 781
Gubboy
    Henry 697

Guesse
    George 468
Guin
    Elizabeth 1693
Gunery
    Mr. 1171
Gunfrie
    William 404
Gurrill
    John 982
Guttery/Guttree/Guttrie/Guttry
    James 650, 1792, 1796, 1797, 1855
Guy
    James 118, 330
    John 907
Gwyn
    Anne 274
Gyles
    John 705

Hack
    Capt. 1717
    Peter 722, 843, 1158, 1170, 1444
Hader
    John 1704
Hadwell
    James 481
Haies
    John 14
Haines
    Thomas 711
Hale
    Nicholas 463
Haley
    Cornelius 568
Halfpenny
    Winnefred 1552
Hall
    Daniell 710
    Elizabeth 355

Hall (cont.)
   Hannah 1687
   John 549, 1267
   Stephen 1489
   Susan 710
   Thomas 1267, 1687, 1977
   William 1088
Haluran
   John 117
Hambrooke
   Henry 1323
Hames
   William 1768
Hamlin
   John 519
Hamman
   Thomas 126
Hammond
   Charles 1552
   Thomas 124, 125
Hammondtree
   Jonathan 1716
Hamon
   Perry 26
Hanch
   John 3
Hancock
   George 670
   John 549
   William 313, 623
Hand [?]
   John 222
   Margaret 1323
Handling
   Manns 991
Hanies
   John 502
Hanks
   John 1845
Hanwell
   William 135

Hapney
   Henry 151
Harbert
   William 453
Harbott
   Joan 920
Harcum
   Abigail 782
   Hannah 1459
   James 782
   Lidia 782
   Mary 782
   Mellicent 1963
   Thomas 1646
   William 782, 1056, 1090, 1166, 1253, 1257, 1343, 1345
Hardey
   John 1862
Hardich
   William 41
Harding/Harden/Hardinge
   Edward 378
   Elizabeth 265
   Henry 1183, 1280, 1316
   John 762
   Mark 1452, 1453
   Sarah 1904
   Thomas 1684
   William 925, 1191, 1812, 1816, 1922
Harkfoote
   Richard 265
Harley
   Margarett 715
   Thomas 981
Harling
   Falix 150
Harman
   Elizabeth 348
Harmestone
   Joseph 713

Harmwood
   William 1452, 1453
Harnesse
   Thomas 138
Harpin
   Henry 215
Harrar
   John 650
Harrington
   Joseph 228
Harriot
   James 1764, 1770
Harris
   Anthony 110
   Charles 970
   George 487
   Hugh 303, 333, 671
   James 1706
   Jer: 795
   John 351, 709, 713, 720, 755, 787, 789, 875, 941, 983, 986, 1173, 1228
   Josias 689
   Lewis 422
   Mathew 535
   Thomas 480
   Timothy 1639, 1654
Harrison
   Andrew 1036
   Jane 1310
   John 684
   Joshua 1582
   Josias 614
   Mary 1845
   Richard 212, 1619
   Robert 770, 1313, 1589, 1613
   Thomas 404
Harrold
   Gilbert 1773, 1775
   James 1286
   John 1256

Harrox
   Mary 836
Harry/Hary
   Charles 471
   Joseph 135
Harsell
   William 1288
Hart
   More 738
   William 1444
Hartgrove
   John 1695, 1707
Hartington
   William 191, 335, 341, 342
Hartland
   William 572, 603, 609, 707, 708
Hartley/Hartly
   Henry 393
   John 1368, 1369
   Richard 314
Hartnell
   Samuel 797
Harvey
   Allen 1547, 1553
   Edward 550, 833
   Onesiphorus 1325
   Richard 294, 517
Harward
   George 623
Harwood
   Anne 426
   Mary 244
   Thomas 368
Harword
   Richard 181
Haskins
   John 208
Hassell
   Rachel 685
   William 685

Hatch
  Amy 1470
Hathaway
  Francis 1275
Haughton
  John 734
Haverfeild
  Thomas 714
Haverson
  Simon 1302
Havliss
  Samuel 840
Hawes
  John 352
Hawkens—see Hawkins
Hawkins
  Ambrose 1143
  Elizabeth 229, 714
  Ellinor 1382
  Hannah 256
  James 662
  Richard 21
  Thomas 38, 47, 77
Hawley
  James 101
  Mrs. 89
  Thomas 712
Hay
  Ann 731
  Daniel 731
Hayden
  Ezekil 1858
Hayes
  James 1631
  John 909, 1048, 1153, 1315
  Mary 4
  Richard 725
  Roger 731
  Thomas 749, 1030
Hayly
  Esther 273
  Hesther 288, 290

Haynie
  Anthony 1014, 1141
  Elinor 1592
  George 1813, 1880
  Jacob 1874
  John 62, 122, 272, 618, 636,
     712, 860, 888, 932, 965,
     967, 981, 1012, 1297, 1308,
     1351, 1352, 1391, 1392,
     1521, 1531
  Ormsby 1646, 1751
  Richard 851, 924, 965, 966,
     971, 973, 982, 996, 1222,
     1289
  Sarah 1813
  Spencer 1956
  Stephen 1697
Hayter
  Charity 281
Hayward
  Nicholas 45
  Thomas 313
Hazelip/Hazellipp
  Thomas 105, 124
Hazelwood
  Elizabeth 1277
Hazlas
  William 844
Hea
  Thomas 734
Head
  William 177
Headnett
  Joseph 239
Heales
  John 478
Heard
  Walter 684
Hearne
  Samuel 1238
Hearty
  Mary Merry 1137

Heath
    Samuel 1481, 1565, 1623
    Thomas 1541
    William 1432
Helbert
    Ellinor 1323
Helps
    Sampson 895
Hemmerson
    John 313
Hemoney
    Jonathan 1320
Henderson
    William 1287
Hendy
    John 734
Henley/Henly
    Anne 348
    Edward 348
    Joane 348
    Sarah 348
    Susanna 348
    William 1287
Henry
    John 1013
Herbert
    Mary 682
Hester
    Isaac 1326
Hewes/Hews
    Ellinor 1262
    James 1210, 1366
    Mary 135
    Nicholas 644
    Richard 1331, 1364, 1380
    Robert 673
Heylen
    John 233
Hickley
    James 484
Hickman
    Nathaniel 27

Hicks
    John 713
    Katherine 1621
    Thomas 1620, 1621, 1624, 1635, 1642, 1650
Hickson
    James 730
    Samuel 680
    William 179
Higgenson
    Humfrey 90
Higgham
    An: 455
Higgins
    Hannah 1925
    Nora 1323
    Thomas 804
    Timothy 1230, 1297
    William 1499
Highland
    John 108
Hill
    Enoch 1101
    Evan 1230
    Francis 281, 516
    George 496, 834, 1306
    James 176, 379, 539, 1042
    John 129, 709, 1211, 1376, 1388
    Mary 180
    Richard 650, 684
    Sarah 254, 607
    William 313, 987, 1635
Hilley
    John 834
Hillier
    John 4
Hills
    Enoch 1336
Hilman
    Thomas 833

Hinderson
  Herman 1473
Hinds
  John 875
Hine
  John 190
Hitchcock/Hitchcocke
  John 171, 180, 222
  Robert 99
Hobart
  James 128
Hoberry
  Lydia 175
Hobs
  Thomas 493
Hobson
  Clark, Mrs. 1731, 1759
  Elizabeth 794, 1261
  Judith 1829
  Thomas 428, 441, 466, 469,
    519, 616, 650, 668, 722,
    735, 955, 1208, 1225, 1251,
    1293, 1574
  William 432, 1502, 1713
Hocar
  Peter 519, 532
  Phil: 532
Hogan
  Edward 1486
  Daniel 1063, 1123, 1242
  Teage 698
Hogherd
  Anthony 1261
Holbrooke
  Thomas 492, 493
Holden
  Richard 36, 71, 81
Holder
  Edmund 249
  John 727

Holland
  Daniel 201, 213, 216, 269, 279,
    283, 292, 338, 339, 344,
    349, 350, 383, 453, 489,
    504, 516, 526, 574
  John 199, 220
  Joyce 568, 570, 574
  Symon 1034, 1288
  William 232
Holley
  Thomas 734
Hollis
  Boaz 224, 417
Hollowes
  Jon 3
  Restitute 3
Holmes/Holms
  Elizabeth 249
  Ralph 1152
  Samuel 1924
Holt/Hoult
  Ann 1460, 1515, 1542, 1569,
    1570, 1571, 1577, 1718
  Joseph 722, 866, 954, 1182,
    1197, 1210, 1225, 1319,
    1332, 1366, 1367, 1395,
    1418
  William 1267
Homes/Hoomes
  Robert 1465
  Samuel 1887
Hood
  William 172, 180
Hooper
  Francis 150
  Mary 306
  Robert 242
Hope
  Samuel 1798
  Thomas 981, 1592
Hopkins
  Grace 464

Hopkins (cont.)
    Hannah 1691
    Henry 935, 1419, 1430
    Mr. 362
    Thomas 103, 121, 365, 478
Hopper
    Thomas 727
Horedome/Horedum
    Elizabeth 906
Horsely/Horsley
    Joseph 179, 246
    Ralph 101
    Rose 179
Hortman [?]
    Mary 722
Horton
    Dorcas 316
    Elizabeth 351
    Thomas 579
Houghton
    James 430
    John 324, 391, 954
Hould
    Ann 1485
House
    Robert 734
Houson—see Howson
Howard
    Dor: 795
    Elizabeth 419
    Henry 706
    Lucy 543, 544, 571, 572, 709
    Thomas 723
    Walker 180
Howe/How
    Jonathan 110
    Joyce 481
    Robert 173, 277
    Thomas 549
Howell
    Alice 244
    Elisha 758

Howell (cont.)
    Francis 106
    George 1609
    John 106, 225, 406
    Peter 944, 956
Howett
    John 116
Howkar
    Adam 754
Howland
    Daniell 1150
Howson
    John 1107, 1287, 1347
    Leonard 314, 429, 432, 454,
        458, 519, 559, 589, 595,
        781, 1277
    Robert 314
    Sarah 1193, 1201, 1204
    Thomas 519
    William 313, 1066, 1158
Howton
    John 1051
Hoyle
    Charles 142
Hubbard
    Steven 358
Hubbart
    William 177
Hubbert
    Stephen 679
Hubburke
    Joseph 245
Hudnall
    Alice 855, 888
    Ezekiel 1885
    John 552, 1593
    Joseph 1055, 1382, 1644, 1689,
        1967
    Richard 1135, 1270, 1304,
        1455, 1646, 1708, 1757,
        1774, 1807, 1858, 1883
    William 1653

Hudson
  Fielding 1850
  Henry 802
  Isaac 362, 464, 478, 709
  John 1640
  Lewis 1748
  Robert 144
  Sarah 1469
Hues
  Katherine 1620
  Mary 1509
  Richard 1425
  Robert 1606
Hughes/Hughs
  Catherine 1440
  David 734
  James 1332, 1418
  John 371
  Mary 153, 1479, 1496
  Prudence 322
  Robert 996, 1289
  Thomas 213, 216, 972
Hughlett
  Ephraim 1555
  John 271, 606, 661, 710, 737, 739, 888, 905, 919, 970, 1307
  Kath: 833
  Mary 1401
  Robert 666
  Thomas 972, 1001, 1016, 1067, 1339, 1458
  William 1662, 1693
Hughson
  Charles 314
  Willliam 204
Hull
  John 52, 314, 804
  Richard 490, 496, 502, 662, 770, 793, 808, 816, 827, 834, 848, 872, 900, 1854, 1856, 1895

Hull (cont.)
  Samuel 404
Humphryes/Humphry
  Joseph 550, 1041, 1250, 1477
  Peter 180, 222
  William 1, 1179, 1181
Humpston
  Edward 238
Hunch
  John 3
Hunt
  Benjamin 404
  Charles 828
  Elizabeth 1145, 1235
  Ellinor 1311
  Jannet 1688
  Martha 1159, 1246
  Nathaniel 44
Hunter
  Jannet 1688
  Martha 1159, 1246
Hurst
  John 1676, 1677
  Michael 959, 962
  Thomas 150, 1676, 1677
Huske
  Thomas 1111
Hust
  Dor: 784
Hutchins
  Sarah 1152, 1380
Hutchinson
  Nicholas 990, 1287
  Thomas 313
Hutson
  Henry 1153
Hutt
  Daniel 217
Hutton
  George 1799
  John 714
  Mary 138

Hynton
    Mary 1929

Ignatious
    Hawett 734
Iland [?]
    John 222
    Richard 141
Ingram
    Abraham 1563, 1579
    Ann 1561
    Charles 1133, 1561
    George 1911, 1913, 1914
    John 1019, 1032, 1115, 1167, 1381, 1394, 1443, 1455, 1517, 1532
    Katherine 675
    Thomas 675
Iron/Irons
    John 1563, 1579, 1705
Itrey
    John 714
Izard
    Robert 351
Izeberris
    Thomas 433

Jackman
    Matthew 1021, 1150
Jackson
    Anthony 1206, 1230
    Barbara 980
    George 1311, 1312
    James 427
    John 1569
    Mary 1390, 1398
    Richard 192, 228
    Robert 1412
    Sarah 130
    Susana 954
    Thomas 770, 1313
Jacob/Jacobs
    Edward 441, 480
    Susanna 689
Jacobus
    Angell 647
Jallion/Jallon/Jallons
    William 322, 559, 579
James
    Daniel 1422
    Elizabeth 102, 174, 208
    Gilbert 404
    James 843, 1225, 1602
    Joane 404
    John 547, 784, 1323, 1782, 1785
    Joshua 1670, 1680, 1681, 1780
    Mary 658, 783, 798, 799
    Mr. 648
    Thomas 899, 1225
    William 245, 505, 1323, 1478, 1692
Jameson
    John 1318
Jamme
    Jamme 1602
Janeway
    William 1294
Jasper
    Joan/Joane 611, 625
Jeanes
    Thomas 722
Jeckell/Jencken
    John 325
Jeffard
    Amos 754
Jeffery
    Elizabeth 32
Jeffs
    William 467
Jenings/Jennings
    David 433
    Edward 211, 226, 255

Jenkins/Jinkins
    John 549
    Lewis 429
    Mary 1632
    Morris 703
    Walter 473, 836, 995
Jenn
    James 734
Jepson
    Joseph 149
Jermin
    Elizabeth 480
Jernew
    Nicholas 118, 195
Jersey
    James 714
Jess/Jesse
    Hester 696, 716
Jewell
    Samuel 249, 553
    Thurlow 721
Joanes
    Mabell 136
John
    Mary Little 904
    Thomas Pretty 1064
Johnson
    Benjamin 317, 370, 784
    Elizabeth 121, 151
    Evan 427
    Henry 41
    James 302, 612, 713, 750, 869, 937, 950, 1779
    John 684, 986, 1594
    Richard 303
Johnstone
    William 1876, 1878
Jollyns
    William 251
Jones
    Ann 1683, 1687
    Barbary 1751

Jones (cont.)
    Catherine 1214, 1572, 1574, 1647
    Christian 1657
    Daniel 13
    Edmund 941
    Edw: 555
    Elizabeth 416, 606, 661, 1294, 1690, 1827
    Evan 313, 1261
    Franc: 55, 797
    George 1827
    James 260, 829, 1294
    Joane 149
    John 881, 1102, 1262, 1809
    Katherine 1285, 1346
    Mabell 135
    Margaret 93
    Martha 669, 673, 674, 683
    Mary 285, 303, 407
    Maurice 1263, 1264, 1268, 1282, 1302, 1424, 1474, 1508
    Mr. 349, 536, 649
    Owen 977, 1230
    Rice 404
    Richard 348
    Robert 4, 232, 241, 262, 287, 298, 495, 524, 1263, 1264, 1268, 1269, 1473, 1520, 1761, 1819, 1825
    Rod 245
    Solomon 1261
    Thomas 26, 44, 355, 784, 864, 909, 931, 1634
    William 28, 83, 408, 433, 711, 713, 953, 955, 971, 984, 1031, 1075, 1110, 1276, 1294, 1539
Jordan/Jorden
    Catherine 1722
    Henry 212

Jordan/Jorden (cont.)
   John 1475, 1611
Journew
   Richard 310
Joyce/Joyse
   Abraham 95, 214, 684
   John 842
Joyne
   John 1294
Jrock [or Jcock]
   Thomas 671
Jude
   Franc: 519
Juice
   John 44
Jurnew
   Nicholas 97, 232
Jury
   Joane 229

Kaine
   Roger 1636
Kalleron
   Will 1323
Kanne
   Judith 800
Kauselaugh
   Arthur 1311
Kay—see also Key
   Thomas 90
Keale
   Thomas 1323
Keaton
   Katherine 1311
Keble
   Cary 1566, 1580, 1601
Kedby
   Thomas 113
Keen/Keene/Keine
   Elizabeth 832
   John 821, 1411, 1528, 1535
   Mary 51

Keen/Keene/Keine (cont.)
   Newton 1909
   Susan 51
   Thomas 51
   William 51, 687, 718, 821,
     990, 1069, 1074, 1261,
     1503
Kehow/Kehows
   Thomas 1236, 1260, 1266
Keire
   Laurence 650
Keley/Kelley/Kelly
   Bridgett 1487
   Edward 378, 1311
   Hugh 1626
   Jacob 1037
   James 1120
   John 29, 568
   Mary 1716, 1725
   Matthew 1287
   Michaell 1323
   Spencer 1979
   Teaugne 1323
   Toby 1323
Kendall
   Margaret 33
Kendy/Kennady/Kenneday/
Kennedy
   Anthony 1241
   Gawen 313
   John 1501
   Michaell 1234
   Richard 1468
   Silvester 1657
   Teige 1079
Kennall
   Edmund 1323
Kenner
   Capt. 1423
   David 1323
   Elizabeth 1026, 1062, 1217
   Francis 1337, 1390, 1398, 1949

Kenner (cont.)
   Hannah 1949
   Howson 1646
   Matthew 1635
   Rhodon 894
   Richard 482, 506, 527, 556, 684, 713, 745, 760, 772, 776, 779, 784, 790, 868, 901, 1714, 1717, 1719, 1737, 1743
   Rodham 939, 952, 1021, 1023, 1024, 1025, 1063, 1081, 1122, 1123, 1150, 1220, 1230, 1242, 1333, 1337, 1390, 1414, 1947
   Winder 1646, 1652, 1726, 1727, 1936
Kenney
   Henry 1507
Kensloe/Kenslow
   Arthur 1337, 1414
Kent
   John 80, 217, 318, 363
   Phebe 356
   William 241
Kerby
   Manderford 136
Kerr
   George 1765, 1927
Kesterson
   George 1362
Kett
   William 262
Kettle
   Susanna 824
Kevie
   Arthur 388
Key
   Elizabeth 154
   Richard 1065
   Thomas 90

Keyne
   William 601, 604, 619, 637, 642, 778, 796
Kickly
   Thomas 313
Kidd
   William 1116
Killpatrick
   Edward 650
King/Kinge
   Adam 232
   Christopher 1001, 1261
   Francis 33
   George 536
   Hannah 211
   John 1595, 1669, 1670, 1748
   Mary 2
   Richard 30, 211
   Robert 211
   Symon 245
   Tagor 1323
Kinneck
   William 240
Kireton [?]
   Augustine 749
Kirk
   Christopher 766
Kirkin
   Richard 1244
Kitchingham
   Elizabeth 605
   Jane 202
   John 202
Kitchinman
   Joane 138
Kneton
   Daniell 734
Knight
   Edward 313
   Frances 1615
   George 812
   John 135, 1154, 1886, 1965

Knight (cont.)
    Peter 11, 250, 337, 343, 369,
        375, 459, 531, 617, 673,
        720
    Thomas 915, 951, 1230
    William 11
Knot/Knott
    John 3
    William 1530

Lackey
    Thomazine 901
Lacy
    John 1512
Ladner
    Anne 969
Lafeazsone [?]
    Marke 679
LaFolly
    Peter 519
Laland
    John 933, 1294
Lambert
    Henry 510, 511
    William 750, 1294
Lamkin
    Lewis 1723
    Mary 374
    Thomas 374
Lamprey
    Richard 729
Lancaster
    Anthony 317
    Nicholas 1465
Land
    Robert 56
Landrum
    William 151
Landy
    Philip 1843
Lane
    Daniel 520

Lane (cont.)
    Elizabeth 406
    Henry 8
    Hester 520
    James 1083
    John 193, 317
    Mary 1311
    Rho: 519
    Roger 193
    Thomas 406, 457, 485, 520,
        582, 1294
Langley
    Elizabeth 218
Langsdon
    Catherine 1261
    John 1083
    William 1261
Lansdale
    Richard 1660
Lansdell
    Richard 127
La-pero
    Peter 294
Lappage
    Edward 562
Larkin
    Edmund 21
Lashly
    Henry 245
Latemore/Lattemore/Lattimore
    Clement 733, 801, 910, 915
    David 1791
    Richard 1129, 1162, 1400,
        1405
Lattes
    James 1709
Laughee
    John 1311
Laurence—see Lawrence
Lawrence
    Charles 1652
    Edward 1295, 1300

Lawrence (cont.)
   John 1248, 1249, 1255, 1258, 1290
   Margaret 1230, 1253
   Mary 1191
   Spencer 1714, 1717, 1719, 1743
   Thomas 690
   William 702
Lawson
   Anne 388
   Elizabeth 388
   John 388
   Margrett 881, 1204, 1208
   Robert 153
   Rowland 432, 565
Lax
   George 1841
Lay
   Margaret 1187
Laycock
   Judith 1527
Layton
   Judith 52
Leasure/Leazure
   Bartholomew 1216, 1321, 1514
   George 1267
LeBay
   Jane 406
Lebreton
   Edward 532
Lee
   Anne 775
   Charles 877, 1185, 1467
   Francis 530, 598, 623, 626
   Hancock 601, 627, 690, 1027, 1105, 1327
   Hannah 96, 152
   Henry 1719
   Hugh 14, 29, 76, 80, 96, 147, 152
   John 312, 313, 371, 775

Lee (cont.)
   Judith 1728
   Ned 1840
   Richard 187, 198, 204, 206, 232, 234, 287, 299, 300, 312, 378, 530, 1728, 1828, 1832, 1861
   Robert 387
Leech
   Anne 143
   William 427
Lee=how
   Nich: 519
Lefevur
   Abraham 109
   Jacob 109
   Jane 109
   Margaret 109
   Peter 109
Lehoot
   Pet: 554
Lehugh
   Nicholas 1109, 1347
Leitch
   Robert 1623
Leland
   John 1966
Leloge
   Daniel 822
Lenard
   Matthew 1954
Lenham
   John 987
Lennam
   Mary 222, 360
Lentail
   Richard 313
Lenton
   Anthony 169
Leonard
   Darby 1115
   Mathew 1917, 1918, 1923

Letherborough
  James 1151
Lewis
  Ann 138
  Edward 1447
  Frances 733
  Hugh 313
  James 1534, 1698, 1758
  John 205, 271, 294, 549, 731, 753, 1037, 1132, 1442, 1631, 1640, 1649, 1656, 1658, 1668, 1673
  Lewis, ap Lewis 1606
  Marg: 419
  Richard 893
  William 1944, 1946
  Willoughly 1844
Levistone
  Mary 458
Ley
  Nicholas 873
Leyton
  Thomas 371
Licett
  Thomas 274
Liggate
  Jane 850
Lightfoot
  Capt. 587
Ligthgow
  Rachiel 1879
Lilley
  Mary 1313
Linch
  Daniell 722, 1225
Lindsay/Lindsey
  David 96, 164, 206, 317, 366, 367, 370, 604
  John 1152
  Susanna 317

Line
  Katherine 1292, 1296, 1357, 1396, 1397
Linsey
  John 1377
  William 38, 57
Liscombe/Liscome
  Nicholas 1216, 1224, 1233
Lishman
  Thomas 934
Little
  Christopher 197
Lloyd
  Alexander 709
  Thomas 234
Lock
  Thomas 1174, 1230, 1399, 1433
Lockiere
  Charles 1198
  John 1508
Lockman
  John 1094
Lockwitt
  Dorothy 237
Logge
  Robert 372
Lolly
  Thomas 1323
Lonard
  Matthew 1954
Long
  Josias 596
Longerwood
  John 1872
Longham
  Katherine 822
Loope
  James 1323
Lord
  Dorothy 1791, 1853
  Robert 275

Lord (cont.)
    Thomas 311
Loth
    Daniell a [O?] 650
Lovell
    Elizabeth 176, 278, 731
Low
    Abraham 1622
    John 1135
    Robert 667
Lowry
    Michael 1446
Loynes
    John 1007
Loyney
    Dennis 1101
Lucas
    Robert 311
Lucson
    James 379
Lugg/Lugge
    Edward 235, 419
Luin
    Catherine 1213
Luitsey
    Cornelius 1084
Lukas
    John 696
Lunceford/Lunsford
    Edwin 1932
    John 1522
Luttrell
    John 1371
Luxmeeze
    Anne 404
Lyle
    George 734
Lylliesse
    Thomas 568
Lyn
    James 650

Lynch
    Ann 1586
    Daniel 495
Lyndsay
    Helena 410
Lynne
    Elizabeth 1336
Lynton
    Anthony 107, 333, 522, 830, 948, 963
    Jane 885, 963
    John 1156
Lyon/Lyons
    Catherine 1448, 1449
    John 1199, 1315
Lyster
    Edm: 451, 568

Macalle
    John 719
    William 719
Macarmick
    Francis 1059
Macbare
    Henry 1261
Macbeth
    James 1225
MacCarty/Macarty—see also MacKarty
    Denis 916, 1022, 1153
    Neal 983
    William 1002
MacDaniell/MacDannell
    Jaine 1290
    John 892, 912, 916
    Mary 892, 912
MacDennis
    Daniel 947
MacDonnell
    Catho: 993
MacDovett
    Thomas 976

Macey
  Elizabeth 1303
Macgaaine
  Owen 764
Macgee
  Charles 976
  James 979
Macgill
  John 981
Macguire
  Cornelius 566
Machall
  John 663
  William 663
Machelvey
  John 663
MacKarty
  Daniel 650
Mackastelly
  Mary 741
Mackaules
  John 684
  William 684
Mackdanell
  John 1225
  Mary 1225
  Teige 980
MacKenell
  Ellin^r 681
Mackey
  Andrew 834
  Robert 1285
Macklangha/Macklanhan/
Macklaugha
  James 667
  Jane 650
  John 651
  Mannas 650
Mackleteer
  William 974
Mackmartin
  Phillip 667

Mackmenis
  Mary 1510
Mack Million
  Mack 1551
Mackmouris
  Patrick 1500
Mackness
  ___ [?] 692
Macksassion
  Jane 1230
Macktire
  William 650
Maclinshaw
  Edmond 672
Maclowghla
  James 834
MacMaghagn
  Joan 893
Macmend
  James 986
Maconald
  Hugh 840
Macquart
  John 1230
Macquire
  Hannah 738
Macy
  Henry 1249, 1255
  William 1249, 1255
Maddin
  Ellinor 1332, 1366, 1367
Maddison
  John 1228
Maddocke/Maddocks/Maddox
  Rice 12, 137, 182
Madix
  Katherine 34
Madrin
  Bennett 420
Mady
  Edmond 1375

Maghley
　Jone 784
MaGill
　John 902
Mag=Jone
　Dax: [?] 650
Magrah
　Phillip 1430
Magray
　Edmund 698
Magregor
　James 168, 221
Magrill
　John 860
Magrillus
　John 594
Maguire
　John 1512
Mahan/Mahane/Mahen
　Samuel 698, 722, 723, 836,
　　917, 940, 1106, 1179, 1189,
　　1195, 1226, 1252, 1273
Mahoany
　Dennis 1112
Mahon/Mahony
　Mary 1494, 1519
Mahughen
　John 1172
Maise
　Christopher 1397
Maith
　John 1820
Maize
　Thomas 914, 946
Makatter
　Roro 95
Makeile
　Jane 246
MaKenny
　Neale 938
Makewaler
　Alexander 74

Malaughny
　Thomas 1272
Maley
　Owen 738
Mallard
　Elizabeth 294
Mallett
　John 113
Mallin
　Patrick 700
Malloy
　Patrick 1919, 1921
Malony
　Hanah 1566
Malpus
　John 865
Maly
　Patrick 734
Man
　Hugh 363
　Samuel 208
Manby
　Anthony 769
Mankins
　Mary 678
Mansfield
　David 103
Marall
　John 69
March
　Arthur 433
Mardam
　Isaac 1261
Markell
　John 1590, 1599
Markin
　John 1578
Marquiss
　John 1583
Marriner
　John 1131

Marrow
    Luke 714
    Richard 770
Marsh
    George 646, 1014
Marshall/Marshal/Martial
    John 43, 702
    Patrick 1735, 1742, 1745, 1747
Marson
    John 1466
Martin/Martyn
    Elias 1647
    James 387, 679
    Mary 1612
    Miles 522
    Patrick 1542
    William 684
Mase
    John 1261
Mash
    Arthur 549
    Thomas 228
Masker
    Sarah 1926
Mason
    Edward 1784
    Henry 240
    Isabell 980
    John 1067, 1261
    Solomon 696, 1313
    William 1305
Mast
    John 1152
Mathews/Matthewes/Matthew
    Capt. 777
    Charles 229
    George 641
    James 241, 636
    Phillip 635

Mathews/Matthewes/Matthew (cont.)
    Thomas 280, 324, 370, 391, 479, 486, 500, 559, 637, 691, 696, 700, 732, 734, 747, 761, 767, 789, 810, 1421, 1547, 1553
    William 448
Mattux
    Joyce 210
Maudley
    Edmond 816, 834, 848, 872, 900
    Elizabeth 848
    Jane 834
Maughan
    Sarah 1904
Maunder/Maunders
    Henry 313
    Wilkes 161, 266, 311
    Willes 286
Maunding
    Peter 418
Maurice
    Laurence 106
Maursh
    Robert 775
Maver
    Alexander 1793
Maxfield
    John 986
Maxwell
    Mary 825, 1182
    Peter 801, 1182
May
    David 41
    Margaret 717, 980
    Mary 905
Mayes
    Henry 380, 400, 412, 602, 643
    John 1803
    Katherine 517

Mayfield
   Abigall 712
Mayse
   Henry 548, 600, 713, 753, 774
McAdam
   Joseph 1903
McCallaugh
   James 1539
McCarty
   Daniel 1243, 1348, 1349
   Dennis 1917, 1918
McColley/McColly
   Elizabeth 1420, 1471, 1504
McComer
   Owen 117
McConner
   Patrick 1188
McCoy
   Duncan 1557
McDaniel
   Eleanor 1811, 1824
McDarmil
   Hugh 1323
McDermot
   Elizabeth 1522
McDonnell
   James 1248
Mceldemar
   John 1605
McEranire
   Sarah 1922
McFarly
   Dennis 1234
McFarther
   Hugh 117
McGennis
   Michael 714
   Nicholas 1810
   Patrick 714
McGibony
   George 1678

McGoo
   James 1752, 1766
McGraugh
   Phillip 1456
McGregory
   Robert 1151
McGuier
   John 1672
McLana
   John 1323
McMillion
   John 1780
Mealy/ Mealey [?]
   Alice 1323
   Mary 69
Meath
   John 986
Mecham
   Thomas 52
Medcalfe/Metcalf/Metcalfe
   Henry 815
   Jane 201
   Sarah 791
   Thomas 180
   William 1274, 1410, 1412, 1446, 1454, 1457, 1551
Medford
   George 1186
Medly
   John 1314
   Margaret 1314
Meeds
   Nicholas 1815, 1816
Meers
   Edward 101
Meese
   Henry 217
Megeneys
   Margaret 1586
Meighon
   Thomas 1077

Meiny
    Thomas 470
Mekinall
    William 1261
Melony
    Hanah 1582, 1586
Melton
    Michael 561
Menhelvey
    John 663
Merredith
    Alice 127
Merret
    Ellis 519
Merrica
    Nicholas 1077
Merrick
    Joane 742
Merrifield
    Thomas 697
Merrill
    Robert 1009
Merriman
    William 541
Merriockes
    Matthew 313
Merritt
    Ellias 722
    Margery 1314
Meryman
    Francis 90
Meuach [?]
    Anne 1323
Mew
    Charles 299
Michaell
    Robert 703
Michell
    Elizabeth 369
Michem
    John 34

Micklehome
    Thurlo 762
Middleton
    Anne 302
    June [or Jone] 303
    Robert 1823
Milbanks
    Mary 1315
Miles
    Elizabeth 368
    Mrs. 684
Millar
    Thomas 1294
Millbank
    Mary 1219
Miller
    Henry 1765
    Hugh 1195
    John 255
    Matthew 1436
    Michael 395
    Miles 394
    Samuel 775
    Thomas 231, 1331
Milligin
    Jamose 983
Million
    Elizabeth 1468
    Mary 445
Mills
    Isabell 1821
    Jane 1943, 1951, 1955, 1956,
        1957, 1959, 1967
    John 319
    Samuel 153
Milner
    Elizabeth 13
Milo
    Susanna 164
Mitchell
    Matthew 1463
    Robert 244, 986, 1230

Mitchell (cont.)
    Samuel 1323
Mockridge
    John 1489
Moglame [or Moglaime]
    Phillip 1084
Mohanny
    Dennis 1261
Moises
    John 140
Molin
    William 406
Monday
    George 307
Money
    Thomas 144
Mongomery
    Hugh 437
Mono
    Silvester 1649
Monohery
    Cornelius 568
Monsloe
    Val: 406
Montgomerie
    James 838
Mony
    Hugh 716
Moo
    Charles 875
Moody
    John 746
Moon
    Sarah 1843
    William 1613
Moor/Moore/More
    Ann 67
    Daniell 2
    Edward 112
    Fran: 527
    James 986
    John 775, 1047, 1916

Moor/Moore/More (cont.)
    Margaret 836
    Mary 1637
    Robert 623, 626
    Roger 1455
    Sarah 735, 1916
    Thomas 153, 359, 1294
    Walter 52, 735
    William 1134
Moorehead
    Charles 1036, 1174, 1313
Mophats
    John 313
Mopsons
    Joanna 424, 425
Morclay
    Ellin[r] 807
Mordey
    John 709
Morgan
    ___ 406
    Andrew 1823
    Anne 240, 323
    Char: 549
    Charles 729
    Evan 1294
    Marg: 409
    Mary 1710, 1754, 1755
    Rowland 258
    Thomas 684, 1544, 1558
Morning
    Peter 754
Morrer
    Roger 256
Morrey
    James 69
Morris
    Abraham 733
    Anthony 582, 763
    Edward 406
    Elizabeth 367
    Ellinor 1323

Morris (cont.)
   Fenley 836
   Margaret 1323
   Mary 795
   Mrs. 89
   Nicholas 34, 323
   Rose 647
   Thomas 734
   William 313
Mortemore
   James 803, 1153
Morthland
   David 1788
Morton
   Isaac 360
   Tomothy 729
Moseley/Mosely
   John 575
   William 180, 222
Moses
   John 684
Mosley
   John 478
Mosse
   Anne 279, 283, 453
   John 747
Mote
   Katherine 215
Motley
   Elizabeth 374
   John 155, 265, 297, 374, 474, 477, 513, 519, 650
Mott
   Jane 1903
   Marbe 623
Mottourne
   John 357
Mottrom
   Capt. 660, 1243

Mottrom (cont.)
   John 58, 60, 78, 82, 85, 105, 124, 125, 126, 153, 154, 359, 376, 405, 608, 677, 851
   Spencer 1010, 1237, 1245
Moughley
   More 784
Mould
   Humphrey 586
Mouseley
   William 236
Moy
   William 365
Muckfannon
   Jane 1015
Muckle
   Turner 650
Muckleteer
   William 966, 968
Mullagan
   James 941
Mulley
   Margarett 1323
Mulloy
   Charles 1038
Mulroany
   James 1100
Mundy
   Robert 734
   William 101
Munroe/Munrow
   Andrew 39
   Elizabeth 709
Murdock
   George 1477
   John 1477
Murfew/Murfey/Murfy
   Joane 1146
   Nicholas 1190
   Margaret 1287
   Patrick 1502

Murfien
　Joan 920
Murphew
　Daniell 1197
　Elizabeth 1457
　Jane 1230
　Terence 1432
Murphy
　Arthur 1701
　James 1701
　Thomas 1723
Murrall
　Ann 96
Murray
　David 1261
　Gilbert 1493, 1495
Murrow
　Charles 1667
　Edmond 1004
　John 1019
　Margrett 877
Murry/Murrey
　Mac 770
Musgraine
　Elizabeth 714
Muttone
　John 635
Myars/Myers
　Jane 1482
　Peter 1813

Namey
　John 117
Naper/Napor/Napper
　James 650, 681, 741
Nash
　Ann 69
　Anthony 697
　Thomas 231, 232
　William 69, 70, 114
Naster
　Patrick 1323

Neale/Neall
　Abner 1650
　Christopher 441, 671, 713, 714, 898, 999, 1015, 1086, 1157, 1163, 1216, 1337, 1390, 1398
　Daniel 235, 441, 497, 515, 565, 651, 664, 696, 730, 734, 797, 839, 855, 874, 1053, 1152
　Edward 1576, 1584, 1596
　Elizabeth 117
　James 1294
　Mary 1712
　Matthew 734
　Richard 1359
　Rodham 1821, 1831, 1835
　Shapleigh 1779
Nellagon
　William 1147, 1261
Nelmes/Nelms
　Charles 979, 1060, 1175, 1304, 1510, 1648
　John 1357
　Richard 127, 210, 232, 421, 455
　Samuel 1699, 1783, 1786
　William 1046, 1281, 1372, 1463, 1512
Nelson
　Alexander 1492, 1545
　Jeremiah 537
Nephew
　Phi: 491
Newberry
　William 48
Newgent
　Dominick 1282
　Mable 1197
Newland
　Emuell 780

Newman
    Frances 255, 291, 373
    Hannah 193
    Robert 79
    Thomas 527, 784
Newton
    George 1323
    Rachell 1310
Nibbs
    Daniell 211
Nicholas
    Morris 34
    Nich: 441
    Richard 45
Nicholls/Nichols
    Margaret 177
    Samuel 55
    Sarah 1588
    William 34, 454, 781
Nicholson
    Ann 1876, 1878
    George 1876, 1878
Nicken
    Hannah 1787
    James 1911, 1913, 1914
Nickless/Nicklesse
    John 922, 938, 941, 1116
Nightingale
    John 10
Ninars
    Ellen 117
Nipper
    James 836, 1104, 1144, 1159, 1246
    Jane 1144
Nishoe
    Shellis 117
Nolt
    Ed: 378
Nonck [or Noncb]
    William 117
Nono
    Silvester 1694
Nooth
    Matthew 37
Norgate
    Phill: 858
Norman
    Elizabeth 28
Nornitt
    Richard 1055
Norris
    Martha 964
North
    Charles 43
Northage
    Thomas 876
Northen
    Solomon 1443
Norton
    Thomas 1308
    Timothy 729
Noskes
    George 179
Nott
    George 1977
Nowell
    Mary 1261
Nowland
    Charles 807, 918, 923
Nuball
    John 873
Nudman
    Joseph 229
Nugent
    Mary 1270
Nulley
    Tigh 117
Nutt
    Joseph 1558
    Phillip 108
    Richard 590, 840, 933, 978, 1164, 1399, 1433

Nutt (cont.)
   William 160, 267, 372, 986

Oakeley
   Samuel 709
Oakland
   Samuel 531
Oasling
   John 679
Obedine
   Gillpatrick 117
Ockland
   Samuel 617
Odohothy/O Dorhoty
   Neale 650
   William 1104, 1144
Odyer
   Gabriel 19
   Mary 19
Ofile
   Susanna 734
Ogan/Ogen
   John 870, 980
Oger
   Morris 4
O Hart
   Gilbert 717
Ohatonne
   Beren 117
Oheart
   Gillicrest 980
Ohunum
   Donough 117
Okeane
   Laurence 822
Okoner
   Phaelin 117
Oldage
   Robert 317
Oldfield
   Susanna 696

Oldham/Oldum
   James 215, 1364
   John 1792, 1796, 1797, 1851
   Mary 1663
   Moses 1686, 1715, 1733, 1744, 1746
   Richard 1094, 1342, 1573, 1614, 1630
Oldis
   Elizabeth 855
Oldwill
   Thomas 717
Olever
   Thomas 28
Olford
   Anne 378
Olive/Ollive
   William 1247, 1257, 1261
Oliver/Olliver
   Ignatius 637, 993, 1006, 1152, 1240
   John 313, 1968, 1972
   Joseph 986
   Mary 717, 1311
Ologney
   Daniell 1261
Omer
   Joseph 452
O Muddy
   Daniell 650
Omullion
   Patrick 857
O Neal/Oneale
   Arthur 650, 834
   Laurence 1261
   Owen 1031
   Roger 676
Onellican
   William 1330
Opalbow
   Francis 1404

Opie/Opy/Opye
  John 1492, 1545
  Linsez/Lindsey 1649, 1739
  Thomas 575, 705, 769, 941
Ordery
  John 1607
Orley/Orlye
  Rebecca 129
  Susan 129
  Thomas 54, 112, 129, 231
Ormond
  Richard 310
Ormsby
  Elinor 982
Ortland
  Samuel 459
Osborn/Osbourne/Osburn
  Anne 1886
  Edward 684
  John 784
  Mary 1877
  William 108
Oslen
  Rawleigh 784
Osmotherly
  William 313
Otter
  Richard 480
Ounesse
  John 133
Outris
  Mary 33
Oventon
  Sarah 219
Owen/Owens
  Anne 417, 1739
  Jane 89
  John 1152
  Mary 1867
  Nicholas 501, 623, 744, 871
  Thomas 734
  Walter 124, 125, 126, 145

Owen/Owens (cont.)
  William 168, 1845
Owsman
  Edward 734
Oxedine
  John 1577
Oxender
  John 1593
Oxx
  Thomas 1294

Packman
  Mary 734
Paine
  Ann 709
  John 927
  Mrs. 684
Palfry
  Jonathan 1294
Pallas
  Mary 250
Palmer
  Elizabeth 493
  Joseph 841, 847, 899, 1103, 1108
  Judith 151
  Katherine 1370
  Mary 1653, 1760
Palonert
  Susana 1323
Pannell
  Sarah 1222
Paragater
  Sarah 275
Parker
  Azariam 523
  Charles 52
  Henry 726
  Jonathan 128, 199, 347
  Rose 256, 320, 329, 648
  Sabrina 518, 521, 529, 534, 648

Parker (cont.)
   Sibbry 563, 564
   William 734, 1153
Parkes
   John 432
   Jonathan 220
   Thomas 79, 175, 223
Parnell
   John 601
Parr
   Thomas 1618
Parris
   John 841
   Joseph 1230
Parrot
   John 1962
Parry
   Ann 64
   Henry 1208
   Thomas 1675
Parsons
   John 438, 654, 1261
   Mary 1288
Passenger
   Martha 215, 256
Pasternell
   John 1171
Patten
   Elizabeth 1323
   William 1107
Paule
   Charles 354, 368
Paw
   Anthony 734
Payne
   Edward 778
   Grace 1882
   John 1902
   Margaret 508, 573
Payton
   Philip 455
   Susannah 1202

Peachey
   Leroy 1964
Peacock
   Andrew 1098, 1225
   Stephen 1850
Peak/Peake
   Mary 1534, 1595
   Thomas 314
Pearce
   Henry 846
   Thomas 69, 70
Pearle
   Anne 1066
Pearson
   Sar: 381
Peart
   Francis 1672
Peckett
   Edward 313
Pedds
   William 1140
Pedley
   George 714
Pedy
   Jeffery 148
Peecox
   Richard 37
Peer
   Samuel 1669, 1670
Peirce/Peirse
   Edward 557
   James 55
   Mary 455
   Richard 206, 305
   Thomas 508
Peirre
   Richard 312
Peirson
   Sarah 222
Pelke
   John 447

Pemberton
　Richard 634, 755, 904, 908, 926, 992, 1200, 1236, 1238, 1259, 1260, 1265, 1266
Pendexter
　George 684
Pendrill
　John 957
　Sarah 957
Penell
　Robert 453
Peney
　John 177
Penning
　Anne 158
Penny
　Christian 1482
Penry
　Thomas 732
Pere-deboutre
　Cesar 314
Perrey
　Jane 76
Perriman
　William 404
Perry
　Elizabeth 236
　Mary 380, 400
Perym [or Peryn]
　Thomas 447
Pes[?]cy
　Marga: 40
Peters
　Edward 994, 1151
　Margrett 942
Peterson
　Edward 181
　Hugh 1132
　Jane 981
　Matthew 734
Petit
　Anne 128

Pett
　John 499
Pettegrea/Pettegrew
　Andrew 358, 424, 425, 536, 539, 605, 679
Pettitt
　John 68
Petts
　William 480
Pettus
　William 187
Petty
　Christopher 1294
　Thomas 1045
Peyton
　Philip 421, 542
Phealand
　Robert 1692
Phelps
　Thomas 308
Philips/Phillips
　Anne 17
　David 17
　Elizabeth 1491, 1531, 1560
　Ellinor 1323
　George 433, 549
　James 398
　Joseph 1184, 1341
　Loveday 504
　Margaret 294
　Mary 897, 1365
　Mathew 187
　Richard 250
　Robert 821, 1152
　Susan 413
　Thomas 18, 26, 372, 1152
　William 1389
Philpot/Phillpot/Philpott
　John 127, 569
　Thomas 110, 118, 175, 223, 226, 255

Phips/Phipps—see also Fipps
    John 930, 973, 1261
Pickerill
    Henry 232
Pickering/Pickring
    Elizabeth 691
    George 1721
    Rosamond 691
Pickmore
    Symon 820
Pigler
    William 314
Pignett
    Elizabeth 107
Piles
    Sarah 696
Pinckard
    John 964
Pine/Pines
    John 1247
    Margaret 1565
    Marguritt 1481
Pingo
    Magdaline 1816, 1839
Pinn
    John 1858
    Rawleigh 1859
Pinnar
    Robert 430, 437
Pinnell
    Robert 292
Pirson
    John 222
Pitchard
    William 793
Pithard
    John 775
Pittman
    Thomas 1462
Pitts
    Anne 825, 866
    Phill: 722, 1225

Plackmett
    Thomas 26
Plankett
    Thomas 547
Platt
    Peter 722, 1225
Player
    Henry 497
Plea
    Edmond 1316
Pledjoell
    Mary 722
Pledwele
    Mary 1225
Plesington
    Alice 136
Plessee
    Maudlin 457
Ploucer
    Thomas 176
Pollick
    Patrick 880, 915, 947, 1187
Pomfrett
    Anne 120
Pomray
    James 327
Pond
    Anne 295
Ponseby
    Mary 1766
Poole
    Hester 318
Poolton
    Thomas 1723
Poor/Poore
    Catherine 1536, 1537
    David 1150
    John 1020, 1069, 1287, 1311,
        1313, 1321
Pope/Poope
    James 316, 517, 723
    John 1085, 1230, 1309, 1427

Pope/Poope (cont.)
   Nathaniel 45
Popler
   John 1973
Porin
   Robert 1511
Porkey
   John 737
Porter
   Frances 1601
Potts
   Patricke 46
Poulson
   Richard 245
Pouzell
   Richard 643
Powell
   Edmund 833
   John 714
Power
   David 1122
Powers
   Daniell 774
Poynting
   John 1838
Poythers
   Francis 2, 4
Presely/Presly
   Jone 193
   Peter 128, 177, 309, 364, 416, 440, 449, 502, 569, 637, 650, 665, 696, 757, 762, 770, 790, 819, 861, 875, 913, 943, 959, 1182, 1594, 1617, 1682, 1689, 1703, 1763, 1764, 1769, 1770, 1814, 1815
   William 98, 104, 105, 112, 193, 264, 279, 292, 351, 502, 525, 568, 581, 689, 692, 696, 713, 762, 770, 875

Price
   Anne 1230
   Edward 512
   Elizabeth 821, 925
   Ellin^r 531
   Fran: 248
   Henry 669
   Hugh 1169, 1318
   Mary 1383, 1384, 1518, 1554
   Morgan 1017
   Richard 1215, 1355
   Thomas 313
   Walter 248, 456, 463
   William 1230, 1434, 1437, 1513
Prichard
   Ann 1580
   Robert 541
   Swanson 1724
   Walter 79
Prichett
   William 1261
Prickett
   Bridgett 119
   Thomas 119
Pride
   Elizabeth 294
Prise
   Mary 1294
   Richard 1294
   Thomas 1313
Proctor
   Abraham 1294
   Stephen 734
Propert
   Howell 833
Prosser
   John 35
Provis
   William 1294
Provish
   William 612

Puckney
  Henry 1294
Pulham
  Thomas 1740
Pullin
  Nathan 1974
Punisby/Punnby
  Mary 1752
Purcell
  Tobias 1874
Purchet
  Elizabeth 1893
Purney
  John 1016
  Katherine 1016
Pursley
  John 1738
Pursline
  Char: 351
Pyle
  Joseph 1861

Quarom/Quarum
  Mary 1750, 1852
Quemy
  Sutton 218
Quesenbery
  John 26
Quick
  Thomas 317
Quiff/Quiffe
  Patrick 1239, 1294, 1314
Quinborow/Quinbourough
  Andrew 3
  William 326, 493

Radforth
  Judith 247
Rainsford
  Edward 1261
Ram
  Ebenezer 1391, 1392

Ramies
  Anne 683
Ramsey
  John 620
Raney
  John 754
Range
  Mary 1726, 1727, 1741
  Nicholas 1936
  Winefred 1934
Rankin
  William 1653
Rann
  Evan 1230
Ransom/Ranson
  John 1614, 1630, 1663
Rapson
  Richard 1600
Rareday
  Michael 1138
Rasee
  Sarah 129
Rattle
  Edward 388
Raven
  John 188, 289, 321, 328
Rawlins
  Mary 1523
Rayner/Raynor
  Henry 53, 151
  Mary 151
Raynes
  Jane 274
Read/Reade
  Archebald 53
  Elizabeth 87
  George 414
  Henry 151
  Mathew 654
  Sarah 74
  Susanna 1208
  Thomas 94, 103

Reader
   Ellinor 1350
Reading
   Henry 404
Reason
   John 680, 1247, 1257, 1296, 1299
Redish
   Thomas 1323
Redman
   Katherine 1045
Reeves
   Robert 637, 913, 1091, 1192, 1261, 1313, 1330, 1516, 1526
   William 1568
Reinon
   Ann 714
Renalls
   William 86
Rennolds
   William 1287
Revir
   Peter 1404
Rew
   Mildright 750
Reynolds
   Jeffery 743
   John 480
   William 38, 47, 57
Rheine
   Margrett 953, 955
Rhodes
   Nicholas 811
Rhodon
   Matthew 74, 483, 584
   Mr. 470, 472, 498, 499
Rian/Rion—see Ryan
Rice
   Dominick 800
   Hannah 1597

Rice (cont.)
   Richard 319, 661, 731, 1213, 1292, 1973
   William 1973
Rich
   Christian 830, 885, 948, 963
   Jane 963
   Mary 1363
Richards
   John 533
   Joseph 1780
   Peter 244, 703
   William 419
Richardson
   Bridgett 900
   Elizabeth 640
   Margaret 249
   Sarah 293, 1230
   Simon 156, 278, 487
Richman
   Thomas 241
Richmond
   Elizabeth 122
Rickett/Ricketts
   Arthur 734
   Benjamin 764
Ridehouse
   John 1815, 1817
Rigin/Riggin
   Nathaniel 1685, 1689
Riley
   Timothy 1159, 1246
Ring
   Ellenore 1488
Ringeade
   David 1668
Ringken
   George 941
Riscott
   Leah 619, 620, 642, 687
Roach
   John 486, 500, 708, 1311

Roach (cont.)
    Laurence 856
Roane
    William 1899
Robbins/Robins
    Elizabeth 501
    Jeremiah 351, 574
    Mary 1158, 1193, 1201
Roberts
    David 821
    Edward 36, 71
    Elinor 555
    Elizabeth 599
    Evan 891, 1205
    Francis 23, 92, 435, 475, 514, 519, 555, 587
    John 1273
    Mathew 493
    Richard 250
    Thomas 44
    William 1763
Robertson
    Christian 1935
    Moses 1790
Robinson
    Annie 721
    Daniel 351
    Elizabeth 677
    James 460
    John 593, 721, 1185, 1222
    Joseph 1661, 1755
    Susana 657
    Thomas 677, 725
    William 1619
Rock/Rocke
    Constantine 1892
    Henry 63, 356
    Thomas 1311
Rodman
    John 120
Roe
    Samuel 645

Roe (cont.)
    Thomas 282, 441, 491, 494
Rogers
    Capt. 337, 638
    Edward 142, 1718
    James 1169, 1309, 1409
    John 95, 147, 222, 306, 443, 554, 628, 655, 671, 724
    Mary 1224, 1233
    Mr. 349
    Phillip 1385
    Richard 855, 882, 977
    William 284, 800
Roles/Rolles
    Matthew 704
Rooarke
    Dennis 1311
Roobert
    William 227
Rookwood
    John 33
Rope
    Anthony 265
Rose
    John 1598
Rosier
    Elizabeth 5
    John 5
Ross/Rosse
    Francis 181
    John 316, 1598, 1867
    Margaret 1874
    Robert 1601
Roston
    John 339
Rotheram
    John 456
Rout/Routt
    Elizabeth 1494, 1519
    John 1722, 1855
    Richard 1576
    Robert 90

Rout/Routt (cont.)
    Thomas 1161, 1335, 1683
Rowes
    Francis 1856
Rowland
    Thomas 722
    William 371
Royla
    Anne 796
Rule
    William 149
Rulpey
    Maudlin 485
Rumley
    John 479, 734
Runey
    Peter 1794
Runkin
    George 983
Russell
    Charles 1477
    Dorothy 130
    Edward 313
    Elizabeth 115
    Hannah 520
    James 568, 943, 1313
    John 450, 520
    Mary 520
    Peter 693
    Richard 112, 1336, 1338, 1341, 1344, 1365, 1402
    Thomas 729
Rust
    William 1393
Rutt
    Mary 1355
Rutter
    Katherine 931, 972
    William 601
Ryan/Rian/Rion
    Daniel 1808, 1836, 1837, 1849
    Edward 1439, 1539, 1543

Ryan/Rian/Rion (cont.)
    John 1302
    Loughlin 1061
Ryder
    Thomas 525, 875, 1313, 1357
Rylie
    Daniel 129
Rytim
    Langhly 1176

Sabrice
    Doro 834
Sack
    William 559
Saddler/Sadler
    Henry 714
    Robert 714
    Steven 380
    Thomas 650, 714, 1230
Saddon
    Thomas 889
Saffin
    John 390, 395, 396, 397
    Mr. 394
Sage
    William 734
Salisbury/Salsbury
    Robert 242
    Thomas 387, 934
Sallaway
    Jane 1505
Salloes/Sallowes
    Stephen 714, 734
Salmon
    Alexander 1287, 1454
    Elizabeth 722
Sampson/Sampsoun/Samson
    Edward 28, 313
    Joseph 1899
    Sarah 1686, 1715, 1733
Samwell
    Richard 313

381

Sanders/Saunders
   Ebenezer 873, 960, 961
   Edward 135, 181, 202, 240,
      323, 409, 480, 519, 533,
      846, 976, 1061, 1176, 1425,
      1428
   Henry 722, 1225
   Joan 714
   John 180, 222
   Mary 1641
   Mr. 441
Sangbail
   Christopher 313
Sarchfeild
   Patrick 1323
Saul
   Jonathan 161
Savage/Savige
   Charles 1105
   David 1082, 1294, 1317, 1379,
      1431
Savoy
   Mary 1261
Sawter
   John 705
Sayer
   Lydia 85
Sayle
   Edward 150
Scallin
   Gillian 1288
Scallion
   Sinah 1901, 1903, 1906, 1907,
      1933
Scanbrook
   Mathew 527
Scannell
   Gilliam 1139
Scerry
   Susan 13

Schreever/Schrever
   Bartholomew 941, 1117, 1214,
      1285, 1346, 1469
   Mr. 1325
Scott
   Daniel 490
   John 852, 1183, 1225
   Leah 620
   William 187, 313
Screech
   George 1230
Screver
   Nicholas 133
Scriven
   John 52
Scrivener/Scrivner
   Ann 1626, 1651
   James 1616
Scull
   Margaret 410
Scuse
   Edward 543, 571
Seabury
   James 734
Seagreens
   Christopher 284
Seaham
   John 1057
Seaman
   Anne 546
   John 444
Sebree/Seebry
   Abigal 1662
   Ann 1691, 1712
   James 1659
   John 1950
   William 1781
Sech
   Robert 307, 527, 770, 807, 820,
      888
Sedbery
   Edward 69

Seddon
    Joane 1294
    Thomas 1294
Seeling
    George 111
Seers
    Joseph 630
Segar
    William 313
Seldon
    Richard 1859
Self
    Thomas 1884
    William 1530, 1884
Seneger
    William 679
Sennett/Sennit
    Mary 1826
    Phillip 1025, 1150
Sentence
    Henry 55
Servee
    Jane 519
    Mary 519
Sesly
    Robert 371
Seth
    Robert 713, 918, 923
Severin
    Colen 519
Seward
    John 1299
    Mary 1299
    William 1261, 1296, 1299
Shadock
    Alice 1402
Shahanghuary
    Timothy 1279
Shapleigh
    Hannah 1625
    John 1718
    Phillip 664, 684, 822, 840, 887

Shapleigh (cont.)
    Thomas 1071, 1072
Shaply
    Phillip 650
Sharpe
    Richard 313
    Robert 61
Sharts
    William 722
Shaw
    James 1102
    John 1348, 1349, 1354
    Katherine 149
    Phillip 1373
    Shahanna 1287
Shea
    Daniel 734
Sheapard
    John 37
Sheares/Sheeres/Sheers
    Abraham 878, 941
    Elizabeth 1035
    William 703
Sheath
    Henry 41
Sheffeild
    Moses 826
Shelly
    Charles 451
Shenton
    John 214
Shepard/Sheppard
    Elizabeth 1289
    John 229
    William 402
Shepherd
    George 1921
Sherly
    Thomas 151
Sherredon/Sherridon
    John 1749, 1776, 1778

Sherry
  John 456
Sherwood
  Edward 170
Shewter
  Mary 433
Shiels
  Robert 1682, 1703
Shirley—see also Sherly
  Jane 819, 1313
Shiverell
  Allen S. 1937, 1938
Shoare/Shoares
  William 467, 699
Sholauan
  Denish 117
Short
  Samuel 1323
Shorthose
  Thomas 1225
Shusy
  Archibald 1287
Sibbalds
  Robert 1889, 1894, 1896, 1905, 1919, 1921, 1928
Sibble
  James 149
Siddon
  William 1323
Simkins/Simpkins
  John 898, 1148
Simmenet
  George 1784
Simmons—see also Symmons
  Laurence 114
  Matthew 1053
  Thomas 303
  William 1703, 1763, 1769, 1815, 1816
Simms
  Samuel 1625
  Thomas 1294, 1625

Simonds
  Matthew 1422
Simpson/Simson
  George 1900
  Henry 684
  John 228, 294, 317
  Thomas 1549, 1900
Sims
  Thomas 869
Sirves
  John 186
Sisco
  Franck 222
Sivillivant—see Suilevant/Suillevant/Swillivant
Skelle
  John 1230
Skimage
  John 1294
Skinbark
  Grace 256
Skip/Skippe
  William 215, 255
Skipper
  Mathew 8
Slightham
  George 153
Sloan
  Elizabeth 946
Sloughman
  William 1668
Slytham
  George 124, 125, 126
Small
  Hester 333
Smallcole
  William 314
Smallpiece [?]
  Thomas 234
Smee
  Robert 1840

Smith/Smyth
  Anne 6, 84, 1825
  Capt. 493
  Christopher 684
  Col. 519, 684
  David 1130, 1504
  Edward 699, 703
  Elizabeth 128, 744
  Henry 152
  Hester 333, 711, 932
  James 1032, 1126
  Jane 781
  Joana 212
  John 35, 238, 241, 266, 313,
    945, 1149, 1576, 1625,
    1757, 1818, 1833, 1926
  John Nicholas 1899
  Katherine 902, 980
  Margaret 820
  Mary 35, 179, 603, 609
  Nicholas 135
  Philip 1561, 1655
  Richard 52, 313, 405, 608, 936,
    1638, 1721
  Robert 6, 84, 1294
  Samuel 87, 88, 138, 438, 684,
    794, 1112, 1182
  Sarah 84
  Terrence 1598
  Thomas 212, 265, 438, 445,
    446, 699, 782, 1023, 1127,
    1150, 1416, 1461, 1472,
    1501, 1507
  William 27, 152, 228, 871,
    897, 1125, 1680, 1800,
    1820
Smithhurst
  Ralph 1479, 1509
Smitton
  Marmaduke 890
Smoot/Smout
  William 1626, 1651
Smythergill
  Anne 754
Snow
  Samuel 1666, 1740
Soape
  Benjamin 984
Soile
  James 313
Solomon/Sollomin
  Alexander 1393, 1410
Sorrell
  John 1857
Souley
  Thomas 190
Souse
  Edward 409
Southerly
  Leonard 409
Southerne
  James 756
  Judith 75
  Sarah 75
Southward
  James 103
Southwell
  Katherine 176
Span
  Cuthbert 550, 798, 799, 833,
    867, 986, 1078
  Dorothy 1218
  Graciana 550, 551
  Richard 20, 254, 411, 422, 452,
    550, 551, 558
Sparhalt
  Mar: 784
Sparkes/Sparks
  Charles 180, 222
  William 150, 466, 469
Sparrow
  Thomas 313
Speke
  Anne 60

Speke (cont.)
    Thomas 10, 43, 48, 59, 60
Spellman/Spelman
    Clement 1407
    Hannah 1407
    Thomas 684
Spence/Spense
    David 1308
    John 1498, 1503, 1506, 1768
    William 49, 718
Spencer
    Judith 50
    Nicholas 153, 851
    Robert 153, 306
Spicer
    William 7
Spilman
    Mary 428, 764
    Thomas 428, 764
Sprage
    Ann 628, 629, 800
Spratt
    James 1141
Squibb
    John 63
Squire
    John 384, 530
Squiren
    Richard 13
Sryer
    John John 1870
Stafford
    Elizabeth 313
    Robert 69
Staller
    Edward 313
Stamps
    Timothy 1596
Standfield/Stanfield
    Elizabeth 1782, 1785
Stanford
    Edward 149

Stanly
    James 1313
Stanton
    Robert 122
Staples
    Richard 965, 967
Statham/Stathem
    Hugh 306, 1079
    Sarah 734
Staynie
    Hannah 1261
Steed
    Thomas 173, 535
Steel/Steele
    John 265
    Samuel 1881
Stembridge
    Roberta 351
Stepfort
    James 1424
Stephens
    John 531, 1802
    Mary 859, 903, 924, 982
    Richard 550, 833
Stephenson
    William 1294
Steptoe
    Anthony 876, 991
    John 1508
Sterling
    Walter 1445
Stevens
    Amy 108
    Arthur 420
    Jacob 351
    Jane 1530
    Ralph 111
    Thomas 272, 314
Stevenson
    Ralph 108
Steward
    Elizabeth 810

Steward (cont.)
    Gowen 1151
    James 1097
    Jasper 1507
    William 914
Stiles
    Robert 150, 184
Stillingfleet
    Francis 180
Stocken
    Ed: 781
Stocks
    Samuel 245
Stone
    Thomas 1541
Stott
    John 1283, 1308
    Thomas 1150
    William 975
Stowe
    Thomas 211
Stratford
    Mary 84
    William 84
Straughan
    David 1294
Street
    Robert 3
Strickland
    John 1649, 1658
Stripling
    Joell 461
Stuart
    James 1752
Stuck
    Sar: 737
Stutson
    Archibald 1091
Suilevant/Suillevant/Swillivant
    Daniel 1149, 1168, 1190, 1254,
        1267, 1271, 1284, 1799
    Katherine 1173

Suilevant/Suillevant/Swillivant (cont.)
    Mary 1207
    Owen 1173, 1175
    Peter 995
    Teigue 1119
Surtherin
    Thomas 785
Sutton
    Elizabeth 131
    George 131
    John 1853
    Joseph 131
    Lidia 131
    Mary 131
    Nathaniel 131
    Sarah 131
Svirton
    Thomas 322
Swaile
    Robert 79
Swan
    Thomas 313
Swanley
    Capt. 78
Swanson
    Elizabeth 1002
    John 519, 698
    Richard 1002
Swath
    Mathew 519
Sweetland
    Richard 549
Swetever
    Dennis 333
Swetman
    Mary 1225
Swift
    Sar: 427
    Thomas 477
Swords
    Mary 1518

387

Sydnor
   John 1920
Symmons—see also Simmons
   Dorothy 346
   Elizabeth 330
   James 284, 346, 1040
   Joane 346
   John 346, 672
   Richard 380
Symms
   Ediff 434
   Jane 317
   Samuel 317
Symson
   John 2

Tadwell
   Richard 127
   Thomas 155
Taite
   Anne 1865, 1929
   William 1694, 1800, 1801, 1830, 1865, 1868, 1887, 1888, 1891, 1917, 1918, 1923, 1924, 1929, 1930, 1952, 1953, 1954
Talbot
   Katherine 1310
Tally
   John 1760
Tap
   Thomas 775
Tarling
   Richard 33
Tate
   Elizabeth 927
Tayler/Taylor
   Anne 694, 1868
   Bridgett 1305
   Elizabeth 420
   Henry 800
   Humfry 478

Tayler/Taylor (cont.)
   Jennett 709
   John 245, 331, 378, 540, 684, 694, 788, 975, 1196, 1234, 1360, 1451, 1453, 1475
   Joseph 686, 1261
   Lazarus 876, 941, 1009, 1136
   Mary 1744, 1746
   Nanny 1865
   Rebecca 1216
   Thomas 304, 771, 837, 945, 986, 1137, 1452, 1453
   William 124, 125, 126, 222, 806
Taypett
   Margaret 722
Teage
   William 1729
Teagins
   Termance [or Tennance] 1803
Tearney
   Robert 1063
Teigue
   Robert 1287
Tellus—see Tullos
Temple
   Anne 146
Tempteer
   William 592
Tenant
   James 314
Terrell
   Arthur 24
   Elizabeth 24
Terry
   John 368, 623
   Thomas 299
Teuxbury
   James 353
Tew
   Elizabeth 254, 550, 558, 613

Thackerell
  Thomas 1212
Thawe [or Thane]
  Katherine 1359
Theary
  James 1311
Thickes
  Robert 313
Thomas
  Ann 1731, 1756, 1806
  Arthur 1170, 1378
  Daniel 637
  David 1164, 1294
  Elizabeth 703, 1675
  Frances 64
  Francis 1294
  Grace 1945, 1948
  Henry 378
  Jane 241
  Jeremiah 650
  Jnkins 313
  John 166, 317, 775, 937, 950,
    1168, 1294, 1912, 1915,
    1916
  Milly 1969
  Mr. 751
  Rebecca 792
  Richard 1713, 1829, 1849
  Robert 294
  Roger 485, 582
  Spencer 1930, 1942, 1944,
    1946
  Thomas 1930
  William 30, 64, 85, 97, 121,
    245, 251, 317, 322, 326,
    491, 492, 493, 494, 540,
    588
Thompson/Thomson
  Alice 899
  Anne 878
  Dorothy 1208
  Dunkan 1113

Thompson/Thomson (cont.)
  James 523
  Jane 548, 600, 980
  John 43, 313, 1208
  Makum 41
  Marmaduke 590
  Richard 527
  Sarah 108
  Symon 314
  Thomas 970
  William 978, 1294, 1310
Thorne
  Thomas 1392
Thornley
  Alice 314
Thornton
  Dr. 1481
  Presly 1940, 1941
  William 1170, 1173, 1234
Thorton
  Anne 333
  John 522
Threader
  William 13
Thurston
  Julius 618
Tibergine
  James 314
Tidwell
  Richard 824
Tignall
  William 471
Tigner
  William 622, 684
Tillitt
  Thomas 12
Tillman
  John 268
Tingey
  John 130, 244
Tinoth
  Sus: 784

Tipto
    John 775
Tipton
    Elizabeth 759
    Richard 433
Tirkbury
    Samuel 368
Tobin
    Michael 1584
Toby
    John 257
Tomlinson
    John 2
Tomson
    Richard 1710, 1737
Toogood
    Edward 79
Tool
    Darby 1649
    James 1656, 1673
Topping
    John 1208
Toulson
    Betty 1934
    James 1960
Tousend/Towsend
    William 1723, 1836
Tovend
    Edward 4
Towers
    Thomas 389, 590, 632, 639, 772, 776
Tozar
    William 775
Tracy
    Timothy 567
Travers
    John 698
    Rawleigh 933, 994, 1151
Trea
    Laurence 1323

Treipe
    Thomas 235
Treit
    Thomas 758
Tresteale
    William 738
Trimell
    John 535
Trimlett
    John 1139
Troth
    Mathew 919
Trower
    John 117
Trussell
    John 99, 165
    William 1521, 1524, 1581, 1900
Tucker
    Thomas 431
Tullos
    Cloud 638, 1145
    John 1371
    Richard 1155, 1215, 1662
    Sarah 1235, 1312, 1371
Tully
    William 1477
Turberville
    John 940
Turloraldy
    Raley 1006
Turner
    Alice 1937, 1938
    Ann 1793
    Diniogh 117
    Elizabeth 1730, 1732
    John 1016
Turney
    Richard 26, 44
Turrainc
    John 734

Tutt
  Mary 813
Twison
  William 980
Tyngey
  John 385

Underhill
  Thomas 193
Unthank/Unthanke
  Susanna 937, 1294

Vallen/Vallins
  Charles 936
  James 43
Vanlandingham
  Michaell 261, 638
Van-Puck
  Mauldin 130
Varley
  Christopher 701, 775
  Elizabeth 701, 775
  James 701, 775
  Jane 775
  Jennett 701
  John 701, 775
  Mary 775
Vaughan
  Christopher 228
  John 30
  Valentine 598, 626
  William 196, 404
Veale
  Humphrey 799, 822, 1261
Venables
  Joseph 1029
Venner
  Martha 718
Violett
  Anne 1288
  George 1288

Vizard
  Mary 455
Vollen
  Charles 1092
  Dennis 1283
Voss
  Richard 465
Voucher
  Elizabeth 1706
Voy
  Henry 1636
Voyer
  Capt. 1239
  Francis 1095, 1096, 1240, 1241
Vritt
  Richard 231
Vuxon
  Richard 1149

Waddington
  Ralph 519
Waddy
  James 813, 941, 986, 1033, 1034, 1288
  John 345, 418, 537
  Thomas 754, 844, 1186, 1211
Wade
  Christopher 446, 784
  Mary 784
  William 79
Wadmore
  Mary 314
Wainwright
  Margaret 1812
Wakely
  Sarah 351
Walcupp
  Thomas 1029
Waldon
  Henry 317
Wale
  George 301

Walker
　James 1958
　John 71, 502, 1313
　Joseph 757, 819, 1711
　Maj. 684
　Margaret 409
　Nathaniel 986
　Susanna 1971
　Symon 244, 703
　Thomas 684, 1377, 1462, 1615, 1675, 1973
　William 1667
　Winifred 1971
Walkins
　William 1930
Wall
　Benjamin 835
　John 835
　Richard 101
　Ruth 835
Wallace/Wallis/Wallise
　Abraham 222, 233
　Mary 1768, 1771, 1772, 1777
　Thomas 1353, 1627
　William 883
Waller
　Ann 32
Walson
　William 1856
Walters
　Diana 773
　Easter 773
　Elizabeth 1396
　Hester 773
　John 773, 790, 1128, 1633
　Mary 773
　Phoebe 773
　Thomas 1153
Walton
　Stephen 734
Wandorill
　William 174

Ward
　Elizabeth 250
　Francis 1225
　James 983
　Richard 163
Warder
　William 111
Ware/Wares
　Fra: 722
　Hannah 753
　John 108, 155
Warner/Warners
　Grace 834
　John 34, 125, 126, 527, 607
　Robert 115
Warren
　John 124
　Mr. 78
Warwick/Warreck
　Richard 1812
　Thomas 171, 180, 222
Washbury
　Edward 753
Waterland
　Michael 489, 526, 570
Waterman
　Thomas 480
Waters
　Anne 1844
　Lelia/Lilia 1448, 1449
　Mary 229, 245
　Thomas 1093
Waterson
　Peter 313, 949
Wathen
　William 501
Watkins
　Edward 1016
　Mary 1669, 1671
　William 1952
Watson
　John 260

Watson (cont.)
  Susan 14, 29
  Thomas 53, 136
  William 1852
Watts
  Alexander 596
  Duglasse 336
  Edm: 767
  Edward 734, 789
  Elizabeth 544, 571, 572
  Henry 284, 413
  Robert 1451, 1453
  Thomas 656
Wattson
  Hester 1655
  Nathaniel 1466
Waughop
  John 1667
Way
  John 313
  Richard 170, 684
  William 1431
Wayland
  William 1438
Weathers
  William 3
Weatherstone
  Alexander 886, 896, 930, 971
Webb
  Daniel 851, 1204
  James 1591, 1612
  John 272, 740, 928, 966, 968, 974, 987, 1045, 1301, 1307, 1378, 1423, 1425, 1877
  Mary 736, 782
  Rachell 1425
  Samuel 171, 180, 228, 1450, 1546
  Sarah 1425, 1428
  Thomas 706, 736, 862, 1507, 1529, 1575, 1602
  Walter 117

Webb (cont.)
  William 1920
  Winifred 1428
Webster
  Elizabeth 1609
  Thomas 1632, 1735, 1742, 1745, 1747, 1793
Wedderilse
  William 1264, 1268
Weekes
  Walter 247
Weels
  Stephen 890
Welch/Welsh
  Edward 1567, 1591, 1610
  Elizabeth 1461
  James 1049
  Matthew 1056
  Phillip 734, 1152
  Thomas 1424, 1464
Welding
  Samuel 26
Wells
  Honno[r] 1323
  Jeremiah 1761, 1809
  Richard 140
  Rosamond 1329
  Thomas 1167, 1381, 1394
Wesson
  Mary 73
West
  George 35
  Henry 58, 59, 60
  Joane 694
  John 1607
  Richard 694
  Thomas 58, 59, 60, 306
Westerby
  Mary 1294
Western
  John 1857

Weston
  Edmon: 671
Wetheull
  Elizabeth 597
Wharwell
  William 79
Whayland
  William 1539, 1543
Wheaden
  Edm: 775
Whealand
  John 1681
Wheeler
  Frances 959
  Francis 1313
  Mary 1311
  Thomas 818
  William 294
Wherrett
  Susan 480, 552
Whilliard
  Frances 913
Whitby
  Edward 231
  William 1801
Whitcrost
  John 294
White
  Alice 10, 1311
  Ann 33, 399
  Edward 399
  Elizabeth 784
  Hanna 399
  James 380, 1072, 1183, 1261, 1351, 1352
  Jane 107
  Joane 399
  John 245, 519, 572, 775, 776, 1757, 1774
  Margery 128
  Millie 684
  Richard 76, 215, 228, 255

White (cont.)
  Robert 1750
  Symon 1073
  Thomas 399, 601, 608
  William 671
Whitebread
  Mary 738
Whitehook
  Anna 404
Whitehorne
  George 455
Whithall
  Erasmus 455
Whitley
  Thomas 427
Whitney
  John 472
Whitson
  Aaron 992
Whitten
  Jonie 1178
Whitter/Whitters
  Phoebe 1209, 1280, 1316, 1334, 1356
Whitthorne
  George 542
Whittington
  John 734
Wicker
  Henry 618
Widsey
  Mary 559
Wier/Wirre
  William 1889, 1894, 1896
Wiggin/Wiggins
  Anne 1237, 1243, 1245
  Jane 307
Wigginton
  George 1155
Wilcox
  Elizabeth 952, 1150, 1192, 1261

Wilcox (cont.)
   John 525
Wildey/Wildy/Willday
   Elizabeth 1577
   Jane 764, 792, 857, 942
   Joseph 1754, 1755
   William 192, 228, 253, 428, 441, 519, 583, 648, 728, 993, 1099, 1577, 1675
Wiles
   William 74
Wilkes
   Elizabeth 1225
Wilkey/Wilkie
   Elizabeth 1783, 1786
Wilkins
   John 875, 1313, 1882
   William 1230
Wilkinson
   Mary 294
   Thomas 601
   William 245
Wilks
   Robert 818
   Thomas 727
Will
   Jerimah 1819
Willia
   Mary 1868
Williams
   ___ 228
   Abell 404
   Anne 321, 679, 1216, 1253
   Benjamin 162
   David 1257
   Edward 456, 1027
   Elizabeth 766, 1506
   Ellin[r] 848, 1166
   Henry 1700
   Howell 816, 848
   Hugh 1230
   Jacob 906

Williams (cont.)
   John 33, 189, 259, 507, 549, 580, 638, 649, 684, 710, 737, 1165, 1290, 1310, 1340, 1385, 1705
   Joseph 1970
   Mary 758, 1128, 1152, 1283, 1336, 1338, 1767
   Peter 831
   Rachell 1257
   Richard 313, 1162, 1400, 1405
   Sarah 245, 306
   Thomas 97, 162, 191, 209, 257, 335, 336, 341, 345, 477, 519, 745, 771, 775, 809, 849, 999, 1230, 1344, 1402, 1416, 1857, 1861
   Wilf 782
   William 1344, 1402, 1416
Williard
   Francis 1261
Willis
   Francis 46
   John 79
   Mary 1801, 1868
   Richard 2
Willon
   Thomas 422
Willoughby
   Jacob 153
Willowbye
   Katherine 21
Wills
   Rosamond 1326
   Samuel 703
   William 181
Willson
   George 1789
   James 1643
Wilmore
   Daniell 306

Wilsford
    Thomas 75, 76
Wilson
    Betty 1940
    Christopher 941
    Elizabeth 943
    George 1820
    Henry 1087
    John 40, 176, 313, 560, 863, 1125
    Mary 1885
    Mathew 1947
    Nathaniel 1848, 1943, 1948, 1951, 1955, 1956, 1957, 1959
    Robert 183, 528, 1471
    Sarah 1847
    William 313, 941, 1003
Wilton
    Cornelius 150
Winberry
    Mathew 784
Winbourough
    Paul 518
Winder
    Thomas 1172, 1191, 1253, 1256, 1277
    William 1126
Winn
    Thomas 91, 135
Winsborough
    Mathew 713
Winstead
    Samuel 1483
Winstone
    Thomas 784
Winter/Wynter
    Henry 237
    Thomas 695, 701, 775, 826, 1017, 1134
Winterne
    Charles 135

Witherall
    Elizabeth 765
Witherstone
    Alexander 1087
Witherton
    Samuel 998
Witter
    Anne 961
    Phoebe 960, 961
    Thomas 872
Woggan
    William 734
Woldridge
    Edward 538
Wolford
    John 441
Wollham
    Elizabeth 1261
Wood
    Anne 180
    Francis 313
    John 518, 521, 529, 534, 563, 565
    Michael 1075
    Thomas 148, 1374, 1387, 1413, 1415, 1427
    William 13, 222, 775, 987
Woodamore
    William 812
Woodard
    Thomas 313
Woodbridge
    George 1587
Woodcock
    John S. 1964
Wooden
    James 1459
Woodman
    Joseph 194
Woodworth
    Kester 876

Woolard
   John 717
Wooldridge
   Edward 1255
   Mary 48
Wooll/Wool
   Elizabeth 1287
   William 1064, 1136, 1152
Woolridge
   Edward 697
Woolse
   John 1298
Woolsteed
   Sam: 390
Woolvin
   John 706
Wooton
   Elizabeth 26
Wormley/Wormly
   Christopher 622
   Col. 684
   Ralph 1872
Wornom
   John 954, 962
Worsly
   Margery 874
Worthingham
   John 536, 539, 679
Wrenn
   Nicholas 684
Wright
   Andrew 986
   Christopher 153
   Elizabeth 709
   John 39
   Mary 579
   Richard 135, 153, 154, 249, 252, 623
   Robert 135, 679
   Thomas 654
   Winfield 1665

Wryon
   Thomas 1458

Yapp
   John 1898
Yarratt
   Adam 685, 693, 907
   Jane 805, 1013, 1202, 1450, 1487, 1546
   Rachell 824
   William 805, 835, 954, 962
Yeomans
   Amy 108
   Bartholomew 167, 281
Youlle
   Thomas 40
Young/Younge
   Jane 667
   John 679, 1869, 1873
   Mary 879
   Reynold 43
   Robert 726
   Thomas 396, 397

Zuill
   Matthew 1622, 1666, 1720
Zwellawen
   Honorah 176

NO SURNAMES

Abigaile 981
Abraham 441
Alex 69
Alic 1964
Alice 180
Andrew 441, 833
Anne 128, 474, 751
Anthony 622
Augustine 1960
Benbow 382
Besse 87
Billy 1245, 1953
Bryand 87
Charles 1697
Charlotte 1960
Christopher 73, 384, 1230
Coezar 814
Cupid 1500
Cyrus 432
Daino 714
Daniel 616
David 62
Dick 384
Elijah 1966
Elinor/Ellinor 437, 1230
Elizabeth 90, 118, 212, 441
Ester 1253
Eve 211
Francis 134
Fransisco 180
Fryer 280
George 185, 751
Grantham 1323
Guillian 483
Hannah 1724, 1900
Harry 384, 751, 861
Hugh 616, 1409
Isaac 1974
Jack 280, 384, 790, 854, 867, 1426
Jacob 1917

James 452, 862, 1513, 1604
Jane 751
Jeffrey 390
Jenny 790
Joan 81
Joe 1960
John 63, 159, 368, 390, 404, 433, 441, 493, 519, 734, 928, 1230, 1418, 1960, 1966
Jonathan 104
Jorie 26
Jude 1974
Judith 833
Lancelot 106
Lawrence 784
Lettice 1960
Luke 441
Lydia 758
Lyon 26
Mabell 115
Maddam 784
Manuel 26
Marea 1395
Margarett 684, 1225
Margery 118
Maria 180
Mary 734, 855
Massco 1960
Mingo 714
Mitchall 404
Nan 1966
Naple 833
Nicholas 441, 749
Peter 1762
Philip 441
Plato 280, 1327
Primus 864
Rachell 784, 928, 1378, 1960
Richard 180
Robert 1513

Samb: 784
Sarah 449, 480, 808, 834, 1441
Saray 751
Simon 159
Spencer 1966
Stephen 1728
Susan 751
Thomas 101, 185, 493, 684, 734,
 751, 833, 1941
Tobey 280
Tom 827, 834, 853, 960, 961
Toney 784
Tony 87, 550, 833
Turner 734
Will 817, 1423
William 404, 626, 714, 1384
Willoughby 1900
Wilt 1448

www.ingramcontent.com/pod-product-compliance
Lightning Source LLC
Chambersburg PA
CBHW051624230426
43669CB00013B/2169